Liguria

the Bradt Travel Guide

Rosie Whitehouse

edition
3

www.bradtguides.com

Bradt Travel Guides Ltd, UK
The Globe Pequot Press Inc, USA

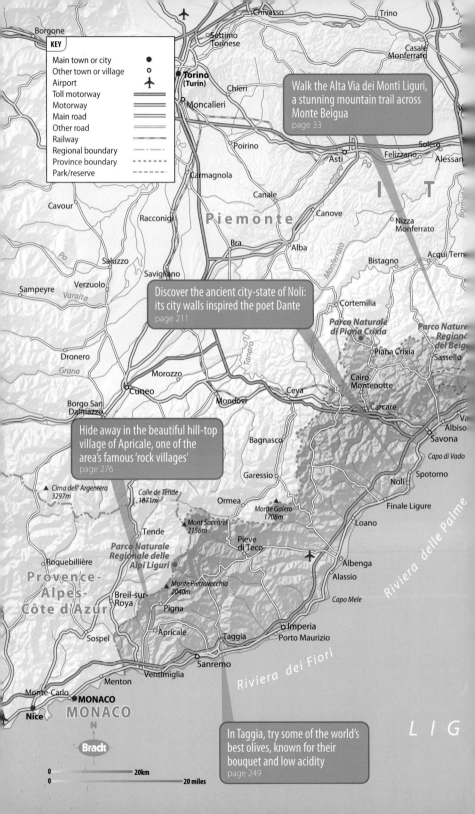

KEY

- Main town or city ●
- Other town or village ○
- Airport ✈
- Toll motorway
- Motorway
- Main road
- Other road
- Railway
- Regional boundary
- Province boundary
- Park/reserve

Walk the Alta Via dei Monti Liguri, a stunning mountain trail across Monte Beigua
page 33

Discover the ancient city-state of Noli: its city walls inspired the poet Dante
page 211

Hide away in the beautiful hill-top village of Apricale, one of the area's famous 'rock villages'
page 276

In Taggia, try some of the world's best olives, known for their bouquet and low acidity
page 249

Borgone
Chivasso
Trino
Settimo
Torinese
Casale
Monferrato
Torino
(Turin)
Chieri
Moncalieri
I T
Asti
Felizzano
Solero
Alessan
Poirino
Canale
Canove
Nizza
Monferrato
Piemonte
Cavour
Racconigi
Bra
Alba
Acqui Term
Bistagno
Carmagnola
Savigliano
Cortemilia
Sampeyre
Verzuolo
Saluzzo
Varaita
Parco Naturale
di Piana Crixia
Parco Nature
Region
del Beig
Sassello
Cairo
Montenotte
Piana Crixia
Dronero
Grana
Morozzo
Tanaro
Ceva
Carcare
Cuneo
Mondovi
Va
Albiso
Borgo San
Dalmazzo
Bagnasco
Savona
Capo di Vado
Garessio
Noli
Spotorno
Monte Galero
1708m
Finale Ligure
▲ Cima dell' Argentera
3297m
Colle de Tende
1871m
Ormea
Loano
▲ Mont Saccarel
2156m
Pieve
di Teco
Tende
Parco Naturale
Regionale delle
Alpi Liguri
Albenga
Alassio
Roquebillière
Provence-
Alpes-
Côte d'Azur
▲ Monte Pietravecchia
2040m
Capo Mele
Breil-sur-
Roya
Pigna
Sospel
Apricale
Taggia
Imperia
Porto Maurizio
Sanremo
Ventimiglia
Menton
Monte-Carlo
MONACO
Nice
MONACO
N
Riviera delle Palme
Riviera dei Fiori
L I G

Bradt

0 ——— 20km
0 ——— 20 miles

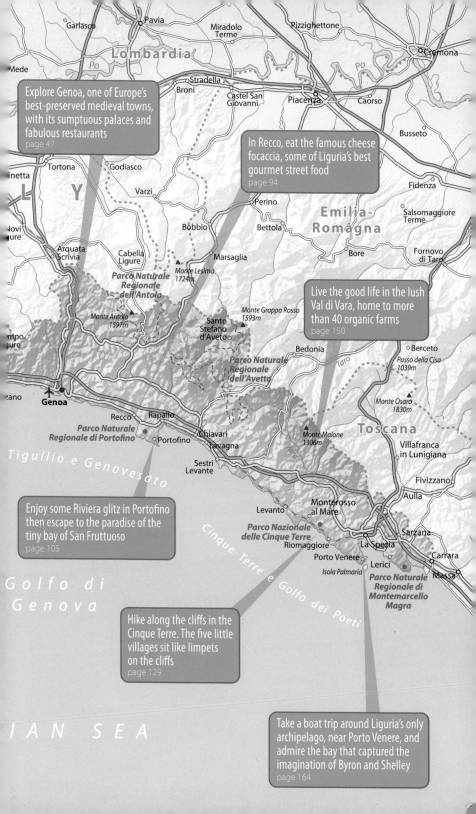

Explore Genoa, one of Europe's best-preserved medieval towns, with its sumptuous palaces and fabulous restaurants
page 47

In Recco, eat the famous cheese focaccia, some of Liguria's best gourmet street food
page 94

Live the good life in the lush Val di Vara, home to more than 40 organic farms
page 150

Enjoy some Riviera glitz in Portofino then escape to the paradise of the tiny bay of San Fruttuoso
page 105

Hike along the cliffs in the Cinque Terre. The five little villages sit like limpets on the cliffs
page 129

Take a boat trip around Liguria's only archipelago, near Porto Venere, and admire the bay that captured the imagination of Byron and Shelley
page 164

Liguria Don't miss...

Spectacular coastal views

An extensive network of walking paths allows visitors to admire the dramatic steep slopes that plunge into the sea in the Parco Nazionale delle Cinque Terre

(SB/S) page 129

Portofino

Late Victorian writers gushed about the beauty of Portofino; though busy, it is still one of Liguria's most picturesque spots

(OZ/S) page 105

Isolated hilltop villages
Best known for its witch trials, the remote village of Triora sits in Liguria's highest valley
(SS) page 253

Genoa's old town
The Porta Soprana are medieval gates that provide one of the entrances to Genoa's old town
(AM/S) page 75

Local cuisine
Food is an essential part of the Ligurian experience: you will find regional variations on hams, pasta and pesto in every deli
(SS) page 34

Liguria in colour

above left   Santa Maria Assunta di Carignano is the greatest Renaissance church in Genoa (AW/S) page 81

above right   The black-and-white striped façade of the Cattedrale di San Lorenzo is typical of medieval architecture (c/S) page 73

left   St George slays the dragon on the exterior of Palazzo San Giorgio (m/S) page 69

below   Containing tropical plants, ferns, butterflies and chameleons, the giant glasshouse of the Biosphere sits next to the aquarium on Genoa's harbour (LA/D) page 70

above   Genoa's old town, with its narrow tangle of alleyways, is one of the continent's largest (AI/S) page 72

below left   The Palazzo Reale stands in opulent contrast to the rough-and-tumble streets of old Genoa (m/S) page 78

below right   Via dei Luccoli in Genoa's old town offers upmarket browsing at its best (SS) page 73

above   During part of the 20th century, Sarzana's Cittadella was used as a jail (E/S) page 174

left   Savona's Fortezza del Priamàr is a superb example of 16th-century military architecture (m/S) page 205

below   Many of the buildings in the sunny hilltown of Apricale date from the 11th century (AAL) page 276

Rosie Whitehouse is a freelance journalist based in London. She has written for a wide array of publications including the *Sunday Telegraph*, *The Independent*, the *Guardian* and the *Daily Mail*. She is the author of a number of travel guides including *Family Guide: Paris* (Dorling Kindersley, 2012) and *Take the Kids: South of France* (Cadogan, 2003), and her own autobiography *Are We There Yet? Travels with my Frontline Family* (Reportage Press, 2007),

which chronicles the experiences of a young family coming to terms with having a front-line reporter as a dad, and centres on the five years she spent as a housewife in the war-torn Balkans with her journalist husband, Tim Judah.

Rosie is one of the UK's leading experts on family travel, and over the last 30 years she has explored every corner of Liguria with her family. While updating the last edition of the guide, Rosie discovered the story of the thousands of Holocaust survivors who passed through Italy after the end of the Second World War. In recent years Rosie has written extensively about the period 1944–48.

PUBLISHER'S FOREWORD — Adrian Phillips, Managing Director

Read the *Author's story* on page vii, or turn to the *Introduction* – or simply close your eyes, riffle the pages and choose to dip at random – and you'll quickly find that Rosie is a Bradt author through and through. Hers isn't text full of formulaic, third-person 'guidebook' speak about population figures and transport timetables. The necessary facts are there, of course – thoroughly updated for this third edition – but they're wrapped in the eager words of a writer keen to paint a picture and to convey her passion for a place she loves. It was with such passion that Rosie convinced us we had to add Liguria to our list of European regional titles – that it was our duty to tempt people beyond the better-known beaches of the Italian Riviera to a hinterland of hilltop villages and winding mountain paths.

Third edition published February 2019   First published April 2013

Bradt Travel Guides Ltd
IDC House, The Vale, Chalfont St Peter, Bucks SL9 9RZ, England
www.bradtguides.com
Print edition published in the USA by The Globe Pequot Press Inc,
PO Box 480, Guilford, Connecticut 06437-0480

Text copyright © 2019 Rosie Whitehouse
Maps copyright © 2019 Bradt Travel Guides Ltd. Includes map data © OpenStreetMap contributors
Photographs copyright © 2019 Individual photographers (see below)
Project Managers: Anne-Marie McLeman and Susannah Lord
Cover research: Marta Bescos

ISBN: 978 1 78477 634 3

British Library Cataloguing in Publication Data
A catalogue record for this book is available from the British Library

Photographs Alamy Stock Photos: Jan Wlodarczyk (JW/A); Dreamstime.com: Leonid Andronov (LA/D), Lianem (L/D); Photos Archive Agenzia in Liguria (AAL); Shutterstock.com: Alberto Masnovo (AM/S), Alex Tihonov (AT/S), Alastair Wallace (AW/S), Anton_Ivanov (AI/S), cre250 (c/S), cristian ghisla (cg/S), Dmytro Surkov (DS/S), Eder (E/S), Federico Rostagno (FR/S), Ion Sebastian (IoS/S), IuliiaSlyshko (IuS/S), Jarous (J/S), leoks (L/S), Marco Maggesi (MM/S), Martin M303 (MM303/S), maudaros (m/S), MeloDPhoto (MDP/S), Miles Away Photography (MAP/S), Nathan Chor (NC/S), Olena Z (OZ/S), paolo airenti (pa/S), Patrizio Martorana (PM/S), s74 (s74/S), Sebastian Burel (SB/S), Sternstunden (S/S), trabantos (t/S), unknown 1861 (u/S), Victor Agostini (VA/S), Yulia Grigoryeva (YG/S); SuperStock (SS)

Front cover Vernazza, Cinque Terre (JW/A)
Back cover View over Sassello (IoS/S); Mirror gallery, Palazzo Reale, Genoa (t/S)
Title page Lerici street (MDP/S); Monterosso tower (L/S); Medieval festival, Taggia (DS/S)
Part openers Palazzo San Giorgio, Genoa (page 91; s74/S); Vernazza, Cinque Terre (page 45; MM303/S); Flag throwing at a medieval festival, Taggia (page 179; DS/S)

Maps David McCutcheon FBCart.S. Colour relief map bases by Nick Rowland FRGS. Regional maps based on mapping © Regional Agency in Liguria. Savona map based on mapping provided by kind permission of Provincia di Savona – Servizio Promozione Turistica

Typeset by Ian Spick, Bradt Travel Guides Ltd and www.dataworks.co.in
Production managed by Jellyfish Print Solutions; printed in India
Digital conversion by www.dataworks.co.in

Acknowledgements

My thanks above all to my kids, who have slogged around old towns in the baking heat and have eaten far too many pastries and biscuits in order to decide exactly which bakery we would recommend. I mustn't omit my husband, Tim Judah, who has more often than not been my chauffeur and without whom I would never have had the chance to learn so much about the place. My three daughters Esti, Rachel and Eve speak wonderful Italian and have helped me decipher many a complicated script and what incomprehensible old ladies and gentlemen in the mountains have just told me. My youngest son, Jacob, took me to my first football match while I was updating the second edition of the book. Proof that anyone who thinks children clip your wings is completely wrong. There are a million things that I would never have done if I had not become a mum. As we watched Sampdoria smash Carpi 5–2, he gave such a fascinating running commentary that I suggested he write a section on football in the Genoa chapter.

I am grateful also for the help given by the Ligurian Tourist Board.

Many thanks, too, go to Sebastiano and Raffaella Musso and Raffaella's family, the Favas, who have for decades welcomed us into their homes both in Genoa and the surrounding countryside, served me some fantastic food and helped me get under the skin of one of the most beautiful parts of Italy. I am also grateful to Marco and Cristina Pratolongo, who have helped me to understand how the country as a whole ticks. There is also a heartfelt thanks to the countless people who offered help, hospitality and kindness, and who gave up their valuable time to explain not only where to eat and what to see, but also helped us negotiate our way out of some tricky dead-end dirt-track mountain roads.

Contents

LIST OF MAPS

Introduction

I love Liguria but am always surprised that when I tell people in Britain that I'm going there, they look blank then slightly puzzled. It's almost as if they feel they should know where it is but have simply forgotten and that is exactly what has happened; as far as Liguria goes, the nation is suffering from memory loss. In the late 19th century it was the place to be and be seen. Thousands of British people wintered in Sanremo, Alassio and Bordighera.

To help to jog the memory, I add, Liguria is the area around Genoa. Then there's a flicker of recognition that you are going to somewhere in northern Italy, but Genoa is in a black hole as far as most tourists are concerned even if Byron, Dickens, James and a whole host of writers have penned thousands of words on the place. Genoa was once a maritime superpower and has the biggest preserved medieval city in Europe, but it's hard to find more than a handful of people who are aware of that these days.

Then I add the magic words 'Italian Riviera' and their faces light up. 'Riviera' conjures up a whole host of images of film stars in speedboats, glistening blue sea and style. Then say 'Portofino' and a dreamy look crosses their faces and there is an intake of breath. It was the fact that most people outside of Italy know very little about this wonderful region where the mountains plunge down to the sea, which prompted me to get in contact with Rachel Fielding at Bradt. Over a cup of coffee I persuaded her that Bradt needed to change the way that foreigners look at Italy, heading for Florence, Venice and Rome and holidaying in Tuscany and Calabria. Italy is in fact an incredibly diverse country with major regional differences. There are things about Liguria that are totally unique. Local people still speak dialect and eat food only found in certain areas even within Liguria itself.

Liguria certainly has all the magic of the Riviera and Portofino still attracts stars and millionaires, but there's far more to it than that. I'm a history buff and there is so much history here, it's a delight. Above all, it's kept a lot of the local charm that many places in western Europe have lost. Yes, there is an IKEA, and there are large supermarkets, but the latter are stuffed with regional products you can't buy anywhere else. There are plenty of local shops that have been in the same families for generations and they are a million times more efficient than the chain stores that have taken over high streets in Britain and other parts of Europe. You can bike down to the local shop to buy a new dishwasher and 5 minutes later you, your bike and the dishwasher are in the back of the van on the way home with a plumber who is going to install it.

All this chaotic efficiency leaves plenty of time to do my favourite things. Number one is stepping out on the balcony to look at the view. There is nothing like watching the sea here; every time you look, it's changed colour. From the top of Monte Beigua, you can look down on the towns along the coast through the clouds as if you're a bird. Then on the way home you can buy something delicious for dinner that won't break the bank.

I fell in love with travelling when my parents bundled my two sisters and I into the car and set off every summer to drive across Europe. In 1972, we went to Liguria. It was a completely chance event. The day before we were all sitting at home, rather depressed as my father had a month off work, but couldn't afford a holiday. Then out of the blue one of his patients at the hospital offered him his house near La Spezia for free and we were on the road at dawn.

I was 11 and I was hooked. The place was full of adorable kittens. I ate far too much focaccia and endless bowls of minestrone, and spent all my dad's money buying trinkets in a vending machine by the café on Lerici's harbour side.

While I was a student at the LSE, I met my husband in the student newspaper office. There was something wonderfully Mediterranean about him. When he told me his father represented the Genoa shipyard and went there often, at first I thought that he actually was Italian (he turned out to be half French, for the record). Things moved fast. When our eldest son was just a month old, we bundled him into the back of the car and set off for Liguria.

We've spent most of our summers there ever since. We've driven up and down almost every road in Liguria and considering the excess of hairpin bends that's quite an achievement. Behind this book is two generations of experience of getting to know Liguria. My father-in-law could banter away in Genoese dialect and my mother-in-law would whisk up a pesto sauce that could hold its own against any Ligurian-born cook's version. Many of the places I recommend in the book are places that they introduced me to. Liguria has got under the family skin to such an extent that, if we go somewhere else in Italy, the kids will all bemoan that there's no focaccia for lunch, and my kitchen cupboard in London is stuffed with walnut sauce, taggiasca olives and anchovies.

Working on the new edition of this book has been a great experience and has given me a chance to go out and meet some fascinating people, many of whom are running small businesses and trying to save the traditional industries and products that have made this region different from the rest of Italy. I have come back laden with jams, olives and basil plants.

I am currently researching a book on the Jewish exodus from Europe, 1944–48, which I regularly tweet about. I tweet also about the Holocaust, history and memory, as well as about Liguria. I am 🐦 @rosiewhitehouse and I am on Instagram at 📷 rosieawhitehouse.

HOW TO USE THIS GUIDE

AUTHOR'S FAVOURITES Finding genuinely characterful accommodation or that unmissable off-the-beaten-track café can be difficult, so the author has chosen a few of her favourite places throughout the country to point you in the right direction. These 'author's favourites' are marked with a ✳.

FOOD AND WINE TRAILS In this guide you can enjoy some food tourism by following the Food Trail, a selection of boxes appearing through this book, marked with a ⑪, and the Wine Trail, marked with a ⑫.

MAPS
Keys and symbols Maps include alphabetical keys covering the locations of those places to stay, eat or drink that are featured in the book. Note that regional maps may not show all hotels and restaurants in the area: other establishments may be located in towns shown on the map.

Grids and grid references Several maps use gridlines to allow easy location of sites. Map grid references are listed in square brackets after the name of the place or sight of interest in the text, with page number followed by grid number, eg: [54 C3].

LIGURIA ONLINE

For additional online content, articles, photos and more on Liguria, why not visit **w** bradtguides.com/liguria?

SEND US YOUR SNAPS!

We'd love to follow your adventures using our *Liguria* guide – why not tag us in your photos and stories via Twitter (🐦 @BradtGuides) and Instagram (📷 @bradtguides)? Alternatively, you can upload your photos directly to the gallery on the Liguria destination page via our website (**w** bradtguides.com/liguria).

Part One

GENERAL INFORMATION

LIGURIA AT A GLANCE

Location In northwestern Italy. It's a thin sliver of coastal territory bordered by Tuscany and Emilia-Romagna to the east, Lombardy and Piedmont in the north, and France in the west.

Size 5,422km^2

Climate Mediterranean

Status One of Italy's 20 regions

Population 1,565,307 (2016)

Life expectancy Men 79, women 84

Regional capital Genoa (Genova) (population 594,733)

Other main towns Sanremo (population 57,000), Savona (61,345) and La Spezia (94,000)

Main airport Genoa (Aeroporto Cristoforo Colombo)

Language Italian. Main dialect Genoese.

Religion Roman Catholic

Currency Euro (€)

Exchange rate £1 = €1.12, US$1 = €0.87, AUS$1 = €0.63 (November 2018)

International telephone code +39 (but keep the first 0 in the number)

Time GMT +1

Electrical voltage 220V/50Hz, two-pin plugs

1

Background information

GEOGRAPHY

Crescent-shaped Liguria is one of the smallest regions in Italy at just 5,422km². It is a thin strip of land that runs along the coast of the Tyrrhenian Sea, bordered by France to the west, Piedmont to the north, and Emilia-Romagna and Tuscany to the east. It is divided into four provinces. From the west: Imperia, Savona, Genoa and La Spezia.

Liguria is split in two with Genoa at its centre. The Riviera di Levante runs east from Genoa and the Riviera di Ponente to the west. The coastal strip is very narrow and the hinterland, known as the *entroterra*, is hilly and mountainous, with the ranges of the Ligurian Alps in the west, and the Apennines in the east. The Giovi Pass behind Genoa separates the two. The watershed line runs at an average altitude of about 1,000m. Liguria's highest peaks are in the west where Monte Saccarello reaches 2,200m. Numerous steep valleys penetrate the mountains and the rivers that run through them are mostly fast-flowing torrents.

Two-thirds of Liguria's land mass is made up of mountains and 35% is covered in hills dotted with olive trees and vines. Plains account for just 1% of the region but these are immensely fertile and highly cultivated. As a result, in order to obtain arable land, mile upon mile of the hills are terraced with dry stone walls (*fasce*). In recent years fewer and fewer of these terraces have been farmed on account of the uneconomical backbreaking work involved. As a result the coast is more vulnerable to mudslides and flooding as the land no longer absorbs the water that it once did. As you travel around you will notice that many of these terraces have been, or are in the process of being, restored and farmed once more for precisely this reason.

There are some interesting geological formations, especially around Finale Ligure, which is famous for its karst; there are also lots of caves and grottos with interesting stalactites and stalagmites and other rocks.

The coast has many tiny inlets and bays. To the west there are wider bays and some sandy beaches (most of the beaches are shingle and pebbles), while in the rocky east there are high cliffs where the mountains plunge into the sea. The continental shelf off Liguria is very narrow, and almost immediately off the coast it reaches a considerable depth. Just north of the island of Corsica the sea is almost 3,000m deep. The only deep natural bays are at Genoa and La Spezia. As soon as you take a dip you'll notice that the sea is exceptionally salty.

CLIMATE

Liguria is protected from cold northerly winds by the mountains and has the mildest winter climate in Italy, especially around Bordighera and Alassio. It was the mild and sunny winters that first attracted tourists to the coast.

It is generally a sunny place with an average of 4 hours of sunshine a day in winter and 9 in the summer. Indeed it is one of the sunniest places in Italy despite its northerly position. Annual average relative humidity is 68%, ranging from 63% in February to 73% in May. Rainfall can be abundant at times, and Genoa and La Spezia can see up to 2,000mm of rain in a year. October and November are the wettest months. Waterspouts, *tromba d'acqua*, have become increasingly common in recent years. They are, put simply, tornadoes that happen over the sea. In bad weather it is advisable to take shelter inside as heavy rain can cause dangerous flooding and when a waterspout hits land it can cause considerable damage. Snowfall is sporadic, but does occur once or twice per year.

The average yearly temperature is around 19°C during the day and 12°C at night. Even in the coldest months of January, February and March, the average daytime temperature is 12°C, which makes for a pleasant stay even in the depths of winter. The average yearly temperature range is only 5.4°C, which is one of the lowest in Italy. In summer, it is usually between 25°C and 28°C, and 21°C at night; temperatures are lower than in other parts of Italy as the sea breezes cool the air, although in a heatwave temperatures can reach 36°C. The sea is generally warm and from June to October is 19°C or higher. It is mainly calm, with a tidal range of 30cm.

Don't be fooled by the sea, which can look like a millpond. The Italian Riviera is particularly prone to fierce storms, heavy rainfall and rough seas, so always check weather reports before setting out (w eurometeo.com).

Liguria is a windy place and the wind usually blows from the southeast, bringing humid and warmer air from the sea. Summer often comes to a close with dramatic thunderstorms that feel like they have jumped out of Mary Shelley's *Frankenstein*.

NATURAL HISTORY AND CONSERVATION

Nature reserves cover 12% of Liguria, of which perhaps the most well known is the Parco Nazionale delle Cinque Terre. In recent years, marine reserves have also been set up on the coast, and in 1999 the Parco di Portofino, which was established in 1935, was extended to cover the seabed.

Liguria is the most densely wooded region in Italy and over half the terrain is covered in trees. As the mountains are so close to the sea, there is a rich botanical world with a juxtaposition of alpine and coastal plants, flowers and animal life. There are many classic Mediterranean species, such as the ocellated lizard, and others that are typically alpine such as the chamois and the black grouse. The vegetation is distinctly Mediterranean up to a height of 500m, with evergreen scrub and shrubbery known as *maquis*, or *macchia*, and vast woods of Aleppo and maritime pines. Beyond this lies the chestnut belt, up to approximately 800m, where black hornbeams, flowering ash, elm and oaks are also to be found. From 800m to 2,000m there are woods of beech, larch and fir. The wild flowers are hugely varied and delightful. Edelweiss grows at higher altitudes in July and August. Hazelnut trees, both wild and cultivated, grow all over Liguria but especially in the Sturla, Fontanabuona and Graveglia valleys. There are tasty wild herbs. Basil, rosemary, marjoram, thyme, oregano, sorrel, borage, wild chicory, chervil and lovage all grow in abundance.

Man has left his mark and the hillsides of Liguria are covered in terraces full of vines and the distinctive grey-green of olive trees. Palm trees, originally imported from north Africa, now grow all along the coast.

Although forest fires, pollution and the use of pesticides have made life difficult for wildlife, it is still possible to encounter some interesting animals and beautiful butterflies up in the high mountain valleys. Among the animals to look out for are the rare red partridge, the small European gecko and the magnificent *Charaxes jasius* butterfly, known locally as the *ninfa del corbezzolo*. There are also rare otters, short-toed eagles and the large speckled lizard.

Wolves put in an appearance when, in 2004, a wolf with a radio collar migrated from the Emilian Apennines to the Maritime Alps. Wolves are a protected species in Italy with an estimated population of 1,200. It is thought that around 50 of them live in Liguria, although some put the figure as high as 200. Seeing one is still a very rare occurrence, but it is worth remembering that they are there if you plan to camp in the remote areas of the hinterland, especially in the Aveto Valley. Wolves that have bred with wild dogs are becoming an issue in Italy's mountain regions as they show no fear of people.

Up in the mountains there are lots of small mammals, foxes, martens, badgers, field mice, hedgehogs and wild boar, the last of which you are most likely to see at night up in the mountains. Roe and fallow deer have been reintroduced in some areas. Wild boars (*cinghiali*, sing. *cinghiale*) are a common sight and in recent years they have been seen along the coast, as the number of wild boar in Italy has doubled in the past decade. If you look online, there are films of them wandering around beach concessions and in private gardens. You are still unlikely to meet one face to face, but it is important to note that there has been a dramatic rise in the number of tick (*zecca*) bites (page 27) in Liguria and the local press blames the boars.

The snake population includes the ladder snake, the Aesculapian snake, the European whip snake, the smooth snake and the viper. Salamanders can be seen during the day, up in the mountains or in small caves.

Many seabirds thrive here, such as gannets, shearwaters, seagulls and cormorants, and in the marshy areas of the river deltas you will find herons and egrets. Owls and birds of prey are common, and during migration periods, swallows and ducks take a break in Liguria. Apart from the typical species such as blackbirds, finches, etc, Liguria is home to many unusual birds. For a list of the latest sightings and a specific list of species see the website w liguriabirding.net.

The sea is not as rich here as one would imagine and due to pollution there are now far fewer fish than you might expect, although over recent years populations seem to be recovering. Furthermore, the narrow coastal shelf and the lack of tides restrict the growth of nutrients that fish need. The catch consists of what Italians call *pesce azzurro*: fresh sardines and anchovies. There are also bass and bream, mussels, cuttlefish, red mullet, squid, tuna, octopus and clams.

HISTORY

ONCE UPON A TIME The first people to live in Liguria were Neanderthals and their remains have been found in caves scattered along the coast. By 30000BC Cro-Magnon man had moved in, although rising sea levels have hidden many of the caves in which they lived. One of the world's oldest artworks was found in the caves of Balzi Rossi near Ventimiglia. The painting of the Przewalski horse dates from 20000BC, and there are hand and footprints in the caves of Toirano that date from 12340BC. Other important prehistoric finds have been made in the caves of Arene Candide, near Savona, and are on display in the archaeological museum in Pegli.

By the Bronze Age a group of tribes collectively known as the Ligures were living in fortified encampments on the hilltops. There are important rock carvings from this period that have been found on Monte Beigua and Mont Bego just over the border in France. Menhirs with faces found near La Spezia can be seen in that city's archaeological museum.

Liguria's maritime position made it inevitable that the first people to navigate the Mediterranean, the Phoenicians and the Greeks, would come into contact with the Ligures. They are first mentioned by Greeks, who settled in Marseille, in the 7th century BC, and the Ligures lived all along the coast as far as Catalonia and traded with both the Greeks and Phoenicians. There is also evidence of an Etruscan presence in eastern Liguria. The towns of Genoa and Chiavari were founded during this period, as were many of the hilltop towns and villages.

THE ROMANS ARRIVE The Romans arrived in 218BC. Liguria was an important springboard for expansion into Gaul and Spain. The Ligures were fierce warriors and did not give up without a fight. Roman writers described their sobriety, the simplicity of their lives and their indomitable courage.

During the Punic Wars, the majority of the ancient Ligurians sided with Carthage, but a minority including the future Genoese backed the Roman legions. The Romans made the area the ninth region of the empire and named it Liguria. It was a vast piece of territory and stretched as far north as the Po Valley and had Milan as its capital.

The great Roman roads, the Aurelia and Julia Augusta on the coast, and the Postumia and Aemilia Scauri, which ran inland, strengthened the territory and encouraged trade. The Via Postumia from Mediolanum, modern-day Milan, was to play an important part in Liguria's history for, as the power of Rome waned in the north and that of Milan rose, Genoa became Milan's port, a role it still fulfils today.

In 177BC the Romans founded two important ports; one at Portus Lunae, near La Spezia and another at Abintimilium, modern-day Ventimiglia. In the years that followed Ingaunum (Albenga), Alba Doclia (Albisola), Genua (Genoa), Portus Delphini (Portofino) and Segesta Tigulliorum (Sestri Levante) joined them. There are important Roman ruins in Albenga, Ventimiglia and Luni, near La Spezia. According to historian David Gilmour, Roman Italy 'was essentially a land of city-states running themselves under the biggest city-state of all.' It was something that was to have an important impact on the way the region developed in the Middle Ages. It also began the Italian tradition of identifying with the city state that you came from more than the greater state itself – something that continues to shape Italian politics today.

THE BLEAK DARK AGES After the collapse of the Roman Empire, there was a series of invasions and Liguria was first taken by the Visigoths, the Byzantines, then the Lombards and the Franks. Liguria, along with the rest of northern Italy, has been one of the most frequently invaded places on the planet. The place to see traces of Byzantine Liguria is Albenga.

On top of the continual invasions, there was a lot of conflict in this area between the various feudal families and bishops. These conflicts were catalysts for the fortification of the city states, which had to defend themselves and their allies against the Saracens who arrived at the end of the 9th century. They had bases in southern France and raided towns and villages along the coast until AD972. Many communities fled inland and founded towns in the safety of the hills. In order to defeat the Saracens the towns along the coast had to develop into considerable maritime powers. In AD961, Italy was invaded by Otto the Great, the Holy Roman Emperor, but the city-states were so powerful that he was unable to establish complete control.

The city states had large fleets that enabled them to grow rich and powerful off the Crusades, which began in 1096. They not only carried knights and troops to the Middle East for a fee, but also took an active part in the fighting, carving out, in the case of Genoa in particular, a trading empire in the Near East.

SO WHO WAS CHRISTOPHER COLUMBUS?

The most famous person in the history of Liguria is undoubtedly Christopher Columbus. For such a renowned character what is odd is that we actually know very little about him. His date of birth is even unsure and is variously recorded as between 1447 and 1469. Genoa, Savona and Cogoleto all claim him as their own and there is no record of exactly where he was born.

To add to the mystery, Columbus never even told his son, who was his first biographer, who his parents were. Some historians say he went to sea as a young boy at the age of 14, but others point out that at 21 he was working in Savona as a weaver. There is also confusion as to how much experience he had as a navigator before he arrived in Spain and, of course, when he actually arrived there. He and his brother, Bartolomé, were gifted cartographers and this has led to speculation that he was Jewish, as the most accurate maps of the day were made by Jewish cartographers. This could account for his desire, in the age of the Inquisition, to hide his identity. It is also possible that he was simply born out of wedlock.

GENOA BECOMES A SUPERPOWER From the year 1000, the history of Liguria was dominated by Genoa. So much so that if you are interested in history but are not visiting the city, you can find out a lot more about Liguria from the Genoa history section on page 49. Genoa was the most powerful of the city-states and built an empire in the Mediterranean and the Black Sea with Liguria as its Italian power base. It took control of the Tyrrhenian Sea after the Battle of Meloria in 1284 when Genoa crushed its great rival Pisa, making it the most powerful maritime republic in the Mediterranean. The defeat of Pisa was followed by the Battle of Curzola, in which Genoa defeated the Venetians, although it was to eventually prove a pyrrhic victory. By 1232 nearly all of the Riviera di Levante was under Genoese control. Many of the more powerful city-states held out against Genoa's growing power, among them Ventimiglia, Albenga and Savona, the last only capitulating in 1528.

These conflicts were complicated by the feudal faction fighting within the Genoese state. Most of this fighting went on in Genoa itself and the city was divided into warring fiefdoms. As one family saw their influence inside the city wane, they often retired to their power base in another part of Liguria and battled against those who were in power from outside the confines of the city itself.

In order to win political battles at home, Genoa's leading families often sought the support of their powerful neighbours. Instability at home between the 14th and 16th centuries meant that overall control of the republic passed backwards and forwards between the dukes of Milan and the French. It was a situation that was only aggravated by the battles between the Ghelphs and Ghibellines, which consumed much of Italy for two centuries. It dragged foreign powers further into local Ligurian politics. The Visconti of Milan, who favoured the Ghelphs, who in turn supported the papacy, gave support to the Fieschis and the Grimaldis. The French, who favoured the Ghibellines, who in turn supported the Holy Roman Emperor, supported the Spinolas and the Dorias. French influence came to an end when the mighty Admiral Andrea Doria allied with Spain in 1528. Under his rule Genoa dominated the western Mediterranean and he imposed a form of aristocratic government, which gave the republic relative stability for about 250 years.

At their peak the Genoese had settlements in Acre, Jerusalem, Constantinople and around the Black Sea. The last was crucial as it linked Genoa into a great trading route, the Silk Road, which led to China.

The Genoese nobility were so rich and their feasts so lavish that in 1484 Cardinal Paolo Fregoso introduced laws regulating the use of sugar and codified what sorts of foods could be eaten at celebrations within the city limits; it was this law that prompted many rich Genoese patricians to build their villas outside the city, in territory not covered by the cardinal's edict.

Genoa's empire in the Near East contracted first with the collapse of the Crusader states and came to an end with the rise of the Ottoman Empire in the 16th century, which brought an end to business in the eastern Mediterranean and the Black Sea, but not to Liguria's growing wealth. The Ligurian nobility now engaged in major financial speculation. Their alliance with Spain meant that the Genoese nobility used their enormous wealth to bankroll the Spanish conquest of the Americas and they took most of the profits in interest on their loans.

THE ROAD TO REVOLUTION The international crisis of the 17th century, which saw the demise of Spanish power and the rise of France, ended for Genoa with a massive bombardment by the forces of Louis XIV that put the republic firmly back in the French sphere of influence. It also put Liguria in the front line of France's battles with Austria and its ally, neighbouring Piedmont. In 1746 the Austrians occupied Genoa but there was a popular uprising in the city, which drove their forces out.

While the nobility were rolling in money, for most Ligurians life was extremely hard. After the fall of the Roman Empire roads were non-existent. As English writer Tobias Smollett described in 1765, 'there is no other way of going from hence to Genoa, unless you take a mule, and clamber along the mountains at the rate of two miles an hour, and at the risque of breaking your neck every minute… What pity it is, they cannot restore the celebrated Via Aurelia.' To get from Nice to Genoa you had to go by sea in an open boat called a *felucca*.

With such disparities of wealth it is no surprise that there was widespread support for French revolutionary ideas in Liguria in 1789. Genoa became a mini Paris. Liberty trees were planted and angry crowds rushed along the streets calling for vengeance. One gang attacked the archives and carried off the *libra d'oro* containing the names of the leading Genoese families and burnt it, together with the doge's sedan chair, on the Piazza Acquaverde, then called Piazza della Libertà.

In 1794 Napoleon arrived in Italy and, during the first Italian campaign, Liguria was transformed into the Ligurian Republic, modelled on the French Republic. In 1805, Liguria lost its name, was swallowed up by the French Empire and was divided into three departments with three regional capitals: Savona, Genoa and Chiavari. During this period revolutionary laws on human rights and education were passed. Many young men went to Paris to study and adopted a more liberal outlook. Under Napoleon the Via Aurelia was laid out and Church property was expropriated. There was a price to be paid, however. Taxes were high, art was looted and 25,000 Italians ended up invading Russia, recruited as part of Napoleon's Grande Armée. Many of them were to perish in the snow in the retreat from Moscow.

DOWN WITH GENOA, LONG LIVE ITALY The Genoese Republic put in a brief reappearance on the world stage in 1814 after the initial defeat of Napoleon. Yet, without any consultation and to the fury of the Genoese, at the Congress of Vienna in 1815, Genoa was handed over to the House of Savoy, the reactionary, monarchist ally of Britain and Austria, which controlled neighbouring Piedmont. Britain and Austria wanted to secure the French border by placing it in loyal hands.

There was widespread resentment and in 1821 there was an uprising against the House of Savoy, which was brutally suppressed. This only roused nationalist sentiment further. This in turn would trigger a new political movement. It is no coincidence that the fathers of the Risorgimento, the movement that was to unify Italy, were born in Liguria: Giuseppe Mazzini, Goffredo Mameli and Nino Bixio. The great military patriot, Giuseppe Garibaldi, although he was actually born in Nice, had his family roots in the valleys behind Chiavari.

Napoleon's legacy in Italy was that he was seen as a protector of nationalities and the oppressed. Mazzini and his supporters wanted to lead a revolution on the Italian peninsula. They were not simply looking to re-establish the Genoese Republic; they had a bigger vision of a united Italy in a united Europe that was liberal and democratic. Hopes of a mass uprising were repeatedly dashed, however, and ended in tatters after the failure of the revolution of 1848.

It was only when the Piedmontese prime minister, Camillo Benso, Count of Cavour, saw an opportunity of aggrandisement in the 1850s that the Risorgimento really took hold. Under his leadership, the House of Savoy reinvented itself as a modern monarchy and was thus in a perfect position to lead a movement like Mazzini's, in an atmosphere in which most Italians felt ashamed of their declining power and wanted to get the Austrians, who controlled large swathes of northern Italy, out of their country. Cavour participated in the Crimean War to gain diplomatic support from Britain and France, and plotted with the French against Austria.

War broke out in 1859. The French conquered Lombardy and Tuscany, while Emilia revolted. France handed Piedmont all three provinces and received what is now the department of Alpes Maritimes and the city of Nice in a rigged plebiscite in return.

In 1860, General Giuseppe Garibaldi set out from Genoa with over a thousand volunteers to begin the conquest of southern Italy. It was a move that electrified Europe. He defeated the Bourbon army and declared himself a dictator on behalf of the King of Piedmont, Victor Emmanuel. The unification of Italy received vital backing from Britain, where the newspapers had whipped the population into a romantic fervour in support of the dashing Garibaldi. The more sober Foreign Office saw it as the perfect solution that would prevent the peninsula from falling into French hands, which would damage Britain's naval power and could impact on its access to the Suez Canal. Thus, in 1861 Liguria became a region of the Italian state, which after ten years managed to settle its capital in Rome.

Despite widespread resentment of the House of Savoy, Liguria prospered in the 19th century and there was considerable economic growth. The industrial revolution was in full swing in Milan and Turin and Liguria's ports of Genoa and Savona were now crucially linked into Italy's industrial triangle. Fiat opened in Turin in 1889, Lancia followed in 1906 and Olivetti began making typewriters in Ivrea in 1908.

The poverty in the countryside, however, remained extreme. In 1846 Charles Dickens described it thus:

> 'Much of the romance of the beautiful towns and villages on this beautiful road, disappears when they are entered, for many of them are very miserable. The streets are narrow, dark, and dirty; the inhabitants lean and squalid; and the withered old women, with their wiry grey hair twisted up into a knot on the top of the head, like a pad to carry loads on, are so intensely ugly, both along the Riviera, and in Genoa, too, that, seen straggling about in dim doorways with their spindles, or crooning together in by-corners, they are like a population of Witches – except that they certainly are not to be suspected of brooms or any other instrument of cleanliness.'

The Risorgimento was to have one unpredicted consequence along the coast that would rocket it out of its sleepy poverty. The Ruffini brothers were, like many young men of their time, deeply committed to the cause. Mazzini's best friend Jacopo Ruffini was arrested in 1833 after a botched uprising and killed himself in prison in Genoa. His brother went into exile in England and wrote a novel, *Doctor Antonio*, in which the hero of the story was a young doctor committed to the Risorgimento who ends up in prison. He no doubt hoped that it would increase popular support for the cause among British readers. The book, however, was the *Fifty Shades of Grey* of its time. The dashing, handsome Doctor Antonio cares for the beautiful British heroine Lucy who has broken her ankle in a carriage accident and while doing so introduces her to the wonders of the coast in and around Bordighera. It caught the imagination of thousands of British readers, who wanted to find their own Doctor Antonio.

The rich and famous had been wintering in Nice since the end of the Napoleonic Wars and the romantic poets Byron and Shelley had put Liguria on the map in the 1820s when they lived near La Spezia. Shelley's death there in 1822 was an

The British naval bombardment of Genoa in February 1941 sank or damaged 20 warships, killing 144 people and wounding 272. The state-controlled Italian press attempted to cover up what had happened but the local paper, *Il Secolo XIX*, broke ranks, publishing a collective letter accusing the Fascist authorities of cheating the people, which fuelled the anger felt in the city.

The bombing of Genoa in October 1941 showed for the first time how close the home front was to collapse. Areas with no bomb shelters saw popular revolts, and protesters, mainly women, forced their way into the private shelters of the upper classes by throwing stones. At the end of 1942, such protests became more widespread and hundreds of families were living in the tunnels in the city centre. During a particularly rainy period, one overcrowded shelter flooded causing scenes of panic, which soon turned into angry protests against the war.

From the very first bombing operations in Italy, RAF planes crossing the Alps were welcomed by the sight of Milan and Genoa fully illuminated. Non-compliance with the blackout was common.

---

enormous story, but it was only after the publication of *Doctor Antonio* that the Italian Riviera was to become the preferred spot to spend the winter for the aristocracy of northern Europe.

The coming of the railways was to make this, for the first time, an easily accessible destination. In 1853 the Genoa–Turin line opened and by 1874 the coastal lines were in operation. The British press took an enormous interest in Queen Victoria's sojourn in Menton in 1882 and her proposed visit to Bordighera. A whole mass of travel guides were produced as tourists flocked to the coast. By the end of the 19th century, the British population of both Bordighera and Alassio far outstripped the local.

In the new Italy, other parts of Liguria prospered as well. Genoa and Savona became increasingly important ports with Genoa soaking up the money to be made from the mass exodus from Europe to the Americas and Australia. In the meantime, La Spezia became Italy's most important naval port.

Politics in the decades after the unification of Italy was dominated by cliques and cartels. Corruption was widespread and the state's finances were in disarray. Umberto I was assassinated in 1900 and there were widespread strikes and political unrest. Tempted by promises of territorial aggrandisement, Italy, who could easily have stayed out of World War I, made a fateful decision when she threw in her lot with the Allies in 1915.

World War I had devastating consequences for Italy. Its forces were routed in the terrible defeat at Caporetto in 1917 which left not just physical scars but also a deeply wounded pride. The war claimed 650,000 dead and another 350,000 casualties out of a population of 35 million. Look out for the war memorials, as in even the tiniest village they carry a long list of names, often from the same family. The war left the economy in tatters; there were strikes and talk of a revolution akin to the Bolshevik takeover in Russia. In Turin the red flag flew over the Fiat factory. The population was hungry, disillusioned and angry, and the middle classes and the factory owners nervous that they were about to lose everything. Liguria was as divided as the rest of Italy and there were running street battles in parts of its port cities between left and right. It was fertile ground for Mussolini and his fascist movement. They were backed by industrialists, and even the king in a desperate gamble to bring some order to the country, and by 1922 they became the driving force in Italian politics.

During the fascist period a number of old buildings were restored, and Genoa in particular was given a large imposing square with a triumphal arch. La Spezia too flourished and has some interesting fascist architecture. Italy again, however, was over keen to throw its weight around internationally and ended up fighting alongside Germany during World War II.

After the Italian capitulation in 1943, the Germans occupied the north of the country and there was widespread resistance followed by terrible atrocities. Genoa and La Spezia and many towns and villages along the coast were badly bombed. There was a widespread insurrection led by partisans who freed large parts of Liguria before the Allied troops arrived. World War II left Liguria a battered place. For information on the Genoa Blitz, see the box on page 11.

Bomb damage was left unrepaired for decades and in the immediate aftermath food was scarce. France took the Val de Roya behind Menton, in what was one of the last frontier changes in western Europe. Fortunately, after 1945, in the words of David Gilmour, 'Italy abandoned its pretensions to become a Great Power and concentrated, with far more success, on achieving prosperity for its citizens.'

In 1946, the country became a republic. Genoa was to play a key role in the economic miracle that followed the war, shipping to the world Fiat's cars and Pirelli's tyres made in Turin and Milan, along with a whole host of other goods. The 50s and 60s were a period of dynamic growth.

The boom brought one important casualty – the environment. There were few building regulations and the coast was quickly developed. People flocked to the cities and in the hinterland whole communities faced extinction. Although a major new motorway was built in the decades after 1960 which improved communications, some roads like the elevated highway in the old port of Genoa were built with almost criminal disregard, while much of the hinterland had dirt-track roads until the 1970s and 80s. Much of it still remains remote.

RATLINES

In the years immediately after the end of World War II, Italy was teeming with displaced people. After the Allied military occupation of Italy ended in December 1945, checks on personal papers became more casual and after the peace treaty was signed in 1947, they were non-existent. As a result, Italy became a highway for escaping Nazis, sympathisers and collaborators. Getting hold of fake papers was easy and forgers abounded.

The Nazi escape route ran through Austria and over the Alps into the South Tyrol and then on to Genoa, where in a murky world of deception and secrets, the Catholic Church provided accommodation, the Red Cross supplied the documentation, the Argentinian consulate the visas and US intelligence played a dubious role in an attempt to fight communism.

Little was done to monitor who was receiving documentation and the signature of a priest was usually enough to suffice. Two of the most notorious Nazis, the Auschwitz Doctor of Death, Josef Mengele, and one of the masterminds of the Holocaust, Adolf Eichmann, both received Red Cross papers in this way and sailed from Genoa in 1949 and 1950 respectively. While Nazis were escaping through Liguria's ports, in a macabre twist and surreal parallel world, so were thousands of Jewish refugees (see box, page 158).

The late 20th century saw cities like Genoa and Savona go into decline, while little changed in the coastal resorts. In recent years, however, Liguria's cities have experienced something of a renaissance, becoming for the first time tourist destinations in their own right. Many of its coastal resorts have been jolted into the 21st century by the construction of some swanky marinas, while the magic of the Riviera lives on.

GOVERNMENT AND POLITICS

Italy is a parliamentary, democratic republic. It uses a proportional voting system to elect the two Houses of Parliament, the Chamber of Deputies and the Senate. Parliament is elected every five years, although few Italian governments run their course. The precarious nature of Italian politics has led to dozens of different governments in the last 50 years.

The prime minister, appointed by the president, is the head of government. The president himself is elected every seven years by a college comprising both chambers of parliament and three representatives from each region. The minimum age for presidential candidates is 50. The Italian prime minister has less authority than some of his European counterparts. He is not authorised to request the dissolution of parliament or dismiss ministers (these are exclusive prerogatives of the president), and he must receive a vote of approval from the Council of Ministers, the Italian cabinet, which holds effective executive power to execute most political activities.

The national government structure is mirrored in the country's 20 regions, where the President of the Regional Government is elected by popular ballot. He is assisted by a vice-president and ten ministers. Legislative power is shared with the Regional Council of 40 members who are elected by proportional representation.

The regions are then subdivided into provinces; four in the case of Liguria. The five 'special status' regions (*regioni a statuto speciale*) of Friuli-Venezia-Giulia, Sardinia, Sicily, Trentino-Alto Adige and Val d'Aosta are autonomous or semi-autonomous and have special powers granted under the constitution. Italy's other 15 regions have little autonomy compared with, for example, those in Germany or Spain. The legislative powers of the regions are subject to certain constitutional limitations, the most important of which is that regional acts may not conflict with national interests. The regions can also enact legislation necessary for the enforcement of state laws and have the right to acquire property and to collect certain revenues and taxes. Regional and local elections are held every five years. Unfortunately, regional government has led to extravagance; in 2004 the entertainment expenses of the president of Campania were 12-times higher than the president of Germany.

The Italian political landscape changed dramatically in the 1990s when the 'Clean Hands' operation exposed corruption at the highest levels of politics and big business, implicating several former prime ministers and politicians. It led to the collapse of the Christian Democrats who had dominated Italian politics in the decades that followed World War II. It was at this point that Silvio Berlusconi entered the political stage. One of Italy's richest men, he has been put on trial no fewer than six times over financial matters, found guilty three times, but eventually acquitted. He's a controversial figure and his sex life has received huge attention. In 2013, he was convicted of tax fraud and for having sex with a minor. He appealed and won the case.

As the eye of the financial storm passed over Italy in November 2011, Berlusconi resigned and the president, Giorgio Napolitano, appointed the economist, Mario

1

Monti, to form a government. His cabinet consisted of technocrats, diplomats and businessmen and not a single politician. He introduced stringent cuts and economic reforms that became increasingly unpopular in Italy and he performed poorly in the February 2013 election. In February 2014, Matteo Renzi became modern Italy's youngest prime minister. Seen as a radical break with the past, he introduced a programme of rapid economic and political reform earning him the nickname Il Rottamatore ('The Scrapper').

Since 2013 Italian politics has become increasingly populist. As the country struggled to recover from the economic crisis of 2008, a vast number of migrants arrived in the country. As a result, votes for the far-right Northern League (Lega Nord) and the Five Star Movement (Movimento 5 Stelle) founded by Beppe Grillo, a shaggy-bearded wrinkly comedian from Genoa, soared. For more information on Grillo, see w bradtguides.com/grillo.

The 2018 elections resulted in a hung parliament and the formation of a coalition between the Five Star Movement and the Northern League. Liguria was traditionally a left-wing stronghold and voted for decades for the Democratic Party, but in 2018 Ligurian votes reflected the national pattern in which the Democratic Party vote collapsed.

The formation of the new government sent shock waves through corridors in Brussels as both parties fought the election using anti-EU rhetoric. Their first steps were to crack down on illegal migration, closing Italy's ports to boats carrying African refugees and migrants, and to introduce a census of Italy's Roma population. The move set alarm bells ringing as it came 80 years after the introduction of racial laws against the Jews in 1938.

ECONOMY

Although Italy is the third-largest Eurozone economy and has a reputation for excellence in the fields of fashion, food and cars, Italy was badly hit by the 2008 financial crisis and has struggled to recover. Italian debt is now the second worst in Europe after Greece and has reached 132% of GDP. It is important to remember, however, that Italy has a huge black economy and economic statistics should be taken with a pinch of salt.

High unemployment has resulted in widespread poverty and many of the jobs created by the Renzi government were part-time with no security. Many analysts also point to Italy's high rates of taxation as an issue.

The country's extremely low growth rates in the 1990s and 2000s and its excessive borrowing have their roots in widespread corruption, bloated bureaucracy, an overpaid political class, low productivity and a poor education system. The problem began in the 1990s when the country's manufacturing sector was overtaken by Asian competitors.

Italy comes 54th in the Corruption Perceptions Index, placing the country lower than Rwanda. Organised crime is a serious issue. In 2012 65% of Italians told Transparency International that corruption had intensified in Italy in the last few years and felt that anti-corruption legislation had had little impact. A 2009 poll by the EU's Eurobarometer found that 17% of Italians said they were asked to pay a bribe in the previous 12 months. Such bribes discourage outside investment.

Above all Italy is dogged by restrictive labour laws that discourage companies from hiring staff and expanding. It is also hampered by the presence of the mafia, which is active in the north, as well as in the south. The task at hand is a major overhaul of not just the economy, but society as a whole.

There is also concern over Italy's birth rate. It's one of the lowest in Europe and is at its lowest in the northwest. In the first decade of the 21st century, 10% of schools in Liguria closed down, some of them becoming old people's homes. The ageing population has serious economic implications that are also adding to the country's woes.

Despite the economic crash, Liguria still enjoys a characteristically high standard of living, and the black economy is certainly a factor in this. Agriculture is specialised in the production of high-quality goods, flowers, wine and olive oil. Flowers are big business on the Riviera di Ponente around Sanremo, where a quarter of Italy's cut flowers are produced.

During the economic boom years, steel was an important local industry, but since the 1980s Ligurian industry has centred on food production, shipbuilding (notably of cruise ships, military vessels, small craft and luxury yachts), electrical engineering and electronics, and petrochemicals. Genoa is one of the biggest commercial ports in the Mediterranean and La Spezia the largest naval base in the country, while Savona is also an important port.

Tourism is a major employer in Liguria. There is a mixture of high-end luxury tourism, especially around Portofino, traditional seaside holiday spots and small

THE SHRINKING CITY

In 1971 Genoa had a population of 816,872 but today just 594,733, live in the city. The city's shrinking population means there is under-use of housing stock in the city centre, which has a significant impact on the economy, public services and education system. Significantly, the population is shrinking across all social classes and in all parts of the city, but this is not a new phenomenon.

Statistics show that since the 19th-century Genoese women have married later than in the rest of Italy and a higher proportion remain unmarried. On average, Genoese couples marry between 34 and 37 years of age. To compound the problem they are more likely to separate than other Italian couples and they have fewer children. As a result Genoa is one of western Europe's 'oldest' cities, with an ageing population who are dying off.

In the late 19th century industrialisation boosted the population as immigrants flowed in from the south and rural northwest of Italy, but in the 1970s the industrial boom years came to an end and immigration from other parts of the country halted. As a result, the old town fell into a state of disrepair and residents moved away from the heart of the city, as municipal social housing was built in the northern periphery. In the late 1980s, Genoa became the destination for African migrants, who created an ethnic enclave in parts of the old town. In the late 1990s, the population was boosted as young women poured in from Ecuador, largely to look after the city's elderly. But as the 1990s progressed and the old port was redeveloped into a tourist attraction, these migrants in turn began to find themselves pushed out of the old city as a process of gentrification began.

Renovated housing was sold or rented at speculative prices to young, single, middle-class professionals and many flats have become offices or B&Bs. As a result there has been the biggest decrease in population the city centre has ever experienced. There are plans to boost the regeneration of the city centre and former industrial areas like Cornigliano, and road connections between outlying parts of the city are being improved. These plans are not without problems of their own. The construction of a highway between Genoa and the Val Polcevera and the Val Bisagno has been opposed by environmentalists, as the hills around Genoa contain asbestos.

holiday resorts. Genoa has, until recently, shied away from making money out of tourism, but as one Genoese businessman said to me, 'If this is what we have to do to make money, we will do it.' Since the Genoese have always been extremely canny at making money, I would say to their old rivals Pisa and Venice, 'Watch out!'

PEOPLE

About 90% of the population of Liguria live along the coast, 40% of them in Genoa. By contrast, the hilly and mountainous inland has been progressively abandoned as the population has moved to the coast where jobs are predominantly in the service industries. Temperamentally, the old adage is that those who live along the western Riviera di Ponente are more open than those who live on the rocky east coast, where people are generally considered to be more taciturn. The Genoese have a reputation rather akin to the Scots of being stingy and dour. Virgil dubbed the Ligurians hard workers and the Romans considered them crafty.

Liguria has produced a disproportionate number of explorers. Probably the most famous Ligurian is Christopher Columbus, who 'discovered' the Americas in 1492, but Recco gave the world Nicoloso da Recco, who claimed the Azores for Portugal, and Varazze Lanzarotte Malocello, who reached the Canaries in 1456. Noli's Antoniotto Usodimare discovered the Cape Verde islands in 1456 and Savona's Leon Pancaldo was Magellan's pilot when he first circumnavigated the globe in 1519–22.

With so many men at sea it is no surprise that the women had a reputation for being tough and hard working. Their beauty was remarked upon by numerous travellers from the era of the Grand Tour, and it is said that one, Simonetta Cattaneo, was immortalised by Botticelli in his Birth of Venus.

While the villages of the *entroterra* are remote, Genoa is a multi-ethnic city. In the 1950s and 60s in particular, it attracted an influx of workers from the bordering regions and from the south. Since then it has attracted a sizeable immigrant community from north and west Africa and South America. At time of writing there were a large number of illegal migrants and refugees in Liguria (see box, page 270).

LANGUAGE

Even if you speak Italian, stop and ask directions from an old man or woman in the mountains and the chances are that you will be left wondering exactly what it was that they said. That's because there are regional versions of Italian spoken right across the country. Italian is derived from 'vulgar' Latin, the language that was spoken every day. This developed in different ways in Italy's regions. One of the reasons it metamorphosed into a mass of different versions was that, until the 13th century, Latin proper was the only written language and the language used in education for far longer. This gave the educated classes a *lingua franca* and left the masses free to speak a dialect.

Modern Italian grew out of the Florentine dialect largely because Dante and Machiavelli wrote in Florentine and their works were the bestsellers of the day. It was also closer grammatically to written Latin than other dialects. In 1861, only one in 40 people spoke what would now pass for Italian. It only began to be established as the national language as literacy levels rose after the introduction of compulsory education in the late 19th century. Many people, however, continued to speak only dialect until the arrival of television in the 1950s.

Ligurian belongs to the Italo-Celtic dialects family of northern Italy. It varies within Liguria and the Genoese, *zeneize*, is the most important version, and is commonly spoken in Genoa alongside Italian. In its differences from standard Italian, Genoese is somewhat similar to French. For example, a raspberry is a *franboâza* and closer to the French *framboise* than the Italian *lampone* and a fig is a *figo*, which in Italian is *fico* and in French *figue*. A popular saying is '*Son zeneize, rizo ræo, strenzo i denti e parlo ciæo*', which translates as, 'I'm Genoese, I seldom laugh, I grind my teeth, and I say what I mean.'

Written literature has been produced in Genoese since the 13th century, but the spelling has never been standardised. Although there are no exact figures it is estimated that over a million people speak the dialect both within Liguria and Corsica.

Dante said, 'If the Genoese through forgetfulness, should lose the letter "z", it would be necessary for them to remain mute, or else to find another means of elocution.' That said, he also adopted a number of Genoese words, which then became part of mainstream Italian.

RELIGION

The Italian constitution provides for religious freedom and there is, therefore, no state religion. The Catholic Church, however, enjoys some privileges. Liguria is, like the rest of Italy, overwhelmingly Roman Catholic and crammed with cathedrals, churches and sanctuaries.

Around 90% of the Italian population are Catholics and about a third of them attend church regularly. Although that number is falling, it is considerably higher than that in neighbouring Roman Catholic France, where just 5% of believers attend church on a regular basis. Most baptisms, weddings and funerals take place in church and attendance is high at Easter and Christmas. The Church still plays a significant role in everyday life, although the political influence it has wielded in the past has declined dramatically in recent years. Religious festivals are an important part of local and national life and even the smallest communities in Liguria celebrate their saints' days with gusto.

Genoa, however, is, and always has been, a large cosmopolitan port with a more mixed religious life than that in the smaller towns and the hinterland. Jews have lived in Liguria since Roman times and today Genoa has a small Jewish community of a couple of hundred people, and a synagogue. The Jewish population of Italy is 30,000 and there are synagogues in 21 cities. The old Jewish ghetto was in Vico del Campo, a narrow street in the old town. It was established in 1660 and the community was locked in at night. Historically the Genoese had a rather contradictory relationship with their Jewish community and while there was an atmosphere of distrust and dislike, violence was far less common than in other parts of Italy and the Genoese, always with an eye on their purses, recognised the important role that Jewish bankers could play in the city. Poor Jews were, however, only allowed to stay three days in the city walls during the early period of the Republic, and during the Inquisition in Spain, Jewish refugees were refused entry to the city and many froze to death on the port side in the harsh winter.

When the Italian state was founded, Jews became an integrated part of the governing classes and there was a Jewish Minister of Defence and prime minister. There were, however, undercurrents of anti-Semitism, which grew under fascism. In 1938 the Racial Laws severely curbed Jewish civil rights.

In World War II Genoa, as a port, came to play an important role in helping Jews to escape from Europe aided by the local clergy. The deportation of the Jews to death camps only began after the capitulation of Italy in September 1943, after which northern Italy was occupied by the Germans. In all, 153 Jews were arrested and deported from Genoa. Then, in the late 1940s Liguria was a major transit point for Jews leaving to settle in Israel (see box, page 158).

As early as the 16th century a mosque was established in the old port for Barbary pirates who had been taken as galley slaves. Liguria now has a growing Muslim population, mainly immigrants from north Africa, south Asia, Albania and the Middle East, which numbers around 15,000. Tensions have risen in recent years and right-wing politicians, mostly members of the Northern League, blocked the construction of a new mosque in Genoa in 2010. Getting permission for the building of mosques in Italy is very difficult, although the total number of Muslims in Italy is approximately 1.5 million. Anti-Semitism and racial attacks have increased in Italy in recent years.

Italy also has some 60,000 Buddhists, 20,000 Mormons and 400,000 Jehovah's Witnesses. Recent polls show that approximately 14% of the population consider themselves to be either atheists or agnostics.

Visitors have also left their mark on the religious life of Liguria. Sanremo is home to a Russian Orthodox church, testament to the resort's 19th-century popularity with the Russian aristocracy, and the English community who flocked to Liguria established Anglican churches in their favourite holiday spots. There has been an Anglican church in Genoa since the early 19th century. The present building, in Piazza Marsala, dates to 1873.

EDUCATION

Children can start school at the age of three, but must be in full-time education by the age of six. Education is compulsory until 16 and there are both state and private schools. At 11 children begin their secondary education. Between 11 and 14 they attend a middle school, the *scuola media*. Students study a set curriculum and at the end of the third year, they sit a written exam in Italian, maths, science and a foreign language. There is an oral exam in the other subjects. They then move on to second grade secondary school, *scuola secondaria di secondo grado*. There are two types of school: the *liceo*, which is like a traditional British grammar school; and an *istituto*, which is more vocational. Specialised courses begin in the third year. The final exam is the *esame di maturità* and to obtain this, students must pass written and oral exams; the diploma is considered to be a university entrance qualification. The average student is 19 when they enter university. Every student who has a diploma is entitled to attend a vocational school or university and most choose to do this in their own region.

On paper all looks fine; in fact, Italian education is in a mess and Prime Minister Renzi won an important victory in 2015 when he pushed through parliament a major programme to reform the education system. It is much needed. At time of writing, the Programme for International Student Assessment, co-ordinated by the OECD (Organisation for Economic Co-operation and Development), ranked Italian secondary education levels 34th in the world, significantly below the OECD average. There was also a significant difference between levels of achievement between the north and the south. Although class sizes are small, the problem is that there are too many badly paid teachers. Education has been used by politicians, especially in the south, for patronage and job creation and doesn't attract the best graduates.

Although Italian universities are among the oldest in the world, only one appears in the Times Higher Education rankings of the top 200 universities in the world. The university system is overcrowded and underfunded, and a majority of students leave without completing their degrees. There is little investment in postgraduate studies and many students leave to continue their studies abroad, which contributes to Italy's 'brain drain'. There is an additional problem of nepotism, which has been highlighted by investigations by the newspaper *La Repubblica*, with some university departments in effect family fiefdoms. A number of Italian universities now teach some courses in English in order to make their students better equipped to compete for jobs, attract foreign students and thus boost their world ranking.

CULTURE

ART Liguria has always been something of an artistic backwater and although the wealth of Genoa attracted some famous artists, the Genoese preferred not to spend their money on too many frivolities. In the early Middle Ages, it was mainly Tuscan artists who worked in Liguria, like Maestro Guglielmo, who painted the *Crucifixion* in Sarzana Cathedral.

The 15th century saw a move to the Lombard and Piedmontese schools. The family of sculptors, the Gaggini, were active in Genoa, as were painters Donato de' Bardi and Vincenzo Foppa of Padua. The big local name of the time was Ludovico Brea, who was born in nearby Nice. His paintings are very impressive and can be seen all over Liguria, especially in Taggia (page 251). Bernardo Strozzi also created a number of masterpieces at this time.

Genoese art began to develop in the 16th century, when the great Florentine painter Perin del Vaga, who worked with Michelangelo, was summoned to Genoa by Andrea Doria to adorn his new Palazzo dei Principe. He was a leading light in the style of Mannerism, which introduced elements of abstraction and distortion into art. In all, del Vaga spent eight years painting in Genoa. His work inspired Ligurian artist Luca Cambiaso, who also painted commissions for Philip II of Spain. Other well-known local artists of the time were the Semino brothers Andrea and Ottavio, Bernardo Castello, and Cambiaso's pupil Lazzaro Tavarone, whose speciality was depicting Genoese epics like Columbus's discovery of America. Also from Cambiaso's school came Giovanni Battista Paggi and Domenico Fiasella.

The 17th century was the heyday of art in Liguria. A new influence on Genoese artists arrived when the Jesuits purchased Rubens' *Circumcision* in 1605 and the *Miracles of St Ignatius* in 1620 to decorate Genoa's church of Sant'Ambrogio. Rubens' friend Cornelis de Wael opened a studio in Genoa in 1642 and spent 50 years painting maritime scenes. In the early 17th century, Sinibaldo Scorza became Liguria's first landscape painter.

Between 1621 and 1627 Van Dyck based himself in Genoa, painting a number of important works for the city's noble families, and had a considerable influence on the local painters, among them Giovanni Andrea de Ferrari and the brothers, Giovanni Andrea and Giovanni Battista Carlone.

Flemish painters like Van Dyck also had an influence on Giovanni Benedetto Castiglione, Il Grechetto, who was one of the best Genoese painters of the century. Pastoral scenes were also the forte of Antonio Travi, Il Sestri, who came from Sestre Ponente. One of the great exponents of the Baroque was Valerio Castello. The plague killed off many in this talented generation of artists leaving Domenico Piola, whose work can be seen in the most important palaces in Genoa, as the master in his field. His rival was Gregorio de Ferrari, with whom he painted some of the ceilings of the Palazzo Rosso.

Genoese painting declined in the 18th century and the nobility looked elsewhere for talent. Sculpture, however, flourished. Both Bernardo Schiaffino and his brother Francesco had outstanding talent. In the late 17th and early 18th centuries, Anton

1

Maria Maragliano worked as a sculptor with his uncle Giovanni Battista, and is especially known for his work in wood. In the 19th century, Carlo Rubatto was the sculptor responsible for statues in the Villa Pallavicini in Pegli and many of those in the Staglieno cemetery, as well as the lions that flank the cathedral.

The new trendy face of contemporary art in Genoa is Emanuele Timothy Costa. He has been taking portraits of people in Genoa for his art project #thousandpeople, including those of my family. The idea is that the city is a crossroads of culture and his thousand faces will reflect the diversity of the place. He is self-taught and took up photography after an accident left him bedridden for six months. He then worked on cruise ships before taking to Genoa's streets to snap some incredible portraits.

ARCHITECTURE Liguria's towns and villages are immediately recognisable by their tall houses painted in pastel colours and decorated with trompe l'oeil paintings that impressed both Petrarch and Montaigne. Trompe l'oeil wasn't invented here, but Ligurians made it their own. Some might say it was their famous miserliness that attracted them to it, as it was easier to paint a balcony than build one.

Many of the villages were built on steep hillsides to protect them from pirate raids and cluster around an elegant central church with a beautiful painted spire. The streets run in concentric circles so if an attack occurred, it was easier to defend.

Medieval buildings are characterised by their black-and-white striped façades. The cathedral of San Lorenzo in Genoa is a classic example of this sort of architecture. It was at this point that large palaces began to be built in Genoa by the city's rich merchants. The running battles raged by the warring families in Liguria led to the construction of many castles and towers.

In the 16th and 17th centuries grand palazzos were built along the Via Garibaldi in Genoa and the city's Molo Nuovo also dates from this period. Galeazzo Alessi from Perugia worked here in the Renaissance and the Gaggini family also left their mark. The Milanese Bartolomeo Bianco designed Via Balbi, the Palazzo Durazzo-Pallavicini and the new walls. In the 19th century the main monuments in Genoa were designed by the city's Carlo Barabino.

Architecturally the 20th century saw the construction of a number of flyovers and the hideous *sopraelevata*, the motorway that runs along the old port. In the 1950s and 60s a number of social housing developments in the suburbs were actually cutting edge in design. The Quartiere Forte Quezzi was built in the post-war boom years when workers flooded into the city, which already had a housing shortage after the bombing. It was inspired by Le Corbusier's designs but, as with so much of this architecture, it did little to right social wrongs. Genoa is the hometown of the famous architect Renzo Piano, who oversaw and designed much of the new port (page 69). Architecture has also been a driving force in rejuvenating the old town. The relocation of Genoa's architecture faculty to the historic centre in the 1980s injected vigour and creativity back into the old town.

MUSIC Liguria's musical life took off in the 19th century when the opera house, the Teatro Carlo Felice, was built. It was bombed in World War II, but rebuilt in the 1980s and is now a cutting-edge theatre. Liguria's music star is violinist Niccolò Paganini, who was born in Genoa in 1782, and the city is home to the Niccolò Paganini music conservatory. Genoa is also the hometown of Fabio Armiliato, the opera star, who played the singing undertaker in Woody Allen's *To Rome with Love*. Genoa was immortalised by cult singer-songwriter Fabrizio De Andre. Sanremo hosts the annual Sanremo Song Festival, which inspired the Eurovision Song Contest.

LITERATURE Liguria has attracted and inspired some of the most famous writers in history. Byron and Shelley both spent a considerable amount of time here and Shelley drowned off the coast between Lerici and Livorno. Liguria fascinated some of the greatest talents, prompting Dickens and Henry James to write long accounts of their travels here. Others, like D H Lawrence, who found the inspiration for *Lady Chatterley's Lover* here, drew on their own experiences of the culture and, for Lawrence in particular, the force of nature. Scottish surgeon Tobias Smollett put the region on the map for the British when he published a series of 41 letters of his accounts of travelling along the Riviera from Nice to Genoa in 1764. Liguria also has its own homegrown writers, among them Italo Calvino, who grew up in Sanremo (for more information on Calvino, see: w bradtguides.com/calvino), and Nobel Prize-winning poet Eugenio Montale. There are more details on these books on page 285.

UPDATES WEBSITE

You can post your comments and recommendations, and read feedback and updates from other readers online at w bradtupdates.com/liguria.

LIGURIA ONLINE

For additional online content, articles, photos and more on Liguria, why not visit w bradtguides.com/liguria?

2

Practical Information

WHEN TO VISIT

With the mildest of climates, tourists visit Liguria at all times of the year, but November and February can be wet and are best avoided. There are things to do all year round: from fascinating museums and fabulous palaces to visit, to beaches and wild mountain countryside to explore.

There is, however, a clearly defined high-season that runs from May to September and the coast can get very busy, especially at weekends. It is hot in Liguria in summer and it is not the best time to explore Genoa. It is essentially a beach experience in this season but it is also a beautiful period to spend time in the mountains, which are degrees cooler than the coast. August can be disappointing for visiting Genoa, as many restaurants close for the entire month and the city can be uncharacteristically empty.

In winter, when the air is clear and the views are at their best, it is a joy to walk along the Cinque Terre path in peace and gaze out across the sea to Corsica. Spring and autumn are best for sightseeing and any kind of sporting activity that doesn't involve cooling off in the sea.

HIGHLIGHTS

Liguria has some of the most stunning coastline in the Mediterranean; it includes the Cinque Terre, one of Italy's top tourist attractions. Dramatic cliffs plunge into a deep blue sea; there are tiny rocky coves and beautiful seaside villages, like the world-famous Portofino. That said, Liguria isn't all about glitz. The Ligurians like the simple life and the hinterland is well off the tourist track. This is somewhere to have a truly Italian experience.

For historians and art lovers, Genoa has sumptuous palaces, stuffed with old masters and was once the powerhouse of medieval Europe. Its old town is one of the continent's largest and refreshingly authentic. It is an excellent option for a short break.

One of the real wonders of Liguria is its fantastic food. This is the home of pesto, and you will never have eaten a version of this sauce as tasty as the one they make here. Genoa once had a vast trading empire that stretched to the Near East, and the Genoese as a result adopted the Arab love of ice cream and candied fruit. What is truly fascinating about eating in Liguria is that, although it is Italy's smallest region, the cuisine is highly varied and changes from valley to valley. Trying the flagship dishes won't break the bank either, as the Ligurians are a thrifty lot and live off simple food.

Fortunately Liguria is an outdoor place, so you can burn off the calories hiking along the mountain tops, which offer stunning views along the coast, snorkelling and swimming in the sea or cycling along the mile upon mile of coastal pathways.

Local traditions are important and Ligurians love an excuse for a party, and especially firework displays. Village festivals, often with very ancient origins, abound; and there are colourful religious processions and events throughout the year (for the main festivals, see page 40).

SUGGESTED ITINERARIES

WINTER WEEKEND Base yourself in Genoa. Spend one full day exploring the city and trying out some of its fabulous restaurants. On the second day take the train to Camogli. Eat lunch in La Nonna Nina in San Rocco and then walk across the promontory down to Punta Chiappa and catch the boat back to Camogli.

SUMMER WEEKEND Base yourself in Porto Venere. Spend the first day exploring the old town and take a boat trip to Palmaria Island, where there are great walks and some lovely beaches. The next day, take a boat trip to the Cinque Terre or across the bay to Lerici.

ONE WEEK Spend two nights in Genoa exploring the old town and visiting the palaces and museums. Then go to Camogli for two nights; from here, take a trip to the monastery of San Fruttuoso and visit Portofino for a day, and then head for the Cinque Terre. Spend a night in Corniglia before moving on to Porto Venere, where it is time to unwind and take the boat to Palmaria Island for a day on the beach. As you journey back up the coast, stop off at Sestri Levante before heading home.

TWO WEEKS Spend four nights in Genoa; this will give you time to see everything that the city has to offer and take a trip on the narrow-gauge railway up into the mountain valleys behind the city. Then spend two nights in and around Portofino or Camogli. Take two nights to explore the Cinque Terre and spend the next night in Porto Venere. Then catch the train from La Spezia to Varazze. If you stop off for two nights here you can get the best of the hinterland as you will have time to discover Monte Beigua. Next stop is the tiny walled town of Noli. Then head for Imperia, stopping en route to see the caves at Toirano. Finish your trip with two nights in Triora, deep in the mountains.

THREE WEEKS With three weeks you have time to see all the highlights of Liguria. Start at the French border. The Mediterranean beckons, so spend the first night in Bordighera. Then head up into the mountains to the hilltop towns of Apricale and Triora. Then it is time to head back for the coast via Taggia to Imperia. Take a trip back up into the mountains, basing yourself for a couple of nights in Borgomaro. Kick off week two exploring the area around Varazze and relaxing by the sea. After this you'll be ready for city life and four nights in Genoa. Week three gives you plenty of time to explore the Riviera di Levante as described in the one-week itinerary, but you will also have time to visit the medieval town of Sarzana.

TOUR OPERATORS

UK

Alternative Travel ☏0186 531 5678; **w** atg-oxford.co.uk. Walking tours of Portofino & the Cinque Terre.
Citalia ☏ 0129 383 9842; **w** citalia.com. Hotels across Liguria.

Classic Collection ☏0800 047 1066; **w** classic-collection.co.uk. Luxury holidays in Sanremo, Portofino, Santa Margherita & Rapallo.
HF Holidays ☏0845 470 8558; **w** hfholidays. co.uk. Cooking & walking tours in Liguria.

Inntravel ☎0165 361 7001; w inntravel.co.uk. Specialising in what they call 'slow holidays', & offering tours of Genoa, Camogli, Portofino & the Cinque Terre.
Kirker Holidays ☎020 7593 2288; w kirkerholidays.com. Trips to Alassio, Cinque Terre, Genoa, Sanremo, Portofino, Porto Venere, Santa Margherita, Rapallo & Camogli.
Ramblers ☎0170 733 1133; w ramblersholidays.co.uk. Walking tours of the Cinque Terre.

Sovereign ☎0129 383 2697; w sovereign.com. Holidays in Portofino & Rapallo.

USA

Rent Villas ☎+1 800 880 1228; w rentvillas. com. 17 properties across Liguria.
The Wayfarers ☎+1 800 249 4620; w thewayfarers.com. Escorted walking holidays in the Cinque Terre.

RED TAPE

As a region of Italy, Liguria is bound by national entry regulations, as well as those required by the European Union (EU) and the Schengen Agreement. Citizens from EU member states and those of Albania, Bosnia-Herzegovina, Macedonia, Montenegro and Serbia do not need visas and can stay in the country as long as they like. The holders of passports from the following countries do not need a visa for a stay of 90 days or less: Andorra, Argentina, Australia, Brazil, Brunei, Canada, Chile, Costa Rica, El Salvador, Guatemala, Honduras, Hong Kong, Israel, Japan, Macao, Malaysia, Mexico, Monaco, New Zealand, Nicaragua, Panama, Paraguay, Singapore, South Korea, Switzerland, United States, Uruguay and Venezuela, and, very likely, the UK post-Brexit. All other nationals should consult their relevant embassy about visa requirements or take a look at the website w schengenvisainfo.com.

In theory all foreigners are required to register their presence with the police; for this reason you will always be asked for your passport details by a hotel or B&B, so keep it with you as you travel about. Individuals in reality rarely do so if they are simply on holiday. If you intend to stay longer, it is advisable, however, to register at the local police station.

Staying for longer than 90 days can be complicated for non-EU citizens. Italy currently offers around 21 types of entry visa. The three most common are:

- **Study visas** A study visa requires you to have proof of the following: intended accommodation, financial support of no less than €350 per month, ability to cover medical costs, funds to return to your country of origin and an intended place of study.
- **Work visas** These are difficult to obtain. You must already have secured a position from an Italian employer, who is then required to file the required paperwork. The government has come down hard on illegal immigrants so working in a bar or restaurant without a work visa is not advisable.
- **Elective residence** This visa requires substantial proof of private income such as property or a pension.

EMBASSIES

ITALIAN EMBASSIES & CONSULATES ABROAD

🇪 **Australia** 12 Grey St, Deakin, Canberra, ACT 2600; ☎+61 2 6273 3333; e ambasciata. canberra@esteri.it; w ambcanberra.esteri.it. There are consulates in Melbourne ☎+61 3 9867 5744; Sydney ☎+61 2 9392 7900; Adelaide ☎+61 3 859 39124; & Brisbane ☎+61 7 3229 8944.

ⓔ Canada 275 Slater St, Ottawa, ON, K1P 5H9; +1 613 232 2401; e ambasciata.ottawa@esteri. it; w ambottawa.esteri.it. There are consulates in both Montreal +1 514 849 8351; & Toronto +1 416 977 1566.
ⓔ Ireland 63–65 Northumberland Rd, Dublin 4; +353 1 660 1744; e ambasciata.dublino@esteri. it; w ambdublino.esteri.it.
ⓔ New Zealand 34–38 Grant Rd, PO Box 463, Thorndon, Wellington; +64 4 473 5339; e ambasciata.wellington@esteri.it; w ambwellington.esteri.it.

ⓔ UK 14 Three Kings Yard, London W1Y 2EH; +44 20 7312 2200; e ambasciata.londra@esteri. it; w amblondra.esteri.it. If you reside in Scotland or Northern Ireland, you must only apply in person for your visa at the Italian Consulate in Edinburgh, 32 Melville Street, Edinburgh EH3 7HA; 0131 226 3631; w consedimburgo.esteri.it.
ⓔ USA Consulate 690 Park Av, NY 10065; +1 202 737 9100; e info.newyork@esteri.it; 3,000 Whitehaven St NW, Washington DC 20008; +1 202 6124400; e info.washington@esteri.it; w ambwashingtondc.esteri.it.

GETTING THERE AND AWAY

BY AIR Genoa's Cristoforo Colombo Airport is 6km west of the city in the suburb of Sestri Ponente (010 60151; w www.airport.genova.it). At time of writing it was undergoing a makeover that is due to be completed in 2021. It will improve connections to Genoa, which are notoriously bad. The number of destinations is set to rise from 26 to 40 over the next few years. Buses are infrequent so it is wise to factor a taxi ride to the centre into your calculations if you are not on a tight budget. The rate is shown on a notice at the taxi rank and is €7 per person for three people, meaning if you are travelling alone, you'll pay €21. It is worth flying into Liguria, however, for the breathtaking experience of landing on the runway that juts out into the sea. Ask for a seat on the right-hand side of the plane and you will get a bird's-eye view of Portofino and Genoa. It takes roughly 2 hours to fly from London.

Ryanair and **British Airways** fly directly from the UK, the former from London Stansted and the latter from London Gatwick. Easyjet fly from Bristol, London Luton, and Manchester. The closest airports with direct flights from North America are Milan and Nice. If you are coming from Australia or New Zealand, you are likely to fly into Milan or Rome. If your destination is the eastern end of the Riviera, then consider flights to and from Pisa Airport (050 500707; w pisa-airport.com), which is just 84km from La Spezia. Trains from Pisa connect with La Spezia in 50 minutes. If your destination is the western end of Liguria, it is well worth flying to Nice, which has direct flights from the UK from Bristol, London Gatwick, London Luton, London Heathrow, Liverpool and Manchester on **easyJet**, **British Airways** and **Ryanair**, and direct flights from North America. Note that some connections are seasonal.

Private jets can use the airport at Villanova d'Albenga (w rivierairport.it).

Airlines flying to Genoa
✈ Aegean Airlines 069 7150 53233 (Italy); w it.aegeanair.com
✈ Air France 0207 660 0337 (UK); w airfrance.com
✈ Alitalia 89 20 10 (Italy); w alitalia.it
✈ BA 0344 493 0787 (UK); w ba.com
✈ Blu Express 069 895 6666 (Italy); w blu-express.com
✈ EasyJet 0330 365 5000 (UK); w easyjet.com
✈ Israir 1700 505 777 (Israel); w israir.co.il
✈ Lufthansa 0371 945 9747 (UK); w lufthansa.it

✈ KLM 020 7660 0293 (UK); w klm.com
✈ Ryanair 0330 100 7838 (UK); w ryanair.com
✈ Scandanavian Airlines 0199 259104 (Italy); w flysas.com
✈ S7 Siberia Airlines +7 495 777 9999 (Russia); w s7.ru
✈ Turkish Airlines 020 7471 6666 (UK); w turkishairlines.com
✈ Volotea 010 60151 (Italy); w volotea.com
✈ Vueling 895 895 3333 (Italy); w vueling.com

BY BOAT Ferries leave from Genoa for Algeria, Tunisia, Corsica, Sardinia, Sicily, Barcelona and Tangier. Genoa is also an important destination for cruise ships. The other two large ports in the area are Savona and La Spezia. The latter is principally a naval port but Costa cruises start in Savona and ferries leave from nearby Vado Ligure for Corsica. Liguria has 34 tourist ports and a growing number of marinas and, with berths for more than 17,000 boats, is Italy's most organised region for hosting pleasure craft.

BY CAR Liguria has excellent road connections and is linked into the main European motorway system. It takes two days to drive from southern England. The motorway (*autostrada*) – the A10, Ventimiglia to Genoa and its continuation, the A12, Genoa to La Spezia – runs the length of Liguria set back from the coast and weaves its way through the mountains in a series of impressive tunnels. The views are great and it is an atmospheric ride (w autostrade.it). Please note that at time of writing the A10 was closed between the exits for Genoa Airport and Genoa West, due to the collapse of the Morandi Bridge in August 2018. Driving the A10 is a challenge if you have never driven it before. There are numerous tunnels and the road curves and twists, so you must drive slower than on a normal motorway. Motorways link Savona to Turin (A6), Milan to Genoa (A7), Santhià to Voltri (A26), and Parma to La Spezia (A15). All motorways in Italy are toll roads. Headlights are legally required on all roads even in daylight. Beware of Saturdays in late July and August; it can be very busy as holidaymakers head to catch ferries from Genoa and Savona. If you can, avoid driving at all on a Saturday in mid-August. The Via Aurelia (SS1) runs along the coast.

Traffic jams and parking can be a major issue in summer, so stick to the *autostrada* until your destination in high season. Italian motorways are rather dangerous as the feeder roads are incredibly short. You have to stop and wait until there is a space to pull out – drivers don't expect people to slow down to let people on to the motorway. You are expected to wait for a gap in the traffic.

Genoa and the main towns have car rental offices, Avis (w avisautonoleggio.it); **Budget** (w budgetautonoleggio.it) and **Hertz** (w hertz.it). Liguria Noleggio (m 320 722 4142; w ligurentnoleggio.com) delivers scooters and smart cars to your hotel.

Inland roads are often winding and narrow. Always make sure you have a full tank before heading into the hinterland as petrol stations are scarce and those that do exist are likely to be self-service; the machines either only take cash or often don't accept foreign credit or debit cards, which is often the case even in larger towns out of hours.

BY COACH Eurolines (**w** eurolines.eu) connects Liguria with an extensive network of coach lines, but it is not the cheap option that it once was and air travel may be just as economical.

BY TRAIN The main line runs along the coast and inland towards Turin and Milan. It is an expensive option to take the train from the UK as it involves first taking the **Eurostar** and then the day-long journey to Nice. It is a better option to come by train if arriving from mainland Europe. The trains that run along the coast from Ventimiglia to La Spezia stop at nearly all the resorts but are, as a result, very slow. You need to validate your ticket in the yellow machine on the platform. If you do not, you can be fined. Genoa is just 2 hours by train from both Milan and Turin, and 5½ hours from Rome (**w** trenitalia.it). It is worth noting that trains in Italy are relatively inexpensive.

HEALTH   *With Dr Felicity Nicholson*

Liguria poses no major health risks. Tap water is safe to drink, but it is wise to be up to date with routine vaccinations in the UK such as measles, mumps and rubella, and diphtheria, tetanus and polio. Mosquitoes are an issue in the summer months at night, and in shady areas during the day, so be prepared with a good insect repellent. Big supermarkets stock a wide range of anti-mosquito ammunition and it is far cheaper than the equivalents sold in pharmacies.

Pharmacies (*farmacie*, sing. *farmacia*) are usually open 09.00–13.00 and 16.00–20.00 on weekdays and some close on Saturday afternoons. They are usually closed on Sunday, but in high season may open in resort towns. A pharmacy that is open out-of-hours on a rotation basis is called a *farmacia di turno*. A rota will be posted on the door of the pharmacy or on **w** federfarma.it.

If you are walking in the spring and summer months, beware ticks that may fall from overhanging branches or be hiding in the long grass. Ticks can carry Lyme disease and may even carry the viral infection tick-borne encephalitis, which exists in other parts of Italy. Make sure that you are wearing long trousers with socks and boots and long-sleeved top when hiking in the spring summer months. Check yourself for ticks at the end of the day. For more information see the box below.

For **emergency telephone numbers**, see the box opposite.

TICK REMOVAL

Ticks should ideally be removed complete, and as soon as possible, to reduce the chance of infection. You can use special tick tweezers, which can be bought in good travel shops, or failing this with your finger nails, grasping the tick as close to your body as possible, and pulling it away steadily and firmly at right angles to your skin without jerking or twisting. Irritants (eg: Olbas oil) or lit cigarettes are to be discouraged since they can cause the ticks to regurgitate and therefore increase the risk of disease. Once the tick is removed, if possible douse the wound with alcohol (any spirit will do), soap and water, or iodine. If you are travelling with small children, remember to check their heads, and particularly behind the ears, for ticks. Spreading redness around the bite and/or fever and/or aching joints after a tick bite imply that you have an infection that requires antibiotic treatment. In this case seek medical advice.

Being aware of the dangers related to swimming in the sea can help to avoid accidents. Children must be supervised at all times. Beware that water currents can be very strong, even in summer.

A topic of conversation on the beach is always whether anyone has seen a jellyfish, *medusa*. If you are stung by a jellyfish, rinse the sting with seawater (not fresh water) or vinegar, wine or alcohol. Tentacles should be removed, preferably lifted off the skin with, for example, a credit card.

The rocks are home to colonies of sea urchins so before putting your feet down always look and see if you can spot one. Many Italians swim in plastic or rubber shoes. The spines of a sea urchin, *riccio di mare*, can puncture the skin, causing swelling and infection. The spines break easily and are difficult to remove. To relieve pain, soak in very hot water, then visit a doctor to have the needles removed if necessary.

Shallow sandy seabeds may hide rays, whose tails can sting. The weaver fish, *trachinidae*, has poisonous spines on its dorsal fin. It rests buried in the sand, with the dorsal sticking up, which, if stepped on, causes intense pain. Soak the foot in hot water and, if the sting remains irritated, consult a pharmacist. The scorpion fish, *scorpaenidae*, often lies concealed in rocky places. It also has poisonous spines that can give painful stings.

EU nationals who are taken ill or have an accident when visiting Italy are entitled to health care. The **European Health Insurance Card** improves access to health care in the EU and speeds up the reimbursement of costs (replacing the E111 form). UK citizens can apply for this card through the EHIC website (w ehic. org.uk), or by calling ✎0845 606 2030, but note that participation in the scheme may change for UK citizens post-Brexit. Only publicly funded health treatment is included in this scheme for the moment. In Italy, while emergency treatment is free for visiting EU citizens, you have to pay the full cost of drugs and non-emergency treatment and then claim a refund. It is important to keep all your bills, prescriptions and receipts.

In Italy free emergency health care is available to foreigners, but any required medication or follow-up treatment will have to be paid for. It is therefore important to ensure that your travel insurance covers medical costs. Take a copy of your policy certificate with you and keep the policy number to hand in case you are obliged to quote it. Keep all receipts.

Prevention being far better than cure, **walkers and hikers** should be conversant with first aid, and know how to deal with injuries and hypothermia. Try to avoid walking or climbing beyond your limits. The majority of accidents happen when you're tired. In the event of being injured, use surgical tape for cuts that would normally be stitched, and then bind the wound laterally with zinc oxide tape.

In the extremely unlikely event of being bitten by a **snake**, try not to panic, as a racing heart speeds up the spread of venom – much easier said than done, of course. Most first-aid techniques do more harm than good. If possible, splint the bitten limb and keep below the height of the heart, then get the victim to hospital immediately.

TRAVEL CLINICS AND HEALTH INFORMATION A full list of current travel clinic websites worldwide is available on w istm.org. For other journey preparation information, consult w travelhealthpro.org.uk (UK) or w wwwnc.cdc.gov/travel

(USA). Information about various medications may be found on w netdoctor. co.uk/travel. All advice found online should be used in conjunction with expert advice received prior to, or during, travel.

SAFETY

There are no major crime issues in Liguria, but do beware of pickpockets and keep your handbag or wallet in a safe place at all times wherever you are. This is especially true in stations. Think twice before sleeping with all the windows open; it is an easy mistake to make if you don't come from a very hot country. Thieves can easily jump in through the window while you are asleep. Use your common sense and ask advice. Genoa's old town has a notorious red-light district; its narrow dark streets can be a little dodgy at night.

Forest fires are frequent in the hot summer months and fed by the almost constant breeze. There is a lot of speculation as to how many of them are actually started deliberately and it is not uncommon to see firefighting planes flying down to the sea to scoop up water to put them out. Up in the mountains it is essential to never light a fire outside of designated areas and to make sure that all cigarettes are put out properly. Be careful walking in forests in October on Wednesdays and Sundays. This is the hunting season!

WOMEN TRAVELLERS There are no real issues involved in travelling alone, or in small groups, as a woman in Liguria, which can't be found travelling alone in any other western European country. That said, it is best to avoid Genoa's old town after dark. The areas around its two railway stations are also a little dodgy at night. Just remember that Italy is a pretty sexist country so make sure you have a thick skin.

LGBT TRAVELLERS Not only is Italy sexist but it is prejudiced on all fronts, so a normal amount of discretion is advised. Hotel workers are unlikely to question a gay or lesbian couple requesting a double room. There is a gay scene in Genoa with a number of gay bars. There is a useful website in Italian: w arcigaygenova.it.

INFORMATION FOR TRAVELLERS WITH A DISABILITY

Liguria isn't an easy place to visit if you have reduced mobility, largely because old medieval cities and villages perched on mountainsides aren't the easiest places to get about in a wheelchair or with a walking stick. That said, one organisation that offers services in Italy to travellers with disabilities is **Accessible Italy** (+378 941111; e info@accessibleitaly.com; w accessibleitaly.com). There is also a guide in Italian and French for visitors with disabilities by local organisation **La Cruna** (w lacruna.com). For pre-travel information, **Gov. uk** provides a useful resource (w www.gov.uk/guidance/foreign-travel-for-disabled-people). In addition, **Accessible Journeys** (w accessiblejourneys. com) is a comprehensive US site written by travellers in wheelchairs who have been researching accessible travel full-time since 1985. There are many tips and useful contacts (including lists of travel agents on request) and articles, including pieces on disabled travelling worldwide. The **Society for Accessible Travel and Hospitality** (w sath.org) provides some general information, too. **Disabled Holidays** (w disabledholidays.com) offers accessible holidays to Italy, including Liguria.

TRAVELLING WITH KIDS Liguria is a great destination for children. Even though Italians aren't having many of them themselves these days, Italy is still one of the most child-friendly places in the world. Don't expect lots of specific things for children in museums, restaurants and hotels, however, but what you do get is a warm welcome. All towns along the coast have carousels, rides or mini cars. Beach clubs are all kitted out to accommodate kids, as Liguria is above all a family destination. There's sun and the sea in summer and fun to be had inland up in the mountains. With an ice-cream shop on every corner and endless vending machines selling trinkets, it is easy to calm the nerves of a trainee traveller. Genoa has a number of attractions that go down well. There is a vast aquarium and a number of museums aimed specifically at children.

There is no need to bring supplies from home if you have babies or tiny children. You can buy everything you need; even special pasta for babies.

You will find that some elderly people, or those who don't have children, are not that tolerant of noise. Italians expect quiet in the early afternoon in summer so they can siesta. Pushchairs can be difficult in hilltop towns and on cobbled streets. Their wheels can get stuck between the stones, so always make sure your little passenger is strapped in or bring a sling. If you are coming from the UK, always be extra vigilant about traffic safety as Italians drive on the right-hand side of the road. Also note that cars don't stop automatically at a pedestrian crossing, even when the light is green. With older children make sure their mobile phones are activated to work abroad and that they have your numbers keyed in with the relevant country code.

WHAT TO TAKE

Italians take their appearance seriously and believe that looking one's best, *fare la bella figura*, is important, so pack some smart casual clothes for evenings. Never leave home without your swimsuit in the summer months and always pack a comfy pair of walking shoes. Buy a plug adaptor before leaving home. English books are difficult to find, so if you like reading, be prepared. Other than that, you can buy everything you need in Liguria.

ELECTRICITY In common with the rest of mainland Europe, Italy uses electricity at a current of 220 volts, but anything requiring 240 volts should work. Adaptors are sometimes necessary for older plugs with two pins. Be careful of electrical surges during thunderstorms. It is advisable not to use a computer plugged into the mains if the storm is especially bad.

If renting a house, be aware that Italians can opt for one of two bands when signing up with the electricity company. Most holiday homes are on the lower band so if you have the oven, the washing machine, dishwasher and TV on all at once, don't be surprised if the system fuses. Always check where the fuse box is in case this happens.

MONEY

Italy's national currency is the euro. Cash machines, *bancomat,* are located at the airport in Genoa and in all towns along the coast, but are few and far between in the mountains. Credit and debit cards are generally accepted in shops and restaurants, but many B&Bs are cash only. Banks are usually open from 08.30 to 16.00 Monday to Friday but close for lunch.

BUDGETING

Liguria is not especially expensive. A tray of peaches in summer costs just €5. On a tight budget, a coffee and a croissant for breakfast are around €3.50. If you picnic for lunch, shopping in the supermarket, you can eat for €5, and eat a pasta dish and have a glass of wine to wash it down with for dinner, for €12. Add in a museum visit, usually €6, and a return bus ticket, €4.00. That's a minimum budget of about €25 a day without accommodation costs. For €60 a day you can do well and eat two simple meals in a restaurant, and stop in a café or two. At the top end, Liguria still isn't too pricey with a gourmet set menu coming in at €80; add breakfast, a simple lunch, an ice cream, a couple of drinks and one of Genoa's more expensive museums, or a boat trip, and you'll still find yourself spending well under €150.

Some of the nicest things to do in Liguria are free. There is no charge to hike across the mountains and swim off the rocks. Although the number of pay beaches is controversial, you can usually find a free spot and the concessions stop at the water's edge, so you can swim freely in front of a pay beach. Churches are free to visit and much of the enjoyment of the towns and cities is to be had wandering around their narrow streets.

Beach concessions and swimming pool clubs can be very pricey, weighing in at between €18 and €35 per person with a sun bed. Prices are often higher at weekends and in August. It is always worth negotiating as you may get a reduction, especially if it is halfway through the day. In very touristy places, seafront cafés will be pricey and you may be charged extra if you buy an ice cream and then sit down. Look out for set menus. A lunchtime set menu, often called *pranzo di lavoro,* is usually €10 for two courses and a coffee. Prices tumble as soon as you go into the hinterland. While doing your sums, don't forget that most restaurants have a cover charge of about €3 and often charge for tap water.

Some typical prices:

Litre bottle of water	€1.50 (€0.30 in the supermarket)
Cup of coffee	€1.50
Glass of wine	€2.50–4.50
Loaf of bread	€0.90–2.00
Street snack	€2.50
Ice cream	€2.50

Postcard	€0.40–1.50
T-shirt	€12
Litre of petrol	€1.75

Tipping is expected in restaurants if there is no cover charge, but optional in bars and cafés. It is usual to tip if drinks are brought to your table. Taxis round up to the nearest euro.

GETTING AROUND

Public transport is good. For timetables and routes, see w www.orariotrasporti. regione.liguria.it.

BY BOAT There are frequent ferries in the summer and a number of companies run whale-watching trips. There are also night-time excursions to see the firework shows that take place throughout the summer. A boat trip is a must as it really puts you in touch with Liguria's seafaring side and it is wonderful to see it from the sea. There are a number of companies who hire small sailing boats, with or without a crew. See individual town listings for details.

BY BUS Buses also run along the coast and up into the mountains. Services are regular but not frequent. Bus fares within towns are usually inexpensive and are likely to cost around €2.

BY CAR To really explore the mountainous hinterland it is better to have a car. Beware, however, that many of the roads are narrow and extremely winding, are often in bad repair and can be dangerous. Ask about before you set off to the remoter parts of Liguria. Some parts of the coast can be very busy in summer and long queues can result.

The collapse of the Morandi Bridge in Genoa in August 2018 has caused considerable traffic problems in the western part of Genoa. The A10 motorway was closed at time of writing from Genoa Airport to Genoa West and likely to remain closed for some years. Check w autostrade.it for updates on the situation.

Parking Although there is a car park at Monterosso al Mare, parking can be extremely difficult in the Cinque Terre. In Italy, the colour of the lines on the parking space indicates the type of parking: white is for free parking, blue is for paid parking and yellow for residents only.

BY MOTORBIKE When Piaggio made their first Vespa in 1946 they revolutionised Italian life. Suddenly it was possible to get out of the city and spend the afternoon on the beach. Since production began, over 3 million Vespas have been manufactured in Italy; today the roads are full of Vespas and hiring one can add an authentic touch to a holiday. You can rent scooters from Ligurent (m 320 722 4142; w ligurentnoleggio. com). Many locals explore the hinterland at the weekend on motorbikes. For more information on the history of Piaggio, see w bradtguides.com/piaggio.

BY TRAIN The railway runs along the coast. Regular services stop at all the stations along the route. The train is an excellent way to visit Liguria's big tourist draw, the Cinque Terre. Some trains also stop in the hinterland en route for Turin, Milan and Parma.

Liguria is a great destination for walkers and is covered in trekking paths, *sentieri*. The most famous links the five villages of the Cinque Terre (page 129), while others are well off the tourist track. The best time to walk is in the drier months from April to October, but the heat of July and August can slow the pace. It is tempting if you have been on the beach to attempt these paths in sandals but you really do need good walking shoes. Many tracks have been damaged by flash flooding in recent years and part of the famous Cinque Terre route was closed at time of writing.

The Alta Via dei Monti Liguri is a 440km footpath that runs the length of Liguria along the top of the mountains, offering stunning views across the sea and north to the Alps. It is Italy's longest continuous pathway reaching its highest point at 2,200m on Monte Saccarello. Paths are well indicated with red and white markers. It begins in Ventigmiglia and ends in Montemarcello. The main trail is crossed by other paths, which go down the Apennine Ridge towards the sea if you fancy a dip. It is divided into 43 sections, each of which requires about 2 to 3 hours of walking. Mountain refuges are dotted along the path. Even if you don't speak Italian, it is worth taking a look at *L'Alta Via dei Monti Liguri* by Andrea Parodi as the maps of the walks are excellent and there are nice pictures to give you an idea of what to expect.

Further details are available from the **Associazione Alta Via dei Monti Liguri** (*0102 485 2200; w altaviadeimontiliguri.it).

BY BIKE Italians are mad about cycling. Elderly men in lycra are to be found even at the top of the highest mountain pass. Along the coast, it is easier going and there are masses of flat routes along the old railway line that has been converted into a seaside promenade in many parts of Liguria.

There is an excellent guide in Italian to cycle routes in Liguria, *Liguria in mountain bike* by Sergio Grillo and Cinzia Pezzani (Edicoloeditore, 2008), which is useful even if you do not speak Italian as the suggested routes with altitudes and length are clearly indicated. Most bikers in the hinterland use the roads. There is not much traffic so this is often a pleasant experience.

Another source of information, w liguriabike.it has a comprehensive list of mountain-bike routes. There are lots of bike-rental shops along the coast and many hotels hire out bikes. Finale Ligure is a popular spot for mountain biking. The best time to cycle is late spring and early autumn although the Italians are at it even in the height of summer.

ACCOMMODATION

There is no shortage of places to stay in Liguria, from super luxury to mountain refuge. Accommodation can get booked up in July and August so if you are planning a trip in high summer, you should think about booking in advance. That said, the economic crisis has had an effect on tourist numbers and on sites like w booking.com you can find very good places at the last minute.

There is a massive choice of where to stay. Hotels, *alberghi*, tend to be mid-range and living on their laurels along most of the coast, but there are also luxury options, notably in and around Portofino. The star system in Italy doesn't make a four-star a classy hotel. You get stars for amenities and location, not quality of service. There are also lots of B&Bs (**w** bed-and-breakfast-in-italy.com) and in many places they are a better option than hotels as they are often more modern and stylish, especially in Genoa, in Dolceacqua and along the Cinque Terre.

There are a vast number of apartments and rooms on **w** airbnb.com. It has brought a wide variety of accommodation on to the market and given much needed competition to hotels along the coast. It has also kept prices down, especially in Genoa. Just be careful to look at the location of the property closely, especially when the motorway and the railway line run close to the coast.

It is easy to find apartments but good campsites (**w** camping.it) are more difficult to come by, particularly in areas away from the coast. Some have closed in recent years as they have been washed away in flash floods. A fun option is a mountain refuge, a *rifugio*. Accommodation is often in dormitories and is very cheap. There are a few hostels in Liguria as well. Staying in an *agriturismo* (**w** agriturismo.it), on a farm, is also a great way to get a real feel for Liguria. You will find them on **w** booking.com as well. Standards vary and be sure to check online reviews before you book. They often serve their own homegrown produce and this is the place to taste some really good home cooking. Religious institutions, like monasteries and sanctuaries, often also rent rooms.

Beware that many B&Bs, *rifugi* and *agriturismi* don't take credit cards, so make sure you have the cash before you set out for a rural bolthole.

EATING AND DRINKING

Restaurants tend to open from 12.30 to 15.00 and from 19.00 until late on the coast. Inland restaurants often close at 21.00. Not all restaurants open for lunch and some only open at weekends. There is a smoking ban in cafés, restaurants and bars. Ligurians don't eat much for breakfast. It's usually a shot of espresso and something sweet. Italian breakfast is a kid's dream. In good B&Bs and *agriturismi* you will get a mouth-watering array of cakes and biscuits. Hotel breakfasts are often a waste of time, so avoid paying for them if you can and go to a café.

Ligurians have a reputation for hard work and are more likely to eat a piece of focaccia, flat bread, than sit down on a daily basis to a large lunch. Part of this culture probably came from the fact that when the men were away at sea, the women were busy keeping the place ticking over, so didn't have time to cook, and preferred to skimp, so there was plenty when their husbands returned home. Meals are less formal in Liguria, and less rigid than in other parts of the country.

Genoa's Chamber of Commerce supports restaurants that use local ingredients and serve local dishes and Ligurian wines. Those that meet their criteria are given the Genova Gourmet stamp of approval (**w** genovagourmet.it), as are local producers making traditional food products.

THE TASTE OF LIGURIA Food is an essential part of the Ligurian experience and a very local affair. All of Italy's regions have their own distinctive dishes, many of which are never eaten out of the area in which they are made. In Liguria the dishes change from village to village much like the dialect, although there is a core group of common ingredients and techniques. The isolated narrow mountain valleys were linked only by dirt-track roads right up until the 1960s and, as a result, each had their own cuisine based exclusively on what was at hand. As a result it is a lean and healthy diet centred on vegetables, fruit, olive oil, wine, pasta and fish. The wild herbs that grow on the Ligurian hillsides are the basis of nearly every dish and were traditionally harvested to make *preboggion*, a mixture of herbs that have been simply boiled and dressed with olive oil and lemon. This mixture is used to stuff the large triangular pasta, *pansotti*, and to fill *gattafin*, a large, fried ravioli from Levanto.

'It was a cuisine made of labour and patience and the love of aromatic herbs', wrote nostalgic regional writer Vittorio G Rossi. 'It was a cuisine of lean folk who lived on lean land – sea cliffs and terraces hewn by hand from solid stone – and lean olive trees.' Rossi echoes Diodorus, who in the 5th century BC spoke of Liguria as 'a hard, sterile land' where men and women 'live a hard, uncomfortable existence full of hardships and toil. Their physical efforts and the sobriety of the foods they eat have made them wiry and tough.'

Away from the coast, fresh fish was a rare commodity in the *entroterra*. Villagers had to make do with salted anchovies, dried or salted cod and other easily transportable preserved fish. The division between coast and hinterland means that just as fresh fish was a rarity in the hills, the abundant wild mushrooms and game, which were staples in the hilltop villages, were rarely seen in the fishing villages along the coast. Today coastal restaurants are most likely to specialise in fish, while in the mountains you'll find wild game on the menu.

Much of this ultra-regional cuisine is also due to the remoteness of Liguria itself which is cut off from the rest of Italy by the mountains. Ligurian recipes did not appear in the cookbooks of Italian cuisine that began to appear in the Renaissance. The flagship dishes that we all associate with Italian cookery like pizza and risotto did not come from Liguria and even today there are many staple products like focaccia and walnut sauce that disappear from the supermarket shelves the moment you cross the border into Piedmont or Tuscany. The dishes that bind Ligurians together tend to be Genoese. The city's cuisine came to dominate the surrounding coast as the Genoese empire spread.

RESTAURANT PRICE CODES

Based on the average price of a main course.

Expensive	€€€€€	€31–40
Above average	€€€€	€26–30
Mid-range	€€€	€21–25
Cheap and cheerful	€€	€16–20
Rock bottom	€	<€15

Note that in Liguria many restaurants, especially at the top end of the range, have only set tasting menus, which are on average between €30 and €80, considerably cheaper than the à la carte option.

Prompted by the plans to open a McDonald's by the Spanish Steps in Rome, the Slow Food Movement was started by Carlo Petrini in 1986, in Bra in Piedmont (w slowfood.it). The movement immediately took off in Genoa, where the Slow Fish Movement was born. Slow Fish (w slowfish.slowfood.it) is now a major biannual event in the city.

The Slow Food Movement opposes junk food culture and the globalisation of agriculture and it encourages locally produced foods made using traditional methods. One important way it does this is by setting up grassroots organisations called *praesidia,* of which there are a growing number in Liguria. The region also has two Mercato della Terra, backed by the Slow Food Movement. Spending time browsing the stalls at any market is a great way to meet local producers and discover some of the region's unusual products. There is a Mercato della Terre in Cairo Montenotte (page 197) every second Saturday of the month and another in Sarzana (page 172) on every second and fourth Saturday of the month.

In this guide you can enjoy some food tourism by following the Food Trail, a selection of boxes appearing through the book, marked with the icon at the top of this box. There are also listings of local shops and restaurants that produce food in the traditional way and are affiliated to the Slow Food Movement.

Nowadays all Ligurians eat local variations of pesto, basil sauce; focaccia, a flatbread with olive oil; *farinata,* a chickpea-flour pancake; rabbit with olives and herbs; rockfish and anchovies in soups, stews and tarts, or stuffed, fried or grilled; *stoccafisso,* dried cod; ravioli or other filled pasta; vegetable tarts and stuffed vegetables; and *pandolce,* a cake with candied fruit. Similarly, every serious kitchen from Sarzana on the edge of Tuscany to Ventimiglia bordering France will be stocked with local olives and oil, pine nuts, salt-preserved anchovies, fresh and pickled vegetables like courgettes, chard, tomatoes and aubergines, white beans, chickpeas and preserved mushrooms, and the region's ubiquitous herbs.

Many of the techniques used date back to ancient times. Cooking on hot slabs of slate, called *ciappe,* was practised by the Ligurian tribes and is still a common way of preparing meat, especially in the Val Fontanabuona behind Chiavari and Lavagna.

Extra virgin olive oil has sat at the heart of Ligurian cuisine since ancient times and is the key ingredient in the best-known Ligurian delicacies such as focaccia, *farinata* and pesto. The most famous varieties are made from *taggiasca, pignola, lavagnina* and *razzola* olives and since the 16th century it has been an important local industry, especially in the hills and mountains behind Imperia. Here the olive oil, thanks to the more temperate climate, is more delicate and fruitier than that produced in other parts of Liguria. *Taggiasca* olives are a tasty aperitif and are used to make the local olive paste.

The king of the Ligurian kitchen is, however, basil. Indeed the word basil, *basilico* in Italian, comes from the Latin translation of the Greek βασιλικός, meaning 'regal'. The best basil in the world is grown in Liguria, in giant greenhouses perched precipitously on the hillside between the motorway and the rather run-down flats of Genova Prà. With a view of the docks and the salty air, it's the perfect stressful environment to grow a really pungent basil plant. Basil is a serious affair and since 1992 the Confraternita del Pesto have guarded the authenticity of the sauce.

Liguria is also one of the four big pasta regions of Italy and home to the Agnesi pasta dynasty. Pasta was eaten in Italy long before Marco Polo described it in his reminiscences. In *Il Millione* he mentions it in a passing comment, saying that the Chinese eat a sort of pasta. If he didn't know what pasta was, he wouldn't have been able to recognise it, say the experts. The Genoese had a monopoly on importing grain from Sicily and the Middle East and it is no surprise that pasta production flourished here in the Middle Ages. Among the varieties to try is the ribbon-like *trennette*, sometimes called *bavette*; *trofie*, small cylindrical twists and *mandilli*, thin flat pieces of pasta, akin to a handkerchief. Indeed, the word comes from the Arabic for handkerchief, *mandil*. It was traditionally served to sailors before they set sail. Another typical Ligurian speciality are *corzetti*, small discs with a cross, a *croxetta*, stamped on them, which are made in eastern Liguria. *Pansotti*, a ravioli stuffed with chard, ricotta and herbs, are unmissable.

Ligurians are great grazers and, living up to their hard-working reputation, often eating on the hoof. It means you can get some really good food on a budget. There are shops selling focaccia on every street corner. The ancient Romans ate *panis focacius*, a flat bread that was baked in the ashes of the fireplace and took its name from the Latin *focus*, meaning 'centre', but also 'fireplace'. Focaccia makes the perfect speedy simple picnic and is one of the great treats of a trip to Liguria.

Alongside the trays of focaccia, especially in the evening, you will see round copper trays of *farinata*, Liguria's oldest dish. *Farinata* is a thin pancake made from chickpea flour, water and olive oil. The legend has it that it was invented by a group of Roman soldiers who had roasted some chickpea-flour pastry on a shield. *Farinata* is best eaten warm, fresh from the wood-burning stove.

Pies play an important part on the Ligurian table. Here they are called *torta*, although in the rest of Italy that is a word used to describe a cake. A classic Easter dish, now sold all year round, is the Genoese *torta pasqualina*. The earliest records of it date back to the start of the 16th century. Thirty-three sheets of paper-thin pastry are overlapped in remembrance of Jesus's age when he was crucified. It's filled with whole hard-boiled eggs and spinach. A typical family meal is *torta verde*, a spinach pie made from a variety of herbs mixed with Parmesan and *prescinseua* cheese. Pumpkin pie, *torta di zucca*, and artichoke pies, *torta di carciofi*, or *articiocche* in dialect, are made all over Liguria, as is *torta de gee*, which is dialect for chard.

Ligurians have a sweet tooth and there are pastry and biscuit shops, many of them well over a hundred years old, in every town. A lot of fun is to be had if you make visiting cake shops part of your itinerary. As with everything in Liguria,

🍴 VEGETARIAN'S DREAM

As a lifelong vegetarian I can vouch that Liguria is a great place for vegetarians. Vegetables grow in abundance and feature highly in the menu. In the countryside everyone has their own vegetable patch, an *orto*, and there is an abundance of cabbages, broad beans, courgettes, aubergines, beans, and tomatoes with an intense flavour.

Stuffed vegetables are a Ligurian speciality. Although some are stuffed with meat, many are not. If the name of the vegetable is followed by *ripieno*, *ripieni* or *farcito*, it is stuffed. I usually avoid soups unless I know what stock has been used, but here it's most likely to be made with a vegetable one. Ask if it has meat stock and the cook will look at you a little oddly and say, 'But it's a vegetable soup, why would I use meat stock?'

🍴 THE PERFECT PESTO

Everyone in Liguria has an opinion on how to make the perfect pesto sauce. Purists use a traditional pestle made of olive wood and a stone mortar. A marble one is considered too cold to pummel or pound the ingredients. *Pestare* in Italian means 'to pound'. The key thing about the pounding of the herbs and nuts is the heat produced by the wood that releases the fragrances from the herbs. Many cooks use a blender, but those who opt for this faster method all have an opinion on what sort of blender will do. Basil leaves are surprisingly tough and can fuse cheap models, so watch out if you get whizzing. The key is to use the leaves of young plants not more than two months old. It is incredibly easy to make and tastes a million times better than anything that comes off supermarket shelves.

Put in a pinch of sea salt, which protects the green colour of the basil, with two large bunches of basil, add two garlic cloves, a sprinkle of pepper, four tablespoons of olive oil and three tablespoons of pine nuts.

Whizz it all up and then mix in a handful of grated *pecorino* cheese. Here again the debate can get quite heated as in some parts of Liguria Parmesan cheese is used, but it lacks the cutting edge of a good sharp *pecorino sardo*. Serve with *trofie*, which are traditionally boiled in water with potatoes and green beans. This can be served chilled in a salad.

In some parts of Liguria walnuts are added instead of pine nuts and ricotta is mixed in instead of *pecorino*.

The key thing to remember is that you do not simply put the pesto on top of the pasta on your plate. Moments before the pasta is ready you add a tablespoon of the cooking fluid to the pesto, then you drain the pasta and mix it with the pesto. By warming the sauce slightly you bring out the aromas. The principle is the same when serving walnut sauce.

regional specialities abound. *Canestrelli*, crumbly, flat, round, shortbread biscuits with a hole in the middle, are now found all over Liguria but originally hail from the Genoese hinterland. They are popular for breakfast or are served after a meal with sweet white wine. Right across Liguria honey is produced and flavoured with flower petals.

What I really love about eating in Liguria is that many of the dishes, among them the fried fish, pies, breads and biscuits, are street food. You don't have to have a million dollars and eat in the most expensive restaurants to savour the best the region has to offer. Nor do you have to shop in the most luxurious delicatessens. Supermarkets, especially Coop, sell regional products. They are usually displayed separately. They support small producers and promote seasonal foods as well. If you want to try some of the local specialities that I have written about in the guide, you often need look no further than the local Coop. Many of the tastiest things on offer don't require cooking or can be brought ready-made, so a picnic in Liguria can be a gourmet experience.

Wine Liguria doesn't produce vast quantities of wine and it is little known outside of the region. Wines are classified according to DOC, Denominazione di Origine Controllata, which means that it has been produced according to prescribed standards and quality. DOCG, Denominazione di Origine Controllata e Garantita, applies to very few wines, notably Barolo from just over the border in Piedmont, which is widely available, and the fortified Sciacchetrà from the Cinque Terre.

🍴 A FISHY TREAT

The sea that laps the coast of Liguria is very salty and, as a result, produces excellent anchovies. Although it isn't as rich as some seas, fishermen regularly haul in octopus, squid, scampi, prawns, sea urchins and sole, and catch lobsters. Anchovies, once known as *pan do mâ*, bread of the sea, are found all along the coast, but those of Monterosso are among the best. Anchovies are cured in salt and olive oil and stacked in layers in chestnut barrels or clay pots. The whole process takes almost two months and anchovies have been an important export since medieval times. They are used to make the soup *bagnun* and *pissalandrea*, a focaccia with salted fish named after Admiral Andrea Doria, which is made in Imperia. In Sanremo the anchovies are replaced with sardines and the dish is known as *sardenaira*.

Even the sea manages to change according to the locality. The rich plankton and the lower salinity of the sea around La Spezia produces excellent mussels, known locally as *muscoli*, which were first cultivated by the Romans and served raw, but also taste great fried, stuffed, in a sauce, and in a soup. Santa Margherita and Sanremo are known for their red shrimps which are at their best simply boiled and dressed in extra virgin olive oil and lemon juice.

A traditional fish dish is *musciàmme*, a preserved fish fillet that was eaten on board ships as early as the 12th century. It is cut into very thin slices after it has been softened in a marinade of olive oil. It is also a basic element of *capponada*, another classic ship's meal. It fitted all the requirements of a cramped wooden ship where there was no possibility of cooking and it was necessary to eat sufficiently moist dishes that quench thirst, while not causing sea sickness. It is made with ship's biscuits, beef tomatoes, *musciàmme* and/or anchovies, black olives, capers, hard-boiled eggs, extra virgin olive oil, vinegar and salt.

Cappon magro was traditionally served during Lent. It was a dish that was born out of poverty and the necessity of using leftover fish, typically capon, a fish of little value, which was then mixed with vegetables.

A word of warning before you reach for a bottle. Some red wines are fizzy and need to be served cold. Most of these wines aren't especially tasty. Look out for the key word *frizzante* on the label.

Try Rossese, a ruby-coloured red that turns a garnet colour as it ages and which complements meat and game dishes. It comes from the vineyards around the ancient village of Dolceacqua near Ventimiglia. The vines grown in the high Arrosica Valley behind Imperia produce Ormeasco, another red wine which comes from the vineyards around the dubiously named Pornassio, which has the same connotations in Italian. This local wine goes under the name of nearby Ormea. Closer to the coast Pontedassio, San Lorenzo and Diano Castello are the home of Vermentino, a fresh white wine that is a good accompaniment to fish and seafood appetisers. The Vermentino produced around Sestri Levante is also good.

Pigato from the Albenga Valley, notably the tiny villages of Salea, Ortovero and Ranzo, is a lightly fragrant straw-yellow white wine with a bitter almond taste. In the vineyards around Finale they produce a particular, fresh and slightly acid white wine, Lumassina, also called Buzzetto, which in dialect means 'still unripe'; so-called as it is made with grapes that ripen late. Close to Genoa the local wine is from the Val Polcevera. It is a white wine which is both still and sparkling.

Sparkling wines are also produced in the Golfo del Tigullio. Further east, in Levanto, the *Colline di Levanto* quality assurance label protects both white and red wines, and both are worth looking out for. The grapes from the precipitous vineyards that cling to the cliffs of the Cinque Terre turn into *Sciacchetrà*, made from grapes naturally dried on mats. The Romans admired the wine from the hills around Luni, *Colli di Luni*, which has become increasingly popular in recent years.

PUBLIC HOLIDAYS AND FESTIVALS

OFFICIAL HOLIDAYS

1 January	New Year's Day, Capodanno
6 January	Epiphany, Epifania
Easter Monday	Pasquetta
25 April	Liberation Day, Festa della Liberazione
1 May	Labour Day, Festa del Lavoratori
2 June	Republic Day, Festa della Repubblica
15 August	Assumption, Ferragosto
1 November	All Saints' Day, Ognissanti
8 December	Immaculate Conception, Immacolata
25 December	Christmas Day, Natale
26 December	St Stephen's Day, Santo Stefano

FESTIVALS Ligurians are *festa*, festival, mad. As Italy is a predominantly Roman Catholic country religious festivals figure highly and many have very ancient origins. Assumption on 15 August is known as Ferragosto, and dates back to Roman times when it was a harvest festival in honour of the Emperor Augustus. It really took off under fascism, however, when it became an important summer holiday taken in organised groups. It is a day to party and along the coast there are often fireworks in the late evening.

Not surprisingly, Easter is a major event. On the evening of Maundy Thursday in Genoa, there is an evocative procession between the seven oldest and most important churches in the old city, a tradition which dates back to the 15th century. There is also a popular Good Friday religious parade in Savona.

At Christmas in Liguria, there are lots of street markets and in Genoa and other towns along the coast a bay tree is burnt in the centre of town. Nativity scenes, *presepe*, are big and peopled with lovely little models of ordinary people, and are found all year round in some sanctuaries and churches.

Every village, however small, has at least one *sagra*. These festivals also often have very ancient origins and some are based around local food specialities or products. They are great fun and usually involve huge cauldrons of food served up at long trestle tables. Some are a little mad. During the mountaineers' *sagra* on Monte Beigua we were once stopped by a road block of *alpinisti*, who were handing out salty doughnuts and red wine. You had to have a glass before you drove on.

SHOPPING

SOUVENIRS Liguria is well known for its ceramics which have been made in Albisola for hundreds of years. Lace has traditionally been made in Rapallo and Portofino. Macramé and woodcarving, especially the making of chairs, is the speciality in Chiavari. Velvet and silk have been made since the Middle Ages in and around Zoagli. Liguria is also a good place to shop for antiques. There are antique markets in many of the towns along the coast. Ligurian olive oil is not easily available outside of the region, so it pays to pop a bottle in your suitcase. There is a useful website (w artigianiliguria.it), which has a list of locally made products.

OPENING TIMES

It has been impossible to list the many exact opening times for **bars and restaurants** in this book as often they don't display them. You are just supposed to know that lunchtime is usually 12.30–15.00 and dinner 19.30–23.00, although in rural areas the restaurant may close much earlier.

Ligurians tend to open all hours when there is the custom and shut up shop in low season, winter time on the coast, and August in Genoa and Savona. They don't often advertise that they do this, again it being simply what you do in this part of the world. Even in summer if the weather is bad or simply for no reason at all, bars, restaurants and discos may be closed. It is a family joke that restaurants tend to shut for lunch, tourist offices are open as little as possible and when updating this guide, I even found a hotel that shut for two weeks in August.

Churches are only open when there is someone to guard their treasures. They usually close between noon and 16.00.

Museums in big cities can close on Mondays or Tuesdays. In the more rural communities they often don't advertise when they are open and tell you to make an appointment. Don't expect them to come running. They may say they can only open next week for example. Don't not go to a museum because the schedule says it may be shut, as I have found them open when they are supposed to be closed and vice versa. You will also see signs to some museums that are only open on special occasions or for school visits. For that reason I've not included some tiny museums that appear on tourist leaflets and you will see signs to, as they are open so rarely.

Most **shops** open at 08.00 and close at 19.30; many close from 12.30 to 15.30, although in the city centre some shops and all large stores stay open all day. Most shops close on Sunday except supermarkets. In August, in the main resorts, some supermarkets are also open all day. On Monday most museums, the majority of restaurants, and hair salons are closed.

ENTERTAINMENT

Along the coast in summer there are plenty of things to keep you busy after dark, from circuses to late-night discos. Santa Margherita and Sanremo have a particularly lively scene. In the latter the main entertainment is the city's casino. Most of Liguria's big towns have a theatre and Genoa has the well-known Teatro Carlo Felice, which has some excellent music and opera performances in winter. Cultural life doesn't stop in the summer though and there are ballet, theatre and operatic performances along the coast in such venues as Savona's Priamàr Fortress. See the individual listings for details.

SPORT

The mountains and the sea mean that there is a vast array of sporting activities available in Liguria and the region is a great destination for outdoor activities all year round. Anyone heading for the mountains will find information about climbing, hiking and skiing on the website of the **Club Alpino Italiano** (w cai.it).

There are traditional sports like *bocce*, a version of the French game boules. Some resorts here even have indoor *bocciodromi*. *Pallone*, rubber ball, is played in the mountains of Liguria and there are championships that receive a lot of local press coverage.

The mild climate makes Liguria a climbing destination all year round and the main centre is around Finale Ligure. Also popular are the cliffs at Muzzerone close to Porto Venere. For more information, see the website of the **Italian Climbing Federation** (w federclimb.it).

The flood of British tourists who invaded Liguria in the 19th century have left their mark. Both Genoa and Rapallo have cricket clubs. The Genoa Cricket and Athletics Club was founded in 1893. Golf arrived in 1903 and one of the best courses is in Rapallo. The first Italian tennis club was the Bordighera Lawn Tennis Club, founded by British residents in 1878, and there are many tennis courts in the region.

Italians are mad about football, *il calcio*, another British invention. Big league matches are played on Sunday afternoons from September to May. Il Genoa was founded in 1893 by a group of Englishmen and it's officially called the Genoa Cricket and Football Club. The **Stadio Luigi Ferraris** (Via Giovanni de Prà 1; ＼010 839 2431) was built in 1911 and renovated for the 1990 World Cup. Here the rival home teams Genoa and Sampdoria battle it out in the annual Derby *della Lanterna*.

The sea is the big draw and there are masses of opportunities for watersports. Liguria has more than 60 sailing clubs and is a lovely place to sail, as many of the tiny bays along the coast are accessible only by boat. A list of sailing clubs in Liguria is available from the Italian Sailing Federation. For more information, see the websites of the **Federazione Italiana Vela** (w www.federvela.it), and the **Italian Yacht Club** (w yachtclubitaliano.it). It is possible to rent canoes and kayaks in most resorts, as well as up in the mountains. Liguria is a relatively windy place so is ideal for windsurfing. Arma di Taggia, Andora and Levanto are the best places to do this. Diving and snorkelling are also extremely popular.

There are two million anglers in Italy and there are lots of places to fish in Liguria. To fish in fresh water you must have a Category B recreational licence, which is available to non-residents. It is illegal to fish in protected areas, to catch fish that do not meet the minimum size standards, or fish during a forbidden period. Freshwater fishermen must apply for a *tesserino segnacattura,* as well as a fishing licence; this keeps a record of where fish have been sighted and how many have been caught. Ask the tourist board for details.

Many resorts and *agriturismi* have riding facilities. In winter there are some basic ski resorts in the mountains in the Val d'Aveto and Monesi (w liguriasci.it). Snow is erratic and this is, therefore, a bonus activity, and not something to build a holiday around.

PHOTOGRAPHY

Liguria is a great place to take pictures. There is an abundance of subjects to snap on your phone, not to mention the changing colours of the sea and the clouds that swirl around the hilltop villages. If you are using a proper camera, keep your equipment in a sealed bag, and avoid exposing it to the sun when possible. Digital cameras are prone to collecting dust particles on the sensor, which results in spots on the image. The best time to take pictures is in the early morning and late afternoon and generally, it is best to have the sun behind you.

You are unlikely to run into any photography problems in Liguria if you apply the usual ethical standards. Respect people's privacy, don't take pictures you know will offend, and especially don't take pictures when you're asked not to.

MEDIA AND COMMUNICATIONS

MEDIA Media, like nearly everything else in Italy, is a local affair. Ligurians read *Il Secolo XIX* (**w** ilsecoloxix.it), which has specific supplements for the region's provinces. The local radio station with the biggest following is *Babboleo*, based in Genoa. It has both a music and a news station.

TELEPHONE AND INTERNET The international dialling code is +39 followed by the local landline code of the person you are calling. Unlike elsewhere in Europe Italians don't drop the first zero in the number if you are dialling from abroad or with a foreign sim card.

Most hotels, but few bars, have Wi-Fi. Some communal Wi-Fi schemes exist and in the Cinque Terre it is possible to buy an Internet card to access the town's Wi-Fi network, though the signal is often very weak.

POST Post offices can be found in all larger towns. They are usually open from 08.00 to 18.30 Monday to Friday, from 08.00 to 13.30 Saturday, and are closed on Sunday. Branches in smaller towns close for lunch. Stamps, *francobolli*, are sold in *tabacchi*, tobacconists. The postal system is notoriously slow, so if your letter is urgent, make sure it is sent *posta prioritaria*. Courier companies like DHL are also very efficient.

BUYING A PROPERTY

Property along the coast in a good position with a sea view is expensive and difficult to find. Oligarchs own villas here. Even small flats in prime positions don't come on the market very often. If you are looking for a property in a condominium, you need to find out which local agent manages it and tell them that you are looking for something. Good property is snapped up, especially small flats.

Up in the mountains property is much cheaper, but you will find complications here too. Buildings, even if they stand empty and crumbling, often belong to many heirs in the same family who can't agree on what should happen to it. Also these communities are very closed and you may find there is a reluctance to sell to someone who is not a local, and by that they mean someone from the immediate vicinity and not simply Liguria, let alone Italy, or abroad.

If you do find something, make sure that you learn Italian. It is impossible to manage a property if you don't speak the language. Making it your residence will reduce taxes and the rates at which you pay for amenities. Agent's fees are usually divided between the buyer and the seller. The market is relatively stable, despite the recent crisis, as property doesn't change hands as fast as it does in the UK, for example. In the long term Italy, with a shrinking population, will face a housing surplus in the coming decades in the mountains where the population is declining, so here you might be left with a house that you cannot sell, although a prime property on the coast is a sound investment.

CULTURAL ETIQUETTE

Italy is a surprisingly formal country. Everyone wishes everyone *buongiorno* and *buona sera*; or uses the more informal, *salve*; friends are greeted with a kiss on both cheeks and everyone always asks how you are, '*Come stai?*', even if they don't care about the answer. In polite company, Italians always use the third person, *Lei*.

You should use first names only when invited. Saying thank you is big too. Italians don't just say thank you but 'a thousand thanks', *grazie mille*.

In towns and cities you will be expected to dress properly, even along the coast. Many resorts actually ban people from walking in the streets in swimwear. When visiting churches, dress modestly and cover shoulders, torso and thighs. Be quiet and respectful. Topless bathing, however, is common, although breast-feeding in public is not.

It makes an enormous difference if you speak Italian, even a few basic words. Italians aren't good at foreign languages and many speak only basic English, if at all. In the west of Liguria, if they speak any foreign language, it is most likely to be French. Once you make the effort to say something in Italian, faces light up and you get far better service. It's easy to take it for granted that people speak English, but always try to think that if you ran a restaurant in Birmingham or Baltimore and someone came in expecting you to speak Italian and got grumpy if you didn't, how would you feel?

TRAVELLING POSITIVELY

It is good to give something back when you travel and that's hard to do in a sophisticated Western country. Italy's economy is not strong and simply by coming and spending your money here you are helping.

Devastating floods caused widespread destruction in the autumn of 2011 in the Cinque Terre and the hinterland. Many of the villages that were affected received no government aid despite promises. Reconstruction has been carried out, but paid for by people who are already suffering from rising taxes. To find out more, see the box on page 4.

Be sure to support local producers. One way of doing this is by looking for the Slow Food label on products and for restaurants associated with the movement (see box, page 36).

UPDATES WEBSITE

You can post your comments and recommendations, and read feedback and updates from other readers online at **w** bradtupdates.com/liguria.

Part Two

GENOA

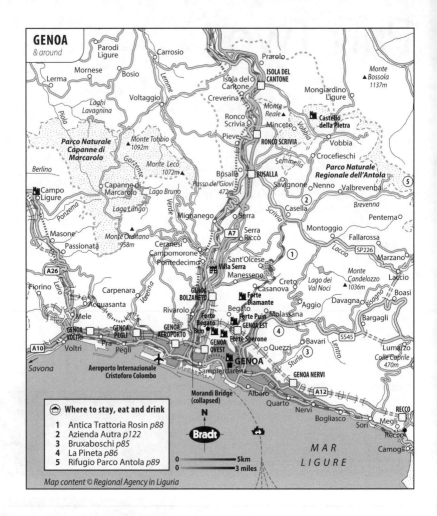

GENOA
& around

Parodi Ligure
Carrosio
Prarolo
Mornese
Bosio
ISOLA DEL CANTONE
Monte ▲ Bossola 1137m
Lerma
Isola del Cantone
Mongiardino Ligure
Voltaggio
Creverina
Laghi Lavagnina
Monte Reale ▲
Castello della Pietra
Ronco Scrivia
Minceto
Piola
Pieve
RONCO SCRIVIA
Vobbia
Parco Naturale Capanne di Marcarolo
Monte Tobbio 1092m
Crocefieschi
Berlino
Gorzente
Monte Leco 1072m▲
Busalla
BUSALLA
Parco Naturale Regionale dell'Antola
5
Campo Ligure
Capanne di Marcarolo
Lago Bruno
Passo dei Giovi 472m
Savignone
Nenno
Valbrevenna
Ponzema
Lago Lungo
Mignanego
Serra
Casella
Brevenna
Pentema
2
Masone
Monte Orditano 958m
Serra Riccò
Montoggio
Fallarossa
SP226
Passionata
Ceranesi
Verde
A7
Laccio
Marzano
A26
Campomorone
Sant'Olcese
1
Monte Candelozzo 1036m
Laccio
Fiorino
Leiro
Carpenara
Pontedecimo
Villa Serra
Manesseno
Creto
Lago dei Val Noci
Boasi
Acquasanta
Vernna
GENOA BOLZANETO
Casanova
Aggio
Davagna
Bargagli
Mele
Rivarolo
Forte Diamante
Begato
Molassana
GENOA PEGLI
GENOA AEROPORTO
Forte Begato
Forte Puin
GENOA EST
4
Bavari
SS45
GENOA VOLTRI
Forte Sprin
Forte Sperone
Quezzi
3
Lumarzo
A10
Voltri
Pra
Pegli
GENOA OVEST
GENOA
Colle Caprile 470m
Savona
Aeroporto Internazionale Cristoforo Colombo
Sampierdarena
GENOA NERVI
Morandi Bridge (collapsed)
Albaro
A12
RECCO
N
Quarto
Nervi
Megli
Bradt
Bogliasco
Sori
Recco
Quarto
M A R
Camogli
L I G U R E

⌂ **Where to stay, eat and drink**

1 Antica Trattoria Rosin *p88*
2 Azienda Autra *p122*
3 Bruxaboschi *p85*
4 La Pineta *p86*
5 Rifugio Parco Antola *p89*

0 ━━━━━ 5km
0 ━━━━━ 3 miles

Map content © Regional Agency in Liguria

3

Genoa

Telephone code 010 (+39010 if calling from abroad)

Genoa is a real port city. When Welsh poet Dylan Thomas arrived here in 1947, he wrote home to his parents, 'The dock-front of Genoa is marvellous. Such heat and colours and dirt and noise and loud wicked alleys with all the washing of the world hanging from the high windows.' Genoa is still a vibrant, sometimes intimidating place, that's definitely on the up.

American writer Henry James described Genoa in 1909 as the 'queerest place in the world', and it is certainly different from any other Italian city. Until recently it wasn't on the tourist trail at all and, despite efforts to clean up the old town, you will still see prostitutes, even on a Sunday morning. Yet, as James pointed out, 'it is not fair to speak as if at Genoa there were nothing but low-life to be seen, for the place is the residence of some of the grandest people in the world'. That is certainly the case. Once a maritime superpower, Genoa has some of the most sumptuous palaces in Italy.

In many ways Genoa is like London: it was badly bombed in World War II and hastily rebuilt in the post-war boom years without any consideration for aesthetics. The Genoese are regarded by their fellow Italians as penny-pinching, and despite the city's extraordinary wealth in the Middle Ages and the Renaissance, they never spent anything doing up Genoa. As a result, it has Europe's biggest and best-preserved medieval town, which James believed, 'it would be almost impossible to modernise'. He might well be proved wrong. There is a trendy feel descending on the old town as in the last couple of years hip bars, cafés and shops have begun to open up.

Genoa sits surrounded by hills dotted with forts. It impressed everyone who sailed in here until the 1960s. Charles Dickens, who spent a year in Genoa in 1844, described the harbour as 'a splendid amphitheatre, terrace rising above terrace, garden above garden, palace above palace'. Be warned, however, that first sights of the city are seriously off-putting these days. Its suburbs, which stretch along the coast to the west around the airport, are particularly shabby. Not surprisingly, as it is one of the Mediterranean's largest ports, the seafront is lined with huge docks and stacks of containers, and stretches for 22km. Across the old port, right in front of the old town, is an elevated flyover, the *sopraelevata*. It was built in 1965 as were many of the modern bridges that carry the motorway across the surrounding valleys. It is easy to see their necessity but frankly whoever thought it was a good idea to build a motorway on stilts in front of the medieval city must have been in the sun too long. Back in the 60s, however, this architectural monstrosity was considered cutting-edge and the shops sold postcards of it. I have one my mother-in-law bought of the Morandi Bridge but never sent. The Morandi Bridge collapsed in August 2018 (see box, page 48).

It is not the case that Genoese ignore the problem of the *sopraelevata*. What to do with it and how to redirect the traffic are a source of debate and numerous

THE MORANDI BRIDGE

The Morandi Bridge [map, page 46], part of which collapsed in August 2018, was not only an indispensable transport link but a source of civic pride. When it was designed in the 1960s by famous architect Riccardo Morandi, it was acclaimed across the world. It was a key part of the A10 motorway, which links the two halves of Liguria. The bridge is situated on the west side of Genoa and links with the motorway that heads north to Milan and along the Riviera di Levante. It ran between the Sampierdarena and Cornigliano districts.

It is thought that the concrete used in the construction was vulnerable to degradation and cracks let water in almost as soon as the bridge opened in 1967. It seems that the necessary maintenance and repairs were not carried out.

The collapse of the bridge set off a bitter debate about why the disaster, which claimed 43 lives, happened. At time of writing an investigation was underway to find out who bears responsibility and what caused the disaster.

A structural engineer, Carmelo Gentile, from the Politecnico di Milano had found troubling signs of corrosion in 2017 and had warned the company that manages the bridge, Autostrade per l'Italia. The company belongs to the Benetton family.

The motorway was privatised in 1999 and there is now a political debate over the extent of privatisation in Italy and the country's ageing infrastructure.

Renzo Piano (see box, page 183), the architect behind London's Shard and the Centre Pompidou in Paris, was born in Genoa and has offered to design a new bridge.

A 12-month state of emergency was declared in the area and there was, at time of writing, severe traffic congestion in this part of the city. For updates check w autostrade.it.

proposals. The latest is to build a tunnel under the port. After the Morandi Bridge disaster, questions have also been raised about the state of Liguria's infrastructure in a debate that is likely to intensify. One factor that is believed to have led to the Morandi disaster is that the bridge was not designed for the current traffic flow, but the bridge's collapse has only increased the number of cars and lorries on the *sopraelevata*.

There are bold plans to take Genoa into the future with the development of offshore wharfs to expand the port. Genoa is also one of the few Mediterranean ports that still builds ships. The city wants to guard its position as a major repair centre and become a ship disposal hub, and the dismantling of the *Costa Concordia* was emblematic of this move. In 2013 the pilot's control tower was destroyed in an accident and Renzo Piano, the city's architectural genius, has designed a new pilot's tower that will rise 70m over the eastern gateway to the port – but it is yet to be built. At time of writing, plans to expand the port were under consideration and the environmental impact of the proposed changes was being assessed.

With a population of 594,733 Genoa is Italy's sixth-largest city and perhaps its most elusive. The Genoese are traditionally reserved with strangers and have, until recently, shunned tourism. It takes time to get under the city's skin and see beyond the ramshackle and the run-down. One reason it is an elusive place is that the old town is a confusing rabbit warren with few squares or parks. 'Genoa is the crookedest and most incoherent of cities; tossed about on the sides and crests of a dozen hills,' wrote James. 'Down about the basements, in the little, dim, close alleys, the people are forever moving to and fro, or standing in their cavernous doorways or their dusky, crowded shops, calling, chattering, laughing, scrambling, living their lives in the conversational Italian fashion'. The city was always open to foreign influences and today has a big immigrant population primarily from Africa and South America.

First impressions of Genoa are nearly always wrong. Dickens was taken aback, 'I never in my life was so dismayed!' and 'the disheartening dirt, discomfort, and decay; perfectly confounded me'. He wrote later, however, 'It is a place that "grows upon you" every day. There seems always something to find out in it... It abounds with the strangest contrasts; things that are picturesque, ugly, mean, magnificent, delightful and offensive, break up the view at every turn.'

When I first sat on the dockside on a rainy day in 1988 contemplating this rather dark and dilapidated place, I was bemused by how much my husband loved it. What's so magical about Genoa is that it's a real working city not overrun with tourists like its great rival Venice. It hides its treasures in its dark alleyways and the fun is to be had in discovering the opulence of its palaces and its fantastic cuisine, which made it, in the opinion of the famous Renaissance scholar Petrarch, 'La Superba', Genoa the Proud.

Today, after much renovation in 1992 to mark the 500th anniversary of the city's most famous son's achievement, Christopher Columbus's 'discovery' of America, the old port is a bustling tourist centre. The old town, with its narrow tangle of alleyways, the *caruggi*, is a place to wander and get lost in a hundred times. It's being slowly gentrified in parts but still has an edge. Real gems, however, lie behind the dark exteriors of its palazzos whose plush, sumptuous interiors are bursting with fabulous art collections in stark contrast to the rough-and-tumble back streets. This is the Genoa that, in 1853, composer Richard Wagner found 'unbelievably beautiful, grandiose and characteristic'.

HISTORY

Genoa was founded in the 4th century BC as a Roman port. Its name derives from the Latin *iuana*, meaning 'gates', which was corrupted into Genoa (Genova in Italian). Little is known about Roman Genoa other than it was an important trading port and was sacked by Hannibal's brother, Magone, during the Punic Wars. The Genoese still say '*avere il magone*' or '*u magun*' in local dialect to mean that someone is depressed.

In the early Middle Ages, as Liguria suffered endless invasions, the city was occupied by the Franks and the Lombards. Then, in AD935, the Saracens sacked it, taking nearly half the population prisoner. It was a wake-up call for the Genoese who roused themselves to protect their harbour and coast from Saracen attack. As a result they embarked upon a course that would make the city, by the millennium, an independent city-state and a maritime superpower.

The Genoese brutally suppressed the coastal population, bringing all of Liguria under their control and repelling an attack from the legendary Holy Roman Emperor Barbarossa in 1158, when the people of Genoa built a new city wall in just 53 days.

Medieval Genoa was a violent and fractious place ruled by deeply divided clans who fought running street battles with their enemies rather like drug cartels in parts of modern-day South America. Each lived in their own fief with their own tall tower for security. There were so many of these towers that Genoa must have looked much like a medieval, mini Manhattan. They used to throw boiling oil and water on people below and were so dangerous that in 1196 a maximum height of

24m was introduced. Only the Embriaco family were allowed to keep theirs, thanks to the important role they played in the First Crusade.

The vendettas, which looked as if they had stepped out of the pages of *Romeo and Juliet*, were aggravated by the wars between the Guelphs and the Ghibellines. The Guelphs, known locally as Mascherati, sided with the Pope and were represented by the Fieschi and Grimaldi families. The Spinolas and the Dorias, the Rampini, sided with the Ghibellines, who supported the Holy Roman Emperor. Large parts of the old town were destroyed in their battles and when wells were dug in Piazza di Sarzano at the end of the 16th century, workmen came across a mass grave of bones mixed with weapons and helmets, some of which contained severed heads.

Periodically, one clan would leave the city altogether as the Grimaldis did in 1346. They moved to their piratical little fiefdom of Monaco and swore allegiance to the French king. As a result, about 12,000 of their clan ended up in the Battle of Crécy, where they were massacred on the front line. When the news reached Genoa, their enemies partied late into the night.

In order to try to bring an end to the incessant infighting, the mercantile classes rose up against the nobles and a doge was elected in 1339. Doges then ran the city until 1805. Only four were ever actually elected. More often than not warring factions called on outside powers to put their man in the job, in what was effectively a military coup. It meant that Genoa was constantly under the tutelage of different outside powers. The extraordinary thing, however, was that, despite all this, Genoa grew immensely rich and powerful.

Genoa clashed with its great rivals, the other maritime republics of Venice and Pisa, which led to some quieter times at home while its young men sailed off to fight elsewhere. Genoa was at war with Pisa for virtually 200 years until its decisive victory at the Battle of Meloria in 1284. The Genoese took over 7,000 prisoners who were unloaded below Piazza di Sarzano on the Campo Pisano, which at the time was a small harbour. The vast majority of them were murdered on the quayside, which ran with blood. The main bone of contention between Genoa and Pisa was the island of Corsica due south of Genoa, which the Genoese took full control of after Meloria. Bloody battles with Venice continued until the Battle of Chioggia in 1380.

Genoa's clans grew rich from the Crusades that began in 1096 and soon established an empire in the Mediterranean and the Black Sea. They played an important part in the siege of Jerusalem and had trading quarters in Acre, Jerusalem, Jaffa and ancient Antioch, in Turkey, and later around the Black Sea. For centuries Genoese galleys sailed the seas loaded with sugar, wheat, salt, gold, silver, spices and slaves, which were all traded through the port and made their way north on the crucial trading route that ran through Busalla. Her fleet sailed under the flag of the cross of St George (San Giorgio), also adopted by the English having put their fleet under Genoese protection, and later adopted as the flag of England. Not everything that arrived in the port was a good thing, however. Genoese traders and Crusaders brought home so many treasures they have been described as 'international robbers' by one historian. Unfortunately, in 1347, they also brought home the Black Death, which ravaged first the city and then Europe.

Genoa was also the financial powerhouse of Europe. The Genoese minted their first coins in 1139. It had a cross on one side and a castle on the other, hence 'heads or tails' is 'croce e grifo', where *grifo* is the dialect word for a castle. The Bank of San Giorgio was one of the continent's first banks and effectively ran the empire. It had considerable influence as it lent money to Europe's kings and queens. In the 16th century, Genoa lost its territories in the east to the Ottoman Empire but still managed to prosper.

Under Admiral Andrea Doria, Genoa grew even richer off trade from the New World and by financing Spanish adventures there. Doria put Genoa under Spanish protection and ran the city through an oligarchy of the old and new nobility. Doria's dictatorial rule did much to cool the infighting, although insurrections continued, and he was almost toppled by the Fieschi in 1547, who mounted a coup that failed when its leader fell overboard fully armed and drowned at the vital moment.

The city's elders may have refused to bankroll Columbus, but as the saying went, 'Silver is born in the Americas, passes through Spain and dies in Genoa'. Although a third of the precious metals from Spain's empire ended up in Genoa, the Genoese were renowned for their miserliness. The big families hoarded their wealth and the riches that flowed into the city did little to help the poor. In 1656, 40,000 Genoese died from plague. The leading families were fabulously wealthy and the Spinolas had an estimated wealth of 16 million lire, a massive sum for the time. In the 17th century many beautiful palaces were built as was a new ring of city walls. More money poured into the city as the Bank of San Giorgio financed the Spanish wars in the Netherlands and, at last, some of the first charitable institutions were established to help the homeless and the needy.

In 1630 Spain was defeated militarily and simultaneously the supply of precious metals from the Americas came to a halt. The Spanish defaulted on their debts and the Genoese, who by now were no longer a naval power, could do little about it. For the next 150 years Genoa was tossed between the French, Spanish Neapolitans, Austria-Hungary and the House of Savoy who bombarded it, sacked it and ruled it. There was one final victory when the city rose up against the Austrians in 1746, sparked by the courage of one young boy, Balilla, who threw a stone at the Austrian troops. Genoa lost Corsica, its final colony, to the French in 1768. When English writer Tobias Smollett arrived in 1764, he found the nobles as proud as ever, living in marble palaces but eating scraps.

Although the Genoese were supporters of the French Revolution, the situation didn't improve and in 1800 during the Austrian siege of Genoa, when Napoleon's forces held out in the city for four months, 30,000 Genoese died. Seen as too loyal to Napoleon and with the British keen to establish a powerful state in northern Italy to see off a future French attack, in 1815 the Congress of Vienna wiped Genoa off the map, without even consulting the Genoese, and handed the city and its possessions to Britain's ally, monarchist Piedmont. It was a resentment that was to fuel a new movement.

Napoleon had, however, left his mark on Italian history. The masses had welcomed the ideas of the French Revolution and the city's intelligentsia were open to liberal ideas. After Liguria had been absorbed into France many of the nobility were even sent to study at French universities. As a consequence, liberal ideas gave birth to the concept of an Italian nation united under a liberal regime within a united European federal state, whose forceful advocate was Genoa's Giuseppe Mazzini. His ideas led to the Risorgimento, the struggle to unite Italy at whose forefront was the military genius, the Ligurian Giuseppe Garibaldi. It would be Garibaldi who set sail for Sicily from the fishing village of Quarto dei Mille, now in Genoa's eastern suburbs, with his 'Thousand' in 1860.

While its old rivals Venice and Pisa became backwaters, Genoa was boosted by the opening of the Suez Canal in 1869 and the industrialisation of northern Italy. Steelworks and shipyards shot up as the harbour grew to be one of Europe's main ports. The mass migration from Europe in the late 19th century also made Genoa rich as millions of passengers passed through the port on their way to the far-flung corners of the world, many of them never to return.

Giuseppe Mazzini was born in Genoa in 1805 when it was part of the French Empire and his father was an advocate of the ideas of the French Revolution. Genoa's intellectual elite resented being handed over to the authoritarian monarchical Piedmont in 1815 and Mazzini, soon after graduating as a lawyer, started writing for newspapers that challenged the House of Savoy and were quickly closed down by the Piedmontese authorities.

In 1831, Mazzini joined the patriotic movement, the Carbonari, and he was arrested and imprisoned in Savona. On his release, he went into exile in Marseille, where he founded Giovine Italia, Young Italy, a secret society who wanted to unify Italy into a liberal republic. Mazzini was convinced that this would be brought about by a popular uprising that would in turn spark a revolution across Europe.

By 1833, Giovine Italia had 60,000 members and Mazzini launched the first of a series of failed revolts in Genoa. The uprising was brutally suppressed, its leaders executed and the head of the Genoa branch, Jacopo Ruffini, killed himself in prison. Mazzini was tried *in absentia* and sentenced to death. Another revolt failed in 1834 but undaunted, Mazzini now founded Young Europe, Giovine Europa, a movement ahead of its time, that envisaged a Europe of liberal republics linked in a federal state. It was a move that saw him arrested in both Switzerland and Paris.

In exile in England he continued to plot revolts. Above all he was impressed by the power of the press and was quick to see it as a potential weapon for garnering support, both in Britain and Italy. It was Mazzini who was to create the great myth of Garibaldi, the military leader of the Risorgimento. After another failed uprising in Genoa, Mazzini was sidelined in the story of the Risorgimento by Camillo Benso, the Piedmontese prime minister, who in 1856 now took a leading role, although he still remained active in Italian politics until his death in 1872. He's buried in Genoa's Staglieno cemetery.

The second branch of the fascist organisation the Fascio di Combattimento was formed in Genoa in 1918 and the port was expanded in the interwar years. Genoa, however, was the first city in the north to rise up against the Nazi occupation and liberated itself before the Allies arrived. The war left its mark on the city, which underwent a series of naval bombardments and bombing raids that killed a large number of civilians. Many buildings were left in a state of disrepair until the 1980s. Economically, the post-war period gave Genoa another high. It benefited from a boom as Milan and Turin's port. The symbol of this second industrial revolution, the container, arrived in the 1960s. In the 1970s the new container port of Prà-Voltri came into being. Unlike its old rivals, it was forgotten by tourists, which is one reason it has retained so much authenticity. Since 1992, when Genoa underwent a face-lift to mark the 500th anniversary of Columbus's 'discovery' of America, under the guiding hand of local architect Renzo Piano, there has been a slow gentrification, and in 2004, it was Europe's Capital of Culture.

GETTING THERE AND AWAY

BY AIR Cristoforo Colombo Airport [map, page 46] is 6km west of the city in Sestri Ponente (✆010 60151). A taxi costs €21 to the city centre, but don't be fooled by the sign saying 'taxi €7'; it's the price per person and you will have to pay the minimum, which is for three. Alternatively, the shuttle bus, Volabus, runs roughly every 45 minutes connecting the airport to Principe [56 C1] and Brignole [56 G3] stations and Piazza de Ferrari [62 G4]. Buy a ticket on the bus for €6, which includes a train, bus or metro transfer within the city.

BY BOAT Genoa is one of the busiest freight ports in the Mediterranean, but also has docking for yachts, ferries and cruise liners. Ferries from Mediterranean ports depart from and arrive at the Stazione Marittima [56 C2] (Ponte dei Mille; \ 010 089 8300; w stazionimarittimegenova.com). You can sail to Barcelona, Sardinia, Sicily and North Africa. The marina near the airport has some 600 berths (\ 010 614 3420; e info@marinagenova.it; w marinagenova.it) and the Porto Antico [56 C3], 270 berths (\ 010 247 0039; e porto@marinaportoantico.it; w marinaportoantico.it).

BY BUS Intercity services depart from Piazza della Vittoria [56 G4] or from Piazza Acquaverde by Principe Station [56 C1].

BY CAR Four different motorways connect the city to the national network from different points. The A12 runs along the coast from the east, the A10 leads west along the Riviera di Ponente, and the A7 heads north to Milan. The A26 from Voltri also goes north to Gravellona. The easiest place to park is in the Porto Antico, the old port [56 C3], where there are three car parks. Following the collapse of the Morandi Bridge [map, page 46], the A10 is closed between Genoa Airport and Genoa Ovest and this is likely to remain the case for some years. As a result there is considerable traffic congestion in the western part of the city. Check w autostrade.it for updates.

BY TRAIN (w trenitalia.com) Genoa sits on the main line between Ventimiglia (2¼hrs) and Rome (5¼hrs). It has direct connections with Turin (1¾hrs) and Milan (1½hrs), as well as Pisa (2hrs). The two main railway stations are: Principe, on the western side of town, where trains arrive from the west and the north; and Brignole, in the east, which connects with trains running eastwards. Buses 33 and 37 run between the two. Avoid arriving at Principe late at night, especially if you are a woman travelling alone.

A FLYING VISIT

If you have only one day in Genoa:

Start your tour in the Porto Antico [56 C3]. Walk up through the old town to the Cattedrale di San Lorenzo [62 E4]. Then visit the Palazzo Ducale [62 F4] and walk over to see Christopher Columbus's supposed birthplace by the Porta Soprana [59 E7]. Walk across Piazza de Ferrari [62 F4] and turn left into the old town and wander its tiny alleyways, the *caruggi*. Eat lunch in the old town at a classic Genoese restaurant like I Tre Merli (page 61). Spend the afternoon exploring the city's impressive palaces on Via Garibaldi [58 D3]. If you only have time to visit one, make it the Palazzo Rosso [58 D3]. Be sure not to miss the view from the roof. Finish the day with a coffee and cake at Fratelli Klainguti (page 65).

ORIENTATION

Genoa is a remarkably thin city, which runs along the coast for 40km. The mountains behind it provide a green backdrop. The main museums and restaurants are to be found in the Porto Antico and the Centro Storico, the port area and the old town. To the northwest of the old town is the area of Pré below Principe Station – it is a bit rough and ready, especially at night. On the other side of the old town the area dominated by the Basilica di Santa Maria Assunta is known as Carignano. Foce is a modern suburb to the east before the more elegant Albaro and Nervi. The shopping area around Via XX Settembre is called Portoria. The smart place to live is Castelletto.

GETTING AROUND

The easiest way to get around Genoa is on foot, especially in the old town. Use the funicular to get a splendid view of the city from the hills. The funicular to Righi leaves from Largo della Zecca [58 C2] and a wonderful Art Nouveau lift takes you from Piazza del Portello [58 E3] to Castelletto. The best way to explore the mountains behind Genoa is to catch the narrow-gauge railway from just above Piazza Manin [56 G2]. To explore Genoa's suburbs, use the suburban trains from Principe or Brignole.

BY BOAT Ferries leave in summer for the Cinque Terre (w golfoparadiso.it), Portofino (w traghettiportofino.it) and San Fruttuoso (w liguriaviamare.it), and there are whale-watching cruises (w whalewatchliguria.it). It's also possible to see the local firework displays from the sea. The Navebus run by AMT links Pegli to the old port and takes 30 minutes.

The Yacht Club Italiano [56 D4] founded at the end of the 19th century is the oldest Mediterranean sailing club and has one of the most prestigious sailing schools in the country (w yachtclubitaliano.it).

BY BUS AND METRO Tickets are sold at newsstands, in tobacconists, *tabacchi*, and also via ticket machines located in the main stations. The standard fare is €1.50, or €14 for a carnet or book of ten. There is also a 24-hour ticket (€4.50), as well as a joint museum and bus card available (see box, page 69). Tickets are also valid for the metro, lifts and funiculars for 100 minutes after validating the ticket. You must stamp your ticket when you get on the bus or you could be fined. City bus tours leave daily from in front of the aquarium and last an hour (w city-sightseeing.it; €8). The Genoa underground is diminutive. It currently runs from Brin to Brignole and has eight stations. It is actually quite a fun ride and surprisingly cool in summer. Bus tickets are valid on the metro.

BY TAXI There are taxi ranks at the two main stations: Principe (℡010 261246); and Brignole (℡010 564007).

Radiotaxi ℡010 5966

TOURIST INFORMATION

The main tourist offices are on Via Garibaldi [58 D3] (℡ 010 557 2903) and in the Porto Antico [62 B3] (℡010 557 2903) by the Banco San Giorgio. There are also desks at the airport and in Principe Station [56 C1]. There is a useful audioguide

(€10.50), which can be purchased at the tourist office.. The tourist board is also very proud of its Genova App, which has good maps and lots of useful information on exhibitions and events.

Guided tours leave from the tourist information office in the Porto Antico (English-language tours ⏱ 10.00 Sat/Sun; €14) as does the sightseeing bus. **AlbaTravel** (☏ 010 529 9206; **w** albatraveliguria.com) organises walking tours and **Genova Guide** offers private tours (**m** 3470 920177; **w** genovaguide.com). There are guided tours of Genoa's forts and walls and the Staglieno cemetery periodically in summer. A tourist 'train' (**w** treninopippo.it) also runs from in front of the aquarium [62 A1] (10.00–17.00 daily). Segway tours are based at Calata Cattaneo 18 (**w** genovasegway.it).

EVENTS
April Every five years, at the end of April, the huge flower show Euroflora takes place in the city. The next Euroflora will be held in 2021.

May Every other year in May there is a Slow Fish food festival. The next one takes place in 2019.

May to June The Regata delle Antiche Repubbliche Marinare (**w** repubbliche-marinare.org), the regatta of the four historic maritime republics, is held at the end of May or the beginning of June. The boat race and costume pageant are a celebration of the history of the republics of Genoa, Venice, Pisa and Amalfi. They take it in turns to host the event, with the next one being held in 2022.

June The poetry festival (**w** parolespalancate.it) is one of the oldest and largest in Italy, celebrating poetry in every form.

But the big day is 24 June, the feast of the city's patron saint, St John the Baptist. There is live music across the town. In the afternoon, there is a religious procession and a blessing of the sea, and at midnight the traditional bonfire is lit.

September The Paganini Violin Competition (**w** premiopaganini.it) began in 1954 in order to spotlight new talent.

Every year in early September, on the Notte Bianca, the city is full of art exhibitions, film screenings, theatre shows, music and museums with late-night openings.

October The Genoa International Boat Show (**w** salonenautico.com) is a huge event with more than 400 boats There is also a science festival in October.

USEFUL WEBSITES
w comune.genova.it
w visitgenoa.it

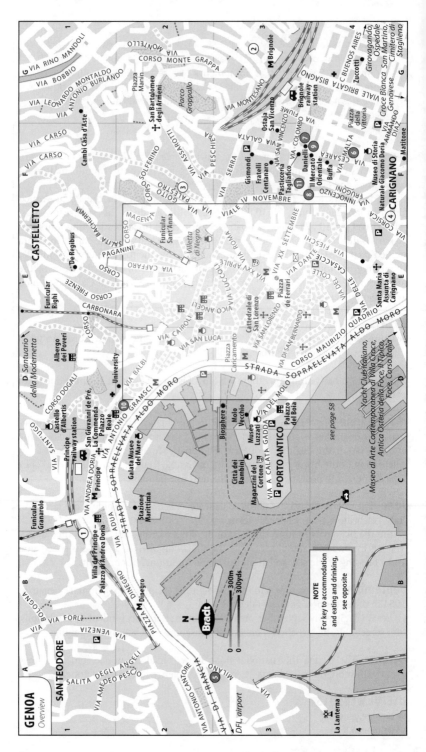

Hotels in Genoa are a little bland at the top end of the mid range and there are no luxury hotels here. The NH chain has two of the best-located ones and the Meliá was done up a few years ago and is now a stylish mid-range hotel. Family-run moderate to inexpensive hotels, apart from a handful of exceptions, are unmodernised and not especially nice. The best accommodation is in B&Bs, which have opened up all over Genoa in recent years and are the best places to get a real feel for the city. Many of the B&Bs are extremely chic, with frescoed ceilings, but affordable, making Genoa a great destination for a city break that won't cost a fortune. If you are travelling with children and want to keep costs down, there is a Novotel, where two kids can stay free in their parents' room, on the harbour near the Lanterna, but it isn't the greatest of locations.

🏠 Bristol Palace [59 F6] (133 rooms) Via Settembre 35; ☎010 592541; e info. bristolpalace@duetorrihotels.com; w hotelbristolpalace.com. Located in the middle of Via XX Settembre, this has all the character of a late 19th-century hotel. It's a bit scruffy at the edges, like the city itself, but full of old-world charm & antiques. The hotel opened in 1905 & among the famous names who have stayed here are Alfred Hitchcock & Luigi Pirandello. The restaurant is sadly not as good as it could be. €€€

🏠 Meliá [56 F4] (99 rooms) Via Corsica 4; ☎800 788333; e melia.genoa@melia.com; w melia-genoa.com. This is the most stylish hotel in Genoa & is in the Carignano district. It used to be known as the Bentley & was built in 1929 as an office building, & has some interesting architectural features. If you want to splurge, go for the Presidential Suite with roof terrace & hot tub. There is a small swimming pool & very stylish

touches to the décor, such as the TV hidden behind the mirror in the bathroom. Wi-Fi. €€€

🏠 B&B Domitilla [56 B1] (3 rooms) Via Pagano Doria 1; m 349 360 1648; e info@ bebdomitillagenova.it; w bebdomitillagenova. it. Nice, modern rooms in a flat, 1 with a balcony, in the former Grand Hotel Miramare, which has a garden with a great view across the port. Free Wi-Fi. €€

🏠 B&B Lercari [58 E2] (1 room) Via Caffaro 8b/4; m 338 431 9838/73 0581. 1 room in a family apt with private bathroom just off Via Garibaldi. Perfect if you want to really feel what it is like to live in Genoa. The ceilings are frescoed. Private parking at an additional fee. €€

🏠 B&B QuartoPiano [58 C3] (3 rooms) Piazza Pellicceria 2–4; m 348 742 6779; e info@quarto-piano.it; w quarto-piano.it. This ultra-modern luxury B&B near the Palazzo Spinola is a top choice. It has a roof terrace with a hot tub & a stylish modern interior. No lift. Free Wi-Fi. €€

🏠 Genova Porto Antico Bed & Breakfast [62 C2] (3 rooms) Via San Luca 1/15A; ☎010 301 3905; e info@bbgenovaportoantico.it; w bbgenovaportoantico.it. On the 5th floor of a 14th-century palazzo in Piazza Banchi. The rooms have a modern, simple, white feel. A fabulous location & friendly hosts. €€

🏠 Girovagando [56 G4] (3 rooms) Corso Torino 31, interno 20 scala B; m 393 328 0593; e info@girovagandogenova.com; w girovagandogenova.com. In the Foce area of Genoa, this B&B is on the 6th floor, but has a lift & the owners are great at giving you a real home-from-home experience. €€

🏠 Le Nuvole Residenza d'Epoca [62 D2] (15 rooms) Piazza delle Vigne 6; ☎010 251 0018;

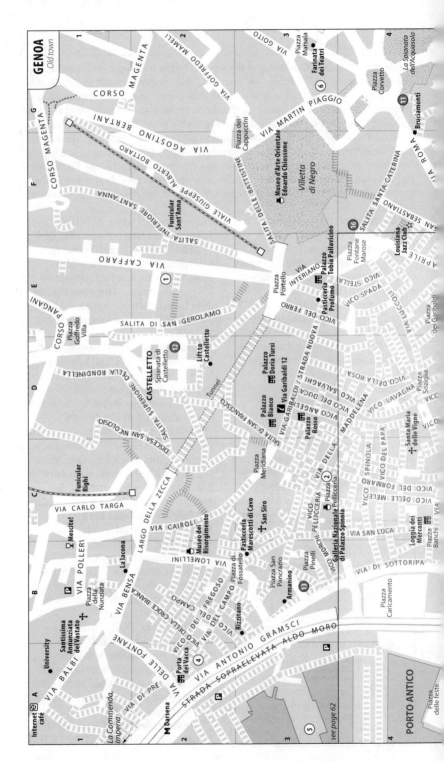

58

La Commenda, Imperia

Internet café A

University

Santissima Annunziata del Vastato †

VIA BALBI

VIA DELLE FONTANE

VIA DI PRE

M Darsena

Piazza della Nunziata

VIA POLLERI

Mescîtee!

La Iacona

VIA CARLO TARGA

Funicular Righi

CORSO MAGENTA

CORSO MAGENTA

VIA GOFFREDO MAMELI

VIA AGOSTINO BERTANI

VALE GIUSEPPE ALBERTO BOTTARO

SALITA INFERIORE SANT'ANNA

Funicular Sant'Anna

VIA GOITO

VIA MARSALA

Farinata dei Teatri 6

Piazza dei Cappuccini

Piazza Corvetto

Villetta di Negro

Museo d'Arte Orientale Edoardo Chiossone

SALITA DELLE BATTISTINE

VIA MARTIN PIAGGIO

Bruciamonti 11

VIA ROMA

La Spianata dell'Acquasola

PANGANI

CORSO Piazza Goffredo Villa

SALITA DI SAN GEROLAMO

CASTELLETTO

Spianata di Castelletto

Lift to Castelletto 12

SALITA SUPERIORE DELLA RONDINELLA

DISCESA SAN NICOLOSIO

VIA CAFFARO

Tunnel

Piazza Portello

VIA INTERIANO

Piazza Pontello

Pasticceria Profumo

VIA DEL FERRO

VICO DEL FERRO

Palazzo Tobia Pallavicino

Piazza Fontane Marose

Louisiana Jazz Club

SALITA SANTA CATERINA

SAN SEBASTIANO

16

A APRILE

VICO STELLA

VICO SPADA

LUCCOLI

Piazza dei Garibaldi

VICO DELLA ROSA

VICO DELLA

Piazza Soziglia

VICC

VIC

Santa Maria delle Vigne †

VICO DEL PAPA

Palazzo Doria Tursi

Palazzo Bianco

Palazzo Rosso

Via Garibaldi 12

VIA GARIBALDI / STRADA NUOVA

VICO DEL DUCA

SALITA DI SAN FRANCESCO

VICO ANGELI

VICO DEL DUCA SAN SALVAGHI

MADDALENA

Piazza Meridiana

LARGO DELLA ZECCA

VIA CAIROLI

Museo del Risorgimento

Pasticceria Marescotti di Cavo

San Siro †

VICO DELLA PELLICCERIA

Piazza 2

VICO DELLA MADDALENA

VICO SPINOLA

VICO DELLE MELE

VICO DEL FORMARO

VIA SAN LUCA

VIA DELLE FONTANE

VIA BENSA

VIA LOMELLINI

VIA DEL CAMPO

VICO DEL FREGOSO

VICO DELLA CROCE BIANCA

VIA DEL CAMPO

Piazza di Fossatello

Rizzitano

Armanino

Piazza San Pancrazio

Piazza Pinelli

Galleria Nazionale di Palazzo Spinola

Pellicceria

VICO NOCHI PELLICCERIA

13

Loggia dei Mercanti

Piazza Banchi

VIA DI SOTTORIPA

Piazza Caricamento

Porta dei Vacca

4

VIA ANTONIO GRAMSCI

STRADA SOPRAELEVATA ALDO MORO

P

P

P

P

5

see page 62

PORTO ANTICO

Piazza delle feste

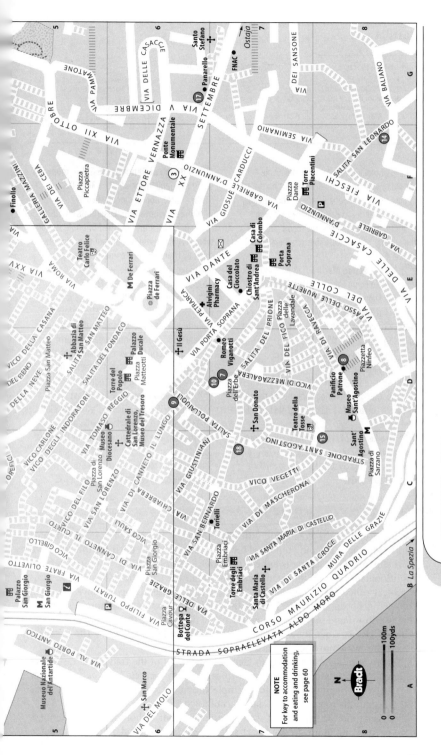

e hello@hotellenuvole.it; w hotellenuvole.it. In the old town in the Maddalena district on the 4th floor of the Lamba Doria Palace. It is eco-friendly & mixes modern & classic Genoese style with beautiful frescoed ceilings. The rooms still have the original 18th-century shutters. A really good choice. €€

🏠 **NH Collection Marina** [58 A3] (140 rooms) Molo Ponte Calvi 5; ☎010 25391; e nhcollectionmarina@nh-hotels.com; w nh-hotels.com. Great location with good-sized rooms with balconies overlooking the harbour right next to the aquarium. Free Wi-Fi. €€

🏠 **NH Genova Centro** [58 G3] (143 rooms) Via Martin Piaggio 11; ☎010 83161; e nhgenovacentro@nh-hotels.com; w nh-hotels. com. Another good location opposite the park just off Piazza Corvetto, in a modernised old hotel. Free Wi-Fi. €€

🏠 **So e Leo** [62 C1] (4 rooms) Via di Sottoripa 1a; m 346 518 5238; w soeleo.it. B&B close to the aquarium. Family suite for 4 & a room with disabled access. €€

🏠 **Il Borgo di Genova** [56 G3] (4 rooms) Via Borgo degli Incrociati 7; m 347 602 5578; e info@ilborgodigenova.com; w ilborgodigenova.com. Elegant B&B with lovely period features north of Brignole station, which is convenient if you want to explore the coast by train. Friendly owners & a fabulous b/ fast make this one of the best B&Bs in Genoa & a bargain at the price. Wi-Fi. €

🏠 **Il Salotto di Lucilla** [56 F2] (3 rooms) Passo Palestro 3/5; ☎010 882391; e info@ ilsalottodilucilla.com; w ilsalottodilucilla.com. Elegant B&B in a residential area just north of Piazza Corvetto with exceptionally friendly owners. Only downside is that it's at the top of a steep flight of stairs, so travel light. €

🏠 **La Superba Rooms & Breakfast** [58 A2] (4 rooms) Via del Campo 12; ☎010 869 8589; m 335 720 8642; e info@la-superba.com; w la-superba.com. In a beautiful palazzo, the Durazzo-Cattaneo Adorno Palace in front of the aquarium. Simple elegant rooms. Terrace with a great view across the port. Excellent value for money. €

✖ WHERE TO EAT AND DRINK

Genoa is one of the great food cities of Europe. It has lots of good restaurants and food shops. To enjoy top-class food you don't have to head for the city's two Michelin-starred restaurants either, there are plenty of authentic trattorias serving traditional local dishes that won't break the bank. The Chamber of Commerce runs a project called Genova Gourmet and they have a useful app, Genova Gourmet (w www.genovagourmet.it). It gives their stamp of approval to those restaurants that use Slow Food ingredients, Ligurian olive oil and serve the four Ligurian CDO wines. CDO is a quality assurance label for Italian food products. The initiative covers the entire province and not just the city.

The great thing about eating in Genoa is that a lot of the traditional dishes are essentially street food and you can buy pies and tasty focaccia from bakers all over the city. When buying focaccia, for example, the rule is to buy it in a place that looks like a dive in the most working-class part of town.

The gastronomic experience starts in the port. For a thousand years Genoese have been eating in the arcaded port-side *sciamadda* fast-food outlets. *Sciamadda* means 'flamed' in dialect and inside roasting ovens are busy baking *farinata* and food is frying in large metal *friggitore*. Fried squid, *totani fritti*, and salted cod fritters, the poor man's fish, *frittelle di baccalà*, are the things to try. They must be eaten fresh and frying starts at 11.30.

RESTAURANTS
Expensive
✗ **Zeffirino** [56 F4] Via XX Settembre 20r; ✆010 897 0079; e info@zeffirino.com; w zeffirino.com. Once a favourite of Frank Sinatra, Pavarotti & Pope John Paul II. Run by 5 brothers with branches in Las Vegas & Hong Kong, this is a beautiful restaurant with flamboyant touches & top-quality fresh Italian food. Pink tablecloths & starched linen help make this Genoese institution, opened in 1939, feel more upmarket. Seafood is always fresh. They have the Genova Gourmet certification. Set menu. €€€€€

Mid-range
✗ **Antica Osteria della Foce** [56 D4] Via Ruspoli 72r; ✆010 302 7696; ⊕ closed Aug & Sat/Sun lunch. Opened in 1932 & famous for its *farinata*, it's absolutely crucial to reserve a table here & is a good place to taste the famous *cima alla genovese*. Great wine list & innovative cakes. €€€
✗ **Beluga** [59 D8] Via Jacapo de Levanto 15; m 349 668 8098; ⊕ closed Mon. One of the best fish restaurants in Genoa in an area that is lively at night. €€€
✗ **I Tre Merli** [62 A3] Calata Cattaneo 17; ✆010 246 4416; e portoantico@tremerli.it; w itremerli. it. Brothers Paolo & Marco Secondo have built a culinary empire since they opened in 1979, with branches in New York, Miami Beach & Chicago. Great traditional Ligurian food. They have the Genova Gourmet certification. €€€
✗ **Il Cadraio** [62 E1] Vico dietro il Coro della Maddalena 26r; ✆010 247 4095. This new restaurant is in a vaulted 600-year-old palazzo that was once a working-class bar. The menu is typically Ligurian. €€€
✳✗ **Il Genovese** [56 F4] Via Galata 35r; ✆010 869 2937; w ilgenovese.com. Unpretentious restaurant in a quiet street off Via XX Settembre. The chef is Australian, but the cuisine is 100% Ligurian & the pesto is made with a pestle & mortar. This is a really good place to eat authentic local food. The restaurant's Roberto Panizza is the organiser of pesto championships & makes a

fantastic pesto himself. There are recipes on the website if you like cooking. €€€
✗ **Le Terrazze del Ducale** [62 F4] Piazza Matteotti 8; ✆010 588600; e ristoro@ leterrazzedelducale.it; w leterrazzedelducale. com. The setting for this restaurant is the big draw as it's on the roof of the Palazzo Ducale. €€€
✗ **Ombre Rosse** [62 E3] Vico degli Indoratori 20–22r; ✆010 275 7608; e ombrerosse@tiscali. it; ⊕ closed Sun lunch/Tue in winter. Halfway between the cathedral & the port, serves simple Genoese food in one of the oldest houses in the city, dating from the 13th century. The interior is dark & lined with books & there is outdoor seating in summer. On Fri they make the classic fish dish *cappon magro*. They have the Genova Gourmet certification. €€€

Cheap & cheerful
✗ **A' Lanterna** [56 A3] Via Milano 134r; ✆010 256425; ⊕ closed Mon/Sun evening. This is more than just a good little restaurant serving good-quality Ligurian food at a decent price; it's a place where you can actually make a difference to the world. The restaurant was founded by the priest Don Andrea Gallo who passed away a few years ago. Over the decades he helped hundreds of destitute young people rebuild their lives by giving them a job in the restaurant. It's not far from the lighthouse. €€
✗ **Da Genio** [59 F8] Salita San Leonardo 61r; ✆010 588463; ⊕ closed Sun & Aug. This trattoria serves excellent fish dishes & homemade *trofie di castagne,* pasta made with chestnut flour with pesto, & is one of the city's best. It's near Piazza Dante. €€
✗ **Eataly** [62 B3] Edificio Millo, Calata Cattaneo 15; ✆010 869 8721. The Eataly store by the aquarium is a bit of a foodie amusement park. It may look touristy, but the chain was started in Turin in 2007 to promote artisan products. What is unusual about this chain is that it is one of the few shops in Italy that stocks products from across the country. The restaurant has a minimalist dining room with huge windows looking out over the port & there is a separate pizza restaurant at the other

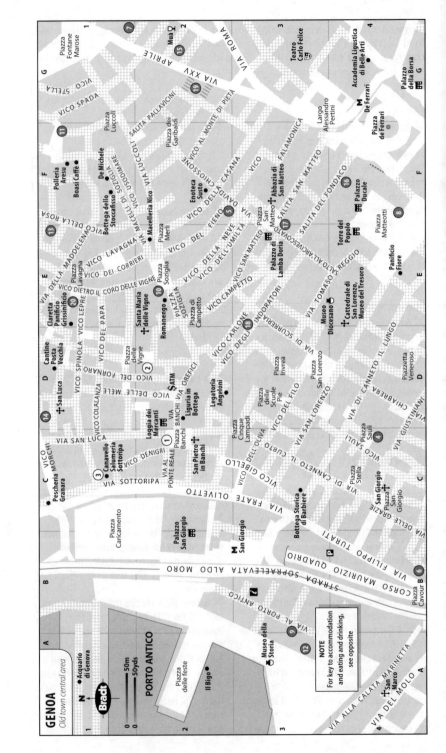

GENOA
Old town central area

PORTO ANTICO

NOTE
For key to accommodation
and eating and drinking,
see opposite

Bradt

end of the shop, which also has a café. The fish comes from Camogli. €€

❌ **Le Rune** [62 G2] Salita Inferiore di Sant'Anna 13; ☎ 010 594951; **w** ristorantelerune. it. Uses local produce & serves classic Genoese dishes. Lovely desserts. It has the Genova Gourmet stamp of approval. €€

❌ **Moa Cashmere & Lobster** [58 F4] Salita Santa Caterina 2/1; ☎ 010 899 2335; **w** moagenova.it. A clothes shop that is also a restaurant serving ice cream & cakes, lobster, & hamburgers made from Piedmontese beef & cheese. Really chic atmosphere & one of the trendy new places that has opened in the city in recent years. Inexpensive for coffee or cake. Lobster dishes are €12–18. €€

❌ **Osteria dell'Acciughetta** [56 D2] Piazza Sant'Elena; ☎ 010 869 3918; **w** acciughetta.it; ⏰ closed Mon evening & Sun. Fish dominates the menu in this rather good new restaurant. It is small so be sure to book. The chef cooks up

a storm with the anchovies the restaurant is named after. €€

❌ **Trattoria da Franca** [62 E1] Vico Lepre 4r; ☎ 010 247 4473; ⏰ closed Mon. A classic Genoese restaurant north of Santa Maria delle Vigne with excellent fresh fish & a bargain at the price. They have the Genova Gourmet certification. €€

Rock bottom

❌ **Antica Trattoria Sa' Pesta** [62 C4] Via Giustiniani 16r; ☎ 010 246 8336; **e** info@sapesta. it; **w** sapesta.it; ⏰ closed Sun & Aug. This family-run restaurant has been famed for its *farinata* & savoury pies served on long wooden tables since 1850. It's very popular so you may have to queue. Classic Genoese trattoria. €

❌ **Antica Tripperia** [62 F2] Vico della Casana 3r. A Genoese institution since the 1800s. Boiled tripe is served with white beans doused in olive oil. Eat in or take it away. Tripe with mushrooms & pine

🍴 **FOOD ON THE GO**

There are plenty of good bakeries in the old town if you want to eat on the go in the true Genoese style. You can sit down on a bench in the old port, in the two parks, or for a more serious picnic head for the forts. **Claretta Panificio Grissinificio** [62 E1] (Via della Posta Vecchia 12r), near the Spinola Palace, has been baking classic focaccia, the local flat bread, pizza and breadsticks since 1953. It also sells *pandolce* cake and *canestrelli* biscuits. **Panificio Patrone** [59 D8] (Via Ravecca 72r), in a curving medieval alley that runs off Piazza di Sarzano, has a wide range of focaccia, tarts and biscuits. **Farinata dei Teatri** [58 G3] (Piazza Marsala) serves some of the best *farinata* in the city. It is just north of Piazza Corvetto in the 19th-century part of town. **Ostaja San Vincenzo** [56 F3] (Via San Vincenzo 64r), off Via XX Settembre on a pedestrianised shopping street, has good *farinata*, savoury tarts and fritters. The *farinata* also comes with onions, cod fish and sausage. It is a real Genoese experience and totally authentic.

Genoa **WHERE TO EAT AND DRINK**

3

The bible of Genoese cooks, *La Cuciniera Genovese* was written by Giovanni Battista Ratto in 1865 and little has changed since. Basil is king of the kitchen and some of the best basil in the world grows in Genoa's suburb of Prà. It's used to make the classic pasta sauce, pesto.

Genoa's empire and maritime past have left their mark on the city's cuisine. Tuna has been part of the local diet ever since the Genoese took control of fishing rights along the coast of Tunisia, an area rich in tuna, and the classic walnut sauce originally came from the Black Sea. Minestrone with pesto was always served to sailors returning from long voyages who were desperate for vegetables and herbs after months at sea and was dispensed from 'floating kitchens' in Genoa's port. Although the Genoese were big spice traders, they did not incorporate spices into their own cooking unlike the Venetians.

A classic Genovese dish is a ravioli called *pansotti*, stuffed with chard, herbs and ricotta. *Ravieu*, a meat ravioli, is traditionally served at Christmas and was a favourite of the violinist Niccolò Paganini, who used to cook it up on tour. In fact the Genoese claim to have invented ravioli and the story goes that it was first recorded as having been made by the Ligurian clan of chefs who came from nearby Gavi Ligure, called Raviolus. As one of the great seafaring city-states of the Middle Ages, it is no surprise that many staple dishes and ingredients were once perfect for long voyages. Dried ravioli was one of them.

Vegetable pies abound and *torta pasqualina*, traditionally eaten at Easter, pops up all year round. It's made up of puff pastry stuffed with cooked chard or artichokes, courgettes, herbs and cheese. In Sestri Ponente they make their *farinata* with pumpkin, *farinata di zucca*.

Although traditionally meat was scarce in Liguria, the wealthy merchants of Genoa, many of whom had country houses or farms in what is now Piedmont, regularly ate beef. The area around Via Macelli di Soziglia in Genoa's old town was the butcher's quarter. Genoese meat dishes were as ostentatious as its palaces. *Cima* is a classic dish of veal stuffed with offal, peas, eggs and cheese, flavoured with marjoram and served in slices. It is sold ready made in many butchers and supermarkets. *Involtini* are rolls of veal filled with eggs, oregano, cheese, pine nuts, parsley, garlic and mushrooms simmered slowly in white wine and topped with fresh tomato sauce. The simpler *vitello all'uccelletto* is shredded veal sautéed with fresh bay leaves and white wine. The pasta sauce *tocco* is always made from meat.

The flagship *pandolce* is a round cake full of pine nuts, raisins, candied fruit, fennel seeds and crushed pistachios, flavoured with orange flower water and traditionally eaten at Christmas, served by the youngest member of the house and cut by the oldest. It was inspired by cakes that the Genoese ate in the Middle East and it in turn inspired English visitors in the 19th century who turned it into Genoa cake back home in England. At Easter look out for the traditional biscuits, *quaresimali*. Other local cakes include the dome-like *torta sacripantina*, made with chocolate cream and liqueur and the almond cake, *torta panarello*.

nuts is called *sbira*, the dialect word for 'miserable', as it was the poor man's food. €

✗ Carega [58 B3] Via Sottoripa 113. Has been selling fried fish & *farinata* since 1942. Cash only. €

✳✗ Cavour 21 [62 B4] Piazza Cavour 21; m 393 851 1140; e cavour21r@gmail. com. The owner of this new restaurant is 86 years old & won the Pesto Championship in

2014. One need say no more! This restaurant is unsurprisingly very popular with the locals. Great atmosphere. €

✕ Da Maria [62 G1] Vico Testadoro 14r; ☎010 581080; ⏱ closed evenings exc Thu/Fri. Simple restaurant serving excellent soup, focaccia & traditional pasta dishes at big tables. It's packed at lunchtime with locals so arrive early. Try the *cima* & the *stoccafisso*. €

✕ Il Ristoro dei Grimaldi Ivana [62 D1] Vico San Luca 1/3. A good hole-in-the-wall pizza & focaccia joint west of the church of San Luca. €

✕ La Forchetta Curiosa [59 C8] Piazza Negri 5; ☎010 251 1289; **w** laforchettacuriosa.com. This traditional little place serves both Ligurian & Piedmontese specialities. All lunch dishes are just €6-9. €

✕ Sciûsciâ e Sciorbî [62 G2] Via XXV Aprile 32r; **m** 348 839 1924; **e** info@sciusciaesciorbi. it; **f**. An excellent stylish pizzeria & very good value. €

CAFÉS

Coffee houses sprang up in Genoa during the 19th century & many still retain their original décor.

☕Caffè degli Specchi [59 D6] Salita Pollaiuoli 43r. One of the most famous cafés, across from the Palazzo Ducale. It opened in the 19th century & was a writers' hangout. Don't be tempted to eat here, however, the food is bland. €

☕Caffè Letterario [59 D7] Piazza delle Erbe 25r. An antiquarian bookshop that became a literary café in the 19th century. €

☕Caffè Mangini [59 G4] Piazza Corvetto 3. Another classic 19th-century place with chandeliers, oak panelling, beautiful hand-painted china & a zinc bar. It's owned by the Rossignotti family, who run a number of classic cafés along the Riviera & have been making sumptuous cakes & pastries since 1840. €

☕Douce [62 F4] Piazza Giacomo Matteotti 84r & [56 F3] Via XX Settembre 62r; **w** douce.it. Run by Frenchman Michel Paquier, this is a stylish hangout & the pastries are excellent if you fancy a taste of France. €

☕Fratelli Klainguti [62 E2] Piazza Soziglia 98r. In the heart of the old town, it was opened in 1826 by 2 Swiss brothers, both pastry makers who hoped to sail to America, but missed the boat. Everything is made in-house. Guiseppe Verdi came here & they created the *Falstaff* cake for him. They sell some excellent candied fruit & marrons glacés. Try a *zena*, a *zabaglione*-filled pastry. They also serve snacks & light lunches. €

☕Murena Suite [59 G6] Via XX Settembre 157r; **w** murenasuite.it. For something a bit more modern, try this slick café designed by Luca Parodi. It serves excellent brioche & *tramezzini*, sandwiches, & has a sunken garden with an olive tree. €

BARS

🍷Bar Berto [59 D7] Piazza delle Erbe 6r. A popular hangout since 1904. €

🍷Calice [58 D2] Spianata Castelletto 9r; ☎010 246 6820; **m** 335 756 8233; ⏱ Mon–Sat lunch & dinner until 21.00. Enoteca run by sommelier Andrea Mescoli. It is a good spot for an *apertivo* & is in a great location. Calice means a goblet or wine glass in Italian. €

🍷Mignone Enoteca [62 E3] Piazza San Matteo 4r. With over 1,200 labels this is an excellent place to try the local wines. It opened in the 19th century & the furnishings date from the 1930s. €

ICE CREAM

The Arab love of ice cream was brought home by the Genoese. The 2 local ice creams are *panera*, an intense coffee-flavoured one, & *paciugo*, a sundae with morello cherries.

🍦Caffè Gelateria Balilla [56 F4] Via Macaggi 84r. Off the beaten track near Piazza Vittoria, but a must on every visit to the city my family has ever made. Balilla was a young boy who defied the Austrians & flung a stone at them, prompting an uprising in the 1740s. Mussolini appropriated him by giving his name to his fascist scouts. This handsome classic café with lavish décor took his name when it opened in 1934. Their ice cream is excellent. €

🍦Cremeria Colombo [56 F3] Via Colombo 37–39r. Totally natural ice creams. €

🍦Gelateria Profumo [62 F1] Vico Superiore Del Ferro 14r. Just below the Strada Nuova, this has wonderful ice cream made from fresh fruit with no colours or preservatives. It was opened in 2007 by

Genoa's footballing scene is dominated by its two biggest teams, Genoa and Sampdoria. Both play at the 36,703 capacity Stadio Luigi Ferraris, nicknamed the Marassi, after the area where it is located. It is one of the oldest stadiums still in use in Italy and opened in 1911. The big moment in Genoese football is the Derby della Lanterna, when the two sides go head to head; it is one of the most intense matches in the Italian football calendar, complete with walls of colour, flares, mock castles and fans dressed as crusaders.

Genoa, the older of the two clubs is officially called Genoa Cricket and Football Club and was originally set up by British expats in 1893. In 1897, it began to admit locals under the guidance of James Spensley, the 'father of Italian football'. A doctor, he arrived in Genoa in 1896 to care for British sailors on the coal ships. Under his management, the team would go on to dominate early Italian football, winning its championship six times in seven years, up to the 1903–04 season. Spensley was also a founder of the Italian scouting movement and would die in World War I. The club was forced to change its name in 1928 because the fascists considered it unpatriotic. It was reborn as the Genova 1893 Circolo del Calcio. Genoa's greatest triumph in recent memory is being the first Italian team to beat Liverpool at Anfield to book a place in the semi-finals of the UEFA cup, prior to stumbling before the eventual winners Ajax.

Recent years have seen a yo-yo of success and failure for Genoa. In 1995, the team was saved from relegation to Serie B, but in 2003, they were saved by a decision of the Italian Football Federation to extend the division to 24 teams. The following season Genoa won Serie B, but allegations of match fixing saw them relegated to Serie C, and hit with a six-point penalty the following season. Despite this, within two years Genoa secured promotion back to the top division for the first time in over a decade. Genoa finished sixth during the 2014–15 season, and were set to qualify for the Europa League, but late paperwork led to their place being passed to arch-rivals Sampdoria.

Genoa's upstart sibling Sampdoria was founded in 1946 when the teams Andrea Doria and Sampierdarenese merged, keen to challenge Genoa's domination of the city. Its colours and name pay tribute to its parent clubs and the club has enjoyed more success than its sibling since its creation, winning four Coppa Italia between 1985 and 1994, and the UEFA Cup Winner's Cup in 1990, before beating Berlusconi's Milan to the Scudetto title in 1991. From then on they threatened to conquer Europe, only to be felled during extra-time at Wembley before Barcelona and Ronald Koeman's boot. In the years that followed, things did not go so well and many of its stars began to leave. Sampdoria spent three seasons in Serie B from 1999, and since then, have yo-yoed in success. A return to Serie B, as well as a Champions League playoff loss in 2010 has seen the club fortunes stabilise, and they secured 7th place at the 2014–15 season, and, at the expense of Genoa, qualified for the UEFA Cup.

Football fans will enjoy the Museo della Storia del Genoa [62 A3] (Via al Porto Antico 4; \010 595 9709; w fondazionegenoa.com; ⊕ 10.00–19.00 Tue–Sun, admission €5). The museum charts the history of the game in Genoa.

Maurizio Profumo of the famous pastry-making family. €

U Gelato [59 C7] Via San Bernardo 91. A gelateria with some unusual flavours, including dates, violets & ginger. €

ENTERTAINMENT AND NIGHTLIFE

Nightlife is centred on Piazza delle Erbe [59 D7]. The Porto Antico is also lively as is the Corso Italia seafront, which is lined with open-air nightclubs in summer around the San Giuliano Abbey, and Via San Bernardo and Via San Donato have a number of lively bars. There's also a lively theatre scene and several cinemas across the town.

BARS

Bottega del Conte [59 B6] Via delle Grazie 47r. Drink cocktails in this beautiful former 18th-century grocery store.

Mescite! [58 B1] Via Sant'Agnese 25r; 010 403 3352; w mescite.it. An ultra-modern bar, with seven huge vats of local wines. 'Mescite!' means 'hurry and pour' in dialect.

Muà [62 G2] Via San Sebastiano 13r; 010 532191; w mua-ge.com. Sleek grey-and-white cocktail bar – the chic *aperitivo* choice.

LIVE MUSIC

☆ Louisiana Jazz Club [58 F4] Via San Sebastiano 36r; 010 585241. The club is one of the oldest of its kind in Italy, opened in 1964.

Many of the famous names in the jazz world have played here.

THEATRE & CINEMA

Magazzini del Cotone [56 C3] Porto Antico; w cinemagenovacentro.it. A multiplex cinema that has a good choice of films.

Teatro Carlo Felice [62 G3] Piazza de Ferrari; 010 5381224; w www.carlofelice.it. A cutting-edge theatre that was bombed in World War II and rebuilt in the 1980s.

Teatro della Tosse [59 D7] Piazza Renato Negri 4; 010 24707; w teatrodellatosse.it. This is the oldest theatre in the city, opened in 1702. The present company was formed in 1975 by, among others, artist Emanuele Luzzati.

SHOPPING

FOOD Food makes a great souvenir or gift to take home. If you are in a hurry, **Liguria in Bottega** [62 D2], a modern, stylish shop on Via Banchi just off Piazza Banchi, stocks a good range of artisan products from the region. Genoa's main market, **Mercato Orientale** [56 F4], is on Via XX Settembre, the arcaded 19th-century street that runs east from Piazza de Ferrari. It is the place to buy fresh fruit, vegetables and cheese. It takes its name not from the exotic East but from its eastern position. Here it is possible to buy *preboggion* – bunches of wild herbs that are the cornerstone of Genoese cooking. There's a supermarket behind the Teatro Carlo Felice.

Bottega dello Stoccafisso [62 F2] Via dei Macelli di Soziglia 20/22r. Opened in 1936 & sells dried fish, pesto & pickled vegetables.

Bruciamonti [58 F4] Via Roma 81r. A historic deli selling walnut sauce & *cima*.

Cantine Posta Vecchia [62 D1] Via della Posta Vecchia 18r. A historic wine shop where the Taducci family once bottled wine directly.

Danielli [56 F3] Via Galata 41. Sells *stocco*, the slow-cooked meat sauce, & some excellent fresh pasta.

De Michele [62 E2] Via dei Macelli di Soziglia 54r. A deli selling a great selection of local products,

which has been run by the same family for 5 generations.

Fratelli Centanaro [56 F3] Via San Vincenzo 103–105r. A family business, near Via XX Settembre, which has been going for over a century selling the best pork sausages & smoked pork products in Genoa.

Macelleria Nico [62 E2] Via Macelli di Soziglia 8r. This butcher's has sold specialities like *cima* since 1790. Head here for red meat.

Pescheria Granara [62 C1] Via di Sottoripa 39r. A fishmonger's that has been selling fish since 1927.

Genoa, with its ancient trading links to Asia, Africa and the Middle East, has long had a sweet tooth. Chocolate bars were first made in Turin and the cocoa that made them arrived in Genoa. **Buffa** [56 F4] (Via D Fiasella 9r) is a pocket-sized family-run chocolate shop south of Via XX Settembre, which dates from 1932. **Romeo Viganotti** [59 D7] (Vico dei Castagna 14r) is one of the oldest chocolatiers in the city, founded in 1866, and everything is still handmade. Try the chocolate-covered chestnuts fitting for the address – *castagna* means 'chestnut'. Zuccotti [56 G4] (Via Sata Zita 36; w zuccotticioccolato.it) has been making chocolates for 80 years and is a must. At La Iacona [58 B1] (Via Bensa 26r) you can not only buy traditional chocolates but also see some on the old confectionery-making equipment from the 17th century.

For the local speciality, *pandolce,* go to **Panarello** [59 G6] (Via Galata 67r). It also has a branch at Via XX Settembre 154r. **Pasticceria Profumo** [58 E3] (Via del Portello 2r; w villa1827.it) is a Genoese institution just off Via Garibaldi. Founded in 1827, it sells the best biscuits and chocolates in the city. It has been run by the same family for generations and has a reputation for its marrons glacés and sugared almonds. Near the San Siro church, **Pasticceria Marescotti di Cavo** [58 B3] (Via Fossatello 35r; w cavo. it), has a maple and rosewood interior and sells fabulous biscuits. It was run by the Marescotti family until it closed in 1979, then sat abandoned until being rescued by Alessandro Cavo in 2008. **Pasticceria Tagliafico** [56 F3] (Via Galata 31r), just across from the Mercato Orientale, has a tempting display of pastries. It has belonged to the same family since 1923. **De Regibus** [56 E1] (Corso Firenze 26–28r), in upper Genoa, near the Castelletto esplanade, is one of the city's best. **Dria** (Corso Torino 93r) in Foce is known for its *canestrelli.*

Genoa is famous for its candied fruit and flowers, and its marshmallow, *pasta di altea.* **Pietro Romanengo** [62 E2] (Piazza Soziglia 74; w romanengo. com) has wonderful frescoed ceilings and has belonged to the same family since 1780. The interior has creaking wood floors, period display cases and even the chocolate wrappers are beautifully old-fashioned. Buy candied fruit and rose drop pastilles. Among its customers were Verdi and Umberto II. They also sell rose syrup, *sciroppo di rose*, and *acqua di fiori di arancio,* orange flower water, both local specialities. There is a second shop dating from the 1930s on Via Roma 51r. **Armanino** [58 B3] on Via Sottoripa 105, have been selling candied fruit since 1905. The shop floor is the original.

Polleria Aresu [62 F1] Vico Inferiore del Ferro 1r. Selling poultry, this shop is much as it was when it started business more than a hundred years ago.

Torielli [59 C7] Via San Bernardo 32r. A shop that has been selling teas, coffee & scented oils since 1930.

OTHER GOODS Via Roma is Genoa's most exclusive designer street with the glass-covered **Galleria Mazzini** [59 F5] built in 1870. Also on Via Roma at 38r is the shirtmaker **Finollo** [59 F5], which has been making shirts for the rich and famous since 1899 and has dressed the Duke of Windsor and Gianni Agnelli. Shirts start at about €375.

For something completely special, try the **Cambi Casa d'Aste** [56 G1] (Castello Mackenzie, Mura di San Bartolomeo 16; ☎ 010 839 5029), the local auction house.

Bids start at €50. For the home, **Via Garibaldi 12** [58 D3] (w viagaribaldi12.com; ⊕ closed Mon & Sun) is an interiors shop in a 16th-century palazzo. It is a beautiful shopping experience, but beware it is very pricey.

One of the big changes in Genoa over the last couple of years has been the arrival of chic boutiques in the old town. It is a sign of the trendy atmosphere that this part of the city has acquired. Moa Cashmere & Lobster [58 F4] (Salita Santa Caterina 2/1; ☎010 899 2335; w moagenova.it) is a clothes shop that is also a restaurant (page 63).

If you like old-fashioned shops, you should take a look at the Alvigini Pharmacy [59 E6] (Via Petrarca 14r; w farmaciaalvigini.com). Legatoria Angeloni [62 D2] (Via Conservatori del Mare 47r) still binds books by hand. Gismondi [56 F3] is the place for silverware (Via Galata 78). The shop opened in 1763.

OTHER PRACTICALITIES

There are **ATMs** on Via Orefici 37 [62 D2] and in the old port. The **post office** [59 E7] is at Via Dante 4B/r. There are all-night **pharmacies**: Farmacia Pescetto [56 D1] (Via Balbi 185r, only a few metres away from Genova Principe Station; ☎010 261609); Farmacia Europa (Corso Europa 676; ☎010 380293); and Farmacia Ghersi [56 G4] (Corte Lambruschini 16; ☎010 541661). The **hospital**, Ospedale San Martino [56 G4] (Largo Benzi 10; ☎010 5551) has an emergency department (*pronto soccorso*). If you need a vet in a hurry, contact the Croce Bianca Genovese [56 G4] (Piazza Palermo 25r; ☎010 363636).

WHAT TO SEE AND DO

Genoa's main sights are all within walking distance of each other, so if you wish, you can visit the places below in order as a walking tour of Genoa.

THE PORT [56 C3] Genoa's story begins with its port and, in an ideal world, the best way to arrive in the city is to sail in. Within living memory, the port was actually separated from the town by a large wall. After extensive renovation, under the direction of local architect Renzo Piano, the area has become a lively place with some major attractions (w portoantico.it). On the quayside is the *Galeone Neptune*, a rather kitsch replica of a 17th-century galleon built in 1986 as a prop for the Roman Polanski film *Pirates*. Boat trips leave from the quay by the aquarium for Portofino and the Cinque Terre. The boat tour of the port is well worth taking to get a feel for the real maritime importance of Genoa (w liguriaviamare.it; admission €6). There is a pleasant walk along the harbourside under the old cranes, which has great views back across the city.

Palazzo San Giorgio [62 B2] (⊕ for temporary exhibitions only) To the east of the flyover, the Palazzo is one of the most important buildings in the city.

GENOA MUSEUM CARD

The Genoa Museum Card (City Card Musei Genoa) gives free admission to 22 of the city's museums. It costs €12 for a 24-hour card, €20 for 48 hours. The card gives discounted entrance to the aquarium and a number of other attractions. It is sold in museums and at the tourist offices. It's also possible to buy a joint card that includes bus travel for €15 for 24 hours and €25 for 48 hours. Buy it at w visitgenoa.it.

More than anything it symbolises the power that Genoa once wielded in Europe. It was, from 1407 to 1805, the home to one of the world's first banks, the Banco di San Giorgio, which issued the first cheque. It ran the empire and lent money to Europe's royals and was, as a result, very influential. It was closed down by Napoleon in 1805. Today it is the headquarters of the harbour authorities.

The oldest part of the building faces the old town. It was here that Marco Polo was held prisoner in 1298. This part of the building was built in 1260 from materials taken from the demolished Venetian palace in Constantinople. In many ways it's a monument to Genoa's hatred for the Venetians. The frescoed façade by Lazzaro Tavarone dates from 1606 to 1608 and was revealed when the building was restored in the 1990s. Prior to this it was in pretty bad shape.

Acquario di Genova [62 A1] (☏ 010 24351; w acquariodigenova.it; ⏰ 09.30–20.00, but times vary – check the website; admission €26, child €18 – there are a variety of tickets but the joint ticket with the Galata Museo is the best value for 2 adults) On the quayside and sticking out into the harbour, this aquarium is Europe's largest and was designed by Renzo Piano. Check the website prior to going as there are lots of deals available. It's one of Italy's top tourist attractions. Beware, however, that for Italy the entrance fee is very steep so if you are travelling with kids and on a tight budget, you might be wise not to mention it exists. It welcomes over a million visitors a year, so expect to queue. If you do have the money, it is well worth it. The aquarium is partly built into a ship and has 74 tanks full of 12,000 sharks, dolphins and every imaginable fish both big and small. The Cetacean Pavilion was designed by the Renzo Piano Building Workshop. Especially entertaining is the penguin tank with its glass wall that allows you to see them swimming underwater. You can visit a recreation of the Red Sea and a Caribbean coral reef, walk through a Madagascan rainforest and don 3D glasses to see a fishy film. Very small children find the latter rather scary.

Biosphere [56 D3] (⏰ daily in summer; admission €5) Next to the aquarium, the Biosphere was also designed by Renzo Piano in 2001. This giant glasshouse has all sorts of tropical plants, ferns, birds, butterflies and chameleons.

Il Bigo [62 A2] (w acquariodigenova.it/bigo-panoramic; ⏰ 10.00–noon & 17.00–22.00, though check online as opening hours vary; admission €4) On the southern side of the harbour, Il Bigo was again designed by Renzo Piano, and inspired by the old cranes that used to dot the quayside. The panoramic lift offers views from 40m across the city and the port, but they are a bit uninspiring. If it's a windy day, it's likely to be closed.

Molo Vecchio [56 D3] The old port, beside Il Bigo, was built in 1257 by the Cistercian friars Oliverio and Filippo and was considered one of the wonders of

---

JEANS FROM GENOA

Ligurian sailors wore trousers made out of a heavy blue cloth, *blu di Genova*. Genoa is Gênes in French and the trousers were soon called 'jeans', a corruption of Gênes. Ligurian sailors in their denim outfits arrived in San Francisco in the Gold Rush in 1849 and Levi Strauss adapted their outfits. Ligurians who stayed went on to found the California wine industry and the Bank of America.

medieval Genoa. Across the piazza is the tiny church of **San Marco** nestling in the walls. It was here that condemned prisoners took the last sacrament. The 13th-century **Palazzo del Boia** is where prisoners were hanged over the quay until 1852. Further round the harbour is the huge stone gate, the **Porta del Molo**, also known as the **Porta Siberia**, which was designed by Galeazzo Alessi in 1553 to defend the port and which also served as a tax collector's office. It levied taxes on foodstuffs, *cibaria*, hence the name. It now contains the **Museo Luzzati** [56 D3] (✆ 010 253 0328; w museoluzzati. it; was closed for renovation at time of writing), which has a collection of paintings and stage designs by the artist Luzzati, and is aimed at children. The port is also home to Genoa's football museum (see box, page 66). Across the car park in a former cotton warehouse is the **Città dei Bambini** [56 C3] (✆ 010 234 5635; w cittadeibambini.net; ⊕ 10.00–18.00 Tue–Sun; admission adult & child €10–13 – adults are not allowed in alone), a hands-on science museum for kids, linked to the Cité des Sciences in Paris. It is divided into two parts: one aimed at three- to five-year-olds, and the other at six- to 14-year-olds, although kids over 11 might find it rather babyish. Language isn't a barrier and among the attractions is a child-sized TV studio where you can have fun presenting the Italian weather forecast. There is also a multiplex cinema here, an ice-skating rink in winter, and an outdoor swimming pool.

Galata Museo del Mare
[56 C2] (✆ 010 234655; w galatamuseodelmare.it; ⊕ Mar–Oct 10.00–19.30 daily; Nov–Feb 10.00–18.00 Tue–Fri, 10.00–19.30 Sat/Sun & public hols; admission €13, child €8 – there are combined tickets with other sights in the city) The Maritime Museum is north of the aquarium, in the old dockyard, the Darsena. It's the largest maritime museum in the Mediterranean and charts Genoa's rich seafaring history. It has some fascinating paintings of Genoa, its harbour crammed with ships that bring the history of the city to life. There's a small collection of Christopher Columbus memorabilia including the famous posthumous portrait of Columbus by Ridolfo di Domenico Bigordi.

The museum may look modern, but it is the oldest building in the dockyard. It was here that the republic's galleys were built, fitted out and repaired. The museum takes its name from the former Genoese colony of Galata in the then named Constantinople, now Istanbul. The collection includes a 17th-century galley, a 19th-century brig, globes and maritime instruments galore. In the Storm Room you can experience a shipwreck on board a small boat identical to that in which the crew of the *Nemesi* survived for 24 days after their ship went down in the Atlantic in 1901. The third floor focuses on the transatlantic liners that left here from 1861 until 1945. Between 1907 and 1914 four million Italians departed for the United States and for many of them one of their last sights of Europe was of Genoa. The SS18 *Nazario Sauro* submarine moored alongside the museum was originally launched in 1976. There is a good view from the glass terrace on the top of the museum.

La Lanterna
[56 A4] (✆ 349 280 9485; ⊕ 14.00–18.30 Sat/Sun & holidays, summer until 19.00; admission €6 – entrance via the ferry boat terminal) The symbol of the city, the Lanterna sits across the harbour to the west. It is the oldest working lighthouse in the world and dates from the 12th century. It was destroyed by the French in 1514 and the present structure, made up of two superimposed towers, dates from 1543. It is 77m high and the beam can be seen for 52km. Visitors can climb the first 172 steps. There is a small museum in the fortifications, which date from 1830.

Below the lighthouse is the 19th-century gate that led into the city from the west and a memorial to 15 British soldiers who died de-mining the port at the end of World War II. There is an interesting view of the working port, much of which is situated on land quarried out of the rock below the lighthouse that once formed a natural boundary for the city. The mountain ran right down this side of the harbour, forming a natural wall. It was blown up in the early 20th century to make room to expand the port, which moved away from the old port and ate up the lovely sand beach at Sampierdarena. It changed the climate, making the city a much colder place in winter.

OLD TOWN
Southern side The 12th-century arcaded **Via Sottoripa** runs along the eastern side of the **Piazza Caricamento** [62 C1] that's next to the elevated highway by the port. It takes its name from the Italian *caricare*, which means 'to load'. The dockers were known as *camalli*, camels. The word comes from the Arabic *hamal*, which means 'pack animal'. Little has changed here over the centuries and this is the place to try some of Genoa's traditional fast food (see box, page 63). A marble plaque, on Vico Morchi 1 [62 C1], marks the spot where the Hotel Croce di Malta once stood and where so many of the famous writers drawn to Liguria, among them James Fennimore Cooper, Mark Twain and Henry James, stayed. In the middle of the square is the statue of Raffaele Rubattino, who supplied the ships used by Garibaldi's Thousand. There are a number of traditional places to eat on Via Sottoripa including Rizzitano [58 B3] (Via Sottoripa 21), which sells fried fish and vegetables, as well as *farinata* (page 63). They may look touristy but are, in fact, very old.

Tiny streets, *caruggi*, run off into the old town. Look out for faded postwar stencilled signs warning Allied troops that certain streets were out of bounds. Paul Valéry, the French poet whose mother was born in Genoa in the mid 19th century, caught the essence of the city when he wrote, 'Caruggi. Multitudes of children playing near poor semi-naked women who – offer not just chestnuts from nearby – but themselves, like immense golden cakes and chickpea tarts. These are like the sensations of Arab stories… concentrated smells, icy smells, drugs, cheeses, toasted coffee, delicious finely roasted cocoa…'. There is still a whiff of exotic danger in the back alleys and the advice given by Edward Hutton in *Florence and Northern Italy* in 1907, still applies: 'Genoa is,' he wrote, 'a city of noisy shadowy ways, cool in the heat, full of life, movement, merchandise and women.'

Take the Via al Ponte Reale to Piazza Banchi.

Piazza Banchi [62 C2] gave its name to banking and until the 18th century this was the commercial heart of the city. In the Middle Ages, there was a bustling grain market and the square takes its name from the moneychangers' tables, *banchi*, that once stood here and later moved into the 16th-century **Loggia dei Mercanti** [62 D2]. The loggia was designed by Andrea Vannone and the arches were glassed in during the 19th century. On the outside is a 16th-century frieze by Taddeo Carlone and inside there is a fresco of the *Madonna and Child and Saints John the Baptist and George* by Pietro Sorri. In 1855, the loggia became the first stock exchange in Italy which then moved to Piazza de Ferrari in 1912. It is now an exhibition hall.

San Pietro in Banchi [62 C2] was founded in the 9th century. It was damaged in the fire that ravaged the square in 1398 during the battles between the Guelphs and the Ghibellines. It was not rebuilt until the 16th century after a serious outbreak of plague in 1579 prompted some pious thoughts. In order to raise money for the project, concessions were sold off as shops in the lower levels and as a result the church sits elevated on a terrace.

Walk up Via Banchi and into **Vico Orefici**. **Via Banchi** is on your right if standing with your back to the church. It is traditionally where goldsmiths had their shops and jewellery is still made here. **Piazza Soziglia** is home to **Fratelli Klainguti** (page 65), one of Genoa's oldest coffee houses. Via dei Luccoli ahead has some swanky shops. On the left Vico di Lavagna leads to Piazza Lavagna and the daily flea market. Opposite Klainguti turn right into Vico di Campetto that in turn runs into Via Scurreria, which leads to Piazza Lorenzo.

The **Cattedrale di San Lorenzo** [62 E4] on Piazza Lorenzo is named after one of the city's patron saints and his symbol is, fittingly for a trading city renowned for its parsimony, a purse. He was unfortunately grilled to death in AD258, an event depicted in the frieze over the main door. The cathedral was consecrated in 1118 and, having no grand square in front of it like so many other Italian cathedrals, retains the air of a local parish church. It was built on the site of a Roman temple, to hold the ashes of John the Baptist brought to Genoa after the First Crusade in 1098 and on 24 June, the feast of John the Baptist, it's supposed to be haunted by the ghosts of its builders. The Romanesque building was never completed and the primarily Gothic appearance dates from the 13th century after it was damaged during battles between the Guelphs and Ghibellines.

Typical of Liguria is the black-and-white-striped façade, which was restored in the 20th century. The steps, flanked by two stone lions, are a 19th-century addition. The rose window was added in 1476 but remodelled in 1869. Only the symbols of the four Evangelists are original. The roof was raised in 1550 and the cupola was added in 1567 and is the work of Galeazzo Alessi. The bell tower was completed in 1522 and the bells were brought from England. This was not just a religious building; important political events also took place here, such as the signing of treaties, investitures and legal rulings.

Inside there are some notable paintings. In the presbytery the 17th-century frescoes of *The Martyrdom of St Lawrence* are by Lazzaro Tavarone. The choir dates from the 16th century and the pulpit is c1526. The chapel, dedicated to John the Baptist (San Giovanni Battista), was made by Domenico and Eloa Gagini in the mid 1400s. In the chapel to the right of the high altar is a painting by Fedrico Barocci and to the left, frescoes by Castello and Cambiaso (c1565–69). The stalls in the apse date from 1514 to 1964. There's an unusual sight in the south aisle: a British naval shell that damaged the cathedral during World War II, but which luckily did not explode.

Don't miss the **Museo del Tesoro** (⊕ 09.00–noon & 15.00–18.00 Mon–Sat, 15.00–18.00 Sun; admission €6), in the crypt. It is a modern museum designed by Franco Albini in 1954, which holds some of Christianity's most important holy relics. Ships came back from the Crusades laden with treasure and this collection shows just how important Genoa was at the time. Among them is the 9th-century Sacro Catino, which was once believed to be the Holy Grail from which Jesus took his last sip of wine. Surprisingly, it isn't a cup but a large green bowl, which according to legend was sculpted from an emerald that dropped from the Devil's head. It's in fact made of green glass and was broken when it was seized by Napoleon's troops in 1806 and taken to Paris.

There's a beautiful red plate dating from the 1st century AD, which was said to be the same plate upon which Salome received the head of John the Baptist. There's also a golden 12th-century crucifix, the Croce degli Zaccaria, and an elaborate 12th-century silver chest believed to hold the remains of John the Baptist which is processed around the city on 24 June. The entrance ticket also covers admission to the **Museo Diocesano** [62 E4] (Via Tommasso Reggio), in a lovely 12th-century cloister, which has a number of works by the notable Ligurian artists, Perin del Vaga and Luca Cambiaso.

Parallel to Via San Lorenzo, on its southern side, **Via di Canneto il Lungo** has some fine doorways, reliefs and friezes, and religious carvings. Walk down Via San Lorenzo and turn left into Via di Canneto il Curto which leads to **Piazza San Giorgio**, an important marketplace in the Middle Ages and home to the church of **San Giorgio**, [62 C4] which was first documented in AD965. In this area many students and young professionals have moved back into the upper floors and as a consequence there is a lively bar scene.

Walk up Via Giustiniani and turn right into the narrow Via Chiabrera. It leads up to the 12th-century **Torre degli Embriaci** [59 B7], one of the best preserved of the 66 privately owned towers that once graced the skyline and the tallest at 41m. Other towers were limited to 24m but in honour of the role played by the Embriaco family in the Crusades and the capture of Jerusalem in 1099, it was decreed that their tower had no limit. Guglielmo Embriaco was a warrior and engineer and had a habit of head-butting his enemies. This is one of the oldest parts of the city. Close your eyes and imagine it as Dickens saw it: 'As it is impossible for coaches to penetrate into these streets, there are sedan chairs, gilded and otherwise, for hire in diverse places.'

Just behind the tower is the 15th-century Romanesque church and convent of **Santa Maria di Castello** [59 B7] on Via Santa Maria di Castello. It sits on the site of the Roman *castrum* and retains some Roman columns. Inside there is a Roman sarcophagus and two beautiful loggias with a fresco by Justus von Ravensburg: *Annunciation* (c1451). There is a small museum with works by two of Liguria's most famous artists, Brea and Maragliano.

Via di Santa Croce to the south of the church leads up to **Piazza di Sarzano**, once the heart of the old town and the largest square within the city walls, which once overlooked the sea. In the Middle Ages jousts were held here.

The **Museo Sant'Agostino** [59 D8] (✆ 010 251 1263; ⊕ 10.00–19.00 (18.30 winter) Tue–Sun; admission €5) sits in the middle of Piazza di Sarzano, inside the former 13th-century Augustinian convent. It was here that the first doge, Simon Boccanegra, was elected. It has an interesting collection of maps, sculptures, Italian and Ligurian frescoes, and tombstones dating from the 10th to the 18th centuries. Its prize treasure is a fragment of the 14th-century monument to Margherita di Brabante, the wife of Emperor Henry VII, who died in Genoa in 1311, which was sculpted by Giovanni Pisano.

At the northern end of Stradone di Sant'Agostino is the 12th-century church of **San Donato** [59 D7]. Badly restored in 1888, it's still worth a visit as it contains some good religious paintings. *The Virgin* by Nicolò da Voltri is above the altar and in the chapel of San Giuseppe is a panelled triptych, *The Adoration of the Three Kings* by Joos van Cleve (c1515). The church has a particularly fine octagonal Romanesque bell tower, which inspired the architects of the modern tower in the port, the so-called Matitone, or 'giant pencil'. It's supposed to be haunted by the ghost of a noble who was killed in one of the endless conspiracies of the Middle Ages. From here walk for a few minutes north and you will emerge into **Piazza Matteotti**.

The **Palazzo Ducale** [62 F4] (✆ 010 817 1663; w palazzoducale.genova.it; ⊕ 14.00–18.00 Mon, 09.00–19.00 Tue–Sun; admission varies by exhibition: tower & prison 10.30–20.00 daily in summer; guided tour 15.00 Sat winter; entry €5, guided tour €12) dominates Piazza Matteotti. This impressive building became the doge's palace in 1339. It is made up of two palaces, which originally belonged to the Doria and Fieschi families. In 1591 it was remodelled on the orders of Andrea Doria. It was badly damaged during the bombardment of Genoa by Louis XIV's fleet and by a serious fire in 1777. The restoration was carried out by Simione

Cantoni, who modelled the impressive reception rooms on the first floor. The **Torre del Popolo** [62 E4] dates from the 13th century and was originally a lookout tower. The rooms below it were a jail for political prisoners and the cells are covered in drawings. Among those who were held here was the notorious pirate Dragut, the terror of the Mediterranean. A number of painters and artists also spent time in the cells accused of rowdy behaviour, among them violinist Niccolò Paganini, who was accused of seducing a minor. Risorgimento hero Jacopo Ruffini killed himself in the cell known as 'the small stairs', Lo Scalinetto, and Garibaldi also spent time locked up here. The Palazzo Ducale organises events for children in English and has an area dedicated to families, Kids in the City.

Il Gesù [59 D6], on the eastern side of Piazza Matteotti, is also known as Sant'Ambrogio. The present building was built by the Jesuits in 1589 over the existing church of Sant'Ambrogio, hence its name. The façade, based on the original designs by Giuseppe Valeriani, was only finished in the 19th century. The rich Baroque interior is adorned with statues and above the altar is Rubens' *Circumcision* (c1605). In the Chapel of St Ignatius there is a second Rubens, *Miracles of Saint Ignatius* (c1620).

On the right-hand side, if facing the church, is the **Via Porta Soprana,** which leads to the city gates, the **Porta Soprana** [59 E7] (Via di Raveca 47; ✆ 010 246 5346; ⏰ 11.30–17.30 Tue–Sun & hols, closes 16.00 in winter; admission €5, joint ticket with Casa di Colombo), also known as the Porta di Sant'Andrea, with its two majestic towers. Chiselled on it are the words, 'If you bring peace you may touch this gate, if you seek war, you will leave afflicted and conquered'. The gate stands on the spot where the walls were opened up in the 9th century to connect Genoa with the Riviera di Levante. The present gate dates from 1155 when a new ring of walls was built to protect the city from attack by Barbarossa, Emperor Frederick I. The building was restored in the 19th century. Next to the gate is the **Chiostro di Sant'Andrea**, which is all that remains of a Benedictine monastery that was pulled down in 1904, to make way for a new building. The architect couldn't bring himself to knock it down.

The **Casa di Colombo** [59 E7] (⏰ 11.00–17.00 Tue–Sun, closes 15.00 in winter; admission €3), next to the cloister, is reputed to be the childhood home of the great explorer, Christopher Columbus, who some people believe was born in Genoa in the middle of the 15th century (see box, page 7). That he was born right here is rather a doubtful claim as this tiny house was put up in the 18th century after the previous building was destroyed in a French bombardment in 1684, and was chosen as Columbus's house in the 1890s during the 400th anniversary of his 'discovery' of America. There is absolutely nothing inside, so save your euros, turn left and head into the modern town down Via Dante to Piazza de Ferrari. In Piazza Dante is another Genoese landmark, the skyscraper, the **Torre Piacentini** [59 F7], built in 1940 by Mussolini's favourite architect, Marcello Piacentini. Genoa was the first city in Italy to build a skyscraper. To finish exploring the medieval town, on the western side of Piazza de Ferrari, take the **Salita del Fondaco**, turn right at the bottom and you will find yourself in Piazza San Matteo.

Piazza San Matteo [62 F3] was, between the 12th and the 17th centuries, the headquarters of the Doria family. Genoa was run by powerful families, each of which had their own stronghold within the city in which the others would not dare to tread. Each had its own church and square, like a city within a city. This is one of the reasons that Genoa's old town is such a maze of tall buildings as whatever a powerful family wanted to build had to be slotted into their fiefdom. At No 15 is the **Palazzo di Lamba Doria** [62 E3]. No 17 is Palazzo Andrea

Doria, which was given to the great admiral in 1528. The little black-and-white-striped **Abbazia di San Matteo** [62 F3] was where the Dorias worshipped and was founded in 1125, although the present building dates from the 13th century. Andrea Doria, who was the ruler of Genoa in the 16th century, is buried in the crypt as is Lamba Doria who defeated the Venetians at the Battle of Curzola in 1298. Inside the church are frescoes by the famous artist Luca Cambiaso. The Dorias chose San Matteo as their patron saint as he had worked as a tax collector, which tells you a lot about them.

Walk along Piazza di Campetto to the southeast of the square. It leads to the Piazza delle Vigne. A thousand years ago the area was planted with vines, *vigne*. The church of **Santa Maria delle Vigne** [62 D2] dates from the year 1000 but the only surviving Romanesque feature is the bell tower. The current church was rebuilt in the Baroque style in 1640. The façade, by Ippolito Cremona, dates from 1842 and the beautiful 17th-century frescoes inside are by Lazzaro Tavarone.

Now walk back up to Piazza Ferrari and explore the rest of the old town.

Northern side When you arrive in Piazza de Ferrari, walk towards the left of the theatre and plunge back into the old town to discover some of Genoa's most sumptuous palaces. Via Roma and Via XXV Aprile lead to **Piazza Fontane Marose** [62 G1], which takes its name from a fountain that once stood here. The Palazzo Spinola dei Marmi at No 6, with its black-and-white stripes, has had to be adapted to the uneven terrain, adding to the general mishmash of buildings. Families could only use stripes if they had a permit and had done some illustrious deed for the city.

For a great view of the city, from Piazza del Portello walk to the north at the end of Via Interiano and take a ride on the lift to **Castelletto** [58 D2]. It's part of the Genoese experience and takes you up to the smart residential part of town. The views back down over the city give a very different perspective if, so far, you have only explored the old town. There was originally a fortress here which was destroyed in the uprising of 1848.

LA STRADA NUOVA **Via Garibaldi** [58 D3] is the absolute must-see sight of Genoa. It leads off the Piazza Fontane Marose and is a UNESCO World Heritage Site. Despite its 1990s facelift, Genoa remains a rough-and-tumble port town that is easy to dismiss at first glance. A walk down Via Garibaldi and a visit to some of the city's sumptuous palaces will change your mind. The palaces are known as the Palazzi dei Rolli (w museidigenova.it; ⊕ winter 08.30–18.00 Tue, 09.00–19.00 Wed & Thu, 09.00–21.00 Fri, 09.30–19.00 Sat, 09.30–19.30 Sun, summer 09.00–18.00 Tue, 09.00–19.00 Wed, Thu & Sat, 09.00–21.00 Fri, 09.30–19.30 Sun; admission €9 – 1 ticket for all museums, panoramic lift €5; cash only) as they were listed on the rolls of a Senate decree in 1576 and were designed by Bernadino Cantone in the mid 16th century. Once finished, it was soon known as the 'Strada Nuova', the new street.

It was so opulent that it was dubbed the 'Rue des Rois', the street of kings, by the French writer Madame de Staël, and it so impressed Rubens that he drew the buildings in detail and produced a book to show the rich families of Antwerp how to build their houses. The Countess of Blessington, a friend of Byron's, was less kind and said that the palaces looked like 'a collection of edifices heaped together for sale' and longed for 'the hand of a magician to transport these fine palaces to suitable sites'. The mansions here were home to the oligarchy of rich merchant families who ran the city. Ironically these palaces that are symbols of the power of Genoa and its noble families were laid out at the precise moment that the republic was about to go into decline. Today they are home to banks, museums and offices.

Palazzo Doria Tursi [58 D3] at No 9, is the largest of the palaces. It was built for Niccolò Grimaldi, whose nickname was *monarca*. In 1596, it was bought by Andrea Doria for his son, who became the Duke of Tursi. The Dorias owned it until 1820 when it was bought by the Piedmontese royal family. Three times the size of the other mansions, it has a lovely courtyard with a double staircase that leads up to an arcaded loggia added in the late 16th century. Since 1848, it's been the town hall and has to be one of the loveliest places to get married. The entrance is made of stone from Finale, west of Genoa. The clock tower was added in 1820. The small museum has a 17th-century violin that belonged to the great Genoese violinist, Niccolò Paganini, and three signed letters from Christopher Columbus.

Palazzo Bianco [58 D3] (w museidigenova.it/content/palazzo-bianco), alongside Palazzo Tursi, was built for the Brignole-Sale family and is now a gallery and home to some beautiful artistic treasures, among them portraits by some of the world's most famous artists: Van Dyck, Veronese, Guercino, Strozzi, Rubens and Caravaggio, to name but a few. It was known as the White Palace because of the white plaster used on the exterior walls.

Palazzo Rosso [58 D3] (w museidigenova.it/museo/palazzo-rosso), across the street, is more atmospheric. It was built between 1530 and 1540 and if you are pressed for time, just visit this palace. It was later bought by the Brignole family. Both palaces were donated by the Duchess of Galliera to the city in the late 19th century. On the third floor the architect Franco Albini, who restored the building after World War II, added the Rationalist apartment that was home to the museum curator, Caterina Marcenaro. Whatever you do don't miss the outdoor viewing platform on the top of the palace, which has a panoramic view of the city.

It is also possible to visit Lorenzo de Ferrari's Golden Gallery in the **Palazzo Tobia Pallavicino** [58 E3] (✆010 270 4561; ⊕ by appointment only), at No 4.

San Siro [58 C3], Genoa's original ancient cathedral, can be reached by walking along Via Garibaldi to Piazza Meridiana. Continue straight ahead along Via Cairoli and turn left into Via San Siro. It was here that French bishops fired up the Genoese with rousing sermons so much that they joined in the First Crusade. The original building, destroyed by a fire in the 16th century, dated from the 4th century. The sumptuous interior is marbled and decorated with frescoes and stuccoes by Giovanni Battista and Tommaso. The façade was designed by Carlo Barabino in 1821.

The street in front of the steps leads to **Via San Luca**, which was the main street in the Middle Ages. Vico Pellicceria leads to Piazza Pellicceria where the powerful Spinola family once lived at No 1.

The **Galleria Nazionale di Palazzo Spinola** [58 C3] (✆010 270 5300; ⊕ 08.30–19.30 Tue–Sat, 13.30–19.30 Sun; admission €6.50) has a fabulous collection of paintings, including work by Rubens and Brea. It's more than an art gallery, however, as the Spinola family who donated it to the state specified that it kept the air of a family home. Despite its sumptuous interior it's actually quite a homely place and has some fantastic maps. The decorations, dating from the 17th and 18th centuries, are almost intact and include the original kitchen. On the top floor, which was damaged in World War II, there are fabulous paintings by the master, Ludovico Brea and the haunting image of Christ, *Ecce Homo* by Antonello da Messina (c1474), which is painted on wood. Walk round the back and see the damage caused by woodworm. Rubens' giant portrait of *Giovanni Carlo Doria* was given on Mussolini's orders to Hitler but was returned to Italy after the war.

The nearby tiny church of **San Luca** [62 D1], rebuilt in 1626, is a fine example of Genoese Baroque. Via San Luca leads back to Piazza Banchi if your legs are tired. Nearby, the **Via della Maddalena** [62 E1], which runs parallel to the Strada Nuova, is the heart of the red-light district. Head north back down Via San Luca until you reach Via Lomellini. The hero of the Risorgimento, Mazzini, was born at No 11.

The **Museo del Risorgimento** [58 B2] (☎010 246 5843; ◷ 09.00–14.00 Tue & Fri, 10.00–18.30 (19.00 summer) Wed & Sat; admission €5) was Mazzini's childhood home and is now a museum dedicated to the movement that unified Italy (see box, page 52). A word of warning: if you aren't absolutely fascinated with the topic, think twice; visitors are escorted through the museum by a guard who stands over you while you watch a long film (all in Italian) about the Risorgimento and makes sure you take a good look at everything. The exhibition begins with the young Balilla and ends with Garibaldi's 'Thousand'. If you are interested and speak Italian, it is well worth visiting, as it is full of interesting memorabilia and the film puts the Risorgimento into context.

FROM THE STRADA NUOVA TO PRINCIPE STATION From the next crossroads, **Largo della Zecca**, take a ride up to **Righi** [56 E1] on the funicular for stunning views, not only of the city but also further afield. In the church of the **Santuario della Modernetta** [56 D1], there is a lovely Christmas crib, a *presepe*, which reproduces part of the old town in miniature. The wooden figures were carved in the 17th and 18th centuries, some of them by the master carvers Maragliano and Gaggini.

From Piazza della Nunziata, Via Belluci leads up to Piazzale Brignole. On the north side, the **Albergo dei Poveri** [56 D1], set up by Emanuele Brignole after the devastating plague of 1656, is one of Italy's oldest charitable institutions. Travel guides dating from the 19th century encourage people to visit the local rest homes and charitable institutions, which were considered remarkable at the time. It's now part of the university.

Via Paolo Emilia Bensa leads down to **Piazza della Nunziata** [58 B1] and the church of **Santissima Annunziata del Vastato**, built for the Lominelli family, who once owned swathes of Tunisia. The piazza was named Vastato, after the Latin *vastinium*, which meant that it sat outside the city walls. The original church was built in 1520 but the present one dates from the 16th and 17th centuries, although the façade is 19th century. The interior was decorated by the Carlone brothers.

Via Balbi [58 A1], on the northwestern side of Piazza della Nunziata, was laid out in 1602 by Bartolomeo Bianco for the Balbi clan, who built seven palaces on the street. The Palazzo dell'Università was originally built as a Jesuit college in 1634–36 and houses the University of Genoa, which is one of Europe's oldest, founded in the 13th century.

Palazzo Reale [56 D1] (☎010 16126; ◷ 09.00–19.00 Tue–Sat, 13.30–19.00 Sun, 09.00–19.00 1st Sun of the month; admission €6) at No 10 is the jewel in the crown of Via Balbi. The wealth and opulence inside are a complete surprise and contrast to the rough and tumble of old Genoa. The gilded Hall of Mirrors glitters with golden stuccowork and Domenico Parodi's frescoes depict mythical gods. Originally built for the Balbi family in 1643–55, it was rebuilt by Eugenio Durazzo in 1705, whose Baroque mansion was modelled on a Roman palazzo. Its rooms house a rich picture gallery with works by many Italian and foreign masters, among them Van Dyck and Tintoretto. The collection of Genoese furniture dating back to the 17th century was assembled by the Durazzo family and the House of Savoy, who used the residence as a royal palace. Luigi Amedeo of Savoy, the explorer and navigator (1873–1933), whose father was King Amadeo of Spain, also lived here. He was famous for his mountaineering expeditions, notably to K2. The courtyard has a fountain with little turtles that delights children and the views across the port remind us where all the money came from.

Via Balbi ends in Piazza Acquaverde at **Principe Station** [56 C1], built in 1854. The statue of Christopher Columbus was put up in 1862.

Villa del Principe – Palazzo di Andrea Doria [56 C1] (Piazza del Principe 4; ✆010 255509; ⏰ 10.00–18.00 daily; admission €9; w doriapamphilj.it) is just below Principe Station. This huge palace was built for Andrea Doria, the most famous Genoese admiral and virtual dictator of Genoa for a large part of the 16th century. It was truly a princely residence and is the most important 16th-century monument in Liguria. It has recently been restored. Here Admiral Doria directed the affairs of the republic and planned his naval battles, testing models of galleons he had commissioned in the pond in the garden. Doria built the palace to show off and that was something he certainly did in style. In 1533, to impress Emperor Charles V, three silver services on which dinner had just been eaten were tossed into the sea, as the table was cleared. The emperor fell for it but what he didn't know was that fishermen had been ordered to have their nets ready to scoop them out once he was gone. Don't miss the famous nude portrait of Andrea Doria as *Neptune* by Agnolo Bronzino, in Doria's private apartments.

There are beautiful 16th-century frescoes by Perin del Vaga, a student of Raphael, and a remarkable collection of tapestries depicting the Battle of Lepanto, one of Doria's great victories, which stopped the westward advance of the Ottoman Empire in 1571. In the garden there is the monumental marble *Neptune's Fountain* by the Carlone brothers.

The garden has a good view of the **Stazione Marittima** [56 C2], built in 1930, and once an important departure point for transatlantic liners and ships for India and the Far East. It's a reminder of how the sea provided the wealth on which families like the Doria grew rich and powerful – and they are still an influential force in Genoa.

Turning back towards the old port you pass the church of **San Giovanni di Pré** [56 C1] and **La Commenda** (✆ 010 557 3681; w museidigenova.it/content/museoteatro-della-commenda; ⏰ 10.00–17.00 Tue–Fri, 10.00–19.00 Sat–Sun; admission €5), founded in 1180 by the Knights of the Order of Saint John and largely rebuilt in the Romanesque style in the 14th century. The bell tower, with its pyramidal top, was left unchanged. It is actually two churches. The upper floor was originally only used by the knights. The arched Commenda next door was Genoa's first hotel and originally built to house pilgrims waiting to set sail for the Holy Land and was also a small hospital. There are lovely frescoes on the third floor. Today the building has an interactive museum that illustrates the life of pilgrims and Crusaders, and has a beautifully restored medieval garden.

Porta dei Vacca [58 A2], a Gothic gateway dating from 1155, is a short walk along the Via di Pré, once 'the road through the fields'. This bit of Genoa is still rather scruffy. The streets behind it are still slightly seedy and frequented by male prostitutes. The **Via del Campo** [58 B2] was made famous by the singer-songwriter Fabrizio de Andrè. He was an anarchist, who often sang in Genoese and had a colourful life that included being kidnapped by bandits in Sardinia. It's quite safe and worth walking through because Genoa's *caruggi* were always thus.

MODERN GENOA

Piazza de Ferrari [62 F4] Laid out in the 19th century, this square was pedestrianised in 2001. It takes its name from the wealthy businessman and benefactor, Raffaele de Ferrari, the Duke of Galliera. The fountain in the centre of the square was designed by Giuseppe Crosa di Vergagni in 1936.

3

Teatro Carlo Felice [62 G3] (ticket office: w carlofelice.it) On the northeast side of the square behind the Garibaldi Monument, Teatro Carlo Felice was gutted by bombs in World War II and rebuilt by Ignazio Gardella, Aldo Rossi and Fabio Reinhart in the late 1980s. It is one of the most modern theatres in Europe. From the original building only the Neoclassical façade survives and the new one includes a massive rectangular tower.

Accademia Ligustica di Belle Arti [62 G4] (Largo Pertini 4; \ 010 560131; w accademialigustica.it; ⏀ 14.30–18.30 Tue–Sat; admission €5) Next to the theatre is Genoa's art school. The Neoclassical building was built by the theatre's original architect, Carlo Barabino. The gallery on the first floor houses paintings by Ligurian artists from the 14th to the 19th centuries. On the eastern side of the square, **Palazzo della Borsa**, built in 1908, once housed the stock exchange.

Via Roma [58 F4] This is the city's exclusive shopping street, and runs from Piazza de Ferrari on the left-hand side of the theatre, if facing the façade, to **Piazza Corvetto**. This is the place to come if you fancy a breath of fresh air. The **Villetta di Negro** [58 F3] park on the hillside was laid out by Carlo Barbino in the early 19th century. There is a statue of Giuseppe Mazzini at the foot of the gardens. It was once the garden of the villa of the Marchese di Negro, who entertained Georges Sand, Dickens, Shelley and Byron here. It was given to the city in 1863, but the villa was destroyed by Allied bombs in World War II. Look out for the tiny 'solpersteine', or stumbling stone, dedicated to the memory of the former Chief Rabbi of Genoa, Riccardo Pacifici. Placed here in 2012, it is located at the start of the Galeria Mazzini just behind the Teatro Carlo Felice. Pacifici was one of 261 Genoese Jews arrested and deported in November 1943. The Jews were rounded up in the synagogue on Via Bertora 6 before the deportation. Only 20 survived. Pacifici was gassed on 12 December 1943 along with his wife and children.

Museo d'Arte Orientale Edoardo Chiossone [58 F3] (Piazzale Mazzini 4; \ 010 543285; w museidigenova.it/content/museo-darte-orientale; ⏀ 09.90–19.00 (18.30 winter) Tue–Fri, 10.00–19.30 (18.30 winter) Sat & Sun; admission €5) The Edoardo Chiossone Museum of Oriental Art is built on the site of the original Villeta di Negro. It was designed in 1971 by Mario Làbo and is an interesting piece of Rationalist design. The museum houses a rich collection of Japanese and oriental art collected by Eduardo Chiossone between 1875 and 1898, some of which is very rare. Chiossone was an engraver who was hired by the Japanese emperor to make banknotes. In all he designed 500 different plates for banknotes, stamps and government bonds during the 25 years he spent in Tokyo and amassed this fascinating collection of weaponry, pottery, lacquer-ware, porcelain, prints and bronze sculptures. There is a great view from the museum back across the old town.

La Spianata dell'Acquasola [58 G4] Across Piazza Corvetto, this is another lovely park. It was here that victims of the plague in 1656 were buried in a mass grave. If you are with children, it's a great place to let them run off steam. Mark Twain observed when he visited Genoa in 1869, that the locals would promenade in the park and eat ice cream all dressed in the latest Paris fashions: 'We went to the park on Sunday evening. Two thousand persons were present chiefly young ladies and gentlemen … The multitude moved round and round the park in a great procession.' It was the ladies that caught his eye, 'I scanned every female that passed, and it seemed to me that all were handsome. There may be prettier women in Europe, but I doubt it … Most of the young demoiselles are robed in a cloud of white from head to foot. They wear nothing on their head but a flimsy sort of veil, which falls down their backs like a white mist.'

Via XX Settembre This is Genoa's main shopping street and runs east from Piazza de Ferrari. Its name commemorates the date that Rome was taken by the forces fighting for a unified Italy in 1870. It's well worth walking down to see the church of **Santo Stefano** [59 G6] (c1217), which is built into a Lombard defensive tower. You reach it by a flight of small but signposted stairs. It is near the **Ponte Monumentale** [59 F6], a viaduct and one of the earliest big bridges to be built with reinforced cement. The **Mercato Orientale** [56 F3] (c1889) is a wonderful market and has nothing to do with the Orient, but gets its name because it sits on the eastern side of town.

Piazza della Vittoria At the end of Via XX Settembre near Brignole Station, Piazza della Vittoria [56 G4] is a fabulous example of fascist architecture, built in 1930 by Marcello Piacentini. In the centre is a huge triumphal arch commemorating those who fell in World War I. Make time to walk in the arcades to see the friezes, which are classic fascist imagery. The flat piece of ground on which it is built was outside the city walls and used for parades and other events. On the hill behind, the stairway dedicated to the Unknown Soldier, the Scalinata Milite Ignoto, leads up to the city wall. From here, you can refuel with an ice cream at Balilla (page 65) and walk back up to Piazza de Ferrari.

AND IF YOU HAVE MORE TIME …
Santa Maria Assunta di Carignano [56 E4] (Piazza di Carignano) High up above the port is the greatest Renaissance church in Genoa. It was designed by the famous Perugian architect Galeazzo Alessi. Construction began in 1549 and took 50 years. The flight of steps was designed by Alessi but only added in the 19th century. Much damaged in World War II, it is one of the few churches in Genoa with a sizeable piazza in front. It has a number of important 17th-century religious paintings by well-known Ligurian artists such as Luca Cambiaso, Piola and Strozzi, and there are panoramic views from the balcony. The powerful Fieschi family once had a villa here that was so sumptuous that it took Louis II of France's breath away. After they fell from grace all remnants of the building were destroyed.

Museo di Arte Contemporanea di Villa Croce [56 D4] (Via J Ruffini 3; ✆ 010 580069; ⏰ 11.00–18.30 Thu–Sat; admission €5–10) The collection of this museum of abstract art dates from 1939 to 1980 and is housed in a grand 19th-century villa surrounded by a park overlooking the sea in Carignano. At time of writing it was closed for restoration.

Castello D'Albertis: Museum of World Cultures [56 D1] (Corso Dogali 18; ✆ 010 272 3820; w museidigenova.it/content/castello-dalbertis; ⏰ 10.00–18.00 daily, closes 19.00; admission €6) High up on a hill, the Castello D'Albertis is a real Genoa landmark. It was built in 1892 for the globetrotting Capitano Enrico D'Albertis (1846–1932), who was the first Italian to sail through the Suez Canal and who re-enacted Columbus's journeys using only Renaissance navigational instruments. He circumnavigated the globe several times and brought home an extraordinary collection of objects that he kept in this mock castle decorated in an exotic, Neogothic and Moorish style. Take the lift from Via Balbi, the Ascensore Montegalletto. There is a nice café.

San Bartolomeo degli Armeni [56 F2] (Piazza San Bartolomeo degli Armeni 2) San Bartolomeo was founded in 1308 but rebuilt in 1775, although the bell tower is original. The church is famous because it's the home of the *Santo Volto*, the Holy Face, also called the *Mandillo* in dialect. It's an image of the face of Jesus Christ painted on a piece of cloth. It was given to the Doge of Genoa in 1362 by the Byzantine emperor of Constantinople in return for military assistance.

Museo di Storia Naturale Giacomo Doria [56 F4] (Via Brigata Liguria 9; ✆ 010 585753; w museidigenova.it/it/content/museo-di-storia-naturale; ◷ 09.00–19.00 Tue–Sun; admission €6) Founded in 1867, this traditional museum's collection includes the skeleton of an ancient elephant found near Rome in 1941, whale skeletons and three-and-a-half million other specimens from all over the world.

Bottega Storica di Barbiere [62 C3] (Vico dei Caprettari 14; ✆ 010 256761) A beautiful barber's shop with original 1920s decoration and a shimmering cobalt-blue and gold frieze. The shop closed in 1980 and was bought over a decade later by FAI, the Italian equivalent of the National Trust. It is a stylish place for a short back and sides.

Cimitero di Staglieno [56 G4] (Piazzale Giovanni Battista Resasco 2; ✆ 010 870184; ◷ 07.30–17.00; admission free) To the north of the city, Genoa's main cemetery is stuffed to the brim with the ornate graves of the city's rich families in marble and bronze. It was laid out from 1844 to 1851 and impressed the writer Evelyn Waugh, who wrote, 'It is a museum of mid-nineteenth century bourgeois art in the full, true sense, that the Campo Santo of Genoa stands supreme.' Among those buried here are the hero of the Risorgimento, Mazzini, surrounded by memorials to Garibaldi's 'Thousand', but there are plenty of the less illustrious here, among them Caterina Campodonico, immortalised with a statue, who sold hazelnuts at local fairs. Unfortunately, it is rather run down and full of mosquitoes and the British military cemetery is the only well-kept part. Other celebrities buried here include Fabrizio de André and Oscar Wilde's wife, Constance Lloyd.

FURTHER AFIELD

WEST ALONG THE COAST
Pegli [map, page 46] The coast road out of Genoa is often congested. It takes you to the airport at Sestri and then on to Pegli. If you are driving, it is worth getting on the motorway for a quicker ride. The rather messy suburb of Pegli was once a popular resort and, testament to the number of British visitors, there was an Anglican church. It has some fine villas. One, the **Palazzo Durazzo Pallavicini**, is home to a surprisingly good archaeological museum, the **Museo di Archeologia Ligure** (Via Pallavicini 11; ✆ 010 698 1048; w museidigenova.it/content/museo-di-archeologia; 09.00–19.00 Tue–Fri 10.00–19.30 Sat/Sun; €5 museum, €12 museum & park). This museum is a good example of decentralised Italy. In Britain, the treasures inside would have been whisked off to the British Museum. The museum's collection includes the Palaeolithic tombs found in the cave of Arene Candide near Finale, among them, at 24,000 years old, the oldest skeleton ever found in Italy. The skull is decorated with a hat of shells. He was about 15 years old and undoubtedly

important because of the treasures buried with him and was thus called, *Il Principe*, the Prince. He died from a huge wound that destroyed the left half of his jaw and which is masked with yellow ochre paint. Also in the museum are two prehistoric carvings from Monte Beigua. There is an interesting exhibition of ancient treasures, including a Greek vase, and finds from the remains of a necropolis discovered during the construction of Piazza de Ferrari and Via XX Settembre. Unexpected too, is an Egyptian mummy which X-rays revealed had been dropped while being embalmed and has a dislocated shoulder. The villa is surrounded by a lovely formal park with ponds and greenhouses laid out by Galeazzo Alessi. It was planted by botanist Clelia Durazzo at the end of the 18th century. The park contains an ingenious folly that on one side looks like a Roman temple and the other a rustic cottage. The pond may be green but it's teaming with wildlife. There are dozens of ducks and fish swimming about in it. The lady at the ticket office told me that there are also hundreds of abandoned *tartarughe* (terrapins) in the lake. You can see pictures of the *tartarughe* and the gardens on the Bradt website (w bradtguides. com/articles/skeletons-and-tartarughe).

In the nearby **Villa Centurione Doria**, the **Museo Navale** (Piazza Bonavino 7; ☎ 010 696 9885; w museidigenova.it/content/museo-navale-di-pegli; ☉ 09.00–13.30 Tue–Fri, 10.00–18.00 Sat, 10.00–13.00 Sun; admission €5) has an interesting collection that charts Genoa's seafaring history. Pegli is 9km from the centre. Catch the train from Principe; the station is right next to the archaeological museum. Alternatively take the boat, the Navebus, from the old port.

There's nothing else to draw you along Genoa's western suburbs, which were, a hundred years ago, dubbed the Manchester of Italy. Now the ruined factories of yesterday are being replaced with large shopping complexes and IKEA has moved in, too.

As the road leads out along the coast you pass through **Voltri**. It's a faded resort town past its best, but it does have a couple of good restaurants. At Pasticceria Sambuco (Via Zaghi 9) and Priano (Via Camozzini 76r) you can buy great focaccia, as well as biscuits and cakes. Hidden away on the SP456 in the Val Leira (signposted from the motorway exit in Voltri) is the Baroque sanctuary of **Nostra Signora dell'Acquasanta** (c1718), with its thermal spring. Take a dip in the waters at the **Terme di Genova Spa** (Via Acquasanta 245; ☎ 010 638178; w termedigenova.it; €25 pp, treatments extra), and even have a basil massage.

✗ **Where to eat and drink**

✗ **Gli Archi di Cerusa** Via Cerusa 39/41r, Voltri; ☎ 010 455 2350. This is Voltri's best fish restaurant & also has good homemade desserts. €€€€€

✗ **La Voglia Matta** Via Cerusa 63r, Voltri; ☎ 010 610 1889; w lavogliamatta.org; ☉ closed Sun. A fusion of modern & traditional cuisine. Excellent fish. This restaurant is one of Liguria's best. Set menus, including children's menu: €18. €€€€

✗ **Il Gigante** Via Lemerle 12r, Voltri; ☎ 010 613 2668; e ilgigantedisteardo@gmail.com; w ristoranteilgigante.it; ☉ closed Sun evening & Mon. This restaurant is famous for its fish dishes, prepared in the traditional Ligurian style. Excellent desserts too. €€

✗ **Osteria dell'Acquasanta** Via Acquasanta 281; ☎ 010 638035; ☉ closed Mon. This is a good place to eat the classic Genoese dish *mandilli al pesto*. €

EAST ALONG THE COAST

Albaro [map, page 46] To the east of the city is one of Genoa's wealthiest areas, full of villas and luxury apartments. A number of well-known people have made their home here including Byron, who lived on Via Albaro. There's nothing to see here, but there is an excellent pastry shop in the same building the poet lived in, **Pasticceria**

Svizzera (Via Albaro 9r; w pasticceriasvizzera.it). Dickens lived on Via San Nazaro in the **Villa Bagnerello**. The **Villa Giustiniani-Cambiaso** (Via Montallegro 1) was designed by Galeazzo Alessi in the 16th century and is now home to the university's engineering faculty, but the grounds are open to the public. The **Cremeria Ciarapica** (Via Guerrazzi 8r) has some of the best ice cream in Genoa.

The Corso Italia that runs along the seafront is a good place to get some sea air and take a dip in the classic swimming pool, the **Piscine di Albaro** (Piazza Henry Dunant 22; ☎ 010 860 8775; w piscinedialbaro.com; €9 or €16 with a sunbed & umbrella), which was built in 1935 and was recently restored. There are three outdoor pools and one indoor. The **Abbazia di San Giuliano**, built in the 1400s, sits on the waterfront. Corso Italia leads to the old fishing port of **Boccadasse**. A part of Buenos Aires, Boca, is named after this pretty little seaside village and was settled by Genoese immigrants; they still make *farinata* there. Further east is **Quarto**, where a monument marks the starting point of the expedition of Garibaldi and the 'Thousand', Il Mille, to Sicily in 1860, which launched a five-year war to unify Italy. In the Villa Spinola, where Garibaldi stayed while he planned the campaign, there is the small **Museo Garibaldi** (☎ 010 385493; ⊕ 09.00–18.00 Thu–Tue; admission free).

✕ Where to eat and drink Stop for an ice cream at the **Antica Gelateria Amedo** (Piazza Nettuno 7r), and try the fabulous pinolata, made with freshly crushed pine nuts.

✕ Trattoria Vëgia Arba Piazza Leopardi 16r; ☎ 010 363324; ⊕ closed Sun/Mon. Established neighbourhood trattoria in Albaro, which is 'Arba' in Genoese dialect. It opened 60 years ago with a mission to conserve the traditional flavours of Liguria. Simple cooking with excellent *cima alla genovese*. The garden is an oasis. €€€

Nervi [map, page 46] Genoa's most easterly suburb was discovered by the British in the mid 19th century and appears in all the early guidebooks to the Riviera. In her guide *Italics*, published in 1864, Frances Power Cobbe describes Nervi as a place to enjoy nature: 'I hold that the spots in Italy, where nature is really to be enjoyed, are, above all, those wherein there are no works of art to compete with her … in a word, where travellers most rarely go….' The British were soon squeezed out by the Germans, who colonised Nervi, and it was common to see menus posted up in German. In 1913, the writer Frederic Lees feared that the British were 'relinquishing our hold on some of the most delectable places in the world'.

Today, Nervi is a good place for a day trip on a sunny day, but not really a place to base yourself for a holiday considering the beautiful coast so close by. Take a walk along the lovely 2km seafront promenade, the **Passeggiata Anita Garibaldi**, which has great views across the rocky shoreline. The Blue Marlin on the *passeggiata* is a lovely spot for an aperitivo. A beautiful park, the Parco Municipale, is made out of the gardens of four villas, which these days do have some artworks to enjoy. There is a joint ticket for all four (€10). The **Wolfsonia** (Via Serra Groppolo 4; ☎ 010 323 1329; 11.00–18.00 Tue–Fri, 12.00–19.00 Sat–Sun; €5) and the **Galleria d'Arte Moderna Villa Saluzzo Serra** (Via Capolungo 3; ☎ 010 372 6025; ⊕ 11.00–18.00 Tue–Sun, closes 19.00 Sat–Sun; admission €6) house modern art galleries. The **Raccolte Frugone Villa Grimaldi** (Via Capolungo 9; ☎ 010 323 1329; ⊕ 09.00–19.00 Tue–Fri, 10.00–19.00 Sat–Sun; admission €5) is home to the collection of 19th- and 20th-century art made by the Frugone brothers. **Villa Luxoro** houses the **Museo Civico Giannettino** (Via Mafalda di Savoia 3; ☎ 010 322673; ⊕ closed at time of writing for maintenance work; admission €5), a family collection of paintings, notably from the 18th-century Genoese school, furniture, china and fabrics. The museum also has a collection of clocks and nativity scenes.

Bogliasco, 11km east of Genoa, is a pretty, old fishing village with painted houses arranged around the mouth of the river Bogliasco.

✕ Where to eat and drink

✕ **Al Solito Posto** Via Giuseppe Mazzini 228, Bogliasco; 📞010 346 1040; w alsolitoposto.net; ⏰ closed Tue & Sun evening. Stylish dining in an American-bar-type atmosphere. Tasting menus €50–70. €€€

✕ **Il Tipico** Via Poggio Favaro 20, Località San Bernardo, Bogliasco; 📞010 347 0754; ⏰ closed

Mon. Beautiful view across the Golfo Paradiso & great fish dishes & pasta. €€€

✕ **Osteria della Castagna** Via Romana della Castagna 20r, Quarto; 📞010 399 0265. One of the area's best seafood restaurants. Good place to eat locally produced food as it is part of the Genova Gourmet initiative. €€€

UP IN THE MOUNTAINS

The hill forts When American writer and author of *Moby Dick* Herman Melville visited Genoa in April 1857, he was struck by the fortifications: 'The height and distances of these forts, their outlying loneliness … seem to make Genoa rather the capital and fortified camp of Satan.' They were built between the 17th and the 19th centuries and were colossal. Each fort housed up to 850 men. They were one of the biggest defensive systems in Europe and no other Italian city has fortifications in such good condition, though they are sometimes a little rundown. They are known as the Nuova Mura and run for 13km in a horseshoe-shaped crescent around the city. They are protected by the **Parco delle Mura** [map, page 46] and are a great place for a picnic, with fantastic panoramic views across Liguria. Look out for eagles and honey buzzards.

If you have a car, drive to Piazza Manin and up past the late-19th-century folly, the Castello Mackenzie, following the signs for the *ferrovia*, the train to Casella. On foot, the easiest way is to take the funicular to Righi. It takes about 30 minutes to walk up to get a good view of the forts. The **narrow-gauge Genoa–Casella railway** (📞848 000030; w ferroviagenovacasella.it) also leaves from just above Piazza Manin [56 G2]. It takes about an hour to make the 25km journey. Stop off for lunch at one of the excellent trattorias along the way. When the railway was built in the 1920s, a number of Roman coins were found that show that this salt road, so named for the vital goods like salt that were traded with the landlocked north, was also important in ancient times.

Forte Sperone is situated on the highest point of the city wall on the top of Monte Peralto. Over the main entrance is the Savoy coat of arms. There were serious battles here in the Napoleonic Wars during the siege of Genoa. Sadly, the castle is in a state of disrepair and the gate padlocked. It certainly hasn't been a venue for cultural events as the tourist leaflets claim for a very long time, if ever. Like Edward Hutton in his guide to Genoa, written in 1907, one is left to wonder if the place is 'so regardless of old things that one might fancy her history only began in 1860'. Nearby **Forte Begato** is also abandoned.

In the distance are **Forte Puin** and **Forte Diamante**, where French troops were besieged in the Napoleonic Wars. This is the nicest fort to picnic by and a good place to take a walk. To get there, take SP80 to Casanova or take the Casella train.

✕ Where to eat and drink *Map, page 46*

✕ **Bruxaboschi** Via Giorgio Mignone 8, San Desiderio; 📞010 345 0302; w bruxaboschi.

com; ⏰ closed Sun evening & Mon. This trattoria opened in 1862 & serves traditional local food.

Liguria's climate is particularly good for rose hips, which are used to make syrup, *sciroppo di rose*, and jams, and there are plenty of local producers who sell directly to the public in the mountains behind Genoa. The rose hips, *rosa canina*, known as *grattacû* in dialect are dried in the sun before they are cooked into jam or added to cakes, biscuits, white wine, tea and also to meat dishes. It is a tradition that was brought to Genoa during the Crusades and rose syrup was believed to help stomach upsets and to calm fevers. In rural areas it was used a sweetener by those who could not afford sugar. Today it is popular as a refreshing cold drink in summer and a hot drink in winter.

In Genoa you can buy rose syrup from the confectioner **Romanengo** [62 E2] (Via Soziglia 74r) who have been producing it for 230 years. It's in the hinterland behind Genoa, however, that the tradition has really been preserved, especially in the Valle Scrivia. The petals used to make the syrup are harvested in May and early June. There is a rose festival in Busalla [map, page 46] on the second weekend in June where you can meet local producers.

At **Agriturismo Da U Gatto di Alessio Gatto** (Località Tre Fontane, Montoggio; ☏ 010 938159) you can eat dishes prepared with rose-based ingredients. **Azienda Agricola Scolaro Maria Giuila** (Via Ronchetto 9a, Savignone; ☏ 010 936912; m 3498 699372) is an organic farm, which grows the local *quarantina* potato, jam made from violet leaves and *sciroppo di rose*. You need to call and ask if you want to buy from the farm and make an appointment.

Other local producers are: **Agrituristica Artemisia di Emanuela Annetta** (Località Carpi Superiore 6, Montoggio; m 347 057 9001; w artemisia-montoggio.it), **Agricola Camporotondo di Mariangela Valente** (Località Gualdrà 15, Savignone; ☏ 010 976 1053), **Il Giardino delle Dalie di Viviane Crosa di Vergagni** (Piazza della Chiesa 4, Savignone; m 339 583 7572), **Azienda Il Roseto di Francesco Bertuccio** (Località Malvasi 29, Ronco Scrivia; ☏ 010 965 1075; w parcoantola.it) and **Agricola di Ugo Traverso** (Via Bonnigher 53a, Sarissola Busalla; ☏ 010 964 0536).

Lovely shady terrace in summer. They have the Genova Gourmet certification. €€€

✗ **La Pineta** Via Gualco 82; ☏ 010 802772; w www.ristorantelapineta.org. In the Val Bisagno, this place is part of the Genova Gourmet initiative & serves local mushrooms & chestnut gnocchi. Steaks are cooked on a charcoal grill in front of you. €€

Further north Either take the Casella train or drive to **Sant'Olcese** [map, page 46] (but don't listen to the GPS; it sends you down a tiny back road that peters out in front of some very friendly people's house and they spend their time helping tourists from all over Europe out of a very tight spot. It put our car in the garage for a week). The town produces Salame di Sant'Olcese, which Dickens found so tasty. It is a delicately flavoured salami made of pork and beef and traditionally donkey meat, seasoned with local herbs and red wine and smoked with chestnut leaves. Buy it in **Salumificio Cabella** (Via Sant'Olcese 38). East of Sant'Olcese is the **Villa Serra** (Via Carlo Levi 4; ☏ 010 715557; w villaserra.it; ⊕ 14.15–20.00 Mon–Tue; 10.00–20.00 Wed–Sun; admission €3), which is used for weddings and conferences, and has a stunning formal garden open to the public – a nice place for a picnic. There are great views from the sanctuary, **Nostra Signora della Guardia** at Ceranesi, built after the Virgin Mary appeared before a shepherd in 1490.

There is a footpath up to the top of Monte Antola from Torriglia, which takes about 3½ hours to walk. If you want to go further, a path leads across Monte Tre Croci [map, page 94] about an hour away. It is part of the Via del Mare footpath that runs from Milan to Portofino.

If you want a shorter walk to the summit, another path begins at Bavastrelli. From Monte Antola you can walk to Crocefieschi in the Valle Scrivia. The walk is marked by two yellow horizontal lines and takes 4½ hours. There are beautiful views from Monte Antola across to the sea and the Alps. The mountain is famous for its wild narcissus.

There's another nice walk around the artificial lake, the Lago del Brugneto [map, page 94], the Sentiero Brugneto, 8km to the east, which supplies Genoa's water and was built in 1957. The path starts just north of Garaventa and the whole circuit around the lake is 14km and takes 5–6 hours. There are plenty of picnic spots. The walk up to the top of Monte Antola takes about 3 hours and is marked by a huge white cross. The views of the coast and the Alps are stunning.

If you are hiking across Monte Antola, you can stay at the Rifugio Parco Antola (page 89). If you hike or drive up from Torriglia to Marzano, you can walk the Anello di Torriglia. It's 22km long and can also be done on a mountain bike. You follow a yellow triangle but it is advisable to ask for a map of the walk from the tourist information office in Torriglia so you don't get lost. If you fancy doing some of the route on horseback, there is a stables in Obbi, Centro Equestre Mulino del Lupo (Piazza Posteggio 1; ✆ 010 944494), which has parking.

From Casella take the road up the pretty **Valbrevenna** [map, page 46], stop for a picnic by the river and then head over the hairpin bends following the signs to Nenno on the SP12, or Clavarezzato for an even more off-the-beaten-track experience over the mountaintop to the wooded **Val Vobbia**. This was part of the old salt road to Tortona in Piedmont. The **Castello della Pietra** [map, page 46] (Strada Provinciale 8; ✆ 010 944175; ⊕ 10.30–17.30 Sat–Sun & holidays; admission €5) is a stunning castle, literally built into a rocky outcrop, which once guarded the salt road. Even if the castle is closed, it is worth walking up the steep path for a closer view as it is quite unlike any other castle in Liguria. The local wildlife is rich and includes wolf, deer and foxes. Just south of Vobbia there's a good walk from Crocefieschi to Minceto which takes about 2 hours but, if you feel energetic, you can climb up to the top of Monte Reale which adds on at least an hour and a half. It is good biking country and you can hire mountain bikes in Casella (✆ 010 967 7520).

Where to stay, eat and drink Look out for the local goat's cheese, *caprino*. You can buy it straight from the farm at **Azienda Autra** [map, page 46] (Località Autra 2, Savignone; m 348 365 5655; w agriturismoautra.it; €). They also have a restaurant (⊕ Sun & holidays).

As you travel about you'll notice signs saying *miele* (honey) as many very small producers sell from tables by the side of the road.

In Vobbia, they make a spreadable sausage, *mostardella*, and an aromatic wine, Coronata. Buy the sausage in **Maccelleria Torrigino Gianni** (Piazza della Posta 13, Vobbia). There is excellent homemade pasta on sale at **Pastificio Alta Valle Scrivia**

Genoa FURTHER AFIELD

3

(Via Milite Ignoto 48b; ☎010 938433). In Montoggio, the *pandolce* cakes with pine nuts and candied fruit are also made with chestnut flour, and are sold at **Pasticceria Flavia** (Via NS della Provvidenza 4) in Torriglia. The local tipples are an alcoholic fizzy drink made with elderflowers (*vin de sambuco*), cider (*vino di mele)*, and *birra di Savignone*. Italy's oldest beer factory **Fabbrica Birra Busalla** (Località Birra 3, Savignone; ☎010 964 0161) is in the Valle Scrivia. They use honey, rose petals and chestnuts in their recipes.

🏠 **Agriturismo Terra e Cielo** (10 rooms) Via Bellavista 29, Serra Riccò; ☎010 772 0271; m 348 365 5655; w agriturismoterraecielo.it. The farm has cattle & grows its own vegetables. A rustic experience 20km from Genoa. In addition to offering intimate & tastefully furnished rooms, it has a spacious terrace with a solarium, & a separate kitchen for guests. The restaurant (€€) serves seasonal home-grown produce & is open only if booked in advance. Set menu €30, child €14. €€

✗ **Il Caminetto** Località Nenno Inferiore 17, Valbrevenna; ☎010 969 0986; m 388 042 8087; w ristoranteilcaminetto.eu; ⊕ Thu/Fri dinner

only, Sat/Sun lunch & dinner. The place to taste some real country home-cooking. On the menu is wild boar, as well as truffles & asparagus from Albenga in season. Vegetarian dishes. €€€

✗ **Osteria della Collina** Salita Giovanni Maria Cotella 47r, Molassana; ☎010 835390; ⊕ closed Mon & Tue. Family restaurant founded in 1980, serving excellent fresh fish & local dishes. €€€

✗ **Antica Trattoria Rosin** [map, page 46] Via Provinciale, 15 Tre Fontane, Montoggio; ☎010 938292. Serves *trofie* with nut sauce, *pansotti* and *torta pasqualina*. The family produced the 86-year-old world pesto champion. €€

Torriglia East of Casella, this little mountain resort is a great place for walking, horseriding, mountain biking, climbing, and if it snows, cross-country skiing. There's a bus service from Genoa which takes about an hour. It is nestled under **Monte Antola** (1,597m), in the **Parco Regionale dell'Antola.** (w parcoantola.it). It's a lovely place full of wild flowers, especially in spring. The roads here are quiet and good for cycling. There is a horseriding centre in Torriglia, Centro Servizi per il Turismo Equestre, and there is rock climbing at the Rocche del Reopasso.

In Roman times Torriglia was an important trading centre on the route between Genoa and Emilia-Romagna. The medieval castle was built by the Malaspina family, then taken over by the Fieschi, and from the 16th century it was in the hands of the powerful Dorias. On the first Sunday in September there is a colourful honey festival, followed by a chestnut festival in late October or early November. The town is famous for its *canestrelli di Torriglia* and there is a food festival dedicated to them in May. Buy them from the family-run shop La Torriglia, Via Canale 3.

There was fierce fighting in the mountains above Genoa during the German occupation from September 1943 to May 1945. In Propata there's a small **museum** (☎010 945910; ⊕ by appointment only), which chronicles the struggle that involved a range of different partisan groups – some monarchist, some communist – who fought here. These valleys are really quite remote and closed. For example, a friend of my father-in-law was a monarchist partisan here and after the war that meant he was accepted and able to buy a house in the Valbrevenna. Other people from Genoa have found people reluctant to sell to them because they are not considered locals. There are also a number of villages that still have no paved roads.

Six kilometres north of Torriglia, **Pentema** is famous for its Christmas crib. If you fancy a walk, there's a footpath from Torriglia. In the Val Trebbia, **Fontanigorda** [map, page 94] is a pretty little town with 13 fountains dedicated to the Madonna Addolorata. The water comes from the nearby Bosco della Fate, the Fairy Wood, which is another nice place to walk.

Where to stay, eat and drink For dessert try the round biscuits, *rotelle di borzonasca*, nougat called *torrone* or the *torta di Torriglia*, an almond cake. *Ciambelline* are biscuits made with chestnut flour. You can buy them in season at Passticceria Guano in Piazza Cavour in Torriglia.

B&B Villa Tiffany (3 rooms) Località Porto 36, Torriglia; m 342 626 2550; w villatiffany.it. Friendly owners make you feel at home. €€

Locanda al Pettirosso (3 rooms) Località Pentema 3, Torriglia; 010 944802. Restaurant (€€€) & B&B. Eat the traditional ravioli & a host of other traditional dishes. There is no menu & there is a set price of €25. Come here for a real Italian experience. €€

Hotel della Posta Via Matteotti 39, Torriglia; 010 944050. Built in the 1900s, the restaurant (€€) makes everything in-house. It's also a cheap place to stay. €

Rifugio Parco Antola [map, page 46] (4 dorms) Via Monte Antola, Porpata; m 339 487 4872; w rifugioantola.com. The *rifugio* has 4 rooms with 8 beds. Linen can be hired for €5. It has a terrace with a beautiful view & a good rustic restaurant. €

Trattoria Via Vai Via N S Provvidenza 14–16, Torriglia; 010 945 1005; ⊕ lunch & dinner Thu–Tue. Friendly, family-run restaurant serving classic, Ligurian-hinterland cuisine. €€

Al Castello Via Giacomo Buranello 40, Torriglia; 010 944339. Good pizzeria that won't break the bank. Also serves simple Ligurian dishes. €

FOLLOW US

Tag us in your posts to share your adventures using this guide with us – we'd love to hear from you.

BradtTravelGuides
@BradtGuides & @rosiewhitehouse
@bradtguides & @rosieawhitehouse
bradtguides
bradtguides

Part Three

THE RIVIERA DI LEVANTE

RIVIERA DI LEVANTE

The Riviera di Levante, the coast east of Genoa, has drawn tourists for almost 200 years. Charles Dickens believed that, 'There is nothing in Italy, more beautiful to me than the coast-road between Genoa and Spezzia.' The mountains are much steeper here than they are to the west of Genoa and plunge down dramatically into the sea.

In high season, the resorts can get very crowded, but as Frederic Lees observed in 1913, 'the fact that they are crowded, during the season, with tourists and convalescents testifies not only to their interest but also to their climatic advantages.' He was of course referring to winter as the high season not August, and indeed this is an all-year-round destination. In the winter, walking is delightful when the air is clear and the views are at their best.

In summer you can do everything that the word 'Riviera' conjures up: sea, sun, yachts and luxury living. The Riviera di Levante's crown jewels are the jet-set resort of Portofino and the five tiny villages of the Cinque Terre. This may be the world-famous part of the Italian Riviera, but it is possible to find beautiful places to stay and eat that don't require a millionaire's bank balance.

The big event along the coast is the boat race, the Palio dei Tigullio, which takes place in the early summer. Teams from all the major towns on the Gulf of Tigullio compete in this colourful festival.

4

Recco to Sestri Levante

Telephone code 0185 (+390185 if calling from abroad)

The coast is lush and green. The villas and hotels are surrounded by pungent Mediterranean forests and exotic gardens, full of palm trees and brightly coloured bougainvillea. Portofino may be the place to cut a *bella figura* and spot the rich and famous but there are some beautiful, peaceful spots too where you can get away from it all, like the tiny hamlet of San Fruttuoso, which is only accessible by boat or on foot. It is a little paradise when the day trippers have all gone home.

The majority of the tourists stick to the coast but inland there are fabulous mountain passes and alpine valleys full of pretty mountain flowers in spring and summer.

This is a land of seafarers; the towns and villages between Nervi and Portofino have produced more sea captains than perhaps anywhere else on earth. They were inspired, I am sure, by the astounding views. From the top of Monte Portofino it is possible, on a clear day, to see as far west as Diano Marina, Corsica to the south and the Tuscan archipelago in the east. Men from this stretch of coast sailed to the four corners of the world, among them Nicoloso da Recco, who 'discovered' the Canaries in 1341, and they still train sea captains in Camogli.

🍴 SAY CHEESE

The absolute must-try is Recco's famous cheese focaccia, *focaccia con formaggio*, a thin savoury bread with a filling of *crescenza* cheese. It is such a local dish that it is impossible to find a version made beyond a 5km radius of the town that can hold its own against the real thing. What is really good about this tasty treat is that, although it is served in restaurants here, you can also buy it in any *focacceria* for a couple of euros.

The dish dates back to the time of the Saracens, when the locals took refuge in the mountains, and cheese, flour and olive oil were available in abundance. Traditionally, cheese focaccia was only eaten in the autumn when the cattle were fed partly on fresh forage and partly on hay, a combination that gave the milk a sour taste, making the cheese especially suitable for filling focaccia. Indeed, Recco is an unusually cheesy place for Liguria and the pesto is often made with *prescinseua*, a soft cheese from the hills behind Genoa.

On the fourth Sunday in May, during the Festa della Focaccia, up to 500kg of flour is used to make a mountain of focaccia. Other local classics are *focaccette*, small fried breads, and *sciumette*, little meringue sponges similar to *oeufs à la neige* that have been eaten at Easter and Christmas for over 300 years.

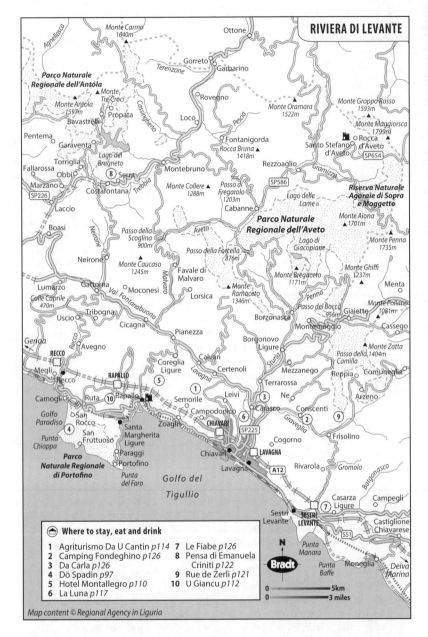

RIVIERA DI LEVANTE

🛏 **Where to stay, eat and drink**

1 Agriturismo Da U Cantin *p114*
2 Camping Fondeghino *p126*
3 Da Carla *p126*
4 Dö Spadin *p97*
5 Hotel Montallegro *p110*
6 La Luna *p117*
7 Le Fiabe *p126*
8 Pensa di Emanuela Criniti *p122*
9 Rue de Zerli *p121*
10 U Giancu *p112*

Map content © Regional Agency in Liguria

0 ⊢━━━━ 5km
0 ⊢━━━━ 3 miles

RECCO

The town of Recco itself is nothing special and was flattened by British and American bombers during World War II in their attempt to take out the railway viaduct. The buildings date from the 1950s and 60s and, at first glance, it appears a little soulless. However, its heart can be found in its amazing cuisine; the locals have hung on to their food heritage so steadfastly precisely because there is little else left.

The big date in the calendar is 7–8 September when they celebrate the Sagra del Fuoco (w sagradelfuoco.it), the firework festival in honour of their patron saint, Nostra Signora del Suffragio.

✕ WHERE TO EAT AND DRINK One of Recco's sights is the weekly Monday **market**, which sells lots of local products, chestnuts and chestnut flour, pasta and cheese. The town has four week-long food festivals, La Settimana Gastronomica, in March, June, September and December, which bring together scores of local producers.

Panificio Pasticceria Moteldo (Via XX Settembre 2–4) sells the best focaccia in Recco, which means it has to be among the best in Liguria. For an ice cream, go to the family-run **Gelateria Cavassa** (Lungomare Bettolo 31), on the seafront. **Caffè Boccia** (Via Roma 40r), has no tables, just a bar, which is why most tourists pass it by, but both the coffee, roasted inland at Avengo, and the pastries are excellent. It is great for kids, with a vast array of sweets all displayed at their eye level.

First opened in 1895, the restaurant **Manuelina** ✱ (Via Roma 296; ☎ 0185 74128; e manuelina@manuelina.it; w manuelina.it; €€€) is named after Emanuela Capurro, who served up *focaccia con formaggio* in her trattoria long before World War I. Eat it here as a starter followed by *pansotti*. Locals celebrate at Manuelina and businessmen from Genoa bring their clients here to impress them. It is on the road that runs towards the *autostrada* and has no view, but it is the food that is the draw and it has the Genova Gourmet certification.

Da Ö Vittorio (Via Roma 160; ☎ 0185 74029; €€€) is another restaurant that is part of the Genova Gourmet initiative. It also serves the classic *focaccia con formaggio*.

Tossini ✱ (Via Biago Asserto 7; ☎ 0185 74137; w tossini.it; ⊕ lunch only, closed May; cash only; €) is a great delicatessen and they make pumpkin *farinata* in season. The company started up in 1899 and now sell their products worldwide.

CAMOGLI

Tall colourful houses look out to the sea and were originally all painted different colours so that the fishermen could recognise their homes while out fishing. In fact, the men were away at sea so much that Camogli actually means 'the wife's house'; *ca* means 'house' in dialect and *moglie* means 'wife' in Italian. Camogli is one of my favourite towns in Liguria. It is set in a steep bay and has a good sandyish pebble beach that is free, and there is a lovely little harbour, all making it a great place to base yourself on a holiday. It has the added bonus of being right next to the Portofino promontory, which is one of the most beautiful places in Liguria.

The big event is the Sagra del Pesce on the second Sunday in May, when vast quantities of fish are fried in a giant, 4m-wide frying pan, the biggest in Italy. The festival is not as old as it looks and began in 1952. It commemorates a night during World War II when the town was starving as the fishermen had not been able to put to sea because of German mines, but the situation was so dire that they set sail anyway. Prayers were offered to San Fortunato and the men returned with a massive catch. There is a huge firework display the night before. The Camogliesi are fed first, then any leftovers go to the hungry tourists. Look out for the giant pan hanging on the wall as you walk into town.

HISTORY From the Middle Ages to the end of the 19th century and the coming of steam ships, Camogli was a bustling seaport, known as the 'city of a thousand white sails', and its harbour was crammed full of its famous tall ships. The fleet was rented out to anyone who had the money to pay for it, and in 1805, it fought alongside

Napoleon in the Battle of Trafalgar. When Dickens visited in 1845, he found it 'the saltiest, roughest, most piratical little place'. The nautical tradition continues and the town is home to an important maritime college.

GETTING THERE AND AROUND If you don't have your own transport, Camogli is a good base for a holiday. You can use the train to visit Genoa and other resorts along the coast. There are good ferry services in summer as well. Alternatively, use your feet and explore the Portofino promontory. It is criss-crossed with trails that start in the town and lead to Portofino, San Fruttuoso and Punta Chiappa.

By bike You can sign up for the bike-sharing scheme at **Pro Loco** (Via XX Settembre 33; ⏱ 09.00–12.30 & 15.00–18.30 Mon–Sat, 09.00–12.30 Sun).

By boat There are 287 berths in the old harbour (❋ 0185 770032; **e** camogli@ guardiacostiera.it), but beware of rocks at the entrance to the port. **Ferries** (**w** golfoparadiso.it) run to Genoa, Nervi, Portofino, Punta Chiappa, San Fruttuoso and Recco from March to September, during the day, and there are also special night-time excursions. Ferries aren't cheap: it costs €11 to go to San Fruttuoso and back, for example, but they are a wonderful way to get under Liguria's seafaring skin. There are also trips to the Cinque Terre in summer. There is a taxi boat service, to Punta Chiappa (**m** 334 254 9868), and to visit the underwater statue of Jesus (**m** 333 435 2502). There are regular, but not daily, excursions to the statue from the harbour in summer, which leave at 14.45 for €6.

By bus There is a good regular bus service to Santa Margherita and Rapallo, both under 45 minutes away. Santa Margherita is just 4km as the crow flies, so it is always quicker to take the train if you can.

By car Camogli is 36km east of Genoa, just off the A12 Genova–Livorno *autostrada*. Take the exit for Recco and then follow the Via Aurelia, the SS1.

By taxi For taxis, call ❋ 0185 771143.

By train Camogli is on the main Genoa–La Spezia line. It is easy to visit for a day trip.

TOURIST INFORMATION (Via XX Settembre 33; ❋ 0185 771066; **w** camogli.it). On the first Sunday in August is Stella Maris, the Star of the Sea, when hundreds of little boats set sail, the town lights are turned off and only the dim lights of the boats can be seen. The boats are blessed and thousands of little candles are set off bobbing in the sea. Each candle represents a sailor's soul.

The **B&B Diving Centre** (Lungomare di Camogli; ❋ 0185 772751; **m** 347 715 4616; **w** www.bbdiving.it) has tours of the Portofino underwater nature reserve and hires boats.

 WHERE TO STAY
Camogli

🏠 **Palazzo Cenobio dei Dogi** (105 rooms) Via N Cuneo 34; ❋ 0185 7241; **e** cenobio@ cenobio.it; **w** cenobio.com. This hotel on the waterfront has a splendid view across to Camogli's church on the promontory. There's a beautiful seawater swimming pool & large garden. It's in a 16th-century palace that once belonged to the doges of Genoa, so has lots of atmosphere. Book a room with a sea view & a balcony to make the most of the setting. There are 3 good restaurants. A dbl with a sea view is more expensive than the rooms that look on to the garden. €€€€

🏠 **Villa Rosmarino** (6 rooms) Via Figari 38; ✆0185 771580; e info@villarosemarino.com; w villarosmarino.com; ⏰ closed Nov. This 1907 palazzo was restored by Milanese businessman Mario Pietraccetta & is above Camogli. Rooms have vintage furniture & modern art. There's a swimming pool, parking & a garden. Ask for a room with a sea view. €€€€

🏠 **La Camogliese** (21 rooms) Via Garibaldi 55; ✆0185 771402; e info@lacamogliese.it; w lacamogliese.it. The Rocchetti family have run this hotel since it opened in 1950 & give a warm welcome. Ask for a room that looks out on to the sea as the hotel is on the seafront with a lovely view across to the church on the promontory. Good restaurant. Free Wi-Fi. €€€

🏠 **Domus Giulia B&B** (3 rooms) Via San Giacomo 50/1; ✆ 0185 773039; m 349 061 9246. Great view & swimming pool. The B&B is surrounded by olive groves. Cash only. €€

On the Portofino promontory

🏠 **Agririfugio Molini** (10 beds in 3 rooms) San Fruttuoso; ✆0185 772291. This old watermill above the bay of San Fruttuoso was converted by a group of young people, who have also reopened the olive mill. They have tended the trees, planted by the monks who once lived here, so they are producing olives again. It may be the budget option but the location couldn't be better. The food is excellent & based on classic Ligurian dishes. It's a 30-min climb up from San Fruttuoso or 1hr from Portofino Vetta. Wi-Fi. It creeps into the mid-range price bracket as it is half board only. €€

🏠 **Da Giovanni** (10 rooms) San Fruttuoso; ✆0185 770047; w dagiovanniristorante.com. The rooms may be basic, but it is in a wonderful location right on the beach. If you want to come in your own boat to eat in the evening, you need to book in advance. The restaurant (€€€) serves classic local food. €€

✖ WHERE TO EAT AND DRINK
Camogli

✖ **Choco Emotion** Via della Repubblica 55. A nice café that serves excellent pastries. €

On the Portofino promontory

✖ **Stella Maris** Punta Chiappa; ✆0185 770285; e info@stellamaris.cc; w stellamaris. cc. A wonderful romantic location with fabulous views. The menu is predominantly fish. Catch the boat from the harbour in Camogli. You can also stay the night (€€€€). €€€€€

✖ **Castel Dragone** Porto Punta Chiappa; m 338 721 6789; w ittiturismocamogli.it. Go fishing with local fishermen & eat the day's catch. €€€

✖ **Dö Spadin** [map, page 94] Via San Nicolo 55; ✆0185 770624. This restaurant, near Punta Chiappa, has a wonderful view & serves traditional dishes. This is the place to come for a romantic meal as the location is the main thing about this waterfront restaurant. €€€

✖ **La Cucina di Nonna Nina** Via Molfino 126, San Rocco; ✆0185 773835; e lacucinadinonnanina@libero.it; w nonnanina. it; ⏰ closed Wed. Simple restaurant with a terrace & a wonderful view. The fish tastes as if it is straight from the sea. There's a handwritten menu, in Genoese, & the dishes, as the name implies (*nonna* means granny), are just like grandma used to make. €€€

OTHER PRACTICALITIES There is an **ATM** at Via XX Settembre 19. The **post office** is on Via Aurelia 199. The **pharmacy** is at Via della Repubblica 4, and the nearest **hospital** is at Via Andrea Bianchi 1, Recco (✆0185 74377).

WHAT TO SEE AND DO A small rocky promontory, the **Isola**, which was once an island, separates the small sandy-cum-pebble beach from the harbour. Walk up the stairs to the 12th-century **Basilica di Santa Maria Assunta**, with its Neoclassical façade and 17th-century pebbled courtyard that is typical of Liguria. The inside is impressive, with gilded columns and chandeliers reminding you that this was no simple little fishing village. It was originally built as a chapel for the castle and the present building dates from the 16th century, although it was altered in the

Onion focaccia is one of the most delicious types of focaccia and in Camogli it was traditionally eaten before the men set off to sea. They would give their wives and girlfriends a big onion-flavoured kiss before they set off, leaving them less desirable to other men. **Panificio Rizzo Rocco**, Via della Repubblica, is the best baker in Camogli, although the family actually hail from Puglia. **Pasticceria Bar Budicin**, Via Aurelia 186, Ruta di Camogli is owned by Marco Budicin who, although born in Istria, is considered one of the region's best pastry chefs. Unmissable is the **Panificio Maccarini**, Via San Rocco 46, in San Rocco opposite the church (w panificiomaccarini.com). They make excellent focaccia and the best vegetable tarts I have ever eaten. They are one of the few bakeries that still make *galleta del marinaio,* traditional ship's biscuits. They aren't eaten dry (if you try you'll crack your teeth), but are softened with oil and, traditionally, seawater.

As wild herbs are so plentiful on the Portofino peninsula, they figure in many of the local dishes like *friseu di borragine*, borage fritters, which are often served with sparkling wine as an aperitif. The town is famous for its cherries. They are called *camoggin* and now grow elsewhere in Liguria, but a unique way of preparing them that is truly Camogliesi is by preserving them in anisette, another local speciality. They are used to make the local ice-cream sundae, *paciugo. Camogliese* are little cakes made with choux pastry filled with flavoured creams and often flavoured with rum.

Don't miss the biscuits at Revello ☀ (Via Garibaldi 183). I think they are the best in Liguria!

The outdoor market is on Wednesday morning. The stalls sell food, honey and cheese made in the mountains and organic produce from the Val di Vara. **Cooperativa Pescatori**, on a steep staircase that runs down from Via della Repubblica, the Salita Priaro, is where the local fishermen sell their fish. The salted anchovies are prepared traditionally, gutted with no head but retaining the fins and bones.

19th century. The religious artwork includes paintings by Cambiaso, Fiasella and Schiaffino. The bones of St Prospero and St Fortunato are housed in the reliquary.

Next to the church is the medieval **Castello della Dragonara**, built to defend the town from the Saracens. There is a fascinating museum, the **Museo Marinaro Gio Bono Ferrari** (Via Ferrari 42; ☎ 0185 729049; admission free), which catalogues the town's golden years in the 19th century with lots of model boats and ships in bottles. There are also interesting exhibitions in the **Fondazione Luigi e Remotti** (Via Castagneto 52; ☎ 0185 772137; w fondazioneremotti.it), a cutting-edge art gallery in a deconsecrated church.

You can go out fishing with the local fishermen at Punta Chiappa on the Portofino promontory (see the notice boards in the park). Budget between €75 and €100, children half price. You eat lunch on board.

The Portofino promontory The Portofino promontory is the star of the show. Rising out of the sea next to Camogli it juts 3km out from the curve of the coast, separating the Golfo Paradiso to the west from the Golfo del Tigullio in the east. It is a miniature mountain covered in lush, dense pine and chestnut forests, which cascade down cliffs that enclose tiny coves. There's a heady mixture of wild strawberry, gorse and wild herbs. The water here is famous for changing colour.

Every time you look it is different. German philosopher Friedrich Nietzsche spent the winter of 1886 in Ruta and described the promontory as a place to 'anchor and never leave'. This is the place to come if you like walking as a large part of the area is inaccessible by car and is criss-crossed with pathways. Although close to Portofino itself, and dotted with the villas of multi-millionaires, it is still a beautiful place to get away from it all. It is wild and peaceful even in the height of summer.

The promontory is part of the nature reserve, the **Parco Naturale Regionale di Portofino** (w parcoportofino.it), which was set up in 1935. It is far larger than the promontory from which it takes its name and covers 18km², taking in the mountains that frame the Golfo del Tigullio behind Santa Margherita. It is botanically rich and there are 700 different plant species growing here and it is home to a colony of peregrine falcons. In 1999, the park was extended to cover the seabed from Camogli to Santa Margherita Ligure. The underwater reserve is divided into three areas: Zone A is enclosed by the creek called Cala dell'Oro between Punta Chiappa and San Fruttuoso and swimming is not permitted here; Zone B stretches from Punta del Faro to Punta Chiappa facing out to sea and here you can see a variety of sea fans, red coral and beautiful sea fauna; Zone C includes the sea around Portofino and the waters from Camogli to Punta Chiappa. The area is particularly good for watersports and diving, especially around the wreck of the *Mohawk Deer*, a cargo boat that sank in 1974. Beware of the strong currents, however.

To explore the western side of the promontory, drive or catch a bus along the Via Aurelia, the SS1. It leads eastwards up the hill from Camogli to **San Rocco di Camogli**. You can also walk up. There's a footpath that starts in Camogli in the car park at the southern end of the town, not far from the Cenobi dei Dogi Hotel. The car park is about 10 minutes' walk from the village. It is possible to drive along this road to drop passengers if needs be.

San Rocco is a sublime little place perched high up above the bay, nestled around its pretty church. There's a small bar, Dai Mûgetti, just after the church on the narrow pathway leading to Punta Chiappa. It has an idyllic view and it is one of the loveliest places to have a drink and watch the sun set. If you are planning a romantic drink you do need to book a table. Buy a picnic at the bakery opposite the church, as there are some pretty spots nearby to sit and eat. It is just down the steps but is closed on Wednesday. There is also a small shop on the road from the car park.

From the square in front of the church there is a beautiful view. From here there are two paths. One goes to San Fruttuoso, which takes almost 3 hours to walk and another leads down to Punta Chiappa, which is about an hour, even though the sign says it takes 40 minutes. The timings of the walks are all on the optimistic side on the park notices. Before you set out make sure you have water and good shoes. Some paths have been badly eroded in recent years, so do pay attention to any signs saying that the path is inaccessible. The early part of this walk through Mortola is very easy and can be done by people of all ages, but after Mortola the path begins to get more challenging. Walking on the slopes of Monte Portofino is beautiful but not that easy or safe with small children, especially as you will probably end up having to carry them most of the way.

The path splits before you reach Punta Chiappa. One path leads down to Punta Chiappa and a second carries along the hillside to the Batterie, the remains of defensive bunkers from World War II. They were built by the Italian army in 1941 and taken under Nazi control in 1943. You can get a guided tour of the bunkers, if you make an appointment (m 348 018 2557). There are two picnic tables and the view, not surprisingly from a gun emplacement designed to protect Genoa from British naval bombardments, is fabulous. From here the path continues on to San

Fruttuoso, which is about 2 hours, or down to Punta Chiappa. It takes 2 hours to walk from San Fruttuoso to Portofino.

The path is very steep down to Punta Chiappa and is difficult without good walking shoes. In wet weather it is very slippery.

In Punta Chiappa fishing nets hang out to dry in front of the fishermen's houses just before the land peters out into the sea in a cascade of rocks, which is a great place to swim. Here you will also find a small fishing museum, Museo della Pesca di Punta Chiappa (m 337 290068; ⊕ May–Sep 11.00–18.00 Sat–Sun) and a lovely trattoria. In the museum you can find out about the unusual net that is just off the coast, the *tonnara*, a long tunnel-like contraption for catching tuna, which is one of the oldest in Italy. There's a fabulous view back across the bay to Camogli and its towering houses. Ferry boats or the water taxi can take you back to Camogli from Porto Pidoccio but remember that in bad weather ferries can be cancelled.

Up the hill from Camogli, on a side road off the Aurelia, is **Portofino Vetta**. It is another good place to start exploring the promontory, as it sits at the axis of the main paths. One leads to the summit of Monte Portofino (610m), which is about an hour's walk and another takes 1½ hours to walk down to San Fruttuoso. From here you can also walk all the way to Portofino. The fun part of these walks is catching the boat back to Camogli, Portofino and Santa Margherita, so be sure to bring plenty of cash.

San Fruttuoso   Facing out to sea in a world of its own, the monastery and little hamlet of San Fruttuoso sit at the head of a steep, tiny verdant bay that's only accessible by sea or on foot. It is a haven when, in the late afternoon, all the day trippers have left, so if you can, stay the night. The nicest trip is to walk down in the morning from San Rocco or Ruta with a picnic and catch the boat back the following day. It is a 30-minute ride but boats only run in summer and good weather. There's no shop so bring everything you need. If your budget is tight, beware that there's a mark-up on ice creams if you sit down.

The **Benedictine abbey** (✆ 0185 772703; ⊕ Jan–Feb & Nov–Dec 10.00–15.45 daily; Apr–May & second half of Sep 10.00–16.45 daily; Jun–mid-Sep 10.00–17.45 daily (in bad weather the times vary); admission €7 (reduction with a UK National Trust card)) sits right on the beach. It was founded in the early 8th century when the Arabs attacked Spain and Bishop Prosperous of Tarragona fled, taking refuge in Liguria and bringing with him the relics of martyr San Fruttuoso. The cult spread quickly in Liguria as it was believed he gave special protection to sailors.

The abbey was sacked by the Saracens in the 10th century and rebuilt in the 13th by the Doria family who added the abbot's palace and, in 1562, the defensive **Torre dei Doria**. The abbey was a monastery until 1885 after which it was taken over by fishermen and severely damaged in a storm in 1915. The family gave the abbey to FAI, the Italian equivalent of the UK's National Trust in 1983. There's not much to see inside. There's a quaint little cloister and the imposing black-and-white tombs of the Doria family, which date from 1275 to 1305. The Doria Tower, emblazoned with the family crest, which commands the cove, has a small exhibition room but it is not possible to climb to the top. The church is free but rather plain inside after it was damaged in the violent storm of 1915. If you don't go in, you won't miss much. San Fruttuoso is just about being in a beautiful place and relaxing.

It may all look idyllic here on a summer's day but the sea can be wild and dangerous. The **Cristo degli Abissi**, a bronze statue by Guido Galletti, was lowered 17m onto the seabed by the entrance to the bay in 1954 and is a reminder of the perils of seafaring; was inspired by the death of a young diver. Old bells, ships' parts and the propellers of an American submarine were melted down to make it. On the last Sunday in July garlands of flowers are scattered in the water above the statue in memory of those who have lost their lives at sea. Ask in the bay if you want to visit, as local fishermen will take you out for a fee.

SANTA MARGHERITA LIGURE

Beloved by writers from northern Europe and America in the 19th and early 20th centuries, Santa Margherita Ligure is a lively, smart, resort town. It is a chic place, with plenty of old-world charm, and set in a pretty lush bay full of exotic plants. A hundred years ago, before mass tourism, it must have seemed not far from paradise, and today it is still a lovely spot outside the high season. The coast that stretches west to Portofino and east to Rapallo is the quintessential Riviera with villas dotted in forests of pine and cypress trees, lush gardens and pleasure boats bobbing in the harbour. Santa, as the town is affectionately known, is also nicknamed the Port of Milan as it is popular with well-heeled Milanese and, as a consequence, there are lots of upmarket hotels and good restaurants. That said the fishermen still mend their nets on the pavement near the fish market. There's lovely walking and plenty of watersports. To appreciate Santa Margherita at its best you need to book a room with a sea view and unfortunately that means that there's no real budget option here.

HISTORY Although it was most likely settled in Roman times, Santa Margherita makes its first appearance in the history books when the eastern part of the town, then called Pescino, was sacked by the Lombards in AD641. The Saracens arrived in the 10th century and sacked it a second time. Santa Margherita was taken by Genoa in 1229. As a result, it was attacked by Venetian ships in 1432 and in 1549. At the end of the 18th century, it was Napoleon's turn to take control and it was he, in 1813, who united the two towns Pescino and Corte, to create Porto Napoleone. Two years later, when it was annexed to the Kingdom of Sardinia, Santa Margherita got its original name back. In the past, the townsfolk made a living making lace and fishing for coral in the sea off Sardinia.

The town has long been a Mecca for writers. Luigi Pirandello, Eleonora Duse and Margaret Duley (the first Newfoundland writer) all stayed at the Imperiale Palace Hotel. Friedrich Nietzsche, André Gide and Samuel Beckett also visited when they stayed in neighbouring Rapallo. Many famous Hollywood stars like Clark Gable and Tyrone Power have also holidayed here over the years. Santa Margherita was also the hometown of poet Camillo Sbarbaro.

GETTING THERE AND AROUND
By bike You can sign up for the bike-sharing scheme at **URP** [102 B2] (Piazza Mazzini 46; ☉ 08.30–12.30 Mon–Fri & 15.00–17.00 Wed).

By boat The marina has 350 berths (🕾 0185 293697; e santamargheritaligure@ guardiacostiera.it). **Ferries** leave for the Cinque Terre, San Fruttuoso, Portofino and Rapallo (w traghettiportofino.it), and in summer for Genoa's old port. You can rent boats, hire a boat with a skipper and order a taxi boat from **Cantieri Sant'Antorsola** [102 D3] (🕾 0185 282687; m 348 359 1488; e cantieri@cantierisantorsola.it; w cantierisantorsola.it).

By bus Bus 82 leaves every 20 minutes from the station for Portofino and buses for Recco, Camogli, Ruta and Rapallo leave from the seafront by the tourist office.

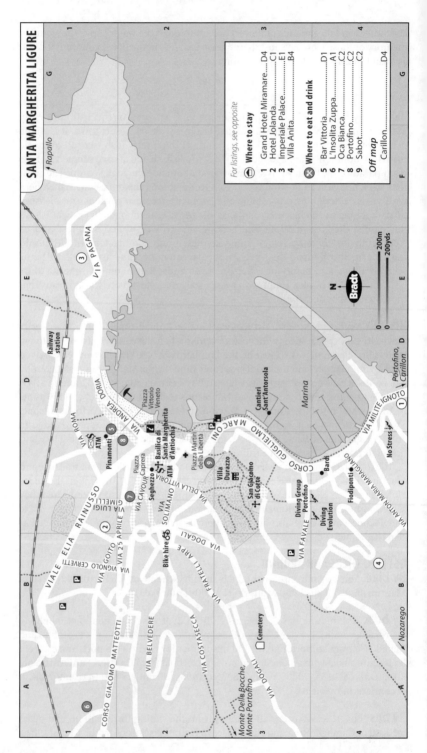

SANTA MARGHERITA LIGURE

For listings, see opposite

Where to stay
1 Grand Hotel Miramare.....D4
2 Hotel Jolanda.............C1
3 Imperiale Palace..........E1
4 Villa Anita...............B4

Where to eat and drink
5 Bar Vittoria..............D1
6 L'Insolita Zuppa..........A1
7 Oca Bianca................C2
8 Portofino.................C2
9 Sabot.....................C2

Off map
Carillon..................D4

0   200m
0   200yds

N

Bradt

102

A shuttle bus goes up to Villa Durazzo every 20 minutes from Piazza Martiri della Libertà for €1.50.

By car Santa Margherita is 35km from Genoa just off the A12 *autostrada*.

By taxi Local taxis are available (m 347 017 6022).

By train Santa Margherita is on the main Genoa–La Spezia line.

TOURIST INFORMATION The main office is on Piazza Vittorio Veneto, right on the seafront [102 D2] (📞 0185 287485; w comune.santa-margherita-ligure.ge.it), and has information on the wide range of watersports available and hiking maps of the Parco Naturale Regionale di Portofino. Diving is offered by No Stress [102 D4] (m 347 420 8543), Diving Group Portofino [102 C4] (Via Favale 25; 📞 0185 282578; w dg.portofino.com), and Diving Evolution [102 C4] (Via Favale 31; m 348 003 7428; w divingevolution.com).

WHERE TO STAY

🏠 **Grand Hotel Miramare** [102 D4] (84 rooms) Via Milite Ignoto 30; 📞 0185 287013; e miramare@grandhotelmiramare.it; w grandhotelmiramare.it. Laurence Olivier & Vivien Leigh honeymooned here in 1947 & the hotel still has a glitzy feel. It was one of the first big hotels opened on this part of the Riviera & in 1933 Marconi sent the first radio signals over 140km from here. Be sure to book a room with a sea view, which is stunning, & on the lower floors for a balcony. Cooking courses. Free Wi-Fi. €€€€

🏠 **Imperiale Palace** [102 E1] (89 rooms) Via Pagana 19; 📞 0185 288991; e info@imperialepalacehotel.com; w imperialepalacehotel.com. The villa was built in 1889 for the aristocratic Costa family, & became a hotel in the early 1900s. It's decorated in Liberty style & is one of the sights to see in Santa Margherita. There's an exotic garden, a seawater swimming pool & a terrace with views across the bay. Wi-Fi at a charge. €€€€

🏠 **Villa Anita** [102 B4] (12 rooms) Viale Minerva 25; 📞 0185 286543; e info@hotelvillaanita.com; w hotelvillaanita.com. A Liberty-style villa with a garden & a small pool. Book a room with a balcony & sea view, although the rooms are somewhat basic. Free Wi-Fi. Close to the starting point for walks across Monte Portofino. €€€

🏠 **Hotel Jolanda** [102 C1] (50 rooms) Via Luisito Costa 6; 📞 0185 287512; w hoteljolanda. it. Central location, minutes from the sea & the railway station. Simple hotel rooms & fitness centre. €€

WHERE TO EAT AND DRINK

Bar Vittoria [102 D1] (Via Gramsci 43) is a wonderfully old-fashioned place run by the same family since 1941, and sells delicious ice creams. If you are looking for picnic supplies, **Portofino** [102 C2] (Via Gramsci 15) has ready-made food and sells good, fresh pasta. There is dancing at **Carillon** [102 D4] (Via Paraggi a Mare 10) and live music at **Sabot** [102 C2] (Piazza Martiri della Libertà 32).

✗ **Oca Bianca** [102 C2] Via XXV Aprile 21, 📞 0185 288411; e info@ocabianca.it; 📘; ⏲ closed Mon, dinner only. This is the place to come for meat dishes & it's not for vegetarians. It's a good alternative to all the fish restaurants that dominate the restaurant scene along the coast. Rack of lamb, duck & steak are centre stage. €€€€

✗ **L'Insolita Zuppa** [102 A1] Via Romana 7; 0185 289594; ⏲ Thu–Tue dinner only. Good simple restaurant away from the tourist part of town. Their speciality is homemade ravioli. €€€

SHOPPING There's a daily fruit and vegetable market. The fish market is on Via Bottaro facing the port. Alternatively nearby **Bardi** [102 C4] (Via Bottaro 23) salts its own anchovies by the pot. The best bakery is **Fiordiponti** [102 C4] (Via Ruffini 26). **Seghezzo** [102 C2] (Via Cavour 1) is a gourmet Aladdin's cave. The homemade amaretti biscuits that made the shop famous are called *ricci* – sea urchins. **Pinamonti** [102 C1] (Via dell'Arco 24), sells the best focaccia.

OTHER PRACTICALITIES There is an **ATM** at Piazza Caprera 22. The **post office** is at Via dell'Arco 40. You can find the **pharmacy** at Piazza Martiri della Libertà 2. The closest **hospital** is in Rapallo.

WHAT TO SEE AND DO The main landmark on the seafront is the castle built by the Genoese in 1550 to defend the town against pirates. In the old town in Piazza Caprera, the **Basilica di Santa Margherita d'Antiochia** was built in 1658 on the remains of a 13th-century church. It is famous for its little statue, the *Madonna del Rosario*. Santa Margherita was the birthplace of famous wood-carver Maragliano and in the church of **San Giacomo di Corte**, on the hillside above the town, is his exquisite statue of the Madonna. It is paraded through the streets on Good Friday.

The Renaissance **Villa Durazzo** (Piazzale San Giacomo 3; ✆ 0185 93135; w villadurazzo.it; ⊕ 09.30–18.00 daily; admission €5.50) is a classic example of the villas that were built here by rich Genoese merchants in the 16th and 17th centuries. It is up on San Giacomo hill set in a beautiful park full of exotic plants, lemon trees, camellias and statues. Under the palm trees there are lovely views across the harbour. It is also home to the library that belonged to Vittorio Rossi, a travel writer and journalist, who wrote extensively about Liguria.

Up on the top of the hill to the west is the village of **Nozarego**. It is the starting point for a lovely walk on the Portofino promontory and the church of **Santa Maria Assunta**, built in 1725, has paintings by the Ligurian master painter, Luca Cambiaso. The beach in Santa Margherita is shingle.

You can walk to the Portofino promontory by taking the footpath from Via Costasecca. It leads up to Monte Delle Bocche. From here you can either walk on the Camogli and catch the train back or return to Santa Margherita on the path that leads through Nozarego. Paths also lead down to Portofino from where you can catch the bus back. Ask for a map from the tourist office (page 103) before you leave. It takes 2 hours to walk from Nozarego to Portofino. The path goes through Gave, Molini and Olmi.

THUS SPOKE ZARATHUSTRA

Ill health brought the German poet and philosopher Nietzsche to the Riviera and long walks in the hills inspired his famous work, *Thus Spoke Zarathustra*. In December 1883, he wrote to his friend Peter Cast, 'My kingdom now extends from Portofino to Zoagli, I live in the middle, that is in Rapallo, but my daily walks take me to the borders of my kingdom. The principal mountain of this zone, which one must climb from my residence, is called Mount Allegro, a fitting name'. Nietzsche spent the rainy cold winter of 1883 in a little hotel, the Marsala, now Hotel Vesuvio. At night the crashing of the waves prevented him from sleeping and he spent the nights writing his masterpiece.

ALONG THE COAST FROM SANTA MARGHERITA The narrow coast road, the S227, runs west to Portofino 9km away and is one of the loveliest in Liguria. It is a single-track road in parts and is controlled by traffic lights. The road passes the **Abbazia di San Girolamo della Cervara** (800 652110; e visite@cervara.it; w cervara. it; ⊕ guided tours 1st & 3rd Sun of the month at 10.00, 11.00 & noon or by appointment), which was founded in 1361. Renaissance poet, Petrarch stayed here and French king François I was held prisoner in the abbey after the Battle of Pavia in 1525. It is now a wedding and conference venue. Miniature **Paraggi** hides away in a small emerald-coloured sandy cove nestled into the hills of Nozarego, just over 2km from Santa Margherita. Surrounded by lush forests with its own castle (now a private house), it was once a fishing village. Today, it makes most of its money from tourism and has just 16 permanent inhabitants. It is a small slice of paradise, but beware as the beach concessions here are very pricey. If you want to stop here on weekends and in high season, it pays to take the bus as parking is impossible.

PORTOFINO

Portofino's tall colourful houses curve around the bay in a cove that forms a perfect miniature harbour protected from behind by steep green hills. When Frederic Lees arrived here in 1912, Portofino was famous for fish and lacemaking. He found it 'as snug and as sunny a little port as ever a mariner could desire, and so picturesque that I know not where you would find a prettier'. The charm of the place was to watch the women sitting on cushions under the porticoes with their bobbins clicking away.

Late Victorian writers gushed about the beauty of the village, not without reason, and began a process that turned this sleepy little harbour into a celebrity Mecca. The woods behind are dotted with the villas of the rich and famous. That said, it is still one of the most picturesque spots in Liguria and best seen out of the main summer holiday season when streams of tourists descend on it during the day.

HISTORY The Phoenicians recognised the importance of its beautiful and secure natural harbour as did the Romans, who called it Portus Delphini, the dolphin port. Portofino was discovered at the end of the 19th century by the British, who fell in love with it to such an extent that architect Sir Clough Williams-Ellis built his own version, Portmeirion in north Wales, between 1925 and 1975. (He denied that it was based specifically on Portofino, however.)

One of the reasons Portofino retains much of its charm is that since 1935 it has been a natural park and thus protected from overdevelopment. At the end of World War II, Portofino narrowly escaped being blown sky high by the Germans. It was saved by Jeannie von Mumm, the Glaswegian wife of Baron von Mumm of the champagne family, who had a villa there. Over a long Ligurian lunch she persuaded the Nazi officer in charge that it was not such a bright idea. In the 1950s and 60s film stars and celebrities flocked to Portofino and still do, many of them marrying in the Castello Brown.

GETTING THERE AND AROUND
By boat From April to October ferries (w traghettiportofino.it) run daily from Portofino to San Fruttuoso, Camogli, Rapallo and Santa Margherita. The marina has limited berths and is one of the most expensive moorings in Italy (0185 269580; e info@marinadiporto.com; w marinadiportofino.com). Glass-bottomed boat trips are popular and the boat taxis in the harbour offer snorkelling and sightseeing trips. Tricoli Charter (m 335 662 5125; w tricolicharter.com) run a

4

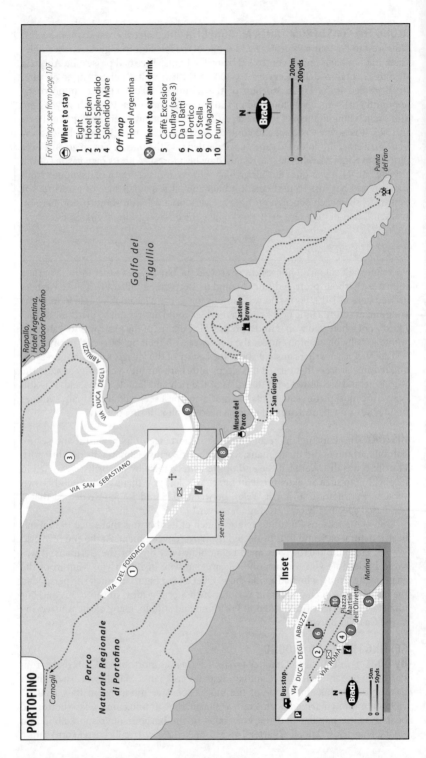

PORTOFINO

For listings, see from page 107

Where to stay
1 Eight
2 Hotel Eden
3 Hotel Splendido
4 Splendido Mare

Off map
Hotel Argentina

Where to eat and drink
5 Caffè Excelsior
Chuflay (see 3)
6 Da U Batti
7 Il Portico
8 Lo Stella
9 O Magazin
10 Puny

Parco
Naturale Regionale
di Portofino

Golfo del
Tigullio

Rapallo,
Hotel Argentina,
Outdoor Portofino

Camogli

VIA DUCA DEGLI ABRUZZI

VIA SAN SEBASTIANO

VIA DEL FONDACO

see inset

Museo del
Parco

San Giorgio

Castello
Brown

Punta
del Faro

Inset

Bus stop

VIA DUCA DEGLI ABRUZZI

VIA ROMA

Piazza
Martiri
dell'Olivetta

Marina

taxi-boat service, rent boats and offer fishing trips, as do Motor Marine (`0185 288408; w motormarine.com).

By bus The 82 bus goes to Santa Margherita train station every 20 minutes from the main square.

By car Portofino is 47km from Genoa. Take the Rapallo exit from the A12 then the S227. The car park is pricey and cash only: another good reason to take the boat or bus from Santa Margherita. Note, the road to Portofino was severely damaged in November 2018 and at time of writing was closed.

On foot One of the nicest ways to reach Portofino is on foot, following the footpaths from Santa Margherita and Camogli, which have the closest train stations.

TOURIST INFORMATION At Via Roma 35 (` 0185 269024). The big event is the festival of San Giorgio on 23 April. They have free maps of the Parco Naturale Regionale di Portofino and information on bike and boat rental. On 24 June, the story goes that the ghosts of lovers divided by fate meet on Monte Portofino where the four footpaths cross. In May there are two regattas: the Rolex Trophy is with period wooden boats; and the SIAD-Bombola d'Oro Trophy is with 4m dinghies.

WHERE TO STAY *Map, opposite*

Eight Hotel (18 rooms) Via del Fondaco 11; `0185 26991; e info@portofino.eighthotels.it; w portofino.eighthotels.it. Smart boutique hotel in a classic Ligurian building. Excellent service, Bulgari toiletries & the rooms have parquet floors. Jacuzzi, sun beds & a shady garden. Book a superior room with a balcony. Free Wi-Fi. €€€€€

Hotel Splendido (64 rooms) Viale Baratta 16; `0185 267801; e reservations.spl@belmond.com; w hotelsplendido.com; ⏀ Apr–mid-Oct. This is where the Hollywood movie stars who made Portofino famous stayed. The golden guestbook is a list of the rich & famous. Wallis Windsor is the first signature just ahead of that of her husband, former British king Edward VIII. There are all the amenities that you would expect in a luxury hotel & the restaurant is top class. The views make the stay. The hotel has a sister, the

Splendido Mare in the harbour; prices are the same. €€€€€

Hotel Eden (8 rooms) Via Dritto 18; `0185 269091; e edenportofino@yahoo.it; w hoteledenportofino.com. It's a basic, rather 1970s hotel that comes at twice the price you might expect to pay elsewhere, but the staff are friendly & if you don't want to pay exorbitant prices this is your best bet. There's a small garden. Free Wi-Fi. €€€

Hotel Argentina (12 rooms) Via Paraggi a Monte 56, Paraggi; `0185 286708; e info@argentinaportofino.it; w argentinaportofino.it. Paraggi is such a beautiful place that this 2-star with a 5-star welcome & surroundings is a lovely place to stay at a more affordable price. If you can, book room 16 at the top with a sea view. No AC. €€

WHERE TO EAT AND DRINK *Map, opposite*

Everything in Portofino comes at a premium so, if you don't have a movie-star budget, the best thing to do is to bring a picnic and eat it on the harbourside or on one of the lovely walks above the town. Also, unless you can afford one of the top-end establishments like the restaurant at the Splendido Mare, the food is some of the worst quality in Liguria. Rather bizarrely the local dish here is *spaghetti poveri*, poor man's spaghetti. Portofino's residents once eked out a meagre living. *Povero* in fact really means 'simple', made from ingredients at hand, and this spaghetti is made with anchovies and local wild herbs, which grow in abundance on Monte Portofino. When the rich from Lombardy and Piedmont began to spend time here after World War II they brought with them a taste for rich cheeses and one tasty hybrid that now appears on menus is *lasagne Portofino*, a lasagne with pesto and gorgonzola cheese. Stop for a drink at **Caffè Excelsior** (Piazza Martiri dell'Olivetta 54) in the romantic booths where Greta Garbo used to drink her coffee.

✗ **Chuflay** Salita Baratta 16; ☎ 0185 267802. Glitzy place overlooking the harbour for the full Portofino experience in the Hotel Splendido. Those who have eaten here include Rod Stewart & James Cameron. Fish & meat dishes but also vegetarian options. €€€€

✗ **Da U Batti** Vicolo Nuovo 17; ☎ 0185 269379. This restaurant is far less touristy as it is not on the seafront. It is known for its shrimps – ask for *scampi alla batti*. €€€

✗ **Lo Stella** Molo Umberto 3; ☎ 0185 269007; e ristorantestella@ymail.com. Has been in the Gazzolo family for 8 generations. Plenty of fish dishes & homemade pasta, with a terrace with beautiful views across the harbour. €€€

✗ **O Magazin** 34 Calata Marconi; ☎ 0185 269178. On the beautiful quayside, from Apr to Sep you can eat on the deck, just metres from the sea. Combining glamour with romance, the restaurant has lovely views of the church & the castle. €€€

✗ **Puny** Piazza Martiri dell'Olivetta 5; ☎ 0185 269037; ⊕ closed Thu. Puny serves tasty homemade pappardelle with pesto & tomato sauce & delicious octopus. Its location & harbour views make this a Portofino favourite, so be sure to book. €€€

✗ **Il Portico** Via Roma 21; ☎ 0185 269239; ⊕ closed Tue. Pizza & fish dishes on the main street near the post office. €€

OTHER PRACTICALITIES Everything you might need is near the car park – the **bank**, the **post office** and the **pharmacy**.

WHAT TO SEE AND DO Portofino is, first and foremost, a place to be seen, and where it is all about cutting a *bella figura*, but all this comes with a price tag. There's no need, however, to spend a fortune to enjoy the beauty of the place.

To see Portofino at its best walk up to the 12th-century church of **San Giorgio**, which stands high up above the harbour. The church was once a Roman sanctuary and served as a lookout post. Portofino's Crusaders brought back the relics of St George, which were kept in the crypt. Jeannie von Mumm, who saved Portofino from being blown up in World War II, is buried here. The church was damaged in the war and rebuilt in 1950. From here the path leads to the **Castello Brown** (m 335 837 1156; w castellobrown.com; 10.00–18.00, until 19.00 summer; admission €5). It was built in the 1500s, on the site of a Roman building and was a strategically important point in Genoa's defences guarding the Golfo del Tigullio. In the late 19th century, it was the home of the British consul in Genoa, Montague Yeats Brown, who gave it its name. The family sold the castle to the local council in 1965. Just beyond it a path leads down to the public beach. There's a beautiful walk, which takes about 10 minutes, to Punta del Capo. Even on a busy day in summer the majority of people stop at the church so you will have time, in peace, to capture the essence of the place, which inspired the book, *Enchanted April* by Elizabeth von Arnim. There are lovely views down to the sea through the pine trees. At the end there's a lighthouse and a café with a stunning view. Be warned the café has no toilet!

On the western side of the harbour, the **Museo del Parco** (Molo Umberto I; m 337 333737; w museodiportofino.it; ⊕ Jun–Sep 10.00–13.00 & 15.00–19.00 Wed–Mon; admission €5) is one of the biggest outdoor sculpture museums in Italy and is surrounded by the garden created by Baron Mumm of the champagne family. He lived in the large white villa above the harbour.

The sea is the big draw here, as well as the walking. **Outdoor Portofino** (Via Duca degli Abruzzi 62, Località Niasca; m 334 329 0804; e info@outdoorportofino. com; w outdoorportofino.com) offers snorkelling and kayak tours led by marine biologists and local experts, as well as sea camps for kids, and marine culture and sailing courses.

RAPALLO

Set in a curving bay below Montallegro, Rapallo's mild climate attracted the Genoese aristocracy who built the villas that dot the hills. Today, affluent Italians living in the northwest weekend here all year round. The golf course is one of the oldest in Italy and there are plenty of places to stay. There is a lively seaside promenade, with a miniature castle and a pretty old town with some good shops. The grand villas on the seafront are surprisingly rather neglected, and there was a spurt of overbuilding here in the 1960s, although even at the beginning of the 20th century Frederic Lees complained about Rapallo's 'moderness'. Today's modern town, however, lies behind the old one in the valley and if you stay here you won't really have anything to do with it.

HISTORY Rapallo gets its first mention in the history books in AD964. In 1229 it came under Genoese control and ships from Rapallo took part in the famous Battle of Meloria in 1284 when the Genoese inflicted a heavy defeat on the Pisans. During the 16th century it was attacked and sacked by Barbary pirates, among them the famous Dragut. For more information on Barbary Pirates, see: w bradtguides.com/ pirates. In the Napoleonic Wars, the French army had some fierce clashes here with

A WRITER'S PARADISE

Rapallo has a rich literary history. English author, caricaturist and parodist Max Beerbohm lived in the Villino Chiaro from 1910 until his death in 1956, returning to Britain during the two world wars. The influential theatre designer and artist Gordon Craig lived in the Villa Raggio, next door to Beerbohm, from 1917 to 1928. Clustered around them, there was a lively literary circle.

American writers in particular were drawn here. Perhaps the most notorious of the town's foreign residents was American poet, Ezra Pound, who lived on the seafront in the attic over the Caffè Rapallo from 1925 to 1945 and in nearby Zoagli from 1962 to 1972. It was here that he wrote his epic, *The Cantos*. A convinced supporter of Mussolini, he made numerous radio broadcasts during World War II condemning his native America and the Jews. As a result he was arrested in 1945 and detained by the US Counter Intelligence Corps in Via Fieschi in Genoa. Poet James Laughlin stayed in Rapallo in 1934 on Corso Colombo 34, where W B Yeats had lived in 1929–30.

Ernest Hemingway stayed in the Hotel Riviera in February 1923 where he set his famous short story, *Cat in the Rain*. William Faulkner also set part of his unfinished novel, *Elmer*, in Rapallo. Poet Robert Lowell visited Rapallo in 1954 with his mother who died there. He sailed back to America with her coffin, an event recorded in his poem *Sailing Home from Rapallo*.

Rapallo hosts two big literary events: the annual National Literary Award, dedicated to woman writers in June; and the International Cartoon Festival in September.

the Austrians. In the 19th century, things were a lot more peaceful and Rapallo became a holiday destination for tourists from northern Europe.

In late 1917, an Anglo–Franco–Italian conference met at Rapallo following the disastrous Italian defeat at Caporetto and the decision was taken to shift some British and French forces to the Italian front. On 12 November 1920, Italy and the Kingdom of the Serbs, Croats and Slovenes (later renamed Yugoslavia) signed the Treaty of Rapallo in the Villa Spinola, which settled the border disputes between the two without reference to the other Allies. Italy's northeastern border was now formed by the strategically important Julian Alps. In 1922, Rapallo again made diplomatic history when the Russo–German Treaty of Rapallo, in which both countries renounced claims to war reparations and renewed diplomatic relations, marked the emergence of the two countries from the diplomatic isolation caused by World War I and the Russian Revolution.

GETTING THERE AND AROUND

By boat In summer ferries (w traghettiportofino.it) connect Rapallo with Santa Margherita, Portofino, San Fruttuoso, the Cinque Terre, Porto Venere and Sestri Levante. There are two marinas: the Carlo Riva has 400 berths (✆ 0185 6891); and the public port, 517 berths (✆ 0185 50583; e rapallo@guardiacostiera.it). There's a taxi boat service in the harbour.

By bus Buses go to Recco about every 45 minutes, to Santa Margherita every 15 minutes and to Zoagli every 30 minutes. Buses leave from the train station.

By car Rapallo is on the A12 *autostrada*, 39km east of Genoa.

By taxi Local taxis are available by calling ✆ 0185 55858.

By train Rapallo railway station, opened in 1868, is on the Genoa–La Spezia main line, 50 minutes from Genoa.

TOURIST INFORMATION (Lungomare Vittorio Veneto 7; ✆ 0185 23 0346; w comune. rapallo.ge.it) On 2 July the big event is the festival of the Holy Virgin of Montallegro, when the whole town makes its way up to the sanctuary of Nostra Signora di Montallegro, 612m up in the mountains, and there is a massive firework display. If you want to dive, visit **Motonautica Ligure** (✆ 0185 231017; w motonauticaligure. it) or **Abyss Diving Centre** (✆ 0185 282578; w abyssdiving.it).

WHERE TO STAY *Map, opposite, unless otherwise stated*

⌂ **Hotel Excelsior Palace** (131 rooms & suites) Via San Michele di Pagana 8; ✆ 0185 230666; e excelsior@excelsiorpalace.it; w excelsiorpalace.it. This grand old *fin-de-siècle* hotel is the best place to stay in the Rapallo area & is in San Michele di Pagana. It has stunning sea views, a beach club & swimming pool. There are 2 restaurants although 1 is closed in winter. One of the first films to be shot outdoors was partially set on the terrace. Be sure to book a room with a sea view & balcony to get the best out of a visit. Fee for Wi-Fi. €€€

⌂ **Hotel Italia e Lido** (50 rooms) Lungomare Castello 1, 16035; ✆ 0185 50492; e info@italiaelido.com; w italiaelido.com. This basic, family-run hotel that opened in 1936, right in front of the castle, is the best budget option. Only stay if you can get a room with a sea view as rooms at the back look on to the noisy road. Those that do look on to the sea, right on the beach, are a bargain but b/fast leaves something to be desired. €€

⌂ **Hotel Montallegro** [map, page 94] (13 rooms) Salita al Santuario 22; ✆ 0185

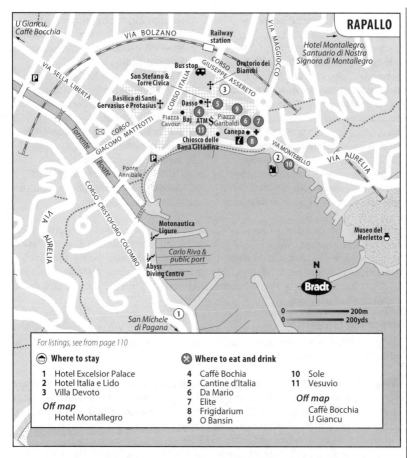

RAPALLO

For listings, see from page 110

🛏 **Where to stay**

1 Hotel Excelsior Palace
2 Hotel Italia e Lido
3 Villa Devoto

Off map

   Hotel Montallegro

🍴 **Where to eat and drink**

4 Caffè Bochia
5 Cantine d'Italia
6 Da Mario
7 Elite
8 Frigidarium
9 O Bansin
10 Sole
11 Vesuvio

Off map

   Caffè Bocchia
   U Giancu

50268; e hotelmontallegro@gmail.com;
w hotelmontallegro.com; ⊕ Jun–Sep & Easter.
A peaceful setting on the path up to the sanctuary
with beautiful views across the mountains & the
sea. There is a Genova Gourmet certified restaurant
(€€€) with a set menu, exc drinks. **€€**

🛏 **Villa Devoto** (3 rooms) Vai Magenta
42 (approach by car from Via Alla Torre Civica);
m 342 664 8550; w villadevoto-rapallo.it. B&B
in a beautiful villa with exquisite frescoes in a
great central location. Parking & garden. Use of
fridge in kitchen. Good for families. **€€**

🍴 **WHERE TO EAT AND DRINK** *Map, above, unless otherwise stated*

There are branches of the local chain **Caffè Bocchia**, on Via Guiseppe Mazzini and
at Via Mameli 261. There's a fantastic array of sweets if you are with children. The
Cantine d'Italia, Via Mazzini 59, is a Rapallo institution, which opened in 1910
and has a wide range of the Riviera's best wines. For ice cream, try **Frigidarium**
opposite the castle. **Sole**, right in front of the castle, is a good spot for a coffee or an
evening drink and also serves some good food, if you fancy staying on.

🍴 **Da Mario** Piazza Garibaldi 23; ☎0185
51736; ⊕ closed Mon. Part of the Genova
Gourmet initiative, it specialises in locally sourced
fish dishes. **€€€**

🍴 **Elite** Via Milite Ignoto 9; ☎0185 50551.
Away from the seafront, this family-run
restaurant serves predominantly fish dishes, but
has meat & vegetarian options as well. **€€€**

✕ U Giancu [map, page 94] Località San Massimo, Via San Massimo 78; ☏ 0185 261212; e ugiancu@mac.com; e ugiancu.it; ⊕ closed mid-Dec–mid-Jan & Wed & Mon–Sat lunch, this sometimes changes so always call. This is a cult restaurant on a hilltop 5km above Rapallo with a great atmosphere. Fausto Oneto was literally brought up in the kitchen of his parents' restaurant, which he now runs. He's a comic book (*fumetti*) fanatic & the restaurant is decorated with cartoons. He's a real character & changes his brightly coloured hats numerous times throughout the evening. He's written a cookbook that's illustrated with cartoons & there are recipes on the website.

He uses vegetables from his own garden when he can & even has a kids' playground. The restaurant's motto is 'everyone's welcome'. Fausto also gives cooking lessons. Always book. €€€

✕ O Bansin Via Venezia 105; ☏ 0185 231119; ⊕ closed Mon & Sun evening. This is the only authentic trattoria in town serving classic Ligurian fare like *ravioli di borragine*. The restaurant opened in 1907. The lunch menu, which changes daily, is especially good value at €10. €€

✕ Vesuvio Lungomare Vittorio Veneto 29; ☏ 0185 271304; e vesuvio2010@live.it ; ⊕ closed Tue. Good budget option with pizza & local dishes on the seafront. €

SHOPPING **Market day** is Thursday. There is a large supermarket by the river at the western side of town. **Dasso**, Piazza Venezia 31, sells excellent fresh *pansotti*, ravioli stuffed with herbs. **Baj**, Via Mazzini 13, is a long-established pastry shop with a wonderful old-fashioned interior. Their speciality is *baci di Rapallo*, chocolate hazelnut kisses. **Canepa**, Piazza Garibaldi 41, founded in 1862, make cakes called *cubeletti* filled with jam.

OTHER PRACTICALITIES There is an **ATM** at Lungomare Vittorio Veneto 26, and the **post office** is at Monsignor Cesare Boccoleri 12. There's a **pharmacy** at Via Milite Ignoto 1 (☏ 0185 231063).

WHAT TO SEE AND DO Art Nouveau cafés with glass verandas line the **Lungomare Vittorio Veneto**, recalling the town's elegant past, so to get into the spirit of things stop for a coffee or an *aperitivo*. The bandstand, the **Chiosco della Banda Cittadina**, in the Piazza, with its beautifully frescoed ceiling, was built in 1929. The money was donated by locals who had emigrated to Chile.

The most striking feature on the seafront is the miniature castle. It was built in 1551 to defend the town from pirates. It was used as a prison until the 20th century and is now an exhibition centre. There is a free shingle beach below if you fancy a dip.

The main street in the old town, Via Mazzini, begins on the western side of the roundabout in Piazza Garibaldi opposite the castle. In the old town there are some nice shops and two interesting churches. The church of **San Stefano** on Via Magenta was founded in 1155. The adjacent **Torre Civica** was built in 1473. There is not much to see inside but there's an interesting collection of processional crosses in the **Oratorio dei Bianchi**. The **Basilica di Santi Gervasius e Protasius** on Piazza Cavour was consecrated in 1118 and restored in the 17th century when a new apse was added. There are paintings by Liguria's top religious painters, Cambiaso and Fiasella. To the west of Rapallo, the church of **San Michele di Pagana** has a painting, *The Crucifixion*, by Van Dyck, who spent nine years in Liguria. Finish a visit to the old town with a look at the medieval Ponte Annibale to the north just off the Via Aurelia. It is also a good spot for a dip in the sea.

Until the tourists came this was essentially a fishing village and, while their husbands were at sea, the women of Rapallo busied themselves with lace making. Lace, from the 16th to the 20th centuries, is on display in the **Museo del Merletto** (☏ 0185 608604; ⊕ 09.00–20.00 Mon–Fri, 09.30–19.00 Sat, 09.30–19.00 Sun; free) in Villa Tigullio to the east of town, including a decorative panel by the Genoese set designer, Emanuele Luzzati. If you're with kids, there's a nice playground with a miniature castle and minigolf in the Parco Casale that surrounds it.

A must is the funicular ride up to the **Santuario di Nostra Signora di Montallegro** (✆ 0185 239000; ⊕ 08.00–17.00 daily; summer until 18.00), where the Virgin Mary appeared to a peasant called Giovanni Chighizola in 1557. The Virgin told him where he could find the icon depicting Mary's transition in the presence of the Holy Trinity, which was supposedly brought from Greece by angels. The church was built to house it and completed by 1559. It was restored in the 17th century; the bell tower was added in 1757 and the stairs in 1896. Inside, there is a vast array of votive offerings including a stuffed crocodile that attacked a missionary from Rapallo in the Congo, who was lucky to escape and brought it home to say thanks to the Virgin Mary. There's also an old master by Luca Cambiaso, and masses of ex-votos from sailors. Taking a trip up here is a good way of experiencing Liguria's mountains if you don't have a car. It takes about an hour to walk back down the path but wear proper walking shoes. The cable car runs every half an hour from 09.00 to 16.30 for €6.50 return.

ALONG THE COAST FROM RAPALLO Just along the coast is **Zoagli**, a little town in a pretty natural harbour and a nice place to stop for a swim. It is quite unlike other Ligurian fishing villages as it is modern and has a large open square in the middle with little jet fountains, which kids love. On 27 December 1943 Zoagli was nearly destroyed when it was bombed by the RAF and many villagers were killed. The aim was to take out the railway bridge but what commanders didn't know was that bombing raids further along the coast had already rendered the railway unusable.

The railway bridge that brought all the trouble still runs between the town and the beach but it's high up and doesn't really get in the way. The beach is pebbly but free and to each side there is a pleasant walkway along the rocks with lovely views. There's another underwater statue here, the *Madonna del Mare* by Marian Hastianatte, which was placed in the sea in 1996. Her feast day is 6 August. On the road between Rapallo and Zoagli, the Spiaggia del Pozzetto is a great place for a swim.

THE SILK ROAD

The art of making silk and damask velvet arrived in Liguria in the Middle Ages and was brought back from the Near East by Genoese merchants, who imported valuable, soft and delicate fabrics known in Arabic as *kahifet*. Ormesion, *hormus velvet*, is a local speciality and originated in the city of Hormuz on the Persian Gulf.

At first, the cloth was produced in Genoa, but the city's trade guilds had extremely strict rules that prompted the weavers to move along the coast to Zoagli, where the guilds had less control. Here it was also easier to supplement their meagre income by farming and fishing. Thus by the Renaissance, Zoagli had became the hub of an industry that centred around the production of *velour de Genes*, which was an overarching name for a range of damasks, velvets and silks. Cloth made here dressed popes, kings and queens and the finest curtains in Hampton Court Palace near London were woven in Zoagli.

To read about the Cordiani family who have been making silk fabrics since 1849, see: **w** bradtguides.com/kahifet.

⌂ Where to stay, eat and drink

⌂ Castello Canevaro (4 rooms) Via Duce Canevaro 7, Zoagli; ✆ 0185 250015; e thecastle@tin.it; w castellocanevaro.com. This is a B&B with a difference, run by the Duke of Zoagli in a castle perched on the cliffs above Zoagli. Antique furniture, breathtaking views & a beautiful garden. Kitchen. No restaurant as yet, but there are plans to open one; private dinners, however, can be arranged. It is a great place to get married. €€€

⌂ Agriturismo Da U Cantin [map, page 94] (4 rooms) Via San Gaetano, San Colombano Certenoli; ✆ 0185 358578; e ucantin@libero.it; w ucantin.it. This farm in the mountains behind Zoagli produces olive oil, wine, fruit & vegetables. Opt for dinner: the food is classic Ligurian & excellent; a meal is €25. Open to non-residents. €€

USCIO

From Recco take the SP333 to the tiny settlement of Uscio. The Trebino family have been making bells and clocks here since 1824 and their bells hang in the Vatican. There is a small museum in the old workshop (✆ 0185 919410; w trebino.it; ⊕ by appointment). In 1906, pharmacist Carlo Arnaldi founded the Colonia della Salute Arnaldi (Via Carlo Arnaldi 6; ✆ 0185 919406; w coloniaarnaldi.com), the first health farm in Italy, which used his own secret potion. You can stay here for €180 for a double room or just spend the day there being pampered. There are lovely walks in the chestnut forests.

WHERE TO STAY, EAT AND DRINK

⌂ B&B La Margherita (2 rooms & 1 apt) Salita Olivi 12, Uscio; ✆ 0185 91725; e info@margheritauscio.it; w margheritauscio.it. Close to the church in Uscio; has garden with lovely views. There are special rates for early in the week. Swimming pool & barbecue. Mountain bikes & pet friendly. €

⌂ B&B Rifugio Uscio (3 rooms) Uscio Salita Olivi 9, Uscio; m 328 401 5992; e info@rifugiouscio.it; w rifugiouscio.it. There is 1 double room & 2 dormitories. Garden with barbecue. Kitchen. Dorm €; dbl €

✗ Antica Osteria da Rasin Via Michelangelo 5, Avegno (southeast of Uscio); ✆ 0185 79003. The food here is typical Ligurian, but as it's in the mountains there are plenty of mushrooms when in season & excellent pasta made with chestnut flour, *trofiette di castagna al pesto.* Cash only. €€

FURTHER AFIELD From Uscio, take the road to Gattorna and pick up the SS225, which runs down the **Val Fontanabuona**, where connections to the Americas are strong. **Neirone** [map, page 94], just north of Gattorna, celebrates perhaps the greatest gift from the New World, the potato, in a festival that began in 1795, when the potato saved the village from famine. The local lord who had the foresight to introduce the crop had been charged with witchcraft by the locals, who thought the harmless spud was poisonous, which was not uncommon at the time. The *quarantina* potato is one of the oldest varieties grown in the hinterland and is traditionally used to make a potato pie, *baciocca,* which is baked on a layer of chestnut leaves.

Val Fontanabuona is ungentrified and rather rough and ready. The Columbus family hailed from the hamlet of **Terrarossa Colombo**. **Cicagna** [map, page 94], the largest town in the valley, is famous for both its bread and slate. Craftsmen produce all sorts of objects made of slate and roof tiles, which are exported all over the world. There is a small slate museum, the **Museo dell'Ardesia** (Viale Italia 25b; ✆ 0185 971091; ⊕ by appointment; admission charge).

Take the SP85 in the direction of Lorsica then the SP23 to **Favale di Malvaro**. Thousands of people emigrated from the valley to the Americas, and especially Argentina, from here. Garibaldi, the Risorgimento leader, spent a chunk of his life there too and his family hailed from the neighbouring valley. Those who left were usually highly ambitious and went on to make their fortunes. Their stories are remembered in the **Museo di Emigranti** in the Casa Giannini (❬ 0185 975195; ⊕ by appointment, but give a few days' warning). The museum is in the family home of Amadeo Pietro Giannini, who went on to found the Bank of America. On the last Sunday in June the locals throw a party, the Festa dell'Emigranti.

Carry on to **Lorsica**, the silk capital of Liguria. You can find out more in the **Museo del Damasco** (Via Casali 109; ❬ 018 977 3020; ⊕ Apr–Oct 16.00–18.00 Sat–Sun; Nov–Mar 15.00–17.00 Sat–Sun; admission €3). The museum charts the development of the industry in the area.

One industry that has been revived in recent years here is the cultivation of hazelnuts, *nocciole* (singular *nocciola*) in Italian. The local variety are called *misto chiavari*. They were once used to produce a wide array of foodstuffs, as well as necklaces.

In **Coreglia Ligure** at **Pian dei Manza** is a notice that tells passers-by that this was the site of a concentration camp during World War II. Originally used to hold prisoners of war, the camp had 44 barracks. On 21 January 1944, 29 of Genoa's Jewish citizens were brought here. They were taken to Milan and then deported to Auschwitz. It is good that it is marked by a notice board, as two other similar sites in Liguria are not.

CHIAVARI

At the eastern end of the Golfo del Tigullio, the coast suddenly flattens as the river Entella reaches the sea. It was a spot beloved by the Renaissance poet Dante. Today the coastline here is rather overbuilt and the coast road is often one long traffic jam in summer. Don't be put off, however; Chiavari is a lovely old town and one of Liguria's great food cities, famous for its *farinata*. There are great restaurants and wonderful shops in its ancient arcaded streets.

HISTORY People have lived on this spot since prehistoric times and there was an ancient necropolis here in the 8th century BC. The Romans called it Clavarium, 'key to the valleys'. In 1178 it was taken by the Genoese. In the Middle Ages, it was an important trading post and was surrounded by some of the best walls in Europe. They were demolished in the 18th century to make way for the Palazzo di Giustizia in Piazza Mazzini. One of Genoa's enduring power struggles pitted the Dorias, who

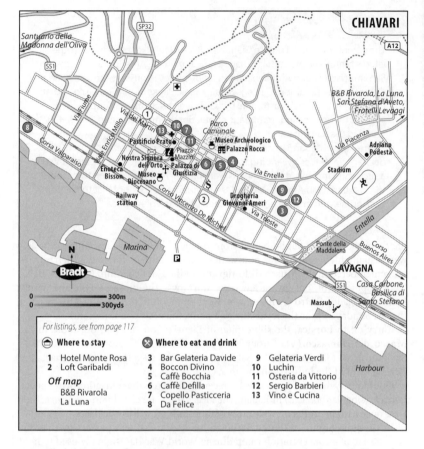

For listings, see from page 117

🛏 Where to stay		✖ Where to eat and drink	
1 Hotel Monte Rosa		**3** Bar Gelateria Davide	**9** Gelateria Verdi
2 Loft Garibaldi		**4** Boccon Divino	**10** Luchin
		5 Caffè Bocchia	**11** Osteria da Vittorio
Off map		**6** Caffè Defilla	**12** Sergio Barbieri
B&B Rivarola		**7** Copello Pasticceria	**13** Vino e Cucina
La Luna		**8** Da Felice	

controlled the city in the 16th century, against the Fieschi, who had a fiefdom that began just across the river Entella, making Chiavari a front-line town.

GETTING THERE AND AROUND

By boat In Lavagna, which has effectively merged with Chiavari, there's a large harbour (↖ 0185 5312626; w portodilavagna.com). With berths for 1,500 boats, it is one of the best equipped in Liguria. Chiavari has a modern marina (↖ 0185 364081; w marina-chiavari.it). Ferries (w traghettiportofino.it) run in summer to Sestri Levante, Portofino and San Fruttuoso. They also organise aperitif trips and pirate cruises for kids. Diving sessions are available from Massub in the tourist port (↖ 0185 599121; m 335 643 5624; w massub.com).

By bus There are buses to Lavagna, just 10 minutes away, and to Rapallo and Sestri Levante, which can be reached in an hour. Buses also go up into the mountains to San Stefano d'Aveto, taking an hour and a quarter.

By car Chiavari is on the main Genoa–La Spezia A12 *autostrada*, 37.5km from Genoa.

By taxi Local taxis are available (↖ 0185 308284).

By train Chiavari is on the main line from Genoa (30 minutes), and La Spezia (43 minutes).

TOURIST INFORMATION Near the train station on Via della Cittadella (✆0185 365400; w www.comune.chiavari.ge.it). Chiavari celebrates its patron saint's day on 2 July and Sant'Antonio on 17 January. There's an antique market every second weekend.

WHERE TO STAY *Map, opposite, unless otherwise stated*

Chiavari isn't somewhere to base yourself for a holiday, but if you want to spend a night or need to be based here, the following are available.

Hotel Monte Rosa (64 rooms) Via Monsignor Marinetti 6; ✆0185 300321; e info@ hotelmonterosa.it; w hotelmonterosa.it. A friendly hotel that opened in 1909 in the old centre, not far from the train station. It has an excellent restaurant. Swimming pool. Wi-Fi. €€€

Loft Garibaldi (3 rooms) Corso Garibaldi 51/4; m 320 221 0328; w loftgaribaldi.com. Friendly hosts in this central stylish apt in a 19th-century building. Use of kitchen. Close to both beach & train station. The owners also have a room in the countryside. €€

B&B Rivarola (2 rooms) Via San Giuseppe 8, Rivarola; m 347 234 7157; w bbrivarola. it. A romantic & relaxing atmosphere, inland of Chiavari. Pet friendly. €

La Luna [map, page 94] (3 rooms) Via Case Sparse 18; ✆0185 382163; e info@bedlaluna. com; w bedlaluna.com. On a hill above Chiavari with views across the sea & surrounded by olive trees. It's run by the friendly Bruce & Pina. Downside is the do-it-yourself b/fast. €

WHERE TO EAT AND DRINK *Map, opposite*

The dish to try here is *ciuppín*, a fish soup made with onions, tomatoes, parsley, white wine, salt and extra virgin olive oil made from Ligurian olives. Originally it was more watery than it is today, as the name *sûppin*, meaning 'a thinner soup', suggests. Little meat fritters, *stecchi di chiavari*, are one of the dishes that made their way here from the Middle East. The local cake is the alcoholic *torta di Chiavari*.

Chiavari has some great cafés and cake shops. The star is **Caffè Defilla** (Corso Garibaldi 4; w grancaffedefilla.com), which has been serving drinks for over a century and is a sight to see with its suite of elegant parquet-floored rooms and the chairs made by local artisans a century ago. The house speciality is the chocolate *sorrisi di Chiavari*. **Caffè Bocchia** (Piazza Matteotti 16; w bocchiacaffe.it) is part of a local chain famous for its array of sweets, tantalisingly displayed at a child's eye-level. **Copello Pasticceria** (Via Martiri della Liberazione 162) opened its doors in 1826 and had an Art Nouveau facelift in 1911. It sells dozens of tiny pastries, among them the *dolcezze di Chiavari*, toasted hazelnut and sponge cakes soaked in liqueur and encased in chocolate. **Bar Gelateria Davide** (Corso Dante 80; 🛈), near the Entella River in the eastern end of town, opened in the 1940s and its loyal customers say this is the best ice cream in town. **Gelateria Verdi** at No 70 isn't bad either and its pistachio ice cream has won awards. **Sergio Barbieri** (Piazza Cavour 10; w www.pandolce.it) produce the classic *pan dolce* Genovese cake.

Boccon Divino Via Entella 18; ✆0185 362964; w boccondivino.info. Traditional simple fish restaurant. Homemade pasta & *cappon magro* are their signature dishes. €€€

Da Felice Corso Valparaiso 136; ✆0185 308016; w ristorantefelice.it; ⊕ closed Mon.

This smart stylish restaurant is the best fish restaurant in Chiavari & has been run by the same family for 25 years. It has the Genova Gourmet certification. €€€

Luchin Via Bighetti 53; ✆0185 301063; w luchin.it. This family-run restaurant is in the arcaded streets in the town centre. Many customers say they make the best *farinata,* which comes in a number of dishes, & they also serve the chickpea polenta, *panissa.* They have their own cookbook & recipes on the website. €€€

✗ **Osteria da Vittorio**   Via Bighetti 33; ☎0185 301093. Opened in 1925, this typical trattoria is the best place to eat *farinata* in Chiavari. €€

✗ **Vino e Cucina**   Via Vecchia Mura 9; ☎0185 305536; e vinoecucina99@gmail.com; ▮; ⏰ closed Mon & Tue lunch. In the old town, this is a great place for vegetarians. Eat outside under the portico. Regional dishes with a modern twist based on a seasonal menu. €€

SHOPPING   The fruit and vegetable market is held on Piazza Mazzini every morning and on the last weekend of the month there's a gourmet market. **Drogheria Giovanni Ameri** (Piazza Roma 27) sells locally produced chestnut flour. **Pastificio Prato** (Via Cittadella 2), founded in 1810, just off the main market square, sells wonderful *corzetti* and fresh sauces. One bottled sauce to look out for is *sugo dei Fieschi,* a blend of duck, guinea fowl and veal. For local wines, try **Enoteca Bisson** (Corso Giannelli 28).

The town has a reputation for its craftwork. The chairs made here are elegant, simple and extraordinarily light and were invented in the 18th century by Giuseppe Gaetano Descalzi. They are also known as Tiffany chairs. French Emperor, Louis Napoleon fell in love with them in the mid 19th century and ordered hundreds of them; there are some in the White House in Washington. Buy them at **Fratelli Levaggi** (Via Parma 469; w levaggisedie.it), and **Adriano Podestà** (Via Gustaldi 17; w podestasedie.com). This is the place to buy leather goods. Macramé has also been made here since the skill was brought back from the Middle East during the Crusades. Chiavari is a well-known shipbuilding centre where they make the classic Ligurian fishing boat, the *gozzo.*

OTHER PRACTICALITIES   There is an **ATM** at Via Martiri della Liberazione 76, and the **post office** is at Piazza Nostra Signora dell'Orto 32. There's a **pharmacy** at Piazza Giuseppe Mazzini 13. The **hospital** is at Via Ghio 9 (☎ 0185 329111).

WHAT TO SEE AND DO   On the other side of the park from the railway station is the temple-style cathedral **Nostra Signora dell'Orto**, built in the 17th century but altered in the 19th and 20th centuries. The façade was added in 1907. Inside are works by Orazio de Ferrari and Anton Maria Maragliano, as well as a painting by Benedetto Borzone of the Virgin, which is said to have miraculous powers. The nearby **Museo Diocesano** (Piazza Nostra Signora dell'Orto 7; ☎ 0185 325250; ⏰10.00–noon Wed & Sun; admission €1) in Palazzo Vescovile has art from the Abbazia di Cervara, near Portofino, Genoese Baroque paintings, and a silk canopy made in China in the 1500s.

Just to the north, **Piazza Mazzini** is the heart of town and the site of the colourful daily food market. To the east runs the main street, the beautifully arcaded **Via dei Martiri**, built in the 14th century. The porticoes are made of locally quarried slate. It leads to **Piazza Matteotti**. On the northern side of the square is the **Palazzo Rocca,** which was designed by Bartolomeo Bianco in 1629. Inside there is the miniature **Museo Archeologico** (Via Costaguta 4; ✆ 0185 320829; ⏲ 09.00–13.30 Tue–Sat; admission free). On display are finds from the necropolis that once stood in the lovely botanical garden below the ruined castle. The **Civica Galleria** (Via Costaguta 2; ✆ 0185 365339; ⏲ 10.00–noon & 16.00–19.00 Sat–Sun; free) is by the park gates and has good examples of Genoese Baroque painting.

Dating from the 14th century, **Santuario della Madonna dell'Olivo**, west of the town, offers great views along the coast and inside there are paintings by two well-known Ligurian artists: Piaggio and Cambiaso.

ALONG THE COAST Across the Entella to the east of Chiavari is **Lavagna**. The two towns are linked by several bridges, including the medieval **Ponte della Maddalena**. Traditionally, Lavagna townsfolk made their living from slate that was mined in the hills above the town. There is a footpath up to the slate quarries on Monte San Giacomo. In Italian *lavagna* means 'blackboard', and many of the medieval buildings are made of slate. The women would carry slabs of slate on their heads down from the quarries to be loaded on to the boats.

Today, the town makes a living out of tourism, as well as building luxury yachts and motorboats, and it is a bit workaday. Do stop, however, to see the **Casa Carbone**, which was the home of Emanuele and Sira Carbone (Via Riboli 14; ✆ 0185 393920; w fondoambiente.it; ⏲ Mar–Jun & Sep–Oct 10.00–18.00 Sat–Sun; Jul–Aug 10.00–

THE CALL OF THE WILD

Horses are a hot topic in this part of Liguria. A small herd of wild horses, some of the locals claim, are causing havoc. Apparently they can't tell a meadow from a vegetable patch and are trampling down crops and destroying fences. It all started when their owner died almost 25 years ago and they were left to fend for themselves. As a result they reverted to the wild. It isn't always a happy story and, in 2009, two of them were shot dead. There are about a hundred wild horses divided into families of eight to ten and they are the only truly wild horses in Italy. Their numbers are dwindling, however, and stories abound of the animals being illegally captured and eaten.

In 2012, naturalist Evelina Isola and, doctor and horse lover, Paola Marinari set up, with the help of the Aveto Park and the WWF, I Cavalli Selvaggi dell'Aveto (Wild Horse Watching), a project that aims to protect the horses and turn them into a tourist attraction.

Wolves are another hot topic in these parts, too. As in other areas of Italy, locals are concerned that they have mated with stray dogs and that a new type of wolf-dog that is not afraid of people has been created. There have been reports of goats being attacked and some of the animals have appeared in villages in broad daylight. It is something to remember if you fancy pitching your tent in the wilds.

If you would like to see the horses, **Wild Horse Watching** organise guided walks from Borzonasca (m 347 381 9395; e icavalliselvaggidellaveto@gmail.com; w wildhorsewatching.webstarts.com).

12.30 & 19.00–22.30 Sat–Sun; admission €5). It is laid out just as it was when they lived there at the end of the 19th century. The old town is overlooked by the **Basilica di Santo Stefano**, built in 1653. Eat *fritto misto* in one of the restaurants on the Via dei Deveto and buy pastries from **Pasticceria Caffetteria Monteverde**, Via Roma 99. There's 4km of sandy beach but unfortunately there is a lot of ugly development and the railway runs the length of the beach, where you can still see the sea-lily planted by Lord Byron.

UP IN THE MOUNTAINS There are four valleys behind Chiavari. The Val Graveglia runs east, parallel to the coast and the Val Fontanabuona to the west (page 114). The Val Sturla runs northwards and across the mountain pass is the Val d'Aveto, where there is beautiful rural countryside with an alpine feel. To explore the mountains behind Chiavari the best thing is to hire a car for a day and make a road trip. Buses do, however, link Chiavari with the main towns.

A short drive up the SP53, or 30 minutes on foot inland, is the village of **San Salvatore di Cogorno** [map, page 94], famous not only for its black potatoes but also for the **Basilica di San Salvatore dei Fieschi**, one of Liguria's most important Romanesque-Gothic monuments. Cogorno was the seat of the Fieschi family, the Counts of Lavagna, and the little complex includes the ruined black-and-white-striped Palazzo dei Fieschi. In 1252 Ottoboni Fieschi commissioned the basilica's construction after he and Pope Innocenzo IV had defeated Emperor Frederick II of Swabia. It is a pretty spot on a little hill surrounded by an olive grove. There's a small museum but there's no indication of when, if ever, it is open.

Val Graveglia The valley takes its name from the river that runs through it, which has its source in Monte Zatta (1,404m), which is the place to pick up the Alta Via dei Monti Liguri. The Garibaldi family hailed from near Zerli, where they grow sweet red onions. The main village in the valley is Ne. It's not much to write home

---

THE FIESCHI END IN FIASCO

From the 13th century to the 16th century, the Fieschi were a powerful bunch, producing two popes: Sinibaldo Fieschi, who became Innocenzo IV; and Ottobono Fieschi, who took the name Adriano V. They also have their own saint, Santa Caterina of Genoa (1447–1510), who worked with the poor and needy, especially when plague ravaged Genoa in 1497.

The Fieschi used the Church as a power-base and the local cardinal was always a family member. This gave them tremendous influence over other important families who usually followed his political line. At the end of the 13th century, the Fieschi founded the town of Varese Ligure on the important trading route to Parma. Niccolò Fieschi, the brother of Innocenzo IV, had dreams of creating a state of his own with its capital in La Spezia. The family were supporters of the Guelphs, and in the battle with the Ghibellines, Niccolò lost his territories in Lunigiana to Genoa. Gian Luigi the Older, his grandson, however amassed a vast fiefdom that included the Pentremoli, now in Tuscany, the Magra Valley, Torriglia and even Loano in western Liguria. As long as they swore allegiance to Genoa all went well.

It didn't last. In 1547, Gian Luigi the Younger organised a plot against Andrea Doria, who was the *de facto* ruler of Genoa and, as a result, all their territory was confiscated and entrusted to the Republic and the Doria family.

about but in the mountains around there's a great B&B and a fantastic restaurant. This is still a mining valley, however, and it is dotted with quarries. At **Reppia** there is an easy walk, the Sentiero Natura Monte Bossea, which takes about 2 hours to walk and takes you up Monte Bossea.

Where to stay, eat and drink

❋ 🏠 **Castagnola 64** (3 rooms) Via Castagnola 64, Ne; m 347 497 9215. There is a lot written about Liguria's winding roads not being for the faint-hearted, but the drive up to this B&B at the top of a mountain is part of the experience. At one point it looks as if the road might peter out altogether & when you arrive there's a long flight of steps up through the garden. The couple who run it, Leo, an Italian, & British Lu, are excellent hosts & cook up some great food. If you plan to picnic, bring everything you need ... it's a long way down. Chill & enjoy the view. There's a small pool & it's good for families with large rooms for up to 4. **€€**

🏠 **Rue de Zerli** [map, page 94] (2 rooms) Località Zerli 51, Ne; ☎0185 334295; w www. ruedezerli.com. Simple rooms in this agriturismo that produces olive oil, fruit, vegetables & chestnut flour. Be sure to try the onion chutney. **€**

✗ **La Brinca** Via Campo di Ne 58, Ne; ☎0185 377480; w labrinca.it. This is a cult restaurant which draws customers from far & wide as it makes some of the best food in Liguria. It serves dishes typical of the valley & uses only local products. **€€€**

Val Sturla The SP586 follows the river up to **Borzonasca**. In nearby Borzone, 4km away, is the **Abbazia di Sant'Andrea** (w abbaziaborzone.it; ⊕ check website for times; admission free). The abbey, built in the Romanesque-Gothic style, is one of the oldest Benedictine settlements in Italy and is built on the ruins of a Roman fortress. It is an unusual building for Liguria, where slate and marble are the norm, as it is made of brick and stone. It was founded in the 12th century by the monks of San Colombano from Bobbio in neighbouring Emilia-Romagna, and donated to the Benedictines of Marseille in 1184. It was rebuilt in the 13th century by the Fieschi. On the road back to Borzonasca is a huge megalithic carving 7m high and 4m wide, the **Grande Volto Megalitico**, a giant face that was once a place of pagan worship.

For something completely different you can climb in the trees at the adventure park **Oasi Belpiano** (Via Belpiano 14, Borzonasca; ☎0185 340012; w oasibelpiano. it). At the top of the valley, the Passo del Bocco, you can pick up the Alta Via dei Monti Liguri if you fancy a walk.

Val d'Aveto From Borzonasca the SP586 zig-zags to **Rezzoaglio** over the Passo della Forcella as the chestnut forests give way to alpine mountain pastures. American writer, Ernest Hemingway was here as a war reporter in 1945 and noted in his diary, 'Today we crossed the most beautiful valley in the world'. At Monasco, south of Rezzoaglio, on the SP654, take a detour to the **Lago delle Lame**. It is a glacial lake and a lovely spot for a picnic in the middle of the woods.

SNOW FOR SALE

In the medieval period the Val Sturla snow was cut into blocks and wrapped in canvas sacks and transported at night to Vico delle Neve, Snow Street, in Genoa. Snow was stored in stone buildings and giant pits on Monte Penello and was used in the great kitchens in Genoa to create ice-cream dishes and to chill food.

The main town of **Santo Stefano d'Aveto** (w www.comune.santostefanodaveto. ge.it) below Monte Maggiorasca (1,799m) is just 20km from the seaside but when it snows you can ski. It is a popular resort throughout the year and clusters around a ruined 12th-century castle. It is popular for cross-country skiing in winter, and in summer people come up from the coast to escape the heat. There are very few foreign tourists who make time to explore this lovely valley and one of the main attractions, along with all the sporting activities, is its food. This is cattle and cheese country, wild game and mushrooms abound and trout are farmed in the rivers. In May there are plenty of spring flowers and the town holds the Sagra dello Spinarolo in honour of the spring mushrooms, *spinaroli*. There is a trout festival on the second Sunday in May and on the last weekend in October the tradition of bringing the animals down from the high pastures is celebrated with the Festa della Transumanza. In early November there is a chestnut festival, the Sagra della Castagna.

This is a place to really enjoy the outdoors in the **Parco Naturale Regionale dell' Aveto** (w www.parks.it/parco.aveto). There's hiking, horseriding, climbing, mountain biking, hang gliding, pot-holing, canoeing and skiing (w sciclubsantostefano.it); ask for full details in the tourist office as times, availability and courses change constantly. The ski lifts work at weekends in July and most days in August, and when it snows, of course. The Val d'Aveto was formed by the Aveto torrent and has a spectacular combination of pine and beech groves, pastures, mountain lakes and high summits, and there are masses of footpaths. Look out for golden eagles and even wolves.

Monte Aiona is the tallest peak in the park (1,701m). There's a pretty walk from the tourist office up to the Fontanabuona. In summer there's a summer sled run in **Rocca d'Aveto**. Don't miss the painting of the *Madonna di Guadalupe* hanging above the altar in the church of **Santi Stefano e Maria**, built in 1928. It was given by the King of Spain to Andrea Doria, who hung the picture from the flagpole of his ship as he sailed to fight the Battle of Lepanto in 1571. There is a statue of the *Madonna di Guadalupe* on **Monte Maggiorasca**.

In **Gramizza** it's possible to visit an old water mill that still grinds grains, chestnuts and corn but, as with many places here, opening times vary according to who can be bothered.

Where to stay, eat and drink The milk of the local cows, the *cabannine*, is used to make both the hard and soft *cabannina* cheese (see box, opposite) and the Aveto Valley is also famous for its rich San Sté cheese, kept in huge yellow rounds weighing between 8kg and 12kg. Look out, too, for *sarasso*, a ricotta-style cheese. A typical local dish is *baciocca*, a potato pie. Buy bread and biscuits and a tasty *pandolce* from **Pasticceria Alimentari Chiesa** (Via Castello 25, Santo Stefano d'Aveto), which opened in 1920.

Residence Grand Hotel Siva (65 rooms) Via Marconi 5, Santo Stefano d'Aveto; m 388 726 6383; w grandhotelsiva.it. This family-run hotel is a little old fashioned but friendly. There are suites with kitchenettes & a swimming pool. Free Wi-Fi. €€

Agriturismo La Casa sul Poggio (5 apts) Via Costigliola 8, Santo Stefano d'Aveto; 0185

FUNGHI EVERYWHERE

Liguria's forests provide a bumper crop of *porcini* mushrooms, *funghi porcini*, which were a favourite of Casanova, and are found all over Liguria, but particularly in the Val Bormida, Val d'Aveto and the Val di Vara. The ideal conditions to grow mushrooms are a mixture of sun and rain, so late summer and autumn is mushroom season. Before heading out to pick them however, it is essential that you have a mushroom licence, a *tesserino*. Ask at the tourist office who sells it in the area where you are.

In Liguria, no more than 5kg of mushrooms may be collected per day, per person. There are no limits on the quantity of mushrooms that may be gathered on private land by the landowner. Mushroom pickers, *fungaioli*, may not use tools that damage the forest floor. There is a hefty fine for those caught breaking this rule. Wicker baskets must be used for collection as opposed to plastic bags, which prevent mushroom spores from being disseminated as pickers walk through the woods.

There is a free service for mushroom pickers wanting to check whether a particular species is edible: **Ispettorato Micologico della ASL** (Via Ghio 9, Chiavari; 0185 329097). In case of poisoning, call an ambulance or go straight to the nearest A&E, the *pronto soccorso*. If possible, take some of the mushrooms, or the remains of the dish eaten. Do not take any drugs, do not attempt to throw up.

88018; **w** lacasasulpoggio.it. This organic dairy & vegetable farm also breeds golden retrievers, & is excellent value. The apts have wood floors & ceilings, adding to the mountain experience. There's a swimming pool, too. €

🏠 **Rifugio Monte Aiona** (50 beds) Monte Aiona; **m** 338 775 9510. Beautiful mountain

setting & there's a good restaurant (dinner €€). €

✖ **Hostaria della Luna Piena** Via Ponte dei Bravi 7, Santo Stefano d'Aveto; 📞 0185 88382. Serves excellent pizza in the evenings (w/ends in winter) & seasonal local dishes, all homemade. €

SESTRI LEVANTE

Back on the coast, life couldn't be more of a contrast. At the most easterly point of the Golfo del Tigullio, the lively, elegant resort of Sestri Levante clusters around a rocky promontory called the Isola. Sestri has two bays and is often also known as Bimare, the two seas. It is a smart upmarket place with some luxury hotels, good shops and cafés, and a lovely sandy beach.

At its heart, the old centre is quintessentially Ligurian with narrow alleyways. On the western side of the Isola, a long promenade extends the length of the sandy **Baia delle Favole**, the Bay of Fables. Hans Christian Andersen stayed here in 1833, hence the name. On the eastern side is the smaller **Baia del Silenzio**, the Bay of Silence, framed by multi-coloured houses that sit right on the beach. It is a lovely place to swim.

HISTORY Sestri was an important Roman port, known as Segesta Tigulliorum. In the Middle Ages, the town was fortified by the Fieschi family before passing into Genoese hands. In 1833, when Hans Christian Andersen stayed here, he 'exulted at seeing that piece of land extending from the shore: what a fabled night I spent in Sestri Levante! The inn was very close to the sea and a strong backwash licked against it. In the skies above the clouds were like fire and in the mountains there alternated the most vivid colours'. The place enchanted both Dante and Byron as well.

GETTING THERE AND AROUND

By boat Ferries (**w** traghettiportofino.it) leave from the Baia delle Favole in summer for Genoa, Rapallo, Portofino, Lerici, San Fruttuoso Porto Venere and the Cinque Terre (**w** navigazionegolfodeipoeti.it). **Silentbay** (**m** 3207 586263; **e** info@silentbay.it; **w** silentbay.it) run sailing tours in a catamaran. The port has 150 berths (📞 0185 44810).

By bus Buses run to Chiavari and Lavagna, taking about 30 minutes, and to Varese Ligure, taking about an hour.

By car Sestri is on the main A12 *autostrada*, 48km from Genoa and 61km from La Spezia.

By taxi For local taxis, call 📞 0185 41277.

By train Sestri is on the main Genoa–La Spezia line, 50 minutes from Genoa.

TOURIST INFORMATION At Corso Colombo 50 (📞 0185 478530; **w** www.comune. sestri-levante.ge.it). The Barcarolata, on the Sunday after 16 July, is a procession of boats decorated with multi-coloured lights in the Baia del Silenzio, which is followed by fireworks. Baia del Silenzio (Corso Colombo 24; 📞 0185 487015;

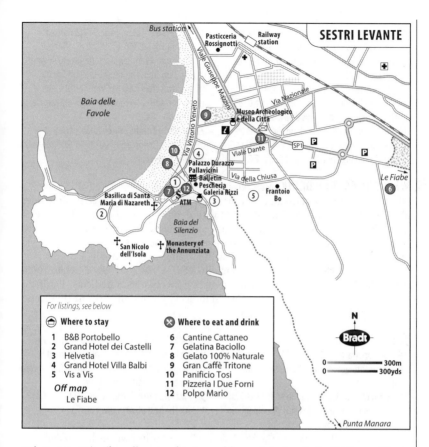

Recco to Sestri Levante   SESTRI LEVANTE

SESTRI LEVANTE

For listings, see below

⌂ **Where to stay**

1 B&B Portobello
2 Grand Hotel dei Castelli
3 Helvetia
4 Grand Hotel Villa Balbi
5 Vis a Vis

Off map
  Le Fiabe

✕ **Where to eat and drink**

6 Cantine Cattaneo
7 Gelatina Baciollo
8 Gelato 100% Naturale
9 Gran Caffè Tritone
10 Panificio Tosi
11 Pizzeria I Due Forni
12 Polpo Mario

0 ————— 300m
0 ————— 300yds

Bradt

w baiaviaggi.it) offers all sorts of tours and excursions by air, foot, bike and boat, not just in Sestri but across the region. Guida di Mountain Bike offers tours of the hinterland (m 3477 757986; e f.castel@libero.it).

WHERE TO STAY *Map, above, unless otherwise stated*

⌂ **Grand Hotel dei Castelli** (50 rooms)
Via Peninsula 26; ☎0185 487020; e info@
hoteldeicastelli.it; w hoteldeicastelli.it. Riccardo
& Cesarina Gualino, wealthy industrialists from
Turin, built their villa on the site of the original
castle in 1925. They were friends of Marconi who
did many of his radio experiments in the garden.
It's a fairy-tale setting but be sure to ask for a
room in the old castle. There's a good restaurant
& a seawater pool cut into the rock. There's also a
beautiful sheltered cove. €€€€

⌂ **Helvetia** (21 rooms) Via Cappuccini 43;
☎0185 41175; e helvetia@hotelhelvetia.it;
w www.hotelhelvetia.it. Excellent family-run
hotel that opened in 1925. Be sure to ask for
a room with a sea view & a balcony. The hotel

overlooks the Baia del Silenzio. Swimming pool.
€€€€

⌂ **Grand Hotel Villa Balbi** (99 rooms) Viale
Rimembranza 1; ☎0185 42941; e villabalbi@
villabalbi.it; w villabalbi.it. Built in the 17th
century, this hotel has a wonderful frescoed
reception. It's on the western side of town, with
a lovely garden & a very good b/fast. It's popular
with tourist groups who get a considerable
discount so don't take the price quoted on their
website as given & be sure to check out internet
prices. €€€

⌂ **Vis a Vis** (46 rooms) Via Della Chiusa 28;
☎0185 42661; w hotelvisavis.com. Lovely hotel
with a great view. Swimming pool & panoramic
terrace. Private beach. Disabled facilities. €€€

Recco to Sestri Levante   SESTRI LEVANTE

4

🏠 **B&B Portobello** (1 room) Piazza Matteotti 54; **m** 331 131 3137. In the historic centre close to the sea. Be sure to book the room with a view of both bays. **€€**

🏠 **Da Carla** [map, page 94] (2 rooms) Località San Bernardo, Via S Quillico, 22; 📞 0185 42819; **w** bebdacarla.it. This B&B is 2km behind the town & has good views along the coast. Rooms are simple & the hosts are pet friendly. Free mountain bike hire & guided tours. **€€**

🏠 **Le Fiabe** [map, page 94] (3 rooms) Via Parma 56; **m** 366 7158002; **e** lefiabe. sestrilevante@yahoo.it; **w** lefiabesestrilevante. it. Just 3km from the centre surrounded by olive groves, this B&B has wonderful views across the gulf. One room has a lovely terrace. Pet friendly. **€€**

⛺ **Camping Fondeghino** [map, page 94] Località Villa La Rocca 59; 📞 0185 409209. Clean & peaceful tent pitches. **€**

✗ **WHERE TO EAT AND DRINK** *Map, page 125*

All along the Riviera di Levante they make a special pasta called *corzetti*, sometimes also called *croxetti*, little disks stamped with designs, often the coat of arms of a noble family. Look out for *bianchetti*, little anchovies, wonderful simply fried with oil and lemon. The local dish is *bagnun*, an anchovy soup, and it has its own festival at the end of July. Traditionally, it was eaten by sailors on board ship.

The best ice cream is at **Gelateria Baciollo** (Piazza Matteotti 55) or **Gelato 100% Naturale** (Via XXV Aprile 126), which uses only organic ingredients. **Panificio Tosi** (Via XXV Aprile 132), makes the best focaccia. **Gran Caffè Tritone** (Piazza Bo 1), is the place for a coffee or a drink.

✗ **Cantine Cattaneo** Via Vicinale della Madonetta 1; 📞 0185 487431; **w** osteriacantinecattaneo.it. Rustic, romantic location for a treat. **€€€€€**

✗ **Polpo Mario** Via XXV Aprile 163; 📞 0185 480203; **e** info@polpomario.com; **w** polpomario.

com; 🕐 closed Mon. The owner owns his own fishing boat & his is the best fish in town. It is very popular; many stars inc Brigitte Bardot have eaten here, so book a table. **€€€**

✗ **Pizzeria I Due Forni** Viale Dante 73; 📞 0185 42398. The best pizza in town. **€**

SHOPPING **Balletin Pescheria**, Via Palestro 7–8, salts its own anchovies and sells amazingly fresh fish. **Pasticceria Rossignotti**, Viale Dante 2, is run by the pastry and chocolate kings the Rossignotti family, who opened here in 1840. Buy their nougat, *torrone*, which is best in the autumn.

Sestri Levante is surrounded by olive trees and the mill **Frantoio Bo** (Via della Chiusa 70; 📞 0185 481605; **w** frantoio-bo.it), founded in 1867, makes the best local olive oil. Locals also bring their olives here to be pressed.

OTHER PRACTICALITIES There is an **ATM** at Via XXV Aprile 176. The **post office** is at Via Caduti Partigiani 10. There's a **pharmacy** at Viale Roma 76, and the **hospital** is at Via Amaldo Terzi 43a (📞 0185 4881).

WHAT TO SEE AND DO Sestri is really all about enjoying the beach and relaxing. The columned **Basilica di Santa Maria di Nazareth** was designed by Gio Batta Carbone in the early 17th century. Its classical design is unusual for Liguria, and the building is particularly impressive when lit up at night. The **Palazzo Durazzo Pallavicini** on Piazza Matteotti also dates from the 17th century, and is now the town hall. The Romanesque church of **San Nicolo dell'Isola** sits at the highest point of the promontory and dates from 1151.

The **Galeria Rizzi** (Via Cappuccini 8; 📞 0185 41300; 🕐 Apr–Oct 10.30–13.00 Sun; Mar–Sep 16.00–19.00 Wed; 10 Jun–10 Sep 21.30–23.30 Fri–Sat; admission €5), by the Baia del Silenzio on Via Cappuccini has artworks collected by the Rizzi family, including works by Giovanni Andrea de Ferrari and Alessandro Magnasco. The former **Monastery of the Annunziata**, which looks on to the Baia del Silenzio, was built in 1496 and, with the Palazzo Negrotto Cambiaso, is now a conference and cultural centre.

The archaeological museum, the **Museo Archeologico e della Città** (Palazzo Fascie, Largo Colombo 50; ✆ 0185 46939; ⊕ 10.00–13.00 & 14.00–17.00; w musel.it; admission €5) showcases locally found artefacts from the Roman and medieval periods.

Take a walk on the headland to Punta Manara. Sestri is also a good spot for diving, as there are two wrecks from World War II just off the coast. The *Betollina*, a cargo boat and the *Cargo Armato*, a German submarine chaser, both sank in 1944. Between Sestri and Riva there's rock climbing at the Punta Manara. There is also a lovely walk to Punta Manara, which takes about 2 hours there and back. It is a bit steep in parts but the views are worth the effort.

UP IN THE MOUNTAINS The mountains behind Sestri are rich in minerals and mining is an important industry. As a result, the **Val Petronio** is rather built up. If you are interested in rocks and minerals in Casarza Ligure, there's the **Museo Parma Gemma** (Via Annuti 31; ✆ 0185 46229; ⊕ by appointment; admission free). In **Castiglione Chiavarese,** you can visit the oldest copper mine in Europe, Mucast Museo e Miniera di Monti Loreto Masso (Via Giuseppe Mazzini 20; ✆ 0185 469139; e info@mucast.it; w ucast.it; ⊕ guided tours 15 Jun–14 Sep 10.30 & 15.00 Wed & Sun; admission €5).

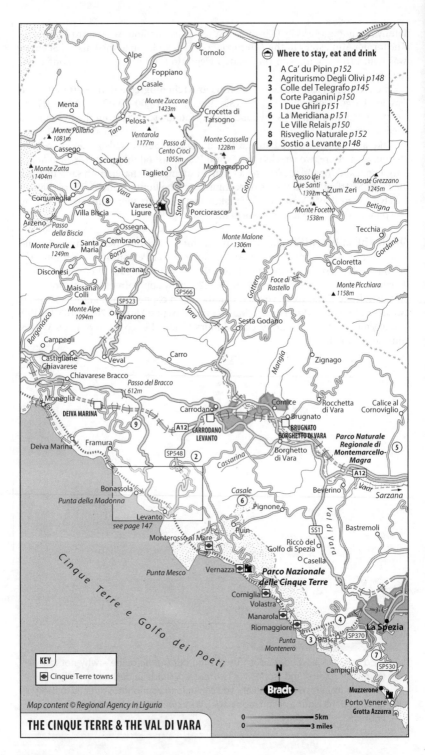

5

The Cinque Terre and the Val di Vara

Telephone code 0187 (+390187 if calling from abroad); Levanto 0185 (+390185 from abroad)

The Cinque Terre, despite its fame, is actually quite a mellow place if you know where to go, and is absolutely stunning. It is made up of five little villages that sit like limpets on the cliffs; *terra* is an old word for village.

The Val di Vara, which lies in the hinterland, is a little-visited area newly opened up to tourism. It is a land of chestnut trees, streams, tiny hamlets and mountain pastures. If you enjoy hiking, you can follow part of the Alta Via dei Monti Liguri here, and it is also possible to explore on horseback and by mountain bike.

Both the Val di Vara and the Cinque Terre are great places for walking. There isn't a list of must-do things to tick off – this is a place to unwind, enjoy the outdoors, take a boat trip, swim in the sea and paddle in the rocky rivers. That said, if you try to go on a day trip to the Cinque Terre in July and August and base yourself in Monterosso, Manarola or Riomaggiore, you can easily end up burnt out and overwrought. These three towns attract the highest number of day-trippers and are very busy in the summer. To avoid the crowds, centre your visit on the coast in Corniglia and Vernazza and inland, in and around Pignone or Varese Ligure. Corniglia, as it is high up on the cliffs, is the one of the five villages that tends to get left out of day trippers' itineraries, and Vernazza retains an ability to rise above it all, as it is simply the nicest of the five. Inland, it is quite off the beaten track even if you only drive a kilometre from the coast, so you will get not only better accommodation at a cheaper price, but also a far more authentic experience and a warmer welcome.

THE CINQUE TERRE

After Levanto, dramatic steep cliffs plunge into the sea, around the five little villages of Monterosso al Mare, Vernazza, Corniglia, Manarola and Riomaggiore. The water here is exceptionally deep and the marine wildlife is the richest along the coast. Their world is enclosed by the two capes. Only 20km lies between Punta Mesco, in the west, and Punta Montenero, to the east. Although Byron called it 'paradise on earth', he was one of the few foreigners to visit before the 1950s, and there is very little evidence that 19th-century travellers went here at all. Frederic Lees gives it only a cursory mention in his *Wanderings in Italy* (1913), leaving the impression he didn't even bother to go.

This was traditionally a very poor place where people eked out a meagre living. Even within living memory people remember villagers from the Cinque Terre begging for beans and potatoes in the richer villages at the start of the Val di Vara.

The five villages have retained much of their original charm and the area was declared a UNESCO World Heritage Site in 1997. Although they are very busy there

The loveliest way to explore the Cinque Terre is on foot. The five villages are linked by the **Sentiero Azzurro**, the Blue Footpath. It's 14km long and takes anywhere between 2½ and 5 hours to walk. The hills are dotted with Aleppo pines and the coastal scrub, *macchia*. Higher up there are chestnut trees, cork, myrtle broom and arboreal heather. The Club Alpino Italiano produces a 1:40,000 map of the area entitled *Cinque Terre e Parco di Montemarcello*.

The Sentiero Azzurro is the only footpath that you have to pay for in the entire country. It can work out as a pricey little walk if you just opt to ramble along the Via dell'Amore, the Path of Love, a half-hour stroll between Riomaggiore and Manarola, as you have to pay the price of the ticket to walk the entire route, which costs adults €7.50. The path starts in the piazza behind Riomaggiore railway station. Although it is the busiest part of the walk, there's a lift for wheelchairs and this part of the coastal path is paved so is easy for visitors with disabilities to enjoy, as well as families with pushchairs. However, the path was badly damaged in the 2011 floods. At time of writing the path from Riomaggiore to Manarola was open only as far as the bar midway along. The second part is due to re-open in 2021.

The Via dell'Amore was cut into the cliff in the 1920s and the path originally led to a gunpowder store that was used to blast the tunnels for the second railway line. The old storehouse now houses the Bar dell'Amore. This part of the trail got its name because someone graffitied 'Via dell'Amore' on one of the barrels and it later became somewhere that young people from Manarola and Riomaggiore would come to meet.

The coastal path between Manarola and Corniglia was still inaccessible at the time of writing following the flooding, and is due to re-open in spring 2019. The coastal walk between Corniglia and Monterosso is a proper hike, which means is no mass tourism. The place has been saved from the developers by three things: its geography, the locals' resistance to outside intervention and its lack of beaches. The area is protected by a national park, the Parco Nazionale delle Cinque Terre, whose headquarters are in Riomaggiore (Via Discolovo Manarola 118; ☏ 0187 762600; w www.parconazionale5terre.it). In 1999 the park was extended to cover the seabed.

The park authorities are currently restoring the terraced farmland that characterises much of Liguria, and the Cinque Terre in particular. Mile upon mile of dry stone walls (*muretti*, or *fasce* in the local dialect) have over the centuries been dug out of the hillsides to enable the locals to grow olives and grapes. The Cinque Terre was devastated by a flash flood on 25 October 2011. These floods were not just caused by global warming but because the locals have abandoned farming for the more profitable money-spinner of tourism. As a result, the untilled land and uncared-for forests have a topsoil that is far more unstable than it was 50 years ago, making it less able to absorb water. More floods like this are expected in the future and the government is doing its best to encourage people back on to the land to till the fields.

Before you go two myths need to be busted. One – this is no secret hideaway. The Cinque Terre is one of Italy's main tourist attractions, with up to 2.3 million visitors a year and a season that never stops. Don't panic and decide not to visit, however, as most visitors come on day trips. To see the Cinque Terre properly, it is best to stay a night or two in order to catch a real feel for the place. The best time to plan a trip here is spring or autumn, although it is also beautiful to visit in winter when the views across the sea to Corsica and Elba are breathtaking.

it is quieter but is relatively easy if you are reasonably fit. Look out for peregrine falcons, ravens and blue rock thrushes.

There are plenty of free footpaths, however – 137km in all.

The **Strada dei Santuari** that links the five pilgrimage churches dotted along the mountaintops, is far less busy. It is also great to mountain bike. The higher coastal footpath runs 45km from Levanto to Porto Venere and starts at Piazza Basteri in Porto Venere, where there is a steep climb up from the castle. It passes through Campiglia, across the Colle del Telegrafo and on to the Santuario della Madonna di Soviore, above Monterosso. Paths lead up to it from each of the villages and the walk is far less touristy than the coastal path.

From Monterosso you can walk along the footpath to Punta Mesco to the northwest of the town. There are fabulous views along the coast from Portofino to Palmaria. At San Antonio you can join the path up to Colle dei Bigari and walk on to the Colla di Gritta. This takes you to Sanctuario di Nostra Signora di Soviore. From here a path leads down to Monterosso. The circuit is not too strenuous and takes just under 4 hours. It is also possible to walk to Levanto and catch the train back to Monterosso. It is just under 3km from Punta Mesca.

There are nice walks at the other end of the Cinque Terre from Campiglia. From here you can walk down to Portovenere and away from the crowds down to Biassa. Sections of this path were also closed at time of writing and in parts dangerous, so it is best to ask at the tourist office before setting off.

A word of warning: wear good walking shoes or boots and never walk along the footpaths if there is a chance of bad weather, as flash flooding is an issue. The national park website (**w** www.parconazionale5terre.it) tells you which paths are currently closed.

Myth number two – the Cinque Terre is cut off from the world. It is certainly true that until the 1970s the villages were inaccessible to cars, but that never meant that they were completely isolated. The railway arrived in 1874, and the villages have always been accessible by boat. Mule tracks linked them with other towns inland and along the coast. Remember that much of inland Liguria had no paved roads until the 1970s, so there was nothing special about the Cinque Terre in this respect. Driving here isn't actually any different from doing so in large parts of the hinterland, but it is, as in many parts of Liguria, tortuous, time-consuming and inadvisable if you have an especially large car. The roads are not in good condition and are sometimes closed. The road to Vernazza is particularly steep so be sure your car is in good shape.

Vernazza is the prettiest and friendliest of the famous five villages. It is best to avoid both **Riomaggiore** and **Manarola** in high season – they will be teeming with tourists as they are the closest to La Spezia, where most visitors catch the train or the boat for a visit. **Monterosso al Mare** is the one to miss if you are in a hurry as it is really nothing noteworthy and in fact a rather tacky place. A car park dominates the bay in the new town and the trappings of tourism have taken much of the charm away. You'll find a much more authentic experience if you base yourself further west along the coast at **Moneglia** or **Levanto**, where there are lovely sandy beaches too. **Framura** and **Bonassola** also have the feel of the way the Cinque Terre once was, and are just minutes away by train.

Most accommodation in the area is B&B style. However, don't take rooms from people offering somewhere to stay at the station as you are likely to be ripped off. If you arrive late and there are no rooms available, ask in the local restaurants as many rent rooms. The best way to find accommodation at the last minute is to go online on w booking.com with a Cinque Terre Wi-Fi card. If you don't have internet access, the agency Cinque Terre Riviera can help. They also organise weddings and a variety of excursions and experiences (✆ 347 703718; w cinqueterreriviera.com).

HISTORY Vernazza was founded by the Romans. Its name comes from the Latin *verna*, meaning 'native'. Wine from the hills around was shipped far and wide and an amphora was found at Pompeii marked with the Roman name for Corniglia, Cornelius. Monterosso popped up in AD643, to be followed by Riomaggiore in the 8th century, founded by Greek settlers fleeing Byzantium, according to legend. Manarola joined the team in the 12th century when the area was a Fieschi fiefdom.

This stretch of coast was controlled by Genoa from 1276 and Genoese warships were made in Vernazza. The villages, like many along the coast, were plagued by pirate raids until 1545 and many locals were taken as slaves. In the 1600s the villages went into decline and although the arrival of the railway in the 1870s gave them an economic boost, it was unable to stem a wave of emigration to La Spezia and the Americas.

GETTING THERE AND AWAY

By air The closest airport is Pisa, 83km away. Trains run from Pisa airport to La Spezia. Genoa airport is 111km away. Take the shuttle bus from the airport to Genoa's Principe Station to catch the train.

By boat In summer boats run from Genoa's Porto Antico (✆ 0185 772091; w golfoparadiso.it); from La Spezia, Lerici and Porto Venere (✆ 0187 732987; w navigazionegolfodeipoeti.it); and from Santa Margherita, Rapallo, Portofino and Sestri Levante (✆ 0185 284670; w traghettiportofino.it). The boats are quite pricey so expect to pay €36 per adult return from Genoa.

By car If you do not intend to use a car while you are there, the simplest thing to do is to park in the car parks at Levanto or La Spezia station and take the train.

The Cinque Terre is off the A12 *autostrada*. The motorway itself loops deep inland behind the Cinque Terre. If you are heading for Riomaggiore or Manarola by car, get off at La Spezia and take the SP350 and then the SP370 from near the Arsenale. For Corniglia, which sits bang in the middle, the choice is yours.

For Vernazza and Monterosso get off at Levanto, then follow the SP566 and then the SP38. It's half an hour's drive from the motorway.

Cars are banned from all the villages unless you have a permit, which is the case in nearly all of Liguria's historic town centres, and **parking** can be a major issue in summer, especially in Riomaggiore and Manarola. If you arrive late in the afternoon, finding a space is not difficult but you may have to walk a little bit. Monterosso is the easiest place to park. Just above the town, the road forks. One leads to the old town where there is a car park, and the other to Fegina, the new town, where there is a large car park by the sea, which is the best option. Car parks are cash only. Budget €12–15 for 24 hours to park in a car park and €8–10 to park in the blue designated areas outside of the towns. Yellow spots are for residents. If you arrive late in the afternoon, however, the chances are that the parking attendant will have gone home. There is no charge for parking overnight until 08.00. Otherwise it is €1.50–2.00 an hour. Each village has a small car park and a shuttle bus service (€2.50), but if you are in good shape, it's only a 10-minute walk uphill to the car park from the sea. Riomaggiore is the most difficult place to park if you are visiting in high season. The policewoman at the entrance in the village is likely to tell you rather curtly to go elsewhere.

It is a stunning drive along the coast road, high up on the mountainside, which offers beautiful views. Not many people drive this road so it isn't very busy, and if you stay on the road, it can be a very stress-free experience. Proof that the roads are not too difficult to drive is that since the flooding we have encountered a number of huge lorries full of road-building equipment carrying out repairs.

By taxi For an airport pick-up, call m 339 130 1183 or m 340 356 5268.

By train For long-distance connections change at La Spezia, Monterosso or Sestri Levante for a local train, which runs roughly hourly. Bags can be left at La Spezia and Riomaggiore stations. Make sure to validate your ticket in the yellow machine in the station as conductors are tough on this stretch of line and if you don't, you will have to pay a fine. It is 30 minutes by train from La Spezia to Monterosso.

GETTING AROUND
By bike You have to be really fit to be able to cycle up and down to the villages, but the road that runs along the top of the Cinque Terre has lovely views and is easy to bike. The tiny roads that link back to Pignone are very quiet and great for cycling.

By boat The nicest way to travel between the five villages, except Corniglia, is by the ferry boat that runs from April to October. The price depends on how far you go, but a day ticket is €25. This is also the simplest way to visit nearby Porto Venere. See w navigazionegolfodeipoeti.it.

By bus Shuttle buses run from the car parks to the centre of each of the five villages and up to the sanctuaries above. A one-way ticket costs €2.50 but the price is included in the Cinque Terre Card. Buses are timed to meet the trains but stop for 2 hours at lunchtime.

By car Once you get to your destination and find a parking space you are better off exploring on foot, by boat or train. It takes longer to drive between the villages than it does to walk. During the day in high season you often have to park a fair hike from the centre if you can find a space. Parking is roughly €2 per hour.

On foot The Cinque Terre has one of the prettiest coastal footpaths in Italy. To walk it you will need to buy a ticket. See box, page 130.

By train The easiest way to get around is by train as the five villages are only minutes apart on the Genoa–La Spezia line. From Monterosso follow signs 'Per La Spezia' and from Riomaggiore 'Per Genova'. It costs €2 to travel between them, so don't use up a Eurail Pass day here. Tickets are valid for 6 hours. The best thing to do, if you plan on hiking, as well as using the train, is to buy a Cinque Terre Treno Card, which includes train travel. A day pass costs €16. The outdoor part of most of the stations are shorter than the trains, especially in Vernazza, so make sure to get off when the train stops, even if it is still in the tunnel. You can leave your luggage at Vernazza station for €10 between 08.00 and 19.00.

TOURIST INFORMATION There is a Cinque Terre information office in every railway station and at the station in La Spezia. The websites w cinqueterre.com and w parconazionale5terre.it are both useful.

i **Manarola** ✆ 0187 762600   *i* **Riomaggiore** ✆ 0187 920633
i **Monterosso** ✆ 0187 817059   *i* **Vernazza** ✆ 0187 812533

FESTIVALS Monterosso has a number of festivals; a lemon festival in May; the feast day of John the Baptist, celebrated from 23 to 25 June; an anchovy festival on 2 September and the feast day of the Madonna di Fegina, 8 September. There are fireworks on 24 June and 15 August. There is a religious procession from the Santuario di Soviore on 15 August. Manarola has an anchovy and olive oil festival in September. On 29 June a giant cake, the *torta dei Fieschi*, is baked in Corniglia, and Vernazza celebrates its patron saint on 20 July.

OTHER PRACTICALITIES There are **ATMs** in each of the towns but beware of those in Riomaggiore and Manarola which, in the height of summer, have a tendency to run out of money, charge your card and not give you any cash. The main **post office** branch is in Monterosso, Via Roma 73.

If you have a medical problem, head for **Monterosso.** The pharmacy is on Via Fegina 42. The nearest **hospital** is in La Spezia (Via Vittorio Veneto 197; ✆ 0187 5331). A Cinque Terre Card includes **Wi-Fi** connections at the local hot spots, including Volastra.

The local tour operator, **Explora** (Via Signorini 402, Riomaggiore; ✆ 0187 920697; w explora5terre.it) organises guided tours, flights over the Cinque Terre, cooking classes, fishing expeditions, sailing courses, weddings and wine tastings.

MONTEROSSO AL MARE Monterosso sits in a cove at the bottom of a deep ravine, but it is the least atmospheric of the five villages. It is divided into two parts – the old town that hides away behind the cliff and modern Fegina. The latter is stuffed with hotels and has a lively evening scene. If you are backpacking, this is the place you are most likely to make friends, but if you want peace and quiet, you will detest it. It is, however, the easiest of the villages to get around as there are fewer stairs. There is a small, sandyish beach that's topped up every spring, the only one in the Cinque Terre.

Where to stay There are more hotels in Monterosso than in any of the other five villages.

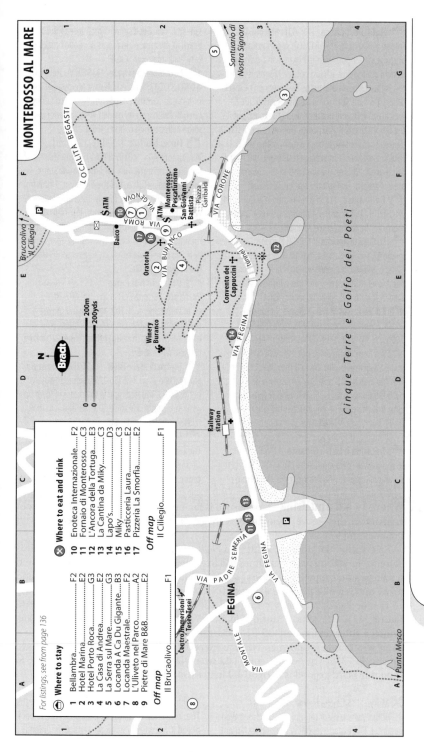

MONTEROSSO AL MARE

For listings, see from page 136

ⓘ Where to stay

1 Bellambra..............................F2
2 Hotel Marina.........................E2
3 Hotel Porto Roca...................G3
4 La Casa di Andrea.................E2
5 La Serra sul Mare..................G3
6 Locanda A Ca Du Gigante....B3
7 Locanda Maestrale................F2
8 L'Uliveto nel Parco...............A2
9 Pietre di Mare B&B...............E2

Off map
Il Brucaolivo...............................F1

✗ Where to eat and drink

10 Enoteca Internazionale........F2
11 Fornaio di Monterosso.........C3
12 L'Ancora della Tortuga........E3
13 La Cantina da Miky..............C3
14 Lapo's...................................D3
15 Miky.....................................C3
16 Pasticceria Laura..................E2
17 Pizzeria La Smorfia...............E2

Off map
Il Ciliegio....................................F1

Hotel Porto Roca [135 G3] (40 rooms) Via Carone 1, 19016; ☎0187 817502; e portoroca@ portoroca.it; w portoroca.it. Perched on a cliff with its own garden & beach just outside Monterosso, this is the classiest hotel in the area, but don't expect super-chic here. The rooms are on the small side & typical of 1960s constructions along the coast, but it's the terrace that is the big draw. The views are 5-star deluxe, so make sure to book a room with a sea vista. Pool & spa. There is an average restaurant, but the b/fast is good. Wi-Fi on the terrace & in the common areas. Free pick-up from the station. €€€€€

Bellambra [135 F2] (4 rooms) Via Roma 64; m 3920 121912; w bellambra5terre.com. Smart rooms in the town centre. €€€€

La Casa di Andrea [135 E2] (5 rooms) Via Milite Ignoto 42, Località Castello; ☎0187 818050; m 335 645 6288; e info@lacasadiandrea.net; w lacasadiandrea.net. A lovely B&B in a peaceful spot with great views. Garden, free Wi-Fi & adjoining rooms. €€€

La Serra sul Mare [135 G3] (3 rooms) Località Serra, Monterosso al Mare; ☎0187 186 2006; m 347 244 7919; w laserrasulmare.com. It is 1.5km from Monterosso but the owners will pick you up & give you a lift down if they aren't too busy. This top-notch B&B is run by a mother & daughter, both fabulous cooks, & it has lovely views across Liguria & the sea. The downside is that there's no Wi-Fi, but it is good for hikers as it's on the trail. Excellent b/fast to set you up for the day. €€€

Locanda A Ca Du Gigante [135 B3] (6 rooms) Via IV Novembre 9–11; ☎0187 817401; w www.ilgigantecinqueterre.it; ⊘ closed mid-

Jan–mid-Feb. Good simple hotel close to the best beach in the area. AC in rooms & a good breakfast. Easy walk into town. €€€

Locanda Maestrale [135 F2] Via Roma 37; ☎0187 817013; e maestrale@monterossonet.com; w locandamaestrale.net. Centrally located family-run hotel with a pretty garden. Atmospheric rooms, some with frescoed ceilings. €€€

Hotel Marina [135 E2] (25 rooms) Via Buranco 40; ☎0187 817613; e marina@ hotelmarina5terre.com; w hotelmarina5terre.com. In a peaceful part of the old town, 100m from the beach, this friendly family hotel is excellent value. Beach towels in the room. Top-notch b/fast served in the garden in summer. Toys for kids, mountain bikes, canoes & snorkelling gear, but don't go here if you're a light sleeper as it's close to the railway line. €€

L'Uliveto nel Parco [135 E2] (5 rooms) Via Mesco, Località Fuisso; m 349 602 2075; w ulivetonelparco.it. This agriturismo grows the famous Monterosso lemons & offers wine & olive-oil tasting. The farm offers dinner & cooking classes. Wi-Fi. €€

Pietre di Mare B&B [135 E2] (2 rooms) Via San Martino 2; m 342 186 0764; w pietredimare.it. This B&B is situated right in the centre of town up a charming little side street. The family run a small takeaway below. Wi-Fi. €€

Il Brucaolivo [135 F1] (3 rooms) Località Campo; ☎0187 817028; m 3319 541866; f; ⊘ closed Dec–Feb. A farm 10mins' walk from the centre of Monterosso. Kitchen facilities & sea views. €

✕ **Where to eat and drink** Monterosso is famous for its anchovies. In the seafront restaurants they serve them fried with lemon juice, salted or cooked up with potatoes and tomatoes.

La Cantina da Miky [135 C3] (Via Fegina 90) is a trendy spot for a drink. It is close to the station and sometimes has live music. They also serve light meals and terrific seafood appetisers. **Lapo's** [135 D3] (Via Fegina 30) serves Italian tapas and pizza, and is a nice place for a drink.

Try the local rich pastry cream and chocolate *monterossina* tart at **Pasticceria Laura** [135 E2] (Via Vittorio Emanuele 59), a family-run bakery-cum-café. **Enoteca Internazionale** [135 F2] (Via Roma 62) is a wine shop and bar with a good selection of local wines. Head to **Pizzeria La Smorfia** [135 E2] (Via Vittorio Emanuele 73) if you want a good takeaway pizza and you don't want attitude to spoil things. Also good is **Fornaio di Monterosso** [135 C3] (Via Fegina 112).

✕ **Miky** [135 C3] Via Fegina 104; ☎0187 817608; w www.ristorantemiky.it; ⊘ closed Wed in winter. This expensive, classy seafood restaurant

is highly popular & serves excellent seafood risotto. The service can be a little uneven & be sure to book ahead if you wish to sit on the terrace. Traditional

🍴 SOMETHING FISHY

Monterosso is famous for its anchovies. It is the saltiness of the sea here that gives them their taste. The fishermen go out every night with a lamp, a *lampare*, which attracts the fish and makes them swim towards the nets. The boats they use are called *gozzo* and are no more than 10m long. The anchovies are called *u pan du ma* – the bread of the sea – in local dialect. Traditionally they were only fished in late spring and early summer but today they are often given the chance to grow to the optimum length of 10cm, which is perfect for salting and preserving in big barrels. Local fishermen complain that the fishing is not regulated enough and that the big swarms of fish that were once seen in the sea are no more due to overfishing by the large boats that catch entire shoals at a time, something a *gozzo* cannot do. Thus while 30 years ago fishing was the mainstay of living in Monterosso, now only a handful of fishermen remain.

The Slow Fish movement is working hard to keep the industry alive and protect the fish. It is a hands-on business and the techniques of catching and preserving the anchovies have not changed for centuries. Each fish has to be salted separately and it is an intensive job usually done by women. The process is complicated by the fact that the fish are very delicate and impossible to freeze. The ageing period lasts from one to six months. Fresh they are often served stuffed or simply fried. There are three anchovy festivals or *sagra* and the fish feature preserved in lemon in May's lemon festival. You can arrange to go out on a boat with a local fishermen through **Monterosso Pescaturismo** (Via XX Settembre 22; 📞0187 817053; w monterossopescaturismo.org).

Ligurian fish dishes & homemade pasta. Tasting menu €78. €€€€€

✕ Il Ciliegio [135 F1] Località Beo; 📞0187 817829. Has the best view in town & a lovely shady terrace 600m above sea level. There's a free shuttle service to & from Monterosso. The food is traditional Ligurian with plenty of excellent pasta & fish dishes. €€€

✕ L'Ancora della Tortuga [135 E3] Via Salita Cappucini 4; 📞0187 800 0065; w ristorantetortuga. it; ⊕ closed Wed & Nov–Mar. Clifftop restaurant serving traditional Ligurian food. €€€

Shopping **Market day** is Thursday. Local products are lemons, white wine, olives and anchovies. **Baico** [135 E2] (Via Roma 4) sells pesto, wine, olive oil and other local products. There's pre-lunch wine tasting at the **Winery Buranco** [135 D2] (Via Buranco 72; 📞0187 817677; w burancocinqueterre.it) at noon daily. The appetisers are very tasty too.

What to see and do This was the first of the five Cinque Terre villages to become a holiday destination and at the beginning of the 20th century had more in common with resorts like Moneglia and Bonassola further along the coast. Wealthy Genoese and Spezzini, as people from La Spezia are called, built large villas here, among them the family of Nobel Prize-winning poet Eugenio Montale, who described Monterosso as 'a plain village made of stone, a refuge for fishermen and farmers'. A remnant from this period is the huge cement statute of Neptune, *Il Gigante*, built in 1910 to hold up the terrace of a villa. It was damaged in World War II when Monterosso was bombed as the Allies were trying to take out the railway line. It stands as a reminder of more elegant times. Sadly, Monterosso has changed a lot, and today it's a tourist hot spot with little of the charm of the other four to save it. There are, however, one or two things worth stopping to see.

A pedestrian tunnel connects the resort of Fegina with the old town, but it's nicer to walk along the seafront with views across to Vernazza. The lookout tower has Ghibelline battlements and was built to defend Monterosso from both pirates and the Pisans in the Middle Ages. The wild Punta Mesco, an important marine sanctuary, lies to the west. There was once a quarry here and this was where Genoa's cobblestones came from.

On the hill that divides Fegina from the old town is the 17th-century **Convento dei Cappuccini** [135 E3]. On the path that leads up to it is a statue of St Francis and a wolf. It is worth the walk up here for the view and to see, in the convent's striped church of San Francesco, the beautiful painting of the *Crucifixion* (c1623), attributed to Van Dyck, who spent many years in Liguria. There are also works by Luca Cambiaso and Bernardo Strozzi.

Under the railway bridge in the old town, the church of **San Giovanni Battista** [135 F2] is the oldest in the five villages and dates from 1307. Outside the church there is a plaque marking the high water mark of the 1966 flood and pictures of the devastation caused by the 2011 disaster. On leaving the church turn left; the **Oratorio** is the most interesting building in Monterosso, decorated with macabre skulls and cross bones. The Black Brotherhood, which once ran it, used to look after the dark sides of life, arranging funerals and taking care of the bereaved.

There's a lovely excursion up the mountainside to the peaceful **Santuario di Nostra Signora** [135 G3], built on the site of an 8th-century church, the remains of which can still be seen. Its prize procession is a 14th-century wooden statue of the Madonna with the body of Christ. It's a haven with a good simple restaurant and a lovely view across Punta Mesco. The walk back down to town takes about an hour and a half.

There are footpaths from Fegina if you fancy a walk to Punta Mesco and its abandoned lighthouse, and Levanto (2½ hours). The coastal path to Vernazza begins by the Hotel Porto Roca. There is a decent public beach in front of the old town. Take a dip in the sea – it is the saltiest part of the Mediterranean. If you fancy diving off Punta Mesco, the diving centre **Centro Immersioni Teseo Tesei** is at Via Padre Semeria 13 [135 B2] (⋂ 0187 818122). The beach concessions by the railway station rent kayaks. You can paddle to Vernazza and back; budget €15 for a kayak for one to two people. Local fisherman Angelo hires his boat out for a cruise, but there's a price tag of €150 for a tour per person (m 333 687 9249; w angelosboattours.com). Fishing trips are organised by Monterosso Pescaturismo (⋂0187 817053; w monterossopescaturismo.org) and Aquamarina offer boat tours (m 371 382 2490; w aquamarinatour.com).

VERNAZZA Vernazza is the prettiest and friendliest of the five villages and, along with being the only village with a proper harbour, this has made it the richest in the area. It is a mellow sort of place and a great base. Colourful houses surround its church, Santa Margherita d'Antiochia, and there are lots of cafés and restaurants along Via Roma giving it a little buzz. There are only about 500 people who live here but it's a tight-knit community that has blocked attempts to widen the road and ease access to the Cinque Terre.

🏠 **Where to stay** *Map, page 141*
Two local restaurants also rent rooms and apartments: **Gianni Franzi** (Piazza Marconi 5; ⋂ 0187 821228; w giannifranzi.it; €) and **La Torre** (Località Preteccia; ⋂ 0187 821082; w camerelatorre.com; €).

LIGURIA'S NOBEL LAUREATE

Eugenio Montale, the father of modern Italian poetry, was born into a wealthy Genoese family in 1896. His writing reflects his revulsion with fascism but also contains some of the most erotic love poems in modern poetry. Another local Ligurian literary legend, Italo Calvino, called Montale's *La Bufera e Altro* (1956) 'the finest book to have emerged from the Second World War'.

At first Montale dreamt of being an opera singer but after seeing action on the Austrian front during World War I he was drawn into Genoa's literary world. As a child he had spent his summers in Monterosso, and with the advent of fascism he took refuge in the wild Cinque Terre. His first collection, *Ossi di Seppia* (*Cuttlefish Bones*), was published in 1925 just three years after Mussolini came to power. The poems draw their symbolism from the stark landscape, which he found 'rough, scanty and dazzling'. From the first, Montale was keen to distance himself from the flowery D'Annunzio, Mussolini's favourite. The poem 'I limoni' ('The Lemon Trees'), which opens *Cuttlefish Bones*, declares war on 'the laurelled poets'. Montale's poems concentrate on the 'little' and the 'insignificant', a world of noisy crickets and red ants, sun-scorched orchards, the sea and the horizon, and 'roads that lead to grassy / ditches where boys / scoop up a few starved / eels out of half-dry puddles'.

However, Montale wasn't just a regional poet and his beloved Liguria also left him with a feeling of imprisonment, isolation and separation. In the poem 'On the Threshold' he calls for the reader to 'watch this solitary strip of land / transform into a crucible'. Then, 'Look for a flaw in the net that binds us tight, burst through, break free!'

In 1927 Montale moved to Florence, then the cradle of Italian poetry, but he soon found himself unemployed when he refused to join the Fascist Party and his poems disappeared from the school curriculum. In 1939 he wrote another masterpiece, *Le Occasioni* (*Occasions*), which critics consider to be the high point of 20th-century Italian poetry. In the post-war years he continued to write poems and wrote widely for *Corriere della Sera*. In 1975 he was awarded the Nobel Prize for Literature and he died in Milan in 1981.

There are guided walking tours of the places that inspired him. Ask for information in the tourist office.

🏠 **Camere Giuliano** (4 rooms) Località Chiappa 1; m 333 341 4792; e giuliano@cdh. it; w cameregiuliano.com. This B&B is run by Michele Sherman, who is one of the founders of Save Vernazza. It has an incredible view & 1 room has a sofa bed so is good for families. €€€

🏠 **Cade Ventu** (6 rooms) Località Cade; m 3311 492791; w cadeventu.com. Rooms high up between Vernazza & Corniglia, with beautiful views. Some have kitchenettes. €€

🏠 **Villa l'Eremo sul Mare** (2 rooms) Località Gerai; m 339 268 5617; e eremosulmare@tiscali.it; w eremomosulmare. com. You will need to hike up above Vernazza to reach this little haven, but it's well worth it as this B&B, hidden in the pine trees, is excellent value & has friendly owners. The view over Vernazza is stunning & the house is on the famous walking trail, the Sentiero Azzurro. Rooms are large enough for extra beds. If you like stargazing, they also have a little telescope. €€

✖ **Where to eat and drink** *Map, page 141*

There are some excellent restaurants in Vernazza, but if you want something more simple, you can buy focaccia at **Da Gino** (Via Roma 7). There is winetasting at

CheO Winery (Via Brigate Partigiane 1; w cheo.it). The Blue Marlin Bar (Via Roma 43) is the hub of evening activity. Alternatively try Burgas, a lively wine bar by the harbour side.

✖ **Belforte** Via Guidone 42; ✆0187 812222; ⊕ closed Wed. The best restaurant in Vernazza, with a terrace overlooking the sea. It's in the old castle & is thus bursting with atmosphere. Fresh fish dishes predominate, but the *trofie al pesto* is excellent. €€€€

✖ **Gambero Rosso** Piazza Marconi 7; ✆0187 812265; w ristorantegamberorosso.net. Right on the harbour, this restaurant has a lovely view & a nice interior for cold weather. Try the *pansotti* (stuffed pasta with walnut sauce), the fried fish mix *paranzella*, or the lemon risotto. Typical Ligurian style with a nice modern twist. €€€€

✖ **La Torre** Località Preteccia; m 388 404 1181. This bar & restaurant offer unmissable views down across Vernazza. Try the local anchovies with potatoes, *tegame*, or a simple *bruschetta*. It's a climb up from Vernazza, which makes it an activity in itself. €€€

✖ **Il Pirata** Via Gavino 36; ✆0187 812047; w ilpiratarooms.com. Popular place known not only for its pasta dishes but also its breakfast. Run by a pair of entertaining Sicilian twins. Basic café with tasty snacks & simple meals. A taste of Sicily in Liguria! €€

✖ **Trattoria Gianni Franzi** Piazza Marconi 1; ✆0187 821003; w giannifranzi.it; ⊕ closed Wed. A local institution with tables in the main piazza. Try the *tegame*. €€

Shopping **Market day** is Tuesday morning. **Enoteca Sciacchetrà** on Via Roma sells local wines, salted anchovies and pesto.

What to see and do Piazza Marconi is the heart of town and it is known locally as U Cantu de Musse, the gossip corner and its makeover after the flood has reinforced its role as Vernazza's meeting place. The church of **Santa Margherita d'Antiochia** [map, opposite] (c1318) sits on the waterfront with its impressive 40m-high octagonal bell tower. It was built, according to legend, after the bones of Santa Margherita were found in a wooden box on the beach and is unique for its east-facing entrance. In the 16th century it was enlarged and as a result grew

---

GIVE SOMETHING BACK

In the dramatic flooding of 2011, Vernazza was particularly badly hit and was covered in 4m of mud and debris, causing €100 million worth of damage, and three people lost their lives. In the aftermath three American women set up **Save Vernazza**, a non-profit organisation dedicated to restoring, rebuilding and preserving Vernazza for future generations. New Yorker Ruth Manfredi is co-ordinating the Renaissance of Vernazza project with architect Richard Rogers, which has so far revitalised Piazza Marconi.

Michèle Lilley, originally from California, runs the **Bottega d'Arte Cinqueterre** in the main street with her husband, local artist Antonio Greco. She runs a volunteer programme for tourists with Busabout and TreadRight. You can work with local farmers to restore their olive groves and vineyards. It is an extraordinary experience that will give you a real feel of local life and as the T-shirt says 'Even Paradise Needs a Gardener'. She also leads Save Vernazza Walking Tours and the group runs a Wine and Food Discovery tour. If you don't have time to volunteer, then you can donate to the fund. Find out more on w savevernazza.com (m 3453 636118; e ruthmanfredi@ savevernazza.com).

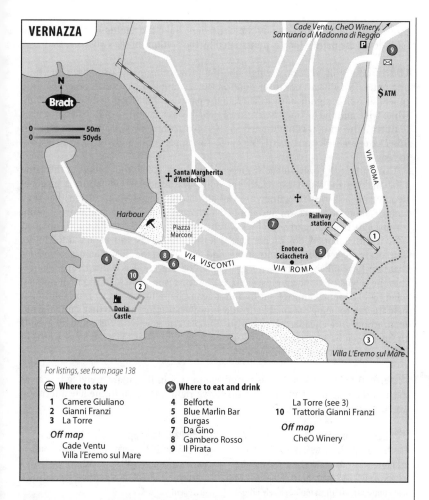

Cade Ventu, CheO Winery,
Santuario di Madonna di Reggio

$ ATM

VIA ROMA

Santa Margherita
d'Antiochia

Harbour

Piazza
Marconi

Railway
station

VIA VISCONTI

Enoteca
Sciacchetrà

VIA ROMA

Doria
Castle

Villa L'Eremo sul Mare

For listings, see from page 138

Where to stay

1 Camere Giuliano
2 Gianni Franzi
3 La Torre

Off map

Cade Ventu
Villa l'Eremo sul Mare

Where to eat and drink

4 Belforte
5 Blue Marlin Bar
6 Burgas
7 Da Gino
8 Gambero Rosso
9 Il Pirata

La Torre (see 3)
10 Trattoria Gianni Franzi

Off map

CheO Winery

disproportionately big for the square. Pop inside to see the replicas of crucifixes taken on the Crusades.

The **harbour** was once used to ship wine and the huge stone near the Burgas wine bar is where animal fat was crushed to make tallow. The harbour was once home to one of Italy's top water polo teams, but when the league's rules were changed and teams needed a home pool, Vernazza was forced to withdraw. There is a small beach and it is possible to rent canoes and small boats here. There are somewhat pricey boat trips to the Acqua Pendente cove, which has a waterfall and is midway between Vernazza and Monterosso. Boat tours are organised by **Nord Est** (m 3387 000436; w nordest-vernazza.it). The trail to Monterosso starts by the church on the harbour side, while the path for Corniglia leaves from by the war memorial just above the station

The ruined **Doria Castle** [map, above] (⏲ 10.00–19.00 daily; €1.50) was built in the 15th century as a lookout tower to protect the village from pirates. It is worth a walk up here as the view is lovely.

An hour's steep walk, about 2km above Vernazza, is the 11th-century **Santuario di Madonna di Reggio** whose black statue of the Madonna is said to have been brought to the Cinque Terre by the Crusaders. Take the shuttle bus up and walk back down the path, which is punctuated by the Stations of the Cross.

CORNIGLIA Built high on a ridge like the prow of a boat, Corniglia is the only one of the five villages not to sit right on the sea and is, as a result, cooler than the others, as well as significantly quieter. In the past Corniglia made a living producing white wine and the fortified Sciacchetrà, which was a favourite of Renaissance poet Petrarch. The wine was mentioned in the 14th century by Giovanni Boccaccio in *The Decameron*. Beware, it is 17% proof! The tipple is celebrated in a wine festival in May.

Corniglia is the only village from which you can see all four others at the same time making the views especially splendid. The resident population is just 240 people and unfortunately, they are rather rude, giving the impression that they would rather you went away and stopped bothering them. We booked a lovely room, for just €70, belonging to a local restaurant and the owner's daughter accompanied us to it with a pained look on her face as if this was the last thing she wanted to do. The locals are actually quite notorious and even the standoffish Genoese consider that they have taken aloofness a step too far. Local legend has it that the problem is that the townsfolk long ago lost their ability to reason. When an old man noticed what had happened and set out to find it again, he returned with a box claiming it held the key to being reasonable. Inside, however, was just a wasp that stung the old man. Rooms are cheaper here and it is the place to stay on a tight budget even if the locals can be a bit sullen. Above all make an effort to speak even a few words of Italian – it might improve things a bit.

Where to stay This is the easiest village to stay in if you are arriving by car as even in the height of summer you can drive right into town in the late afternoon and unpack your suitcases.

B&B Le Terrazze (3 rooms, 7 apts) Via Fieschi 102; \0187 812096; m 349 845 9684; e info@eterasse.it; w eterasse.it. Two friendly sisters run this B&B in the heart of the town with a hilariously kitsch b/fast room & lovely little garden. Cash only. €€€

Corte del Gallo (5 rooms) Via Alla Stazione 31; \0187 812336; w cortedelgallo.com. By the train station, 1km from the centre. All rooms have sea view. Garden with fabulous view. AC. €€€

B&B Da Beppe (2 rooms) Via Serra 2; m 338 495 2022; e info@vacanzeilgatto.com; w www.vacanzeilgatto.com. A 2-room apt with a kitchen, in a dreamy location above the harbour. Excellent value. €

Ostello di Corniglia (2 8-bed dorms & 4 rooms with en suite) Via alla Stazione 3; \0187 812559; e ostellocorniglia@gmail.com; w ostellocorniglia.com. Opened in 2009 & the best budget option in the area. €

Where to eat and drink There is a take-away pizza joint on Via Fieschi if you want a picnic.

Enoteca Il Pirun Via Fieschi 115; \0187 812315. Serves wine in a small glass jug, a *pirun*, which aerates the wine to give the alcohol more of a kick. It's a bit touristy but fun. They also have a restaurant with a set menu, always a local dish. The price includes wine. €€€€

Osteria a Cantina di Mananan Via Fieschi 117; \0187 821166. The best bet for eating out & serves traditional Ligurian recipes, but they are rather 'purist' in their attitude. Don't dare ask for Parmesan cheese with fish pasta, for example, or you will be put in your place! The food is good, so go with the flow. Reservations recommended. €€

What to see and do A steep staircase with 382 steps, the *ladarina*, leads up from the railway station to Chiappa. Alternatively, you can hop on the shuttle bus. The beautiful Gothic church of **San Pietro** to the north dates from 1334. The village proper stretches along the main road, Via Fieschi. The Fieschi family controlled the area in the early Middle Ages and the houses have one side facing this road and the other facing the sea. The diminutive main square is **Piazza Taragio**, which is overlooked by the Oratorio di Santa Caterina. To its side, a stairway leads up to the medieval lookout tower, where the local kids play football. Documents dating from the Middle Ages mention a castle, but no remains have yet been discovered.

Via Fieschi leads to the **Belvedere Santa Maria**, named after a church that once stood here. It's a great place for an evening picnic and has lovely views along the coast. Back on Piazza Taragio, steps lead down to a rocky cove signposted *marina*. It is the nicest place to swim in the Cinque Terre. Near the station an old railway tunnel leads to Guvano Beach. It is a 15–30-minute walk in the dark, so take a torch but, at time of writing, it was inaccessible. The beach was created by a landslide in 1893.

The **Santuario di San Bernardino** is up above the town. It is possible to rent rooms here and the terrace has splendid views back across Corniglia. There is also a footpath that runs up the mountain from the car park if you fancy a peaceful walk.

If you want to visit a local winery, try **La Polenza** (Via Fieschi 107; ✆ 0187 821214; ⏱ visits by appointment only); it is the place to try some of the classic local wines that delighted the Romans.

MANAROLA Manarola's colourful pink, brown, yellow and light-green houses have been immortalised by artists Paul Klee, Llewelyn Lloyd and Antonio Discovolo. The town takes its name from the huge olive oil wheel in the lower part of the town: *magna roea* means 'big wheel' in the local dialect. The main street, just as in Riomaggiore and Vernazza, was once a river criss-crossed by little bridges.

Where to stay

🏠 **Hotel Marina Piccola** (10 rooms) Via Lo Scalo 16; ✆ 0187 920770; w hotelmarinapiccola. com. Simple modern hotel that is 2mins from the sea. €€

🏠 **La Torretta** (13 rooms) Vico Volto 20; ✆ 0187 920327; e torretta@cdh.it; w torrettas. com. This trendy B&B is undoubtedly the best place to stay in Manarola. They greet you with a prosecco & there is attention to every detail; there are Nespresso machines in the rooms & complimentary soft drinks. It's even possible to have b/fast in bed. €€€

🏠 **Ca' d'Andrean** (10 rooms) Via Discovolo 101; ✆ 0187 900040; e info@cadandrean. it; w www.cadandrean.it; ⏱ closed mid-Nov–Christmas. Good-sized rooms, each with a balcony. B/fast is served in the garden under the lemon trees. Cash only. €€

🏠 **Il Saraceno** (7 rooms) Località Ava; ✆ 0187 760081; e hotel@thesaraceno.com; w thesaraceno.com. A quiet hotel 2km above Manarola, next to the old town of Volastra. Ample parking. There's a rooftop terrace & free Wi-Fi. €€

🏠 **Luna di Marzo** (10 rooms) Via Montello 387c, Volastra; ✆ 0187 920530; e info@albergolunadimarzo.com; w albergolunadimarzo.com. This hotel is in Volastra so you need a car to stay here as buses are infrequent. Has a great view & is away from the hustle below. No AC but Wi-Fi. €€

✗ Where to eat and drink
Manarola is a bit of a tourist trap, so often food isn't as good as you might have come to expect in Liguria. The best place for a drink is **La Cantine dello Zio Bramante** (Via Renato Birolli 110).

✗ **Cappun Magru** Via Volastra 19, Località Groppo; ✆ 0187 760057; ⏱ lunch Sun & dinner Wed–Sat. This is a top-class restaurant. The food is all Ligurian & is delicious. If you are saving for a splurge, this is the place to spend. This is the best restaurant in the Cinque Terre & is run by a husband-&-wife team, which gives a homely feel to the fine-dining experience. It's well away from the bustle of Manarola & the views are wonderful too. Set menu. €€€€€

✗ **Il Porticciolo** Via Renato Birolli 92; 📞0187 920083; w ilporticciolo5terre.it. A fish-based menu with excellent grilled octopus & pesto lasagne. €€€€

✗ **Marina Piccola** Via Lo Scalo 16; 📞0187 920923; w hotelmarinapiccola.com. This excellent restaurant wins hands down on location. You need to book in advance. Try the local dish, *muscoli ripieni* (stuffed mussels). €€€

What to see and do When you come out of the railway station, walk up the hill to the church of **San Lorenzo** (c1338). The bell tower across the square once doubled up as a lookout tower. In the **Oratorio della SS Annunziata** are some notable paintings including *Madonna and the Saints* by Vittorio Sgarbi.

A little path leads up from the village through the vineyards on its eastern side, where the nativity scenes are the work of Mario Andreoli who started work after he recovered from a serious illness. The Christmas crib is illuminated on 8 December and is fuelled by solar panels. There are 300 figures and 15,000 lights.

If you fancy a swim, there is a rocky beach by the harbour (but watch out for jellyfish), and great views from the **Santuario di Nostra Signora della Salute** above the town.

Legend has it that there was once a wealthy town called Oleastra near Manarola. One night when the Saracens attacked, the townsfolk buried all their gold and silver but they were all taken into slavery and never came back to claim it. You never know; you might strike lucky!

RIOMAGGIORE Riomaggiore is the largest of the five villages, with 1,693 inhabitants, it is a giant by Cinque Terre standards. The main river in the area, the *rio* in dialect, once ran through the town centre, giving the town its name. Colourful houses fill the steep ravine and it looks much as it did when painted by the Impressionist Florentine painter Telemaco Signorini.

🏠 **Where to stay**

🏠 **Locanda del Sole** (10 rooms) Via Santuario 114; 📞0187 920773; m 340 983 0090; e info@ locandadelsole.net; w locandadelsole.net. Friendly little B&B with Wi-Fi in the b/fast room. They provide picnic lunches. Terrace & parking. €€€

🏠 **Ciao Bella** (9 rooms) Via della Valetta; w ciaobellacinqueterre.com; 🐦 @ciaobella.

Modern colourful B&B in the centre of Riomaggiore. Can organise cooking classes & wine tastings. They are too cool to reveal a telephone number so message them on the website. €€

🏠 **L'Arcobaleno** (6 rooms) Via del Santuario; 📞0187 760554; w larcobaleno5terre.net. Simple B&B 5mins' walk from the centre. AC, parking. €€

✗ **Where to eat and drink** **Panificio Rosi** (Via Colombo 188) makes the focaccia for most of the bars and restaurants in town and has a lot to do with Riomaggiore's reputation for excellent focaccia. Try the *schiacciata,* another flat bread, and the *torta Cinque Terre,* a rich sponge cake with cream and chocolate chips. **Bar Centrale** (Via Colombo 144) has excellent ice cream, especially the one made from local lemons. This is a lively place late in the evening and provides what passes as nightlife in Riomaggiore.

✗ **Ripa del Sole** Via de Gasperi 4; m 3475 155810; w ripadelsole.it; ⊕ dinner only Tue–Sat, lunch only Sun, closed Jan–Feb. Run by a brother & sister & situated by the car park. The menu is always based on the latest catch. €€€€

✕ Enoteca Dau Cila Via San Giacomo 65; ☎0187 760032; w ristorantedaucila.com. Fish is the thing to eat in this stylish bar-cum-restaurant in the port. Book if you want to eat on the terrace. €€€

✕ Colle del Telegrafo [map, page 128] Località Colle del Telegrafo, Monte Parodi; ☎0187 760561; ⏲ closed Thu evening. Situated 1,800m above sea level where the old telegraph line used to cross the ridge. The restaurant is run by the National Park & serves simple fish courses & chestnut-based dishes. €€

Shopping Luciano Capellini (Frazione Volastra, Via Montello 240B; ☎ 0187 920632; w vinbun.it) sells wines by appointment.

What to see and do A tunnel leads out of the railway station. Turn right to the harbour, and the town's rocky beach is 2 minutes' walk to the east; beware of strong currents if you decide take a dip and look out for jellyfish. Then go back up the main street, Via di Riomaggiore. The church of **San Giovanni Battista** was built in 1340 by Antonio Fieschi, the Bishop of nearby Luni, but rebuilt in 1870. Inside is a wooden crucifix by the local master, Maragliano and *The Sermon by John the Baptist*, attributed to Domenico Fiasella. On the right of the church, Via del Santuario leads to the 16th-century **Oratorio dei Disciplinati**. Inside, the wooden statue known as the *Madonna delle Catene*, the *Madonna of Chains*, is a reminder of the raids by Barbary pirates that plagued the coast. The pirates often took the locals prisoner and sold them on into slavery.

ⓠ ALL IN A GLASS

There are three vines that produce Cinque Terre wine and Sciacchetrà: Bosco, Albarola and Vermentino. Bosco accounts for about 60% of production and is little grown elsewhere. The wines grown here are some of the nicest produced in Liguria in my opinion and it is worth paying the extra euros for a bottle. The **Cantina Cinque Terre** (Via Piave, Località Groppo, just above Manarola; ☎0187 920435; w cantinacinqueterre.com; ⏲ 08.00–19.00 Mon–Sat, 09.00–12.30 & 14.30–19.00 Sun) sells a good range of all the local wines.

If you fancy a trip to a winery, **Luciano Capellini** (Via Montello 240B, Volastra; m 339 723 2578; w vinbun.it) sells wines by appointment. Samuele Heidy Bonanini (Via Sant'Antonio 72; m 348 316 2470; w possa. it) produces the famous local wines including Sciacchetrà and also makes own honey. Initiatives like this are important for maintaining the environment in the Cinque Terre. Even if you are not interested in wine and honey, it is worth looking at their website, which has an image of the area as it was once, covered in terraces. Wine production in the Cinque Terre is tough work and it takes 220 days of labour to cultivate 1ha here, compared with 48 days in the undulating hills of nearby Emilia Romagna. Renovating the terraces is pricey, too, and costs €120 per m², but is vital if more landslides are to be prevented.

Cantine Litan (Via G Matteotti 32; m 340 765 5840; w litan.it) is another company that has also returned to the traditional local wine-making industry. Three cousins have been busy reviving the family vineyards and besides producing award-winning labels they organise guided walks around the vineyards, wine tasting and lunches in the fields. You can stay in their holiday house in Piandibarca, 10km away, where they have more vineyards in the Val di Vara. Their shop is in the heart of Riomaggiore.

These days the **castle** (c1260) is used for cultural events, but in the 19th century it was filled in and used as a cemetery. Nearby is the **Oratorio di San Rocco** built during the terrible plague of 1480, which is refreshingly simple inside. There is a watersports centre on nearby Via San Giacomo (5 Terre Diving; ☏ 0187 920011; w 5terrediving.it) for kayaking and diving. They also rent boats.

In addition to the coastal path (see box, page 130), there are walks to the 13th-century **Santuario di Nostra Signora di Montenero e Campiglia**. A shuttle bus also runs up to the sanctuary. A Byzantine icon, reputedly painted by Saint Luke, was buried here to save it from the Lombards and when it was rediscovered, a spring magically arose on the exact spot. The actual icon disappeared in the 16th century but it is still worth visiting as it is a beautiful place with splendid views along the coast, and most tourists don't make it this far. Another path leads up the Montenero promontory. A short walk east out of town leads to the **Torre Guardiola**, where there is a botany and wildlife centre housed in a former naval installation.

ALONG THE COAST

If the Cinque Terre is a little too touristy for you, you'll love the stretch of coast from Moneglia to Levanto. There are three little resorts, all rather sleepy, and the tiny port of Framura with its picturesque villages above. Deiva is not so nice and best avoided as it's a bit scrubby and downmarket and, when there are so many nicer places that cost the same close by, there's no need to compromise.

LEVANTO Levanto is a sleepy, relaxing place and it has a genuine Italian feel as many people from Genoa have holiday homes here. The town has a pretty, historic centre and is family orientated. It has a good sandy beach and is one of the top spots for surfing in Italy. The best time to enjoy the waves is in autumn. The town and the surrounding resorts are a real contrast to the busy Cinque Terre but as they are all linked by train, this stretch of coast is a great base for exploring the Cinque Terre villages. Bonassola and Framura are lovely peaceful resorts and linked to Levanto by the coastal path.

Useful information There is a tourist information office for the Cinque Terre in the railway station and the main tourist information is at Piazza Cavour 1 (☏ 0187 808125; w visitlevanto.it). The local taxi company is contactable on ☏ 0187 808247. The town celebrates its foundation on 22–25 July.

 WHERE TO STAY *Map, opposite, unless otherwise stated*
There's a good campsite, **Campeggio Acqua Dolce,** in Levanto (w campingacquadolce.com) and another in Framura (☏ 0187 808465), on the hill above the station, but be prepared for a hike up and down to the beach.

🏠 **Abbadia San Giorgio** (8 rooms) Piazzale S Giorgio, Moneglia; ☏ 0185 491119; e info@abbadiasangiorgio.com; w abbadiasangiorgio.com. This is a couples-only type of place, & a very romantic one at that – children are not welcome. If you're looking for a honeymoon hotel, this is a candidate. It's a little oasis in an old 14th-century abbey with stylish rooms. The hotel also hosts events,

concerts & theatrical performances. Guests can use the pool at the nearby Hotel Edera. €€€€
🏠 **L'Amandola** (8 rooms) Località Amandola 14; ☏ 0187 801354; m 328 456 8158; e info@agriturismolamandola.it; w www. agriturismolamandola.it. Beautiful 17th-century boutique villa with splendid views, surrounded by a lush garden, olive groves & vineyards. The junior suite has a fabulous open fireplace & is perfect if

146

LEVANTO
& around

Where to stay

For listings, see from page 146

1 Cà du Ferrà
2 Campeggio Acqua Dolce
3 I Pipetta
4 L'Amandola
5 La Rossola
6 Villa Belvedere
7 Villa Caterina

Off map
Abbadia San Giorgio

Where to eat and drink

8 Bar Barolino
9 Da Marisa Antica Liguria
10 Gelateria delle Rose
11 Il Laboratorio del Pesto
12 L'Igea
13 Osteria Tumelin
14 Pasticceria Bianchi
15 Panetteria Raso
16 Piper Bar

Off map
L'Agave
La Ruota

you are travelling in early spring or late autumn. Cooking classes. Bikes. €€€

🏠 **Cà du Ferrà** (4 rooms) Via Gavazzo 46; ☎0187 814083; w agriturismo-caduferra.it. This B&B is a 5min walk from the station in Bonassola & has bikes for guests to use. Nice garden & lovely homemade cakes for b/fast. They advertise themselves as gay friendly, which is unusual in Liguria. They produce wine & lemons. Outside kitchen. Pets are allowed. €€

🏠 **I Pipetta** (4 rooms) Via San Giovanni Bosco, Legnaro; ☎0187 801342; m 349 463 9038; e info@agriturismo-pippetta.it; w agriturismo-pipetta.it. Rustic B&B with simple rooms. The farmhouse has 2.5 acres of land with vineyards & olive trees & is on a hill 3km behind Levanto. They also grow fruit & vegetables. €€

🏠 **La Rossola** (17 rooms) Località Rossola 11, Bonassola; ☎0187 808109; e larossola@gmail. com; w larossola.it. Small hotel with excellent food & a small swimming pool, but you need a car to stay here & it's a bumpy ride down 1km of unpaved road. Good for families with trpl & quad rooms. Free Wi-Fi & mountain bikes for hire. €€

🏠 **Sostio a Levante** [map, page 128] (10 rooms) Località Montebello 1; ☎0187 824284; e info@sostioalevante.com; w sostioalevante.

com. Farm with swimming pool in a tranquil setting. Be sure to eat here as the hosts are excellent cooks. The family grow their own vegetables & make their own wine. €€

🏠 **Villa Belvedere** (16 rooms) Via A Serra 15; ☎0187 813622; w bonassolahotelvillabelvedere.com. Above Bonassola in a lovely garden with hammocks & deck-chairs. The views from the shady terrace make the stay & the restaurant is good. There's a shuttle service to the station. €€

🏠 **Villa Caterina** (4 rooms) Località Pie di Gallona; ☎0187 804013; e info@villacaterina. com; w villacaterina.com. This B&B is 2km from the beach & has a nice garden. It is run by a friendly young couple & the atmosphere is cosy & relaxed. €€

🏠 **Agriturismo Degli Olivi** [map, page 128] (4 rooms) Località Bardellone-Ca'Vagine; ☎0187 1851922; m 328 291 0799; e aziendaagricoladegliolivi@cdh.it; w agriturismodegliolivi.com. Authentic home cooking up in the mountains at this rustic farm. Hiking paths run directly from the door. The couple raise their own animals, grow their own vegetables & make cheese. You need a car to get here as it is 12km from the coast. €

✖ **WHERE TO EAT AND DRINK** *Map, page 147*

Levanto has two gastronomic specialities: *gattafin*, a deep-fried savoury pastry stuffed with chard and onions; and *torciglione*, a sweet pastry made with strands of sugary dough and shortbread dough twisted together, and full of raisins, chocolate powder and sugar. There are decent pizzerias in Sette and Costa above Framura Station. Buy pesto at **Il Laboratorio del Pesto** (Via Dante 16; w laboratoriodelpesto.it).

Bar Barolino (Corso Italia 29) is Levanto's oldest café founded in 1921 and it still has a 1920's feel. Try a *barolino*, which is Barolo Chinato, a fortified wine served with ice. **Piper Bar** (Via Arenile Gavazzo) is right on the beach, perched on wooden poles and is also a lovely spot for a drink. **Pasticceria Bianchi** (on Via Dante, on the corner with Via Vinzoni 33) is the oldest cake shop in town, founded in 1889. It still has a 19th-century feel to it and has a few tables for coffees and tea. Try their small almond pastries, candied cherries and orange peel. **Panetteria Raso** (Via Dante Alighieri 25) is the place to buy focaccia.

In Bonnasola buy focaccia from **Da Marisa Antica Liguria** (Via Risorgemento) and ice cream at **Geletaria delle Rose** (Via Rezzano 22).

✖ **La Ruota** Via Perlemeglio 6, Moneglia; ☎0185 49565; w laruotamoneglia.it. This is the place to splurge on a truly romantic meal. There are fabulous views & the restaurant runs a pick-up service from Moneglia. They serve the

Ligurian classics with a refreshing modern touch. It's a set menu of multiple courses & dinner starts at 20.30. They serve some excellent local wines. €€€€€

✶✘ L'Agave Località Chiama 1, Framura; m 328 862 6222; ✦; closed Wed & Nov–Mar. Tables with a view. The menu features fish. Don't miss this restaurant if you are in the area. €€€

✘ Osteria Tumelin Via D Grillo 32; ✆0187 808379; e info@tumelin.it; w tumelin.it; ⊕ closed Thu in winter & 12 Jan–12 Feb. This is Levanto's best restaurant. It's in a

beautiful 13th-century house with a romantic atmosphere. Always reliable. Booking advisable. €€€

✘ L'Igea Via G Semenza 5; ✆0187 807293. This restaurant is a real favourite with locals & is the place to taste the area's speciality dishes. They also make good pizza so it can cater for a wide variety of tastes & ages. €€

SHOPPING There is a good street market on Wednesday in Levanto. **Antica Pasta Fresca Maria** (Piazza Staglieno 26) is the place to buy pasta, which is handmade by the owner Marco Del Bene, who also makes the sauces and the famous Ligurian speciality *cima*. This is a wine-producing area and there are two places near Levanto where you can taste the local wine and buy some to take home at **Lagaxio** (Via Zoppi 11; ✆ 0187 807137) and **Enoteca Vinum** (Piazza Staglieno 34; ✆0187 800141). Make a call before visiting to check they are open.

WHAT TO SEE AND DO Levanto is a handsome medieval town with some of its walls still intact. The key attraction is the church of **Sant'Andrea**, which is a good example of the Ligurian Gothic style. There are some fine paintings inside. You can rent boats and kayaks on the seafront. Its castle was built by the Malaspina family in 1165 and expanded by the Genoese in the 16th century. The hillsides are dotted with some impressive villas, many of which are now hotels.

The little town of **Bonassola** has a wide pebble beach and some excellent diving. It is full of charm, largely because it is small and the holidaymakers here are all Italians who come on a regular basis, so much so that many of them are almost locals. The town has some handsome old villas and the old railway track that runs to Framura has been turned into a promenade.

There are lovely walks towards Punta Baffe and Punta Manara or towards the Bracco mountain pass before La Spezia. The 2½ hour hike to Monterosso begins in Levanto. It is wonderful in winter when the air is at its clearest, and the views to Corsica and Elba are stunning. Hire a bike by the station and pedal through the cool breeze in the old railway tunnels to Bonassola. Stairs lead down to a tiny beach if you fancy a dip. There's rock climbing at Punta Baffe. There is a nice walk to the tiny church of Madonna della Punta on a cliff jutting out into the sea. There's a taxi boat from the harbour in **Framura**, just below the station. If you ask them to drop you on one of the little beaches or on the rocks along the coast, you'll experience the wild Liguria that inspired Montale's poetry. The taxi can pick you up when you have finished with your Robinson Crusoe experience. The snorkelling is among the best in Liguria and the mountains make a sheer drop into the sea so it is deep and rocky, perfect for fish.

Above **Moneglia** are two little castles built by the Genoese in the 12th century to protect the town from pirates. In the 11th century nearly all of the town's inhabitants were taken into slavery. To the west, inside the church of **San Giorgio**, within the grounds of Castle Monleone, hangs the masterpiece *The Adoration of the Magi* by Luca Cambiaso. The artist was born in Moneglia, as was the poet Felice Romani, who wrote librettos for Bellini, Donizetti and Rossini. Another of Cambiaso's works, *The Last Supper*, is in the striped church of **Santa Croce** (Via Vittorio Emanuele 147), built in 1726. Inside are two links from the chain that once closed the harbour at Pisa, and trophies from the Battle of Meloria at which the Genoese smashed the

Pisans. It also houses a Byzantine cross that was washed up on the beach and the painting *San Giorgio*, attributed to Rubens.

The road from Moneglia to Riva Ligure is a fun drive through the old railway tunnel. It is a single-file road regulated by traffic lights every 20 minutes.

UP IN THE MOUNTAINS

Whereas all the world and his wife may be surging out of Riomaggiore railway station into the August sunshine, in the hinterland it's easy to find oneself bouncing down an untarmacked road, driving through sleepy valleys and spending the night in untouristy towns with chatty, friendly locals.

The hills east of La Spezia are well off the beaten track. Just 20 minutes' drive up into the woods on the SP370, the road for Riomaggiore, is **Biassa**, which has a panoramic view back across La Spezia and the Apuan Alps. On a little hill next to the village is a ruined 12th-century Genoese castle, the **Castello di Coderone**. But if you want some peace and quiet, take the winding wooded road up to **Campiglia**, a pretty medieval village that clings to the cliff side on the old mule road that ran from Porto Venere to Levanto. There are more stunning views across the sea from one side, and from the other a bird's eye view of La Spezia and across to the marble mountains of Cararra. You can walk to the Cinque Terre from here, although it's a real hike. Two thousand steps lead down to the beach at Punta del Persico. Take a deep breath! This is the place to come for a workout holiday. Just a little further westwards it gets even more remote, and there are a number of dirt-track roads near Perodi if you really want to get away from it all. Campiglia is known for its saffron and you can buy it in the village shop, which also sells *fichi d'India chinotti* and local sea salt.

The Via Aurelia heads west towards Sestri Levante crossing the Passo del Braco. It is a route that is popular with mountain bikers as it takes far longer by car to take this road than it does to go on the motorway. It offers fine views down to the coast. Immediately after World War II it was notorious for its bandits.

WHERE TO STAY

Le Ville Relais [map, page 128] (6 rooms) Località Campiglia, Salita al Piano 19; 0187 751518; e info@levillerelais.it; w levillerelais.it. A B&B with a swimming pool & fantastic views back across La Spezia. Restaurant (€€€) serving classic local dishes. All rooms have panoramic views & there is a family suite. €€

Locanda Tramonti (4 rooms, 1 apt) Località Campiglia, Via della Chiesa 56; 0187 758514; e info@locandatramonti.it; w locandatramonti.it; ⊕ closed Jan–Feb. This is a pretty basic hotel, but the point of staying here isn't luxury. The 5-star bit is the view & the surrounding countryside, away from the bustle of the Cinque Terre. €€

Corte Paganini [map, page 128] (5 apts) Via Castè 41, Castè; m 333 249 1254; w www.cortepaganini.com. These apartments in the ancient village of Castè have lots of traditional Italian charm & are tucked away in the hills above La Spezia. They are basic but a good price. Courtyard with deckchairs & barbecue. €

THE VAL DI VARA

The lush Val di Vara is more undulating than the steep valleys that make up much of the Ligurian hinterland. Above all, it is an agricultural area, and organic farming is a key part of the local economy; almost 70% of the local farms are organic. Beef and dairy farming are predominant, but there are also plenty of smallholdings producing berries, honey, vegetables, cornflour, chestnuts, wine and oil. You can stop and buy cheese and vegetables as you drive around. Many Spezzini, who originally hail from here, have weekend bolt-holes in the valley. You need your own transport to explore it properly. Budget for one or two days.

If you like walking, pick up the Alta Via dei Monti Liguri north of Varese Ligure at the Passo Chiapparino. At Beverino there is a good walk along the trail known as the Strada dei Tedeschi, so called as it was used during World War II by German soldiers.

GETTING THERE Take the exit on the A12 *autostrada* for Brugnato or, on the A15, exit at Borgo Val di Taro. That said, **buses** run up the SP523 from Sestri Levante and La Spezia along the SP566.

WHERE TO STAY, EAT AND DRINK A word of warning. If you look on the web for a room around Pignone, a number may pop up in **Riccò di Golfo**. This is a place for dealing with practicalities, like getting cash to pay for a B&B, but the village is an uninteresting drag along the main road, and is not a good place to base yourself.

Pignone & around

Casa Villara (5 rooms) Via Castagnarossa 8, Beverino; 0187 883356; m 349 818 1269; e casavillara@hotmail.com. The house is surrounded by woods on an organic farm that produces wine & olive oil, chestnuts, fruit & vegetables, saffron & honey. Cookery courses & guided walks. Rooms sleep up to 4. Pet friendly. It has a wonderful restaurant where you can taste the local cuisine & it is also linked to the Slow Food Movement (€€€). They raise the local red rooster. €€

I Due Ghiri [map, page 128] (8 rooms) Località Usurana; 0187 576500; m 335 806 1067; e info@agriturismoidueghiri.it; w agriturismoidueghiri.com. A farmhouse stay near Calice Cornoviglio. You can eat here (€€) & even join in cooking your own dinner or simply stop to buy their produce. €€

Il Cigno Ligustico (3 rooms) Via Raffaele Bellani 10A, Pignone; 0187 887681; e info@ cignoligustico.it; w cignoligustico.it. A family-run B&B in the sleepy main square. Delicious homemade b/fast & a friendly welcome from the owners & all the villagers alike. All rooms are doubles but a single bed can be added, & if you ask in advance, you can use the kitchen. €€

Il Nido nella Bionda (6 rooms) Via Bionda 4, Brugnato; m 3498 803450; e info@ ilnidonellabionda.it; w ilnidonellabionda.it. An 18th-century stone farmhouse with a swimming pool which also has a garden. €€

La Giara (6 rooms) Via M Federici 15, Beverino ; 0187 883129; m 347 911 2232; e info@agriturismolagiara.it; w agriturismolagiara.it. Open all year. This lovely farm is perfect for families as it has a swimming pool & children's playground. The restaurant is the big draw (€€€) & serves the local speciality, *testaroli*, with pesto, mushroom sauce or simply oil & cheese. All the fresh pasta is handmade. The meat is barbecued. The restaurant is linked to the Slow Food Movement. Pets welcome. €€

La Meridiana [map, page 128] (5 rooms, 1 apt) Via Valletta 27B, Casale; 0187 887020; e info@lameridianacasale.it; w www. lameridianacasale.it. Lovely B&B run by a charming couple, Edda & Ubaldo. The b/fast is great, with Edda's homemade cakes. They couldn't do more to make you feel at home. The rooms are large & some can sleep 4 people. There is a terrace to relax on just by the rooms, so if you have kids, it's a great option, as you can enjoy the cool of the night with a glass of wine just moments away from them. Cash only. €€

La Taverna dei Golosi Via Borgo San Bernardo 16, Brugnato; 0187 895007. Cosy restaurant in Brugnato. Traditional dishes made with organic produce from the Val di Vara. €€€

Trattoria Puin Via Monti, Località Puin, Pignone; m 331 416 5243; w ristorantepuin. it. This restaurant opened in the 1960s & has a dedicated following. It is the place to taste the meat & vegetables from the Val di Vara as well as the best fish from Monterosso. Local wines feature on the menu. €€€

Locanda da Marco Via del Campanile 139, Pignone; 0187 887950; w locandadamarco.it. Local cooking & traditional dishes, including *gattafin* (deep-fried pastry with a herb filling) and *sgabei* (deep-fried pastry with salami filling). They also rent rooms. €€

✗ **Pizzeria Il Castellaro** Via Superiore (in the old town), Pignone. This place wins for atmosphere & location, even if the food is rather basic. €

Varese Ligure & around

🏠 **Albergo Amici** (8 rooms) Via Garibaldi 80; ✆0187 842139; e info@albergoamici.com; w albergoamici.com. This is a typical family-run Italian hotel, which has a good restaurant (€€) that serves local organic beef. This is just one of the local businesses that were saved by the initiative to go green. €

🏠 **Il Gumo** (1 room, 1 apt) Località Gumo 69, Varese Ligure; ✆0187 842282; e ilgumo@ tin.it; w ilgumo.it. The farm produces seasonal organic vegetables, fresh herbs, homemade jams & liqueurs. Min stay 2 nights. €

🏠 **Risveglio Naturale** [map, page 128] (4 rooms) Località Valletti-Colea 99; ✆0187 185 4393; m 392 219 5962; w risveglionaturale.it. Tranquil accommodation in the countryside 9km from Varese Ligure in an old stone farmhouse. Wi-Fi & a wonderful option of a great homemade dinner. A very friendly place. €

✗ **A Ca' du Pipin** [map, page 128] Località Toceto 82, Comuneglia; ✆0187 849041; ⊕ Sat & Sun only. Luigino & Orietta serve a fixed menu of traditional dishes. The bread, pasta & desserts are all homemade, the fruit & vegetables come from the cottage garden & the organic meat is from the Val di Vara or locally raised rabbits. €€€

✗ **L'Osteria du Chicchinettu** Piazza Manzzini 5, Varese Ligure; ✆0187 842052; ⊕ closed Wed & some hols. Traditional dishes, among them vegetable pies, *testaroli* with pesto & stuffed vegetables. Best to book a table. €€€

Off the beaten path

🏠 **Ca' du Chittu** (7 rooms) Isolato Camporione 25, Carro; ✆0187 861205; m 335 803 7376; e caduchittu@virgilio.it; w caduchittu.it. Lovely farm with a really authentic feel, which produces organic fruit, honey, vegetables & meat. The project is sponsored by La Spezia Slow Food. Rooms have 1950s furniture. It is also possible to camp here. Cooking classes. Horseriding & sailing. The restaurant has a set menu of classic local dishes at €25 not inc wine. Reservations recommended. €

PIGNONE Just 16km inland from Monterosso, life in Pignone couldn't be more different. This is a very quiet place where you will find Italian families kicking around footballs and mama calling them in for dinner as if they were in a pasta advert. The ancient bridge was washed away in the 2011 flood and this part of the Val di Vara is struggling to get over the devastation it inflicted. It is a good reason to visit, as the area needs help to get back on its feet – it received no state assistance.

🍴 THE BLACK ROOSTER

Farmers in the Val di Vara have reintroduced a huge black chicken that almost disappeared after World War II. It has a silky black plumage with metallic green hues and a bright red crest. It almost died out as it was considered too large for the small families that have been so typical of Italy in the last 50 years, as one bird can make at least six meals. Without the passion and drive of Luciano Stagnaro, the breed would have completely disappeared. He carefully rebred the bird over a number of years and it now sadly only differs from the original in the fact that it no longer has pink legs. The roosters grow to a size of 3kg in ten months and 6.5kg by the age of two. They are free range as this is an organic valley. A number of farmers have joined forces and formed a local association of breeders based in Varese Ligure. The roosters and hens can be bought from November until February. To raise the breed to the strength it once had, this Slow Food project needs to make sure that farmers can sell the birds at a profit.

You can see and taste the birds at **Azienda Agrituristica Il Pellegrino** (Pelosa 201, Tornolo; m 328 747 3502; e info@ilpellegrino.eu) who also do donkey trekking.

above   The villages of the Cinque Terre have retained much of their original charm, including Riomaggiore, the largest of the five (IuS/S) page 144

below   Camogli – Dickens dubbed it a 'piratical little place' (AT/S) page 95

above left   UNESCO-listed Porto Venere sits at the tip of a rocky promontory (u/S) page 164

above right The Ligurian coast isn't just about picture-perfect villages — the Grotte di Toirano are among the most beautiful caves in Italy (SS) page 224

below   The elegant resort of Sestri Levante developed around the picturesque Isola promontory (AAL) page 124

above left A defensive tower at Monterosso once protected villagers from pirates (L/S) page 134

above right Liguria is a great climbing destination all year round (AAL) page 42

right Enjoy the views from Corniglia, which looks out to all four of the other Cinque Terre villages (S/S) page 142

below Medieval Porto Maurizio is the historic centre of Imperia (pa/S) page 240

above   Chamois are occasionally seen in Liguria's high country (J/S) page 5

left   *Charaxes jasius* is known locally as *ninfa del corbezzolo* or 'nymph of the strawberry tree' (PM/S) page 5

bottom left   The Aesculapian snake is one of several species found in the region (MM/S) page 5

below   A variety of sea mammals such as blue dolphins and sperm whales can be seen along Liguria's coast (VA/S) page 6

bottom right   The Eurasian eagle owl is present in Liguria, but is rarely seen (MAP/S)

above The Parco Naturale Regionale del Beigua is the largest protected area in Liguria (IoS/S) page 191

right The Abbazia di Sant'Andrea at Borzone is built on the ruins of a Roman fortress (L/D) page 121

below Claude Monet painted several scenes at Dolceacqua in the Val Nervia in 1884 (NC/S) page 273

above left There are shops selling fresh focaccia on every street corner in Liguria (AAL) page 34

above right Chiavari is well known for a range of different crafts, including macramé (AAL) page 118

left All manner of local produce can be found in Genoa's atmospheric Mercato Orientale (YG/S) page 81

below Taste the famous fortified Sciacchetrà wine made from grapes grown in the Cinque Terre (AAL) page 38

above left   Ceramics have been made in Albisola for more than 500 years (AAL) page 198

above right   Liguria produces the world's tastiest basil — a key ingredient in the regional dish, pesto (FR/S) page 36

right   A fisherman sells his catch on the beach at Monterosso al Mare (SS) page 134

below   Italy's largest frying pan is put to use at Camogli's famous Sagra del Pesce every May (SS) page 95

above Religious celebrations are an important part of local life: here residents celebrate St Benedict in Taggia (DS/S) page 249

below left A procession parades through the streets of Savona on Good Friday (SS) page 202

below right Every five years the colourful Euroflora flower show takes place in Genoa (cg/S) page 55

Staying here is a good option if you want to see the Cinque Terre yet avoid the crowds and there is a bus service if you don't have a car. There is a nice bar in the main square, which is directly opposite some graffiti dating from World War II. It is an atmospheric place to stop for a coffee. There's also a market of local products the last weekend in August, but that's about it. There's not much going on, but if you have spent a summer's day in the Cinque Terre, this will come as something of a relief.

The old mule path leads to Levanto from here and it is a lovely 17.5km walk. The path, however, was damaged during the 2011 flood, but new wooden bridges have replaced the old ones that were washed away.

You can buy vegetables from **Agnese Barilari** (Via Calcinara 198; m 360 457116) who sells the famous local potatoes. **La Ferriera Casale** (Via Ferriero 240; 0187 887778) sells the renowned local beans.

Nearby **Casella** is built around the remains of an old castle. There's not much left of it, however. The village has been spruced up and a number of the houses are Milanese holiday homes, to the displeasure of the locals. Drive up here to enjoy the panoramic views across the Val di Vara.

CRISIS IN CASALE

At lunchtime on 25 October 2011 the village of Casale was hit by what local residents describe as 'a water bomb'. Floodwaters burst down the valley like a huge tsunami, and in seconds the ground floors of nearly all the houses in the village were engulfed in water. The water brought with it tons of mud and trees that crashed down on the town, filling the streets and making them impassable.

'I was in La Spezia that day, but normally I would have been in my kitchen, and I would have been killed instantly,' says Edda Battolini. 'It was lucky that the local children were not back from school, or they might have been killed too.'

'We had spent years raising money to restore the 15 paintings in the church. They were very old and we had restored all but one. Now they are in a terrible state, covered in mud, and have been taken away for cleaning,' she adds.

Edda had just done up her little B&B by the old bridge and, like all the local residents, has had to foot the bill for putting things back to normal. She says, 'There was no money from the insurance as it was an act of God, and the government have no money to help us.' It's clear that the locals feel abandoned; most of the press coverage and state assistance went to the Cinque Terre, who quickly got themselves back up and running. Away from the tourist trail, it's a different story.

Edda repeatedly says, 'Thanks for listening to what happened here', as her husband pours us another glass of his homemade limoncello.

In 2012, after I had visited for the first time, I wrote: 'There's a future for Casale, but it's going to be a long haul.' Returning in 2018 I was shocked how true my observation was. Although much rebuilding work has been done, the work in the area is far from complete.

Vernazza may have got the attention of the international rich and famous and had its main square remodelled by the architect Richard Rogers, but Casale is a forgotten corner. If you want to help, you simply visit and spend your money here.

The quaint little village of **Casale** had its medieval bridge washed away in the 2011 floods, as well as part of the **Oratorio** and the small mining museum. The people here are very friendly and, if you stay, you will certainly be giving something back.

Borghetto di Vara, to the northwest on the SS34, is also getting itself back on its feet after the horrendous flood of 2011 devastated the heart of the village, claiming eight lives. Progress is, however, being made; the hotel that was on the banks of the river is now being renovated. From the centre of the village, the left-hand fork leads to **Brugnato**, which has a centre laid out in the unusual shape of a key, built around a Romanesque church with a couple of pretty frescoes and the tiny 12th-century bishop's palace. The palace was extended in the 17th century when the loggia and staircase were added. There's a museum with, to all accounts, an impressive collection of religious art, but it only opens when festivals are taking place. These are not listed, so it's best to assume you won't see inside. The area is a centre for white-water rafting and canyoning: **Kayak Brugnato** (m 327 108 8219).

The Val di Vara behind Brugnato is dotted with prosperous villages, many of which are of little interest to visitors, but among those worth a look are medieval **Cornice** and **Calice al Cornoviglio**. The area is known for its honey, which you can buy in the nearby hamlet of Santa Maria, from **Apicoltura Ribaditi** (Via Santa Maria 44; m 328 672 6264; w apicolturaribaditi.it). **Caseificio Esposito** (Via Regurone 13; ☏ 0187 894103; w caseificioesposito.com) sells milk, cheese and yoghurt.

VARESE LIGURE The salt route from the coast to Emilia-Romagna ran through the Val di Vara, and Varese, at the top of the valley, was a key town on the trading route that brought goods north from the Roman ports on the coast at Luni and Sestri Levante. It's known as the 'round little town' after its arcaded medieval central square, the Borgo Rotondo, which runs around one side of the tiny castle in an arc. The town was once heavily fortified but this is all that remains of its defences. From the air, however, the town is actually laid out in the shape of the euro symbol. The castle at its heart was once a stronghold of the Fieschi family, who donated the land and promised to protect any merchant willing to build a house here.

Opposite the castle is the pretty pink church of **San Filippo Neri** (c1676). Inside on the left-hand wall is the masterpiece *San Francesco Saverio* by Gregorio de Ferrari. The church is part of a convent.

A visit to Varese is essentially about the countryside and there are a number of lovely walks on Monte Zuccone (1,423m), north of Varese, where you can pick up the Alta Via dei Monti Liguri. It runs just north of the village of Cassego over Monte Zuccone and Monte Scassella. North of Varese is the Passo di Cento Croci (1,055m), named after the number of travellers killed by highwaymen, which leads into Emilia-Romagna.

Tourist information Food festivals are held in Piazza Castello throughout the year (w comune.vareseligure.sp.it). On 16 August, the **Fiesta San Rocco** is celebrated with a religious procession, including a blessing for dogs. It was a dog that brought the saint food when he lay dying of plague. There is a cook-up on the sports field on 11 November to celebrate the feast of San Martino, and the streets are full of stalls selling local produce.

Shopping Across the old bridge next to the little parking area by the river is a tiny workshop making the wooden stamps used to fashion the local *croxetti* pasta, little discs with a pattern or heraldic symbol printed on them. Pop into **Alimentari**

Blenci (Piazza Mazzini 4), a well-stocked grocery and fresh pasta shop, which also sells a good range of local cheeses. This is the place to buy dried *croxetti* pasta and some excellent jars of nut sauce, *salsa di noce*. It's pricey but very tasty, and is made with dried mushrooms and white wine. Also good is **Antichi Sapori del Borgo** on Piazza Vittorio Emanuele. The local cattle producers **Cooperativa San Pietro Vara** (Via Municipio 1; ☎ 0187 842501) sell top-notch organic beef and salami, while 1km south of town the **Cooperativa Casearia Val di Vara** (Località Perassa; ☎ 0187 840507; w coopcasearia.it) sells local cheeses and you can see them being produced.

FURTHER AFIELD The outdoor adventure playground **Parco Avventura** (2km southeast of Tavarone; m 339 532 4177; e parcoavventura@giandriale.it; w parcoavventuravaldivara.it; ⊕ Jun–Sep daily, w/ends rest of year) is great if you are travelling with kids. Opening times and prices vary, so check the website before you go.

6

La Spezia and the
Gulf of Poets

Telephone code 0187 (+390187 if calling from abroad)

La Spezia sits at the head of one of Italy's most beautiful bays, which shelters
Liguria's only archipelago. The **Golfo dei Poeti** inspired Petrarch, Dante, Shelley,
Byron and D H Lawrence, to name just a few of the famous writers who have spent
time here. La Spezia is Italy's most important naval port, with a population of over
94,000 people, and home to Italian defence company OTO Melara.

The resorts of Lerici, Porto Venere and Tellaro are great bases for a holiday.
Inland is the little gem of a city, Sarzana, which is usually overlooked by tourists in
the rush to get to the coast and the nearby Cinque Terre. There is plenty to see and
do, lovely beaches to unwind on, cliff-climbing at Muzzerone and lots of beautiful
walks. The 44km Alta Via del Golfo footpath connects the two sides of the bay with
unforgettable views.

LA SPEZIA

La Spezia is a working city and, if you give it time, it has much authentic charm.
Less touristy than the other places on the gulf and with excellent transport
connections, it is the perfect base to explore the area. It has some good restaurants,
a nice landscaped seaside promenade and a couple of interesting little museums,
and there is a handy train link to the Cinque Terre, as well as good bus connections
to Porto Venere. There is ample choice of accommodation and an ever-growing
number of affordable B&Bs. There are also B&Bs, some on farms, outside the city,
which make a great base for exploring the area if you have a car.

HISTORY *Spezia* means 'spice' in Italian and the city is named after all the spices
that were shipped through here from the Middle Ages onwards. The area around
La Spezia has been settled since prehistoric times and there are important Roman
remains in the province at nearby Luni (page 175). As the city was a port, plague,
which was brought from Asia aboard Genoese ships, was a continual problem.
It was because of this the republic constructed a contagious disease hospital in
1724, to quarantine goods and sailors who arrived in the port. English writer
Tobias Smollett, who visited in 1763, observed, 'The whole bay is surrounded with
plantations of olives and oranges, and makes a very delightful appearance. In case
of a war, this would be an admirable station for a British squadron.' Napoleon,
however, was to beat the British navy to it and he declared the bay the best harbour
in the world and wanted to build his own naval base here. Events overtook him and
it fell to the House of Savoy to develop La Spezia's potential. In 1862, Garibaldi and
his troops were headquartered in the Hotel Milan.

By 1901 the city had a population of 73,000 people. In 1913, Frederic Lees described La Spezia in his *Wanderings on the Italian Riviera*: 'Militarism is the dominant note of its streets, its incomparable harbour, and the surrounding circle of hills. Its gardens and shady avenues are ever crowded with smartly-dressed officers and blue-jackets. Pyramids of shells are on the quays, and long rows of torpedo boats are moored alongside. Out in the bay blue-gray ironclads ride at anchor and are continually reminding you that nothing would be easier than to crush you out of existence.'

The city was badly bombed in World War II and after the Italian capitulation to the Allies in 1943 it was from here that a good part of the Italian navy left to turn its ships over to the Allies in Malta. The Germans arrived too late to stop the departure of the fleet, so they summarily executed the remaining Italian captains.

In the late 19th century, La Spezia was a popular tourist destination. It was here that composer Richard Wagner first heard the E-flat chords that begin *Das Rheingold* and set the stage for the monumental *Der Ring des Nibelungen*. The tune, which suggests the churning of the River Rhine, came to him as he lay in bed in a hotel at Via del Prione 45, recovering from a journey from Genoa across a rough sea in 1853. A plaque marks the spot.

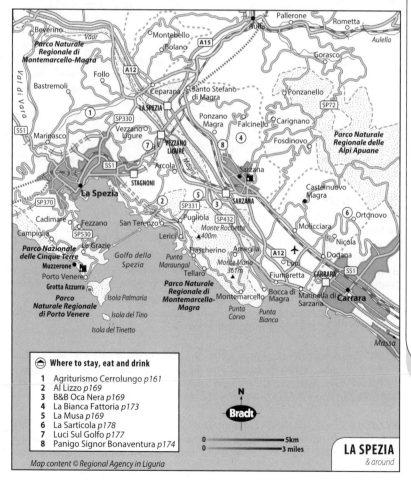

6

Where to stay, eat and drink

1   Agriturismo Cerrolungo *p161*
2   Al Lizzo *p169*
3   B&B Oca Nera *p169*
4   La Bianca Fattoria *p173*
5   La Musa *p169*
6   La Sarticola *p178*
7   Luci Sul Golfo *p177*
8   Panigo Signor Bonaventura *p174*

N

0 ————— 5km
0 ————— 3 miles

Bradt

LA SPEZIA
& around

Map content © Regional Agency in Liguria

An €11 million redevelopment of the old military docks has destroyed the Pagliari pier, where over a thousand Holocaust survivors went on hunger strike in 1946 when the occupying British forces blocked their illegal ship from sailing to Palestine. Once the new marina is built, visitors will, however, thanks to pressure from local activists, be able to visit a new monument to this little-known part of the city's history.

The hunger strike inspired the novel and Hollywood blockbuster *Exodus*, starring Paul Newman as Yehuda Arazi, the Israeli secret agent, and head of Haganah operations in Italy, who led the survivors to Palestine. The actual *Exodus* was fitted out on nearby Porto Venere, which had been a major dockyard at the time. At the time, Palestine was under British control and Jewish immigration was severely curtailed. With the help of left-wing Italian partisans, Arazi cared for and helped to secretly spirit away many of the 75,000 Jewish refugees who flooded into Italy after World War II.

When the British discovered that a thousand Holocaust survivors were trying to leave La Spezia for Palestine, soldiers tried to drive them off the ship. The refugees fought them off the pier and Arazi called a hunger strike to try to force them to let them set sail. The British, however, were no push-overs and a Royal Navy ship sailed into the bay. From the deck the British demanded that the survivors disembark immediately. Arazi shouted back that he would blow the ship sky-high if the British tried to forcibly remove them. As the British sealed the port off with tanks, the news of the Holocaust survivors' plight made headlines across the world. Arazi sent radio messages to world leaders, including President Truman, informing them that the thousand survivors of Hitler's camps were crowded into a small ship in an Allied port being besieged by the greatest navy in the world. It would have a major impact on American policy in the Middle East. Arazi hung a sign on the port gates proclaiming it was 'The Gateway to Zion' and

GETTING THERE AND AROUND

By air The closest airport is Pisa, 80km away. Trains run from Pisa airport to La Spezia. Genoa airport is 113km away. Take the shuttle bus from the airport to Genoa's Principe Station to catch the train.

By boat The yacht club Assonautica has 622 berths (✆ 0187 770229). Tourist boats [160 F3] (w navigazionegolfodeipoeti.it) leave from the seafront promenade for Genoa and Lerici, as well as coastal towns including Porto Venere, the Cinque Terre, Portofino, and Viareggio in Tuscany. Budget €35 for a round trip. It is also possible to hire a small boat to explore.

By bus Buses leave from La Spezia from Via Chiato for the resorts around the Golfo dei Poeti, Sarzana, and for the towns along the Cinque Terre (w atcesercizio.it). Buses for Porto Venere, Sarzana and Lerici also leave from Via Chiodo [160 F4] and all take well under an hour. Tickets cost from €1.50. Fewer buses operate on Sunday.

By car La Spezia is on the A12 *autostrada*, 111km from Genoa and the A15, 125km from Parma. Parking is not an issue here. There is a small car park by the station or a much larger one in the Porto Mirabello, a marina complex on the seafront next to the Arsenale.

flew the Zionist and Italian flags side by side. On the fifth day of the hunger strike Harold Laski, a high-ranking member of the British Labour Party and scion of an influential Jewish family arrived. He tried to persuade Arazi to call the hunger strike off while he interceded on their behalf, but Arazi refused, informing Laski that the next morning ten of the refugees would commit suicide and every dawn ten would do the same until they were allowed to sail. Finally Laski returned from London with news that the Labour government had agreed to let the ship set off. Before they left, the survivors celebrated a hasty Passover on the pier. The ship was dangerously overloaded so an extra boat was brought in and after 45 days in La Spezia, in front of a huge crowd of local well-wishers, a whistle announced their departure and the *Fede* and the *Fenice*, now renamed *Elahu Golomb* and the *Dov Hoz* finally set out to sea.

Surprisingly this drama was immediately forgotten in La Spezia until 1996 when journalist Marco Ferrari came across a story on the wires of a concert being held to commemorate the event in New York and Tel Aviv. 'I am the son of a partisan and I have lived all my life on the left but I had never heard people talk about the aid the partisans gave to the Jews.' He says that 'the partisans did not want to remember the part they had played in the creation of the state of Israel and the conflict with the Palestinians.' As the then cultural director of the local council, Ferrari set up the Exodus Prize for intercultural cooperation, but says that in recent years interest in the story has waned:

'Local people are apathetic but it is important for the world to remember what happened here. Historical facts are in danger of being forgotten and that leads to historical revisionism. The partisans helped over 25,000 Jewish refugees leave for Palestine in the run up to 1948 and they also illegally trafficked arms that were used in the battles against the Arabs. Not to remember the true facts is to leave history open to distortion.'

By taxi [160 F3] Taxis are available via 📞 0187 523523. Expect to pay over €50 for a trip to either Lerici or Porto Venere depending on the traffic.

By train La Spezia Centrale [160 A2] is on the coastal Genoa–Rome line, stopping at Genoa (1¼hrs), Milan (3hrs), Turin (3½hrs), and Parma and Pisa (50mins). La Spezia is also a starting point for visiting the Cinque Terre by train.

TOURIST INFORMATION There is a tourist office at Via del Prione 222 [160 D3] (📞0187 026152; w myspezia.it) and the Cinque Terre Park office is in the train station [160 A2] (📞0187 743500). The Discover La Spezia App is useful.

La Spezia's bustle peaks on 19 March, the feast day of the city's patron saint, San Giuseppe (St Joseph). Celebrations see a giant market fill the port and surrounding streets, and the naval base (off limits the rest of the year) opens to the public for the day. San Venerio, the patron saint of the Gulf, has his saint's day on 13 September. The first Sunday in August is the Palio del Golfo, a rowing race between the seaside towns on the Gulf. It only lasts 10 minutes but is really exciting. The Palio is part of the larger Festa del Mare, which also includes acrobatic parachutists, a costume parade and a commemoration of those lost at sea. The Spezzini eat well and have a love of chocolate, so no surprise that there is a chocolate festival here in October and November. There is an antiques market on the first Sunday of the month except in July and August.

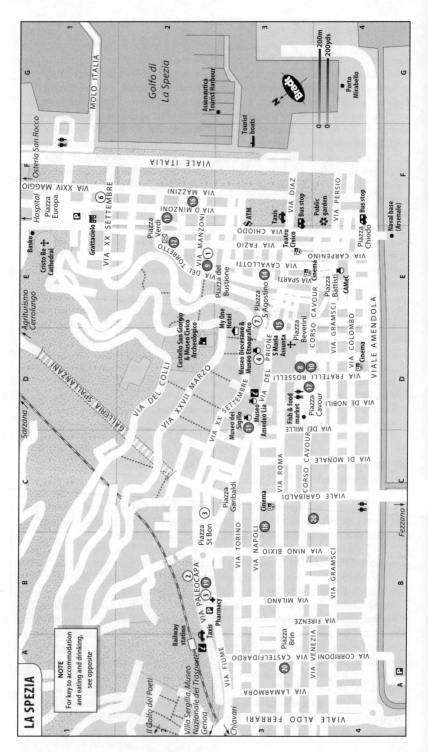

LA SPEZIA

NOTE
For key to accommodation
and eating and drinking,
see opposite

0   200m
0   200yds

WHERE TO STAY

🏠 **A 4 Passi dal Mare** [160 E2] (4 rooms) Via Vanicella 15; m 333 248 8038; e info@ a4passidalmare.com; w a4passidalmare.com. B&B in the old town with friendly hosts & good-sized beds. €€€

🏠 **Agriturismo Cerrolungo** [map, page 157] (6 rooms) Via Montalbano 211/213; 📞 0187 706176; e info@cerrolingo.it; w cerrolungo.it. Beautiful coastal views from this farmhouse, which is surrounded by its own vineyard, a 10min drive from the city centre. A good choice if you have a car & great for families. Booking for min 2 nights. €€€

🏠 **Casa Danè** [160 B2] (3 rooms) Via Paleocapa 4; m 338 535 3103; w casadane.it. This modern B&B is right by the train station. There's no reception & the owners don't live here so be sure to make an appointment to check in. B/fast is in a nearby bar. Free Wi-Fi. €€€

🏠 **Cinque Terre Bridge** [160 C2] (4 rooms) Piazza Saint Bon, 15; m 339 759 6082 w cinque-terre-bridge.business.site. In a block of flats built in the 19th century, with brand new interiors, these basic apts are just across from the station. I found the owners extremely helpful & friendly. €€€

🏠 **Del Prione** (4 rooms) [160 D3] Via del Prione 152; m 320 880 6977; w iremidelprione. com. B&B with AC & Wi-Fi in a 13th-century house on the old town's main street. €€€

🏠 **Hotel Firenze e Continentale** [160 B2] (68 rooms) Via Pietro Paleocapa 7; 📞 0187 713210; e info@hotelfirenzecontinentale.it; w hotelfirenzecontinentale.it. Old-style hotel. No restaurant but room service. Conveniently next to the train station for visiting the Cinque Terre & right next to the car park. B/fast is served in a room at the top of the hotel with a great view. €€€

🏠 **Il Golfo dei Poeti** [160 A2] (1 room & 7 apts) Via Proffiano 34; 📞 0187 711053; m 347 695 5141; e info@agriturismogolfodeipoeti. com; w agriturismogolfodeipoeti.com; ⏰ open all year. *Agriturismo* in the hills above La Spezia. Accomodation in traditional stone cottages with

sea views & kitchenettes; 2 swimming pools, children's play area, ping-pong & barbecue; b/ fast €8. The farm, which is linked to the Slow Food Movement, produces olive oil, honey & breeds the rare Montecristo goats. Pet-friendly. €€€

🏠 **NH La Spezia** [160 F1] (110 rooms) Via XX Settembre 2; 📞 0187 739555; e nhlaspezia@ nh-hotels.com; w nh-hotels.com. Although it's a rather characterless chain, it's a good bet if you are coming by car as there is free parking. The other plus is the location just a second's walk from the seafront & 5mins from the historic centre. There is a nice terrace restaurant (€€€) overlooking the sea. I like this hotel for its convenience & feel its ratings online are unfair. Ask for a room with a view of the gulf. €€€

🏠 **Pandora Apartment** [160 E3] (1 apt) Via Indipendenza 2; m 345 428 4789. Lovely stylish B&B studio apartment with a good-sized kitchen. Owner leaves ample b/fast supplies in the fridge. Off Via del Prione, the main pedestrianised street. €€€

✗ **WHERE TO EAT AND DRINK** If you are looking for picnic supplies, the covered market [160 D3] in Piazza Cavour, which is more often than not called Piazza del Mercato, is one of the best in this part of Liguria. There's a large supermarket, Basko [160 E1], on Via Veneto by the cathedral. **La Pia Centenaria** [160 E3] (Via Magenta

12) has been the place for *farinata*, pizza or the sweet *castagnaccio* since 1887. **Panificio Rizzoli Marcello** [160 B2] (Via Fiume 108) is a family-run bakery and has some good vegetable tarts.

Stampetta Panificio Pasticceria [160 C4 & A3] (Corso Cavour 245 & Corso Cavour 375) sells tasty *pandolce*. **Fiorini** [160 F2] in Piazza Verde is another popular *pasticceria* (⊕ closed Mon). **Caffè Terrile** [160 D3] (Via del Prione 265) has been serving coffee since 1900. Alternatively, for something new, the **Porto Mirabello** is a pleasant spot for a coffee and an ice cream.

While you are in the area, look out for the local beer, produced by artisan brewers Birrificio del Golfo. It is a golden beer with a hint of hay and herbs.

✗ **La Posta** [160 F2] Via Minzoni 24; ✆0187 760437; e info@lapostadiclaudio.com; w lapostadiclaudio.com. Gourmet restaurant in the centre of La Spezia serving modern takes on traditional dishes. This is the place to go if you are looking for something a bit classy. €€€€

✗ **Antica Trattoria Sevieri** [160 D3] Via della Canonica 13; ✆0187 751776; ⊕ closed Sun. Romantic & elegant, it was founded in 1907. Predominantly fish dishes. Bread, focaccia & desserts are all homemade. Outdoor seating. €€€

✗ **Il Restaurantino di Bayon** [160 E3] Via Cavallotti 23; ✆0187 732209; ⊕ closed Sun. Taste the mussels from the bay & *trofie* with shrimps. It's an institution in La Spezia. €€€

✗ **Osteria della Corte** [160 C3] Via Napoli, 86; ✆0187 715210; e info@osteriadellacorte. com; w osteriadellacorte.com. Outstanding service & fabulous local dishes in this characterful restaurant. There's a garden in summer. The desserts are a work of art so be sure to go all the way! €€€

✗ **Osteria San Rocco** [160 F1] Via Costa di Santa Lucia 25, Foce; m 3487 626428; ⊕ Wed–Mon dinner & lunch Sun. A drive out of La Spezia up in the hills behind the city in

Foce, this restaurant has a great view & excellent tasty seasonal food. Traditional *spezzini* cuisine. €€€

✗ **Arci Origami** [160 E2] Via Manzoni 39/41; m 320 815 0119. An excellent choice for vegetarians & vegans. Original tasty dishes & excellent desserts. €€

✗ **Bellavista** [160 D4] Via Rattazzi 54–56; ✆0187 738720; ⊕ lunch daily exc Sun, dinner Thu–Fri only. An atmospheric place with wooden tables covered in paper & a menu of local dishes that changes daily. Just off the market square to the southeast. €€

✗ **Da Bartali** [160 E2] Via del Torretto 64; ✆ 0187 730 0889; ⊕ closed Mon. This restaurant opened in 2009 & has built up a loyal local clientele. It specialises in fish but offers both a meat-based & a vegetarian set menu. €€

✱ ✗ **Osteria all'Inferno** [160 D3] Via Lorenzo Costa 3; ✆0187 29458; ⊕ closed Sun. This busy little restaurant has a laid-back atmosphere & serves Ligurian specialities in a vaulted cellar. The soups are tasty & the homemade pesto is made with both pine nuts & walnuts. There is an array of local dishes to choose from. €€

OTHER PRACTICALITIES There is an **ATM** [160 F3] at Via Chiodo 56/64. The **post office** [160 E2] is at Piazza Giuseppe Verdi 1. It is a classic example of Futurist architecture and well worth popping in to see in its own right. It was designed by Angiolo Mazzoni and built in 1933. There is a **pharmacy** [160 B2] at Via del Pione 9, and the **hospital** [160 E1], Sant'Andrea, is at Via Vittorio Veneto 197 (✆0187 5331). There is **internet** access in the tourist office [160 A2] at the station.

WHAT TO SEE AND DO La Spezia is quite unlike any other town in Liguria for the sense of space it gives off. Even the streets in the old town are unusually large, just as American writer and journalist, Ernest Hemingway described them in his short story, *Che Ti Dice La Patria*.

La Spezia's flagship dish is *mesciua*, a bean soup made with cereals flavoured with olive oil and pepper. Traditionally it was made with grain that fell from the bags being unloaded in the port.

La Spezia traded its salt with Emilia-Romagna, which needed it to make Parmesan and cure its hams and salamis. In return the Spezzini bought all three and as a result an extra touch of meat and cheese makes the cuisine much richer than in the rest of Liguria. One local speciality to try is *gizzoa*, a sausage focaccia. Pork dishes pop up on the menu too but with a Ligurian twist. Look out for *maiale alle olive*, pork with black olives.

Taste the fried little pies, *gattafin,* that are stuffed with herbs. The bay of La Spezia is famous for its mussels, known here as *muscoli* even if the rest of Italy calls them *cozze*. They are often served with *trennette* pasta or *croxetti*, discs of pasta, or in a *bruschetta*. For dessert, try some of the wide array of dried fruits.

The old town lies just below the railway station and the main street, **Via del Prione**, runs down to the landscaped gardens along the seafront. The top is rather touristy, but it has some nice shops and gets more authentic the closer you get to the sea. From here a large white pedestrian bridge leads to the marina, Porto Mirabello [160 G4], where you can admire huge private yachts and the view back across to the city. Via del Prione is the heart of the old town and is named after a *pietrone* or large stone, in local dialect a '*prione*', which once stood here and from the top of which public announcements were read out.

The locals were great collectors and La Spezia has a number of museums made up of former private collections that are well worth a visit. They are all small and each makes an entertaining half-hour diversion. (There is a ticket for €12 that gives access to all the main museums; w laspeziacultura.it.) It is a short walk from the station along Via Prione to the **Museo Amedeo Lia** [160 D3] (Via del Prione 234; ☎0187 731100; ☉ 10.00–18.00 Tue–Sun; admission €10), opened in 1997. Lia was a patron of the arts and collected the works that now hang in the restored 17th-century convent of San Francesco da Paola. This is one of Europe's most important private collections of religious art and there are some beautiful illuminated manuscripts. Not many people stop here unfortunately and when I arrived, they had to turn on the lights. There are paintings by Titian, Tiepolo, Lorenzetti and Bellini, as well as miniatures, medals, precious bronzes and archaeological artefacts.

Next door at No 236 is the **Museo del Sigillo** (Seal Museum) [160 D3] (☎ 0187 778544; ☉ 15.00–18.00 Wed–Thu, 10.00–18.00 Fri–Sun; admission €3.50), which has the world's biggest collection of seals dating from the 3rd century BC and was another private collection donated to the city. A little further along the street is the **Museo Diocesano** [160 D3] (Via del Prione 156; ☎ 0187 258570; ☉ 10.00–12.30 Thu, 16.00–19.00 Fri–Sun; admission €4.50) in the deconsecrated oratory of San Bernardino, which is near the site of the old town gate. At No 156 is the **Museo Etnografico** (☎ 0187 727781; ☉ 10.00–12.30 Thu, 10.00–12.30 & 16.00–19.00 Fri–Sun; admission €4.50), which has a collection of local artefacts from the 19th century.

On the hill behind Via Prione is the **Castello San Giorgio** [160 D2], built in the 13th century and expanded by the Genoese in the 17th century. Inside is the small **Museo Civico Archeologico** [160 D2] (Via XXVII Marzo; ☎0187 751142; ☉ 09.30–17.00 Wed–Sun; admission €5.50). It is well worth a visit to see the precious Bronze

Age stele from nearby Lunigiana and objects from the Roman settlement of Luni (it is best to visit after you have seen the ruins), which were originally part of two 19th-century private collections. There are also a number of Stone Age artefacts from the island of Palmaria in the bay. There are two lifts to take you there, which operate daily from 07.00 to 21.30 (winter until 20.30), from just off Via del Prione by the My One Hotel. From the top there is a good view of the bay, the defensive stone wall that runs across it and the naval ships. There is also a modern art museum, **CAMeC** [160 E4] (Piazza Battisti 1; ✆0187 734593; ⊕ 10.00–18.00 Tue–Sun; admission €5) but its collection does not merit putting it at the top of your must-see list.

Just off Via del Prione on **Piazza Beverini** is the unusual church of **Santa Maria dell'Assunta** [160 D3]. While its exterior is striped in black-and-white stone in the traditional style, the interior is refreshingly bare in comparison with the region's Baroque churches, as it was restored in 1954 after the air raids of World War II. That said, it has some notable artworks, including *The Martyrdom of Saint Bartholomew* by one of Liguria's greatest painters, Luca Cambiaso. This was once the cathedral but has handed the baton on to the extraordinary round, modern **Cristo Re** [160 E1] on **Piazza Europa** on the seafront, which was designed by Rationalist architect Adalberto Libera in the 1920s and 30s, but only finished in 1975.

The area around the cathedral has some notable fascist buildings, among them the Futurist post office [160 E2] on Piazza Verdi. There are also some interestingly decorated 19th-century edifices, among them the Palazzo Ghiaccio on Via Colombo/Via Mille, which is decorated with penguins and polar bears. The **Grattacielo** [160 F1], the skyscraper, was built in 1927.

Back on Via del Prione heading towards the seafront, the Art Deco **Teatro Civico** [160 E3] was the symbol of 1930s La Spezia. Now walk across to the western side of town to the **Arsenale** [160 E4], the naval base, whose construction put La Spezia on the map in the late 19th century. There is an interesting museum inside, the **Museo Tecnico Navale** (✆ 0187 78111; ⊕ 08.00–19.30 Mon–Sat, 08.00–19.00 Sun; admission €1.55). Even if you aren't really interested in ships, it is worth popping in to get a feel of the naval tradition that created modern La Spezia. It will also give non-Italians an alternative perspective of World War II. In the centre of the museum is the crest of British ship HMS *York* that was sunk in 1941, and there are also the remains of an Italian submarine torpedoed off Haifa in 1942. In the garden is a memorial to sailors who died during World War II. The large lamp in the main hall comes from the lighthouse at nearby Tino. Marconi, the pioneer of long-distance radio transmission, carried out important experiments here and some of his equipment is also on show. Train fans will like the tiny **Museo Nazionale dei Trasporti** [160 A2] (Via Fossiterni; ✆0187 718912; w museonazionaletrasporti. it; ⊕ 09.30–12.30 & 14.30–17.00 Sat; admission €3), which runs excursions in a 1920s steam train along the Aulla–Lucca line once a year.

WEST ALONG THE GULF OF POETS

The road west from La Spezia, which follows the bay, leads to **Le Grazie**. On the headland are the 16th-century sanctuary and the **Convento degli Olivetani**. There is also a **Roman villa** built in the 1st century BC (✆0187 794800; ⊕ by appointment only; admission free). The road skirts above the little seaside village of **Fezzano** and on to Porto Venere, 15km from La Spezia.

PORTO VENERE Porto Venere sits at the tip of the rocky promontory that separates the Golfo dei Poeti (also known as the Golfo di La Spezia) from the Cinque Terre.

It was once a fortified fishing village and is now a bustling little resort surrounded by green hills and olive groves. The area is a natural park (w parconaturaleportovenere. it) and is a UNESCO World Heritage Site.

Its rows of gaily painted houses face the sea like a wall and there was originally no seafront promenade. If the town was attacked, the locals would defend themselves by throwing boiling water out of the windows. Inside the town there is a maze of medieval alleyways. Small and friendly, Porto Venere is a great base to explore the area and the Cinque Terre.

History The area around Porto Venere has been inhabited since prehistoric times and it was once a Roman fishing port, the port of Venus. There was a temple to the goddess on the promontory where the 12th-century church of San Pietro now sits. After the fall of the Roman Empire, Porto Venere was a base for the Byzantine navy and was sacked by the Lombards in AD643. It was tormented by Saracen raiders until it was bought by Genoa in 1113. This was the front line in their 200-year war with the Pisans who held the other side of the bay, so it is no surprise that they built a massive castle here in 1162, which was expanded in the 16th and 17th centuries. Often on the front line, Porto Venere was bombarded in 1494 by the Aragonese fleet. War didn't always bring disaster, however, and while Porto Venere was under French control in the years following the French Revolution, the coastal road to La Spezia was built, and called the Route Napoleone.

Getting there and around

By boat There are **ferries** (w navigazionegolfodeipoeti.it) to La Spezia, Lerici, the Cinque Terre and to Palmaria. Budget €13 per person for a tour of the islands and €30 to visit the Cinque Terre and other towns in the gulf. Prices are often higher in August. There are just 32 berths in the harbour (✆ 0187 793042; w portodiportovenere.it). You can hire a taxi boat from **Porto Venere Taxi Boat** (m 3383 952994, 3668 264110; w portoveneretaxiboat.com).

By bus Bus 11 leaves from Via Chiodo in La Spezia, and takes about 30 minutes to reach the town centre, depending on traffic.

By car Take the SP530 from near the Arsenale in La Spezia. In high season, parking can be a real issue but a shuttle bus runs from the car park at Cavo, which is just before the town. Book a hotel with private parking, or consider leaving the car in La Spezia.

On foot Porto Venere is the starting point of a large network of footpaths that runs high up above the Cinque Terre to Levanto via Campiglia, and on to Manarola. There is also a lovely walk around Palmaria island (page 167), which can take up to 3½ hours. A leaflet with detailed directions is available from the tourist office.

Tourist information The tourist office is by the gate that leads into the town (✆ 0187 790691; w prolocoportovenere.it). There are religious processions on 17 June and 29 August. Porto Venere is very busy not just in high season but on bank holidays, so if you want to avoid the crowds, plan your trip midweek out of season.

⌂ Where to stay

⌂ **Grand Hotel Porto Venere** (54 rooms) Via Garibaldi 5; ✆ 0187 777751; e info@ portoveneregrand.com; w portovenerehotel.it.

Recently renovated, the hotel is a former 17th-century monastery in a beautiful position just outside the city walls. For a special event treat yourself to a room with a sea view, though they are exorbitantly expensive. The restaurant serves fresh fish & specialities from the Cinque Terre. €€€€

🏠 **L'Ancora** (3 rooms) Via Capellini 167; m 338 118 6143. Rooms have private bathroom, TV, free Wi-Fi & price includes b/fast. Two rooms with sea view & one looks on to the old town. Situated 20m from the sea, near the church. €€€

🏠 **Le Ville Relais** (12 rooms) Salita al Piano 18/19; ℡0187 751518; e info@lavillerelais.it; w levillerelais.it. Up in the hills above Fezzano. Smart designer-style rooms, all with a great view. This little hotel has a gym, sauna & swimming pool. There is a good restaurant & the friendly owners will drive you into La Spezia or Porto Venere if they are not too busy. €€

✖ Where to eat and drink

For picnic supplies, there is a supermarket on the road that leads back to La Spezia near the car park. In the old town there are tourist shops selling regional products but it is worth calling in at **Bajeico** (Via Capellini 70; w bajeico.it), who have been making pesto with basil grown in Porto Venere for over 60 years. Stop for an *aperitivo* at **Bacicio** (Via Capellini 17), which serves some great antipasti. In the sea you can see poles. These support 'sea vines' which are mussel and oyster nurseries. Fresh from the sea, you can't go wrong if you order a plate for dinner.

✖ **O Chi O A Ca Toa** Via Paita 6, Fezzano; m 3284 688876; ⊕ closed Mon. This place is known for its set menu, which is mainly fish & serves local specialities with an original touch. €€€

✖ **Portivene Un Mare di Sapori** Via Capellini 94/8; ℡ 0187 792722. Family-run restaurant offering local dishes. Great food at a fair price. €€

✖ **Bar Lord Byron** Via Olivo 19; m 3383 588446. This bar & pizzeria has a very family-orientated feel. When we were there, in the inside of the restaurant where there are only a couple of tables, it was full of families & locals eating lunch. Food is basic – salads, pizza & the like, but they are also happy to make you what you fancy. €

What to see and do

Walk up to the old gateway built in 1160. To the left is a marble basin once used to measure quantities of grain and wine. Above the gateway is the 15th-century fresco of the White Madonna. The main street leads out on to the promontory and the 12th-century striped church of **San Pietro,** which sits on the craggy cliff at the end of town as if guarding the entrance to the bay.

The church is dedicated to the patron saint of fishermen, St Peter, and parts of it date from the 6th century. A Romanesque loggia looks out towards the sea with views across to the Cinque Terre and the cliffs of Muzzerone. There are also fabulous vistas from here back across the bay to the marble mountains of Carrara in Tuscany while the church's beautifully simple striped interior makes it one of the prettiest churches in Liguria. Beware, however, the stone path that leads up to it is slippery and dangerous when wet.

Just before the church is the entrance to the **Grotta Arpaia** where the poet Byron used to recite poetry. He was, to the amazement of the local fishermen, an extraordinarily strong swimmer and a plaque commemorates his daring swim from Porto Venere to Lerici across the bay in 1822. The tiny cove inspired his poem, 'The Corsair'. The actual grotto collapsed in the 1930s but the bay is still a lovely place to swim off the rocks.

From the promontory, it is a steep climb up to the **Castello Doria** (w castellodiportovenere.it; ⊕ 10.30–18.30 daily; admission €5), a formidable example of Genoese military architecture. The current castle dates from the 16th century and there are more wonderful views over the bay that are well worth the walk up to see.

Below the castle is the Romanesque 11th-century church of **San Lorenzo**, which is built on the site of a former temple to Jupiter. It houses some important religious relics including a piece of the Holy Cross and one of San Lorenzo's teeth. Much more precious, however, is the painting of the *Madonna Bianca* that is said to have floated to the town hidden in a cedar log in the 13th century. On the night of 17 August, there's a torchlit parade in her honour.

There is a small, free, sandy beach at the entrance to the town and more places to swim along the road out of town towards La Spezia, but for a real beach experience head for the island of Palmaria. There is excellent scuba diving and snorkelling in its clear waters. Porto Venere is also a popular spot for climbers who can scale the steep cliffs at Muzzerone, where there are even climbing courses for children (w parconaturaleportovenere.it). There are a number of walks of varying difficulty in and around Porto Venere. The easiest is to nearby Le Grazie but for a tougher hike, walk up to Campiglia and on along to Levanto.

THE ISLANDS OF PALMARIA, TINO AND TINETTO Liguria's only archipelago lies just off Porto Venere and the islands are a must-see of any visit here. There are regular boats across the narrow strip of water to Palmaria, the largest of the three islands, where there are some lovely beaches, especially on the side that faces out to sea. This is also a good place to walk. Boats leave from the harbour side for a tour of all three and take you close up to the towering cliffs that are striped with black stone just like the pretty church of San Pietro. Rare black portor marble was once quarried here. It is still possible to see where the stone was brought down and loaded on to boats and the area where it was quarried looks like it has been literally cut by a knife, like a slab of butter. Palmaria's **Grotta dei Colombi**, the Doves' Cave, looks out over the island of Tino and is the most important cave in eastern Liguria, not only in terms of its size, but also because of the prehistoric remains that have been found here.

The two smaller islands of Tino and Tinetto are military zones. Access to Tino is only permitted on 13 September for the Festa di San Venerio in honour of the patron saint of the bay. Visitors are also allowed on the following Sunday. On the island there is a ruined 11th-century abbey and a chapel where the hermit saint once lived. The sea around Tinetto is a popular diving area as it has a rich seabed. This is also a good spot for birdwatchers as 70 species of birds, among them the peregrine falcon and the pallid swift, nest in and around Porto Venere in the karst rock face. Tino and Tinetto are also home to the smallest Italian gecko, the rare *tarantolino*.

Where to stay, eat and drink

La Casa del Pescatore (6 rooms) Via San Giovanni, Isola Palmaria; ✆0187 791199; e andrea@palmariaisland.com; w palmariaisland.com. This is a B&B with a difference (you are collected by the owner in his boat) on the island opposite Porto Venere. A peaceful retreat with lovely views across the town & great walks right on the doorstep. All in all a wonderful peaceful place to stay. Free Wi-Fi. €€

Ostello Palmaria (9 rooms) Isola Palmaria; ✆0187 715693; e info@aganziaviaggia5terre.it. On the beautiful island of Palmaria, this is a budget hostel with dorms, 5 rooms & a kitchenette. €

✗ Locanda Lorena Via Cavour 4, Isola Palmaria; ✆0187 792370; e info@locandalorena.com; w locandalorena.com; ⊕ closed Nov. The 5-star setting on the island opposite Porto Venere makes it a real event to eat here. Fresh pasta & local fish. They also rent rooms & a villa (€€€). €€€

EAST ALONG THE GULF OF POETS

Across the water on the eastern side of the bay are the resorts of San Terenzo and Lerici. Legend has it that a sea monster was trapped in the bay and, in its frantic attempts to escape, it scratched out the numerous little coves that dot the shoreline.

A BITTER PARADISE

The Shelleys' summer on the Golfo dei Poeti was not as idyllic as you might imagine. Mary Shelley hated the Casa Magni and later wrote, 'My nerves were wound up to the utmost irritation, and the sense of misfortune hung over my spirits. No words can tell you how I hated our house and the country about it.' She found the people 'wild and hateful' and 'the very jargon of these Genoese was disgusting.'

Although Shelley loved the place and his new toy, his sailing boat, his nerves were also on edge and he was tormented by terrible nightmares. As soon as they arrived, it was Shelley's task to tell his stepsister-in-law and most possibly former lover, Claire, of the death of her daughter, Allegra, whose father was his friend Byron. Throughout the summer Shelley had repeated visions of Allegra rising up naked from the sea.

Mary was pregnant and on 16 June 1822 miscarried, losing so much blood that she too almost died. Shelley saved her life by putting her in an ice-cold bath. All was not well between the two, however, and Shelley spent most of his time with Jane Williams, the wife of his friend Edward Williams, than with his depressed and debilitated wife, who had already lost two children, and the poetry he wrote here was addressed to Jane not Mary. Shelley was also deeply depressed and wrote of 'such sweet and bitter pain as mine'.

On 1 July, Shelley went to Livorno by boat to discuss the launch of a new liberal magazine with Byron and the poet James Leigh Hunt. He was in political exile from Britain, which was at the time very authoritarian. Although the local fishermen tried to persuade Shelley not to take his boat out as the weather forecast was bad, he refused to take their advice and on 8 July he set sail for Lerici with his 18-year-old boat boy and Edward Williams. In summer, the sea can appear far less dangerous than it in fact is and can easily fool anyone who is not well versed in its treachery. No local boats ever set sail if there's a storm in the air.

As if he had been tempting fate, the boat disappeared and Shelley was eventually washed ashore on the beach at Viareggio half eaten by fish. He was cremated on the beach, where his skull cracked open and his brains sizzled in the fire.

The SP331 leads out of La Spezia past the docks, naval buildings and luxury boat builders. After the tunnel is **San Terenzo**. Once a small collection of fishermen's houses clustered along the beach by a castle on a rocky promontory, the village was rocketed to fame when it became the last home of the British poet Percy Bysshe Shelley and his wife Mary, who lived at the white villa **Casa Magni**, with its arched arcade on the eastern side of the seafront (not open to the public). The house was originally a monastery and it was here in June 1822 that Shelley began work on *The Triumph of Life*. He wrote, 'Me, as the swallow of Anacreonte, I have left my Nile and I migrated here for the summer, in an isolated house in front of the sea and surrounded by the sweet and sublime scenery of the Gulf of Spezia.' For a short account of Shelley's fateful visit, see the box above.

There's another British connection here. The town was originally called Portiolo, as it was an olive port, but took the name San Terenzo in honour of a wealthy pilgrim who came from Scotland and, after he had been cared for by the villagers, donated considerable sums of money to help them. He went on to become the Bishop of nearby Luni.

Swiss painter Arnold Böcklin also stayed here and captured the town on canvas, while in a little tower on the top of the Villa Marigola, surrounded by its lovely gardens, the poet and librettist Sem Benelli wrote *The Jest* in 1909. The villa was also visited by the Florentine Impressionist painters known as the Macchiaioli and poet Gabriele D'Annunzio. Anthropologist Paolo Mantegazza lived on Via Campo. A stone plaque on the wall of Via Matteotti near the church commemorates Paolo Azzarini who rescued Garibaldi from the stormy seas. The castle at the edge of the bay is now used for cultural events and there is a small exhibition dedicated to the Shelleys.

Don't be put off by the overbuilt suburbs: the place still has lots of charm down on the seafront where there is a good sandy beach and seafront promenade linking the town with Lerici, with which it has virtually merged. Stop off for biscuits at **Gino Oriani** (Via Matteotti 13); they have been satisfying sugar cravings since 1918.

If you are on a budget, note that there are few good free beaches in the immediate Lerici area.

LERICI The town of Lerici is the main hub on the eastern side of the Golfo dei Poeti and is 13km from La Spezia. Take the SS331 and then the SP26; there's a bus from La Spezia but no railway station. It is a little bit overbuilt here but it is not noticeable once you are down on the seafront where there is a lovely old town. It is so lush here that many of the buildings are hidden in the trees. The bay is dominated by a massive castle built by the Pisans in the Middle Ages. There are beautiful views across the bay to medieval Porto Venere and the archipelago. The area is primarily a holiday destination for Italians and a place to unwind on the beach, walk and explore the area by ferry.

Legend has it that the town was founded by the Trojans after the fall of Troy, but there is evidence that the Etruscans lived here in the 7th century BC. Lerici was a bustling port in the Middle Ages and was on the front line in Pisa's 200-year war with Genoa. The area finally came under Genoese control in 1479. In the 17th and 18th centuries Lerici became an important shipbuilding centre and many of the villas that dot the hills date from this period.

🏠 **Where to stay** There is a good choice of places to stay in this area on Airbnb.

🏠 **Piccolo Hotel del Lido** (12 rooms) Lungomare Biaggini 24, Lerici; ☎0187 968159; e info@hoteldellido.it; w www.hoteldellido.it. Elegant, modern, 1-storey hotel by the sea, with minimalist rooms with panoramic views. The rooms have private sun decks & are about 10m from the shoreline in a sublime setting. Indoor swimming pool but no restaurant. €€€€

🏠 **Il Nido** (31 rooms) Via Fiascherino 75/122, Tellaro; ☎0187 967286; w hotelnido.com. This hotel has a stunning position looking out over the sea above its own beach. Rooms are simple. To get the best from your stay ask for a room with a sea view, but be warned there are lots of steps. €€€

🏠 **Il Senatore** (8 rooms) Via Byron 11, Fiascherino; ☎0187 967236; e info@ locandailsenatore.com; w locandailsenatore.com. Small hotel with a fantastic seafood restaurant on the beach in the lovely cove of Fiascherino. €€€

🏠 **Al Lizzo** [map, page 157] (3 rooms) Località Tre Strade 5; m 3487 742006; e info@allizzo.it; w allizzo.it. B&B with lovely garden, swimming pool & castle views. Around 15mins' walk from San Lorenzo & the friendly owner can give you lots of local tips. Use of kitchen. Cash only. €€

🏠 **B&B Mare di Stelle** (2 rooms) Via Fiascherino 5; ☎0187 968720; e info@maredistelle. it; w maredistelle.it. Great B&B in Fiasherino with fabulous hosts & a stunning view across the bay to Porto Venere. Close to footpaths. €€

🏠 **B&B Oca Nera** [map, page 157] (3 rooms) Località Monti San Lorenzo; m 393 904 1844. A peaceful spot 3km from Lerici with a garden & lovely views. Countryside atmosphere. €€

🏠 **La Musa** [map, page 157] (6 rooms, 2 apts) Località Guercio Carpione 12; m 3483 844014; e info@lamusa.it; w lamusa.it. A lovely B&B furnished with period furniture, 5mins' drive above

Lerici surrounded by beautiful exotic gardens with a swimming pool. €€

🏠 **Locanda Miranda** (7 rooms) Via Fiascherino 92, Tellaro; 📞 0187 964012; e locandamiranda@libero.it; w locandamiranda. com. Family-run hotel with an excellent seafood restaurant. Rooms are decorated with antique furniture. Excellent value for money. €€

✖ **Where to eat and drink** Market day is Saturday and you can buy fresh fish at the harbour in the morning. For top-quality homemade pasta, go to **Pasta Fresca Franzi**, west of Via Cavour on Via Fornara 7–9 (📞 0187 968662; w pastafrescafranzi. com; ⊕ closed Sun afternoon & Mon). Try the unusual pesto-filled *gnocchetti*. **Arcobaleno** (Piazza Garibaldi 20) serves the best ice cream; try the caramel and roasted pine nut. For biscuits go to **Illice** (Via Roma 45). The best place to stop for a drink in Lerici is **Enoteca Baroni** (Via Cavour 18). **Vertigo Bar**, Spiaggia Marinella, in San Terenzo is the evening haunt.

✖ **I Doria** Via Carpanini 9, Lerici; 📞 0187 967124; e info@doriaparkhotel.it; ⊕ evenings only, closed Sun. Chef Davide Santoni has a fabulous touch & the restaurant has wonderful views across the bay. €€€€

✖ **Pescarino** Via Borea 52, Montemarcello; 📞 0187 601388; e randell@alice.it; w pescarino. it; ⊕ closed Mon–Tue. Popular with the trendy residents of Montemarcello, serving elegant dishes & local fish. €€€€

✖ **Dei Pescatori** Via Andrea Doria 6, Lerici; 📞 0187 965534; ⊕ closed Mon. Hidden up an alleyway that leads southeast from the main square, this fish restaurant is a bargain at the price as the set menu is copious. There's no choice; you get what's in season. Set menu with wine only. €€€

✖ **Il Frantoio** Via Cavour 21; m 393 851 1140. Simple menu including local mussels & fish. €€€

✖ **L'Orto di Ameste** Via Casamento 19, La Serra; 📞 0187 964628; ⊕ evenings only, Wed–Sun. Cosy restaurant with a good atmosphere & splendid view. Menu predominantly fresh fish. €€€

✖ **Mare Blu** Via Cavour 9, Lerici; 📞 0187 021503. Fish & meat dishes dominate the menu in this excellent but simple restaurant. It has a loyal following & is not just a tourist hangout. €€€

✖ **Trattoria dai Pironcelli** Via della Mura 45, Montemarcello; 📞 0187 601252; ⊕ evenings only exc Sun when it is open for lunch, closed Wed & 1st week of Jan. Traditional trattoria serving classic local dishes & delicious chestnut *semifreddo*. The restaurant is linked to the Slow Food Movement. €€€

FANCY A WALK?

If you like walking, Lerici is a great place to base yourself, and if you intend to explore on foot, it is best to visit when the weather is cooler, in the early autumn, mid-winter or in late spring. From San Terenzo castle you can climb up towards **Falconara**, where there is a beautiful view. From there you can walk to the 16th-century Santa Teresa Fort. The circuit takes about 1¾ hours. From Lerici you climb up Via Canata to **Barcola**, where an old cart road leads to **Pugliola** and on to **Solaro**. Along the route you can see the remains of Roman thermal baths. There is a panoramic walk from the Church of San Andrea in **Bocca di Magra** up to Montemarcello and over Monte Marcello to Tellaro, which takes about 2½ hours to walk.

There are lovely walking trails through the **Parco Naturale Regionale di Montemarcello-Magra** (w parcomagra.it). Well-marked footpaths run down to the sea through rich Mediterranean flora or up to Monte Murlo (361m) and Monte Rochetta (400m). The path across Monte Murlo starts just north of the church in **Montemarcello** and you can walk from **La Serra** up to the fort on Monte Rochetta. On the road from Lerici there is a botanical garden, **Orto Botanico di Montemarcello**, which encompasses Monte Murlo.

✕ Bontà Nascoste Via Cavour 52, Lerici; ✆0187 965500; ◷ closed Tue. Tiny restaurant north of the main Piazza Garibaldi serving good *farinata*, Ligurian dishes & pizza. €€

✳ ✕ Locanda della Nonna Via Nuova 50, Montemarcello; 📱 366 479 4602. Nice outside terrace. Pizza in the evening. Pasta, salads & basic fish & meat. Good place to stop for a quick lunch. €€

What to see and do

You can't miss the huge **Castello di San Giorgio** (◷ usually 08.00–sunset; free) the best-preserved castle on the Riviera, on the rocky promontory that dominates the bay. It is a 10-minute walk up from the harbour along the **Via del Ghetto**, where Jewish merchants once lived. The castle was built in 1152 by the Pisans to counterbalance the Genoese presence on the other side of the bay at Porto Venere. Most of the present structure dates from the mid 1500s. There is a lift in the tunnel below if you cannot face the steps.

A Roman shipwreck is the centrepiece of the Parco Subacqueo Archeologico, which is a great place for diving; the tourist office has lists of local diving companies. There are boat trips to La Spezia, Porto Venere, the Cinque Terre, Portofino and San Fruttuoso in summer (Consorzio Marittimo Turistico; ✆ 0187 732987; w navigazionegolfodeipoeti.it).

Two pretty fishing villages, **Fiascherino** and **Tellaro** lie south of Lerici facing the bay against a backdrop of green hills. **Fiascherino** has a beautiful beach and the cliffs have coves accessible only by boat. D H Lawrence, English novelist and author of *Lady Chatterley's Lover*, lived in the **Casa Rosa** (Pink House) from 1913 to 1914 with his lover, the German Frieda von Richthofen, who was later to become his wife. They were sheltering from the scandal that erupted over their relationship, and one of the reasons that they came here is that, at the time, it was extremely remote. Frieda was a married mother of two, which only added to the furore.

Lawrence thought that Fiascherino was one of the most beautiful places he had ever visited and wrote, 'I sit on the rock-cliffs in front of the sea for the whole day and I write. I tell you that it is a dream.' In letters, he overflows with enthusiasm as he describes his peaceful garden close to the sea where oranges and lemons grow abundantly: 'I'm so happy that I found this place, at last. It is perfect: A lovely bay that is protected, on one side, by sharp rocks, whereas its other side is bordered by gracious olive trees.'

The classic Ligurian fishing village of **Tellaro** is just up the coast, surrounded by olive groves that produce an oil with a slightly salty taste. The village juts out into the sea as if it was about to sail off and probably gets its name from the Latin *telus*, meaning 'arrowhead'. The tall houses are built on different levels as they teeter down to the tiny harbour.

On the pointy rock that sticks out into the sea sits the Baroque church of San Giorgio. It is a pleasant place to picnic, stop for a drink and take a dip in the sea.

Legend has it that the village was saved by an octopus that rang the church bell to warn of a pirate raid. The story was written down by D H Lawrence and *polpo*, octopus, is very much on the menu here. It is served *alla tellarese*, boiled with potatoes and seasoned with olives, garlic and parsley, salt, pepper and lemon juice. Lawrence used to walk across to Tellaro every day to collect his mail and was spellbound by the women who worked in the olive groves. The place oozed an earthy spirit that he loved. 'I am always expecting when I go to Tellaro for the letters, to meet Jesus gossiping with his disciples as he goes along above the sea, under the grey, light trees.' There are lovely walks to both Ameglia and Montemarcello but, if you are driving, double back to Lerici to drive to **Montemarcello** on the eastern end of the bay. The views from this rocky outcrop are worth the journey to Montemarcello, which was built high up on the hill to protect it from the Saracens. Unsurprisingly, the Germans used it as their local headquarters in World War II.

The village takes its name from the Roman consul Marcellus who defeated the Ligurians. Unlike other hill towns, which are laid out in concentric circles, it follows the pattern of the Roman military camp. It is now a trendy upmarket resort popular with well-heeled Milanese VIPs and was voted one of Italy's most picturesque villages in 2007. The pleasure is to be had strolling around the medieval alleyways although it lacks some of the authentic charm of some of Liguria's more remote villages in the hinterland, but crucially it also lacks the hordes of tourists who pound the streets of the Cinque Terre.

In the church there is an interesting crucifix known as the *Cristo Nero*, the Black Christ. The village is also renowned for its figs, which are celebrated in a local festival in June.

SARZANA

Dominated by its huge fortress and encircled by the city walls, Sarzana is nevertheless overlooked by tourists, who flock south to Tuscany. It is an important agricultural and commercial centre with an old town that's full of character even though the plain around it is now covered in suburban sprawl, but so is the plain around Florence for that matter. The main street follows the route of the old Via Francigena that ran from Canterbury to Rome and was an important trading and pilgrimage route. Today the town is a popular meeting place for antique dealers and is a good destination for food lovers.

HISTORY Sarzana was built in the 11th century by people escaping the nearby marshes that grew around the old Roman town of Luni. The city took over Luni's bishopric in 1204 and changed hands between Pisa, Lucca and Florence until it was taken by Genoa in 1572 and became the easternmost outpost of the republic on the Italian mainland. On 31 March 1353 the Guelphs and the Ghibellines signed a peace treaty here which sadly only lasted a few months. During the early part of the 20th century, many of the inhabitants of Sarzana were politically to the left and in 1921 there was a major shoot-out when fascists from Marina di Carrara tried to storm the town. One of the fascist leaders was Amerigo Dumini, who went on to assassinate Giacomo Matteotti. Twelve of the fascists were killed and the reprisals were bloody.

Sarzana was bombed in World War II as it was still a strategically important place on the route north.

GETTING THERE AND AROUND Sarzana is small enough to explore on foot but you'll need a car to reach some of the nicer hotels in the area.

By bus Bus S runs from La Spezia to Sarzana and takes around 45 minutes, depending on traffic.

By car Sarzana is on the A12 Genova–Livorno and A15 La Spezia–Parma *autostrade*, 20km from La Spezia.

By taxi Local taxis are available by calling \ 0187 627777.

By train Sarzana is 15 minutes by train from La Spezia.

TOURIST INFORMATION The office can be found in Piazza San Giorgio (\ 0187 620419; w comune.sarzana.sp.it). Children's shows are held in the main square, Piazza Matteotti, in summer and an antiques fair in August followed by a Napoleon festival in September.

The local delicacies are *spungata*, a little puff pastry cake stuffed with jam, dried fruit, pine nuts, almonds, raisins and spices; *torta di riso*, both a savoury or sweet rice tart; and *buccellato*, a cake flavoured with grated lemon and orange peels. The *torta di riso* is believed originally to have been a Jewish dish as there was once a sizeable community in this part of Italy, especially in Livorno. Here focaccia is baked with raisins, pine nuts and aniseed, and was traditionally a festive dish. Also look out for *torta scema*, stupid cake, or more literally poor cake: it's made of stale bread and rice. You can buy it at the market on Thursdays.

Most restaurants serve *testaroli*, discs of pasta embossed with a crescent, and in the shops it is possible to buy the wooden or metal *testi* that are used to make them. In Sarzana the vegetable pies are small and round and known as *scarpazza*. You will also see restaurants advertising that they sell *sgabei*, fritters of fried bread dough.

The fertile land around Sarzana has been irrigated by canals since the 14th century. Look out for the local milk, called Marinella di Sarzana, the local courgette, known as *zucchino alberello* which originally came from South America in the 16th century, apples known as *mela rotella della lunigiana*, peaches and plums. The local cherries are often served in liqueur, *ciliegie sotto spirito*.

WHERE TO STAY There's a shortage of good hotels in the town centre, so to stay in the area you really need a car, although at time of writing there were some good options on **w** airbnb.com.

La Bianca Fattoria [map, page 157] (7 rooms) Via Turi 121, Sarzana; 0187 621087; **e** biancafattoria@alice.it; **w** labiancafattoria. com. B&B just outside Sarzana in an old farmhouse with delicious home-cooking. Good for families as there's a kids' climbing frame & table football. €€

Antico Casale (8 rooms) Via Navonella 7; 0187 622543. B&B with a swimming pool, kitchenette & barbecue facilities in the countryside outside Sarzana. Children's playground. Can organise fishing trips, hiking & mountain-bike tours & horseriding. €

B&B In Piazzetta (3 rooms) Piazza Calandrini 13; **m** 333 408 6065; bebinpiazzetta@ gmail.com; **w** bebinpiazzetta.it. Modern rooms with Wi-Fi in the historic centre. €

WHERE TO EAT AND DRINK The food experience here, as in most of Liguria, is not something that is going to break the bank. Many of the local specialities are sold in bakeries, delicatessens and supermarkets. You can try the cakes for a few euros with a cup of coffee. A foodie walking tour of Sarzana is offered by **Le Terre di Mezzo** (**m** 339 868 3544, 338 379 1325; 🇫). **Lu.ne Verdi** (Via Emiliana 4; **w** luneverdi.com) sells organic fruit and vegetables grown at a local farm.

Mamagamma Via Sotto Gli Uffizi 2; **m** 340 987 8472; **w** arcimamagamma.wixsite.com/ arcimamagamma. Rustic feel to this restaurant that has a great unusual tasting menu at €40 not including wine, which is beautifully presented. €€€€

I Tre Anti Via Rossi 3; 0187 603688; closed Sun. A simple traditional Ligurian restaurant in a former convent, serving a good mix of fish, meat & vegetable dishes. €€€

Il Lupo Via Cisa 72; 0187 622619; closed Mon. A good little osteria where you can try all the local specialities from Monterosso anchovies to the famous *spungata* cake. €€

La Pizzeria Sopra il Calcandola Piazza Matteotti 44; 0187 620062; 🇫; closed Tue in winter. A smart, modern pizzeria with tables in the main square in summer. A busy spot as the pizza is very tasty. €€

✕ Panzallegra Via Mascardi 21; ✆ 0187
610606; ◷ closed Mon–Tue. Traditional Lunigiana
cuisine inc mussels, herb pies & *torta di riso*. €€
✕ Riccardo Bugliani Via XXV Aprile 4; ✆ 0187
620081; ◷ Wed–Mon, evenings only. This
pizzeria serves excellent *farinata* & the local *torta
di riso*. Swill it down with a locally produced beer.
€€
✕ Panigo Signor Bonaventura [map, page 157]
Risveglio Naturale, just north of Sarzana on the SR62;
m 338 594 6620. This is the place to try the local
flatbread, *panigaggci*. They are typical of the valley &
served with various sauces, cheese & meat. €

⊑ Caffè Costituzionale Piazza Matteotti 65.
Another historic café, which has good ice cream.
As its name implies, it was a well-known left-wing
café before World War II. €
⊑ Forno Bugliani Via XX Settembre 10.
Opened in 1946, it is a great place to buy a picnic of
pizza, *farinata* & focaccia. €
⊑ Pasticceria Gemmi Via Mazzini 21.
Sazarna's most famous café-cum-bakery, it opened
in 1840 & is the place to go for a coffee. It is an
atmospheric place with frescoes, marble floors &
antique display cases. €
♀ Biagi Via Muccini 11. Good ice cream. €

OTHER PRACTICALITIES There is an **ATM** at Piazza Garibaldi 8. The **post office** is at
Via Ippolito Landinelli 76. There's a **pharmacy** at Via Mazzini 94, and the **hospital**
(✆ 0187 5331) is in the northwestern suburb of Santa Caterina, on Via Cisa.

WHAT TO SEE AND DO Take a stroll around the old town with its distinctively
Tuscan architecture. Its hub is the huge main square, **Piazza Matteotti**, at the
northwestern corner of the old town.

Along the southern side runs **Via Mazzini**, the old Via Francigena, which is lined
with palaces and houses. If you think Napoleon was a thoroughbred Frenchman,
think twice. No 28 was the family home of the Bonaparte family before they
emigrated to Corsica in 1529. The Bonapartes were an important family here
and a number of them were prominent local politicians. Corsica was, of course, a
Genoese colony before it was taken by the French.

On Via Mazzini, the Romanesque-Gothic **Cattedrale dell'Assunta** was rebuilt over the
Gothic church of San Basilio in 1474 and retains the older tower. Construction started
after the bishops of Luni upped sticks and moved to Sarzana in 1204. It was completed
in the 15th century but modified in the 17th century. There's a fine 14th-century door
and elaborate carved wooden ceiling, which is quite unusual for Liguria. In the Gothic
chapel is a monument to Sarzana's most famous son, Pope Nicolas V. The cathedral's
prized holy relic is an ampoule of the blood of Christ that is said to have arrived from
the Holy Land on a vessel without a boatman in AD782. There are two marble altarpieces
from the mid 1400s by Leonardo Riccomanni and wooden crucifixes by Guglielmo.

Take a left turn up to the **Museo Diocesano** (✆ 0187 734503; ◷ Jun & Sep 16.00–
19.00 Sat & Sun, Jul–Aug 18.00–23.00 daily; admission free), in the former Oratorio
della Misericordia on Piazza Firmafede, which has a collection of religious artefacts
from around the Magra Valley and a collection of works by local artist and master
Domenico Fiasella.

Just behind the museum is the giant **Cittadella** built in 1488 by Lorenzo the
Magnificent, a member of the powerful Florentine Medici family. Among the
architects was famous Renaissance fortress builder Giuliano da Sangallo. The 16th-
century walls were added by the Genoese. Unfortunately, it's only open when it is
being used for cultural events, but you can walk around the moat. **Via Domenico
Fiasella** leads back to Piazza Matteotti.

Just north of Sarzana is the **Fortezza di Sarzanello** (Via Alla Fortezza; ✆ 0187
622080; w fortezzadisarzanello.com; ◷ times vary so check the website; admission
€4), built on a commanding hilltop by Castruccio Castracani, the lord of nearby
Lucca, in Tuscany in 1322. His name means 'dog castrator' and he was indeed a

real tyrant, so it's no surprise that the castle is said to be haunted. The castle was altered by the Florentines in 1493. When I first visited this castle as a child, there was a bell by the door and you rang it to get the custodian who lived there if you fancied a visit. The custodian lived in the keep and there was washing hanging out to dry on the ramparts. My mother thought it must be one of the best places to peg out the sheets. They have long since moved on, but the stunning views across the sea to Elba and Corsica remain, and it's still off the beaten track, with a big empty car park to prove it.

THE VAL DI MAGRA The countryside around Sarzana is flat and fertile and spreads out from the banks of the River Magra. The hills that surround the valley are dotted with pretty medieval villages and interesting castles that were built to defend this crucial north–south trading route. Although, sadly, a lot of the valley has been covered with a mish-mash of motorway and urban sprawl, there are still some lush flat green fields, which produce fantastic fruit and vegetables. The valley has been inhabited for centuries and the finds from the ancient necropolis at Cafaggio are now on show in the Archaeological Museum in La Spezia.

South of Sarzana From Sarzana the road south leads down to the resort of **Bocca di Magra**, where the river Magra flows out into the sea; *bocca* means 'mouth'. Swanky boats line the riverbank. Novelist Cesare Pavese stayed here after the war, as did Marguerite Duras, Moravia, Pasolini and poet Eugenio Montale. Further back in time, so did the poet Dante. There are the remains of a Roman villa on the sloping terraces on the clifftop. On the river in September you can see flamingos and white storks.

Boats take visitors to the lovely beaches of Punta Bianca and Punta Corvo in summer, which avoids the walk back up the steep stairs that lead down to the beach. This is also a great place for diving, canoeing and kayaking. Birdwatchers should look out for some of our feathered friends that don't pop up in other parts of Liguria, like kingfishers and herons. You can hire bikes, boats and scooters from **Nolo Mar** (Via Poggio Scafa 16, Fiumaretta; m 329 731 7543; w nolomar.net).

The western side of the valley is very verdant and a beautiful spot for cycling and walking. Above the river in **Ameglia**, the houses cluster around a ruined castle with a large round tower, which is unusual for a Ligurian village, as they normally huddle around a church. The castle was built in 1174 by the bishops of Luni, once a prosperous town in the valley below. There are views across to the Carrara marble mountains and the plain of Luni from the piazza in front of the church.

Elio Vittorini, who wrote the anti-fascist novel *Conversations in Sicily* (1941), lived here and the village is also the birthplace of the novelist Roberto Pazzi. Ameglia earned its place in history when 15 American soldiers were executed here by the German army in 1944. Their murder, in contravention of the Geneva Convention, led to a ground-breaking judgment that an illegal military order by a superior is not a defence to a war crime.

Liguria's best Roman ruins sit in the middle of the suburbs, motorway and downtown drag that has taken over much of the plain near the Tuscan border in the heart of the valley, 30km from La Spezia off the SS1.

Luni (Via Ortonovo 37; ☏ 0187 66811; w luni.beniculturali.it; ⊕ 08.30–19.30 Tue–Sun, in winter check the website as times vary; admission €4) was originally a Roman fortress laid out to fight the Ligurians in 177BC. It soon developed, however, into an important port shipping wine, cheese and marble from the mines in Carrara in the mountains behind the city. The Romans were particularly fond of the wine from the hills around Luni: the white is especially nice.

After the fall of the Roman Empire things went badly in Luni. First, the marble trade declined and then the harbour silted up; now the coast is 2km away. The marshes that resulted were malarial and the population sensibly upped and left for nearby Castelnuovo Magra, up on the hillside. In 1204, the bishops moved to Sarzana just to the north and Luni disappeared from the map. All that was left was its name; the local area is known as Lunigiana.

The site was first excavated in 1837. There's a small museum. It is possible to see the remains of the forum, to the south of the museum, the theatre, a temple of Diana, to the north, and a number of mosaic floors. The most interesting part of a trip to Luni, however, is a visit to the amphitheatre, which is by guided tour just twice a day (⊕ 10.30 & 15.00, afternoon tour Jun–Sep 17.00), otherwise you will have to put up with peeping through the railings. It's east of Luni, a few minutes' walk down the road. It once held 7,000 spectators seated according to social class, and was faced in gleaming white marble from Carrara. The building was reinforced with a type of cement and sand-filled arches to support the seating area. Much of the stone was later taken to build Castelnuovo but it is possible to see some of the remaining marble steps in the amphitheatre.

There are good sandy beaches at Marinella di Sarzana and Fiumaretta di Ameglia. Here, visitors can enjoy the waves and it is a popular spot for surfing and windsurfing.

The eastern side of the valley is dotted with a number of interesting hilltop towns that testify to the valley's wealth. There are also numerous castles guarding this strategic route between the north and south. One village certainly worth a visit is **Castelnuovo Magra**, a sleepy place with a ruined castle at one end and, at the other, the parish church.

In the castle the poet Dante negotiated peace between the warring clans of Vescovi and Malaspina in 1306, an event celebrated with a procession on the last Saturday in August. It's a nice spot in the evening and for a picnic. There's a lovely view and a small kids' playground on the ramparts. Round the back of the castle you can see old men playing the local version of boules.

The large houses that line Castelnuovo's main street are testament to the town's past wealth, as is the church of **Santa Maria Maddalena**, built in the late 1600s with marble columns taken from Luni. Inside is a real gem, Brueghel the Younger's *Calvary* and a crucifix is attributed to Van Dyck. Proof that Liguria is certainly full of surprises.

Equally important in these parts is the fact that Castelnuovo Magra is famous for its salami and ham. The place to buy them is from the Bertini family's **Antica Salumeria Elena e Mirco** (Via Canale 52; w prosciuttacastelnovese.com). The hams are cured using mountain herbs and olive oil. Each ham absorbs 2.5 litres of oil while it's hung for nine months. Curing ham is a complicated art and Mirco produces fewer than 300 hams a year so they don't come cheap. They also sell local olive oils and bottled sauces. Along the walls are vats of Carrara marble in which *larsciac*, a sort of lard pâté, is made, which is eaten on crusty bread. Or you can buy directly from the Bertucci family (Via Canale 52, Località Molicciara; ☏ 0187 673510; e info@prosciuttacastelnovese.com; w prosciuttacastelnovese.com).

If you need to walk off all this good food, there is a pleasant footpath to **Ortonovo** from Castelnuovo, which is another pretty little hilltop village at the very edge of Liguria, which clusters around the Baroque church of San Lorenzo. In 1537, in the white marble 14th-century **Santuario di Nostra Signora di Mirteto**, some local women saw tears of blood run from the statue of the Madonna.

🏠 Where to stay, eat and drink

🏠 **Il Fortino Montemarcello** (6 rooms)
Strada Provinciale 29, Via della Pace, Ameglia;

☏ 0187 1676470; e info@ilfortino.net; w ilfortino. net. This eco-friendly hotel in an old military

The Etruscans first planted vines in the Magra Valley and the Romans shipped the wines produced here all over the Mediterranean. The wine to try is the Vermentino of the Colli di Luni.

In Castelnuovo Magra, try the local wines Colli di Luni and Golfo dei Poeti at **Il Mulino del Cibus** (Via Canale 46) and in the cavernous, vaulted cellars of the town hall, the **Palazzo Comunale** by the church, is the **Enoteca Regionale Ligure** (Via Vittorio Veneto 2; ☏ 0187 677937; w enotecaregionaleliguria.it; (🕒 official opening hrs are winter 15.00–19.00 Sat & Sun; summer 16.00–20.00 Wed–Sun, closed Wed & Sun afternoon, but it is wise to call ahead to make sure it is open).

Many of the local wineries are open to the public. The tourist office can give you a full list, but you need to make an appointment with the wineries to be sure they are open.

The small winery of **Azienda Agricola Giacomelli** (Via Palvotrisia 134, Località Palvorisa; m 349 630 1516) is usually open, but be sure to call ahead. The 18th-century **Ca Lunae** (Via Palvotrisia, 2, Castelnuovo di Magra; ☏ 0187 693483; w calunae.it; 🕒 09.00–13.00 & 14.30–19.30 Mon–Sat, 09.00–13.00 Sun) has a small museum and offers wine tastings.

Cantine Il Monticello (Via Groppolo 7; ☏ 0187 621432; w ilmonticello.it) produces all the local classic wines and offers wine tasting and tours of the vineyards. You can also buy wine and olive oil from **Santa Caterina** (Via Santa Caterina 6; ☏ 0187 629429; w santacaterina-sarzana.it).

barracks makes an unusual place to stay. Good-sized rooms & bike hire. €€€

🏠 **Locanda Il Monastero** (4 rooms, 1 apt) Via Casanova 2, Loc Annunziata, Ortonovo; ☏ 0187 669022; e info@locandailmonastero.it; w locandailmonastero.it. Atmospheric old house with lovely views. Garden & free parking. €€

🏠 **Luci Sul Golfo** [map, page 157] (3 rooms) Via Delle Ville 48; m 3382 595915; w lucisulgolfo. it. B&B with a swimming pool & lovely view. Be sure to eat here as the food is excellent & costs €25 per head (€€€). €€

🏠 **Monteverde** (3 rooms, 14 apts) Via Molino del Piano 65, Castelnuovo Magra; m 3357 048536; e info@agriturismomonteverde.it; w www. agriturismomonteverde.it. Nice little place on a farm in the hills with great views, a swimming pool & gym. Apts are modern & well appointed. Free Wi-Fi. €€

✕ **Locanda delle Tamerici** (5 rooms) Località Fiumaretta di Ameglia, Via Litoranea 106; ☏ 0187 64262/ 65336; w locandadelletamerici.com; 🕒 closed Jan & Oct–Dec, evenings only, closed Mon–Tue. Elegant beachside restaurant in a tranquil setting, with 1 Michelin star. The chef

is Mauro Ricciardi (w chefmauroricciardi.com). Among the specialities are seafood salad & an excellent dessert menu. The restaurant also has a cookery school. €€€€€

✕ **La Lucerna di Ferro** Via Fabricotti 126, Bocca di Magra; ☏ 0187 601206; w lalucernadiferro.it. Fantastic fish restaurant on a pontoon sticking out into the river. Set menu without wine only. €€€€

✕ **Il Mulino del Cibus** Via Canale, 84 Molicciara, Castelnuovo Magra; ☏ 0187 676102; w mulinodelcibus.it; 🕒 evenings only, closed Mon. The place to taste the best of the local wines & enjoy salami, cheese & olives. €€€

✕ **Trattoria Armanda** Piazza Garibaldi 6, Castelnuovo Magra; ☏ 0187 674410; e info@ trattoriaarmanda.com; f. A family-run trattoria by the entrance to the village serving local dishes made from local ingredients. It has been in business since 1908 & is linked to the Slow Food Movement. €€€

✕ **Da Fiorella** Via per Nicola 46, Ortonovo; ☏ 0187 668657; w ristorantedafiorella.com; 🕒 closed Thu. Slow Food-endorsed restaurant with classic local dishes & a good wine list. €€

✕ **Il Tagliere 2** Via Valentina 218; ☏ 0187 987553. Crispy *farinata* & pizza. €€

✕ La Sarticola [map, page 157] Via Sarticola 19, Ortonovo; m 3387 264359; w lasarticola.it. Farmhouse restaurant. The farm produces olive oil, wine, honey & vegetables. Set menu €28 inc wine. They also rent out rooms & apts (€). €€

✕ La Tana del Riccio Santo Via Mazzini 14, Santo Stefano di Magra; ☎ 0187 699428; e latanadelriccio22@libero.it; ⊕ closed Mon. Cosy, excellent-value restaurant with plenty of fresh fish & seasonal vegetables on the menu. €€

North of Sarzana

In the north of the Magra valley there are some pretty villages that are well off the tourist track. Liguria here borders Tuscany and Emilia-Romagna and the borders are not always indicated. If a place is not in this guide, that's because it's not in Liguria – not that it has been overlooked!

Due northwest from Sarzana is the pretty village of **Arcola**, which has a lovely central piazza. Take the SS432 and then the SS1. The nearby village of Trebiano has a ruined castle. At the coffee company **Crastan Caffè** in Romito Magra on the road for Armeglia, there's a small museum in the factory (☎ 0187 988492; ⊕ by appointment). Arcola has the only vineyard, **Conte Picedi Benettini**, which produces *ruzzese* wines that date back to Roman times. The red is a light wine, while the white is a fruity, straw yellow. The area around the vineyard is called the **Baccano di Arcola**, and gets its name from the noise followers of Bacchus made in the fields, '*baccano*', which means 'din'. Arcola's castle dates from the 10th century and is now home to the town council. The Virgin Mary appeared before five sisters in 1556 on a rosemary plant in the village surrounded by angels and asked them to build the **Santuario di Nostra Signora degli Angeli** on Via Garibaldi, which they duly did.

The SS1 leads north to **Vezzano Ligure**. It has stunning views across both the Gulf of La Spezia and the Magra Valley. It has a nice hotel with an excellent restaurant (see below). From here you can walk to the hilltop medieval hamlet of **Valeriano**, which looks out across the Val di Vara. On the Sunday before 15 August the village celebrates the local *torta di riso*.

Cross back across the Magra river to **Bolano,** which has lovely views across to the Tuscan village of Caprigliola. Nearby, **Santo Stefano di Magra** was founded in AD1000 and was an important stopover on the Via Francigena. Its enormous church was built in the 18th century. You can buy olive oil and a wide range of local specialities from: **Ambrosini** (Via dei Molni 396), **Badia** (☎0187 620453) and **Lucchi e Guastali** (Località Vincinella; ☎0187 633329; w frantoiolg.com; ⊕ 08.30–12.30 & 14.30–17.30 Mon–Fri, 08.30–12.30 Sat). On the way back to Sarzana drive or cycle up to the pretty villages of **Ponzano Superiore** and **Falcinello**, which have good views back across the valley.

⌂ Where to stay, eat and drink

⌂ Al Convento (18 rooms) Piazza Regina Margherita 1, Vezzano Ligure; ☎0187 994444; e info@hotelalconvento.com; w hotelalconvento.com. Former 19th-century cloister in the heart of this pretty village. Private garden, spa & a good restaurant (see right). Free parking. €€

⌂ B&B Il Cielo in Una Casa (3 rooms) Piazza Il Giugno 15, Arcola; m 3386 418708. Friendly but elegant B&B just outside Arcola with a shady garden. €€

✕ Locanda del Viandante Piazza Regina Margherita 1, Vezzano Ligure; ☎0187 994725. Traditional Ligurian cooking in this authentic little town away from the bustle of the Cinque Terre. €€€

Part Four

THE RIVIERA DI PONENTE

RIVIERA DI PONENTE

The Riviera di Ponente, the western Riviera, is known as the coast of the setting sun. It stretches 150km west of Genoa to Ventimiglia and the border with France. Less glitzy than the Riviera di Levante and although a favourite spot of the European aristocracy, especially British and Russian gentry in the 19th century, these days large tracts of the coast are almost exclusively the preserve of Italian holidaymakers.

The coast is less dramatic than on the Levante but the upside is that, as a result, this stretch of Liguria has far more beaches. The hinterland here, however, is at its most impressive. One of Liguria's loveliest valleys is the Val Nervia behind Ventimiglia and from the top of Monte Beigua there is a dizzying view across nearly all of Liguria and the plain of Piedmont to the Alps in the north. Deep green valleys and medieval hilltop towns are just moments from the coast and when it snows, it is even possible to ski.

7

Arenzano to
Savona

Telephone code 010 (Arenzano and Cogoleto only; +39010 if calling from abroad); otherwise 019 (+39019 from abroad)

The Via Aurelia winds out of Genoa through run-down suburbs, many of which contain ruined factories that testify to Genoa's industrial history, and past its huge modern container port. Today there is little of interest, although be sure to stop and buy both focaccia and *farinata*, as the more run down the area, the better the bakery. Otherwise it is best to get straight on to the *autostrada* and make a fast getaway.

After the urban sprawl, all of a sudden the road opens up, offering an invigorating breath of fresh air after the intensity of Genoa's busy streets. If you are using public transport, take the train – the bus takes forever. The views from the motorway here across both the mountains and the sea are testament to the elements of contrast on offer along the coast to Savona. Unlike other bits of Liguria, which have either wonderful mountain valleys or stunning coastlines, this area has both.

The seaside is dotted with family resorts centred on medieval fishing villages that are packed to the brim on holiday weekends and in the summer months with Italian holidaymakers. The mountains, just minutes from the sea are remote, rural and home to two of the region's national parks. This part of Liguria is relatively unknown to tourists from outside of Italy and offers the visitor a uniquely Italian experience.

ARENZANO

The first place worth stopping at along the coast is **Arenzano,** which, depending on the traffic, is half-an-hour's drive along the *autostrada* from Genoa. It also has its own train station and a bus service from Voltri. It is a diminutive, rather exclusive all-year-round little resort below Monte Reixa and is popular with well-heeled Genoese. The narrow streets of the old town are full of stylish boutiques and it is bustling both in the day and the evening.

The old town is still laid out on the Roman grid pattern and was originally called Arentianis, as it was the property of the Arenti family. There are a number of impressive villas, notably the 16th-century **Villa Negrotto Cambiaso,** which is now the town hall and is surrounded by a pretty public park full of exotic plants.

On a little hill above the town is the **Santuario di Gesù Bambino di Praga** (\ 010 912 5785; **w** gesubambino.org; ☉ church: 07.15–21.00 daily, crib: 07.15–13.00 & 14.30–19.00; daily admission free), which was built in 1905 by the Carmelites and is the only sanctuary dedicated to the Infant Jesus of Prague. The original statue that came from the Czech capital is said to have belonged to Saint Theresa and has been venerated by the Carmelite order for over 500 years. If you are travelling with children, they'll love the crypt, which has a large nativity scene full of ceramic figures that's open all year round.

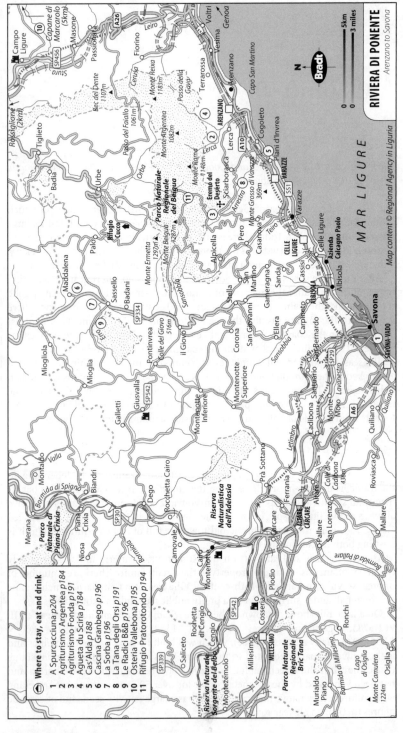

Where to stay, eat and drink

1. A Spurcacciuna p204
2. Agriturismo Argentea p184
3. Agriturismo Fonda p191
4. Agueta du Sciria p184
5. Cas'Alda p188
6. Cascina Granbego p196
7. La Sorba p196
8. La Tana degli Orsi p191
9. Le Radici B&B p196
10. Osteria Vallebona p195
11. Rifugio Pratorotondo p194

MAR LIGURE

RIVIERA DI PONENTE
Arenzano to Savona

Map content © Regional Agency in Liguria

There is an interesting little museum, the **Itinerario Marinaro** (Via Olivette 83; m 342 766 6821; ⊕ 15.00–17.00 Sun or call to make an appointment; admission free) in the Santuario delle Olivette. One of the objects on show is the neck of the bottle of champagne that launched the *Rondine* in 1946. Like the *Enzo Sereni*, the *Rondine* was part of a clandestine fleet that took Holocaust survivors to run the British blockade of Mandatory Palestine in the immediate years after World War II.

The old railway line to the west of Arenzano is now a pleasant seafront walk that leads to Cogoleto and on to Varazze. There are small rocky coves with both beach concessions and free beaches. This is a great place to bike along the coastal path. The bay in front of Arenzano is popular with divers and there is both an 'underwater gym', specially designed for diving practice, and the wreck of the tanker the *Haven*, which sank in 1991, which lies 1.5km off the coast. **Haven Diving** (Via del Porto 8; ↘010 911 3071; w havendiving.com) organises trips to the wreck. The **Sant'Anna Golf Club** at Pineta has a good nine-hole course with mountain views. A marathon, the **Marcia Internazionale Mare e Monti** takes place on the second weekend in September on the scenic paths behind Arenzano (w maremontiarenzano.org). There is also a riding school near the motorway exit opposite the Ekom supermarket. Just beyond the Ekom a road leads up into the mountains; take the left fork until it peters out. Here there's a pleasant walk in the foothills of Monte Reixa. The strawberries grown

THE ARCHITECT

Renzo Piano is one Genoese who has left his mark on many of the world's leading cities. He gave London the Shard, Paris the Pompidou Centre and Manhattan the New York Times Building. In 2013 he was appointed Senator for Life in the Italian Senate.

Born in Genoa's western suburb of Pegli in 1937, these days he divides his time between his homes in Paris and on the cliffs near Arenzano. Here Piano says he likes to sit and watch the sea and simply think. His extraordinary house and workshop in Vesima, just outside Arenzano, is built on land that he inherited from his father. It is a low-level one-storey glass construction, which was inspired by the greenhouses that dot the hills around Genoa.

Piano's father was a builder and the architect spent much of his childhood on building sites. Family holidays involved detours to the famous Carrara marble mines on Liguria's border with Tuscany. Piano has often said his work reflects the very essence of Genoa. On a Sunday his father would take him to the harbour to watch the boats, which to the young Renzo, seemed like immense moving buildings. It drew him to designs that fight against gravity. Light is also an important part of his work and the washing that dries on Genoa rooftops fed his imagination. For Piano design is one of the great adventures of life.

Piano masterminded the facelift of the old port in Genoa in the 1990s and has a new bold vision for its waterfront that would give the city a continuous 3km stretch of seaside walkway, extending from the old port all the way to the Genoa Trade Fair. Part of the port will become an island connected by a pedestrianised walkway. The plan is to make Genoa the largest seafront port city in Europe, strengthening its ship repair activities and relocating and extending its docks for leisure boats. The new pilot's tower he has designed will, he hopes, become the symbol of the new city.

The Building Workshop in Vesima is a retreat for architects and engineers and is sometimes open to the public (w fondazionerenzopiano.org).

here were once so famous that they were shipped to Japan in 1959 for the wedding of the crown prince. These days the fields have largely been built over, but in the market it is still possible to buy them from local producers.

COGOLETO In the next bay, and the next stop on the train line, is Cogoleto. Not quite as classy as Arenzano, it once made its living from a now defunct chemical and metallurgical factory. The factory ruins greet you as you drive down the hill, evidence of a typical disregard for the beauty of the countryside.

During the Napoleonic Wars, in April 1800, there was a little-known but bloody battle here between the French and the Austrians, the Battle of Cogoleto. In 1943 the town was in the wars again when it was badly bombed by the Allies, and the Roman bridge was destroyed.

There's a tiny little old town with some nice food shops and a long seafront with plenty of good free pebble-cum-sandy beaches. There is a religious procession and fireworks on the feast of San Lorenzo on 10 August. However, the town's main claim to fame is that mystery man Christopher Columbus was thought to have been born here (see box, page 7). There is a plaque on the house where he is supposed to have been born, which was originally placed there in the 1650s, but debate rages as to where he actually came from in Liguria.

🏠 Where to stay

🏠 **Grand Hotel Arenzano** (110 rooms) Lungomare Stati Uniti 2; 📞010 91091; e info@ grandhotelarenzano.it; w grandhotelarenzano. it. An old-fashioned hotel dating from 1915, right on the seafront next to the old town, and which attracts an international clientele. Swimming pool (🕐 May–Sep). €€

🏠 **Agriturismo Argentea** [map, page 182] (4 rooms) Via Val Lerone 50; 📞010 913 5367;

w agriturismoargentea.com. B&B in which 2 of the rooms have kitchenettes. Up in the hills on a small farm behind Arenzano. Each of the rooms has a double & a single bed making this a good family option, if a little basic. They are also happy to cook for their guests. They serve their own veal & pork, but they also cater well for vegetarians as the little farm produces a wide variety of fruit & vegetables. €

🍴 Where to eat and drink Some of the lightest and tastiest focaccia I have eaten is sold at **Panperfocaccia** (Via Francia 20), on the road from Arenzano to Cogoleto. Cogoleto has a pleasant bar scene in the evening and some lovely shops. It still has specialist shops, like a poultry shop and a red meat butcher's, which have disappeared in other towns along the coast.

🍴 **Class** Piazza Stella Maris 7a, Cogoleto; 📞010 918 1925. This restaurant lives up to its name & serves excellent fish dishes & risotto made with artichokes from Albenga. The pasta is homemade under the guidance of head chef Gianluca Palmieri. Chic & minimalist, it has a dedicated local clientele. €€€

🍴 **Agueta du Sciria** [map, page 182] Via Pecorara 18/a; 📞010 911 0762; m 339 602 9460; e aguetadusciria@yahoo.it; w agueta.it; 🕐 evenings Tue–Sat, lunch only Sun. In the hills

behind Arenzano, this traditional restaurant has a variety of set menus, inc a vegetarian one. There is an à la carte menu, too. Best to book in advance. €€

✳🍴 **La Cambusa** Lungomare Stati Uniti 3, Arenzano; 📞010 455 4569. This restaurant serves some extremely tasty pizza & excellent *mandilli* pasta with pesto. €€

✳🍴 **Piro Piro** Via Buranello 28, Cogoleto; 📞010 918 3646; w pizzeriapiropiro.it. Slow Food pizza. Proof that the best food does not come from the nicest looking restaurants. €

FROM COGOLETO TO VARAZZE Carry on along the coast to Varazze either by train or bus; it is better to opt for the latter if you are using public transport as to go by train would be to miss the fantastic views along the coast road. It is also possible to walk, or even better to bike the 5km along the old railway track, now a seafront promenade called the Lungomare Europa, beginning in Cogoleto. The Via Aurelia climbs up to the Punta d'Invrea. Just off the road on the left-hand side is a restaurant, **Il Volo dei Gabbiani** (✆019 9220015; w volodeigabbiani.it), with a good-sized pool, which you can pay to use for the day. It is surrounded by a large lawn and is a peaceful spot with nice views and minigolf.

On the wooded headland sits the **Castello d'Invrea**. The local marquis once owned much of the land around here, but the family lost their fortune gambling and were forced to sell large tracts of their estate in the 1960s. Piani d'Invrea, halfway between Varazze and Cogoleto, is the net result and is a pleasant complex of condominiums built above the Lungomare Europa. It is also home to a pricey but top-notch swimming club and disco, the **Orizzonte** (page 189) (m 348 696 1701; ⨍). Open to the public, the seawater pool is perched on the cliff edge with magnificent views across the bay to Genoa and Savona. It is signposted on the Via Aurelia. The **Baia del Corvo** nearby has a café, car park and good pebbly beach, with a small beach club in summer, where it is possible to rent kayaks.

VARAZZE

Varazze is the main seaside resort between Genoa and Savona and an excellent place to base yourself for exploring this stretch of coast. From here it is possible to visit both cities for a day trip. Decidedly upmarket and family-orientated, it is a lively place with a long seafront promenade lined with pretty painted houses. The promenade curves around the palm-fringed bay that lives up to the name of this stretch of coast: the Riviera delle Palme. There is a long beach that is covered in colourful sun umbrellas during the summer and popular with surfers, especially in the autumn. Outside the town there are numerous small rocky coves, some partially sandy, which are completely free of charge.

Varazze is a resort with a real Italian feel and is almost a caricature of the popular song *Stessa Spiaggia, Stesso Mare*, which means 'Same Beach, Same Sea'. Italians are creatures of habit and spend weeks every summer sitting on the same deckchair staring out at the same stretch of sea, year in, year out. In keeping with this, Varazze has a band of regular devoted fans and, in high season, it is usually packed out with holidaymakers from Milan and Turin. It is rare to see a foreign car here or hear anything other than Italian being spoken.

In the summer of 2012, Varazze made it into the news headlines when a well-preserved Roman trading vessel from the 1st century BC was discovered off the coast. Fishermen had been finding bits of pottery in their nets for years and this prompted a search. At the moment it is still underwater but watch this space…

Behind Varazze stands the mighty **Monte Beigua**, home to a national park and criss-crossed with walking and biking trails. The mountain, which towers over the town, couldn't be more of a contrast to the world below and offers wild, rural countryside with breathtaking sea views. All this makes Varazze a great base for exploring the hinterland, as well as for lazing on the beach.

HISTORY The Romans called the town Ad Navalia because they built ships here and the thickly forested hillsides around the town provided an abundance of wood. Later it came to be known as Varagine, a name which derives from the word *varo*, which means 'launch'. This name was in turn corrupted into Varazze, which grew rich on the shipbuilding business. As a result it was coveted both by Genoa and its archrival Savona. The town was briefly an independent city-state before being sold to the Genoese in 1290.

Varazze was put on the map in the Middle Ages by Jacopo da Varagine (1228–98), who was an important religious scholar and Archbishop of Genoa. His most famous book, the *Golden Legend*, was a compilation of the lives of the saints and was one of the most widely read books of its time and one of the earliest to be printed, making it one of Europe's first bestsellers.

GETTING THERE AND AROUND
By boat The marina has 900 berths (019 935321; e info@marinadivarazze.it; w marinadivarazze.it).

By bus Buses run from the seafront along the Via Aurelia east to Cogoleto and west to Savona, as well as from the Viale Nazioni Unite up to the summit of Monte Beigua and then on to Sassello, taking about 45 minutes. To explore the mountains properly, however, it is necessary to have a car.

By car The A10 *autostrada* runs across the steep valley on a viaduct literally over the suburbs of Varazze. The motorway exit is on the eastern side of town. From here, turn right on to the Via Aurelia, the SS1 that soon runs down along the seafront. Varazze is 30km west of Genoa and 11km east of Savona. Park in the town centre – turn right at the small roundabout that divides the town in two (there is also a small car park here), or at the port at the western end of the town.

By taxi For local taxis, call 019 931010.

By train The railway station is just above the port and has direct connections to Genoa and Ventimiglia. The trains stop all along the coast, so it is easy to hop from one resort to another.

On foot or by bike Everywhere is accessible on foot. Bikes can be hired at the start of the eastern stretch of the pedestrianised seafront walkway, the Lungomare Europa, at the little *tabacchi*, or newsagent, **Tabaccheria La Mola** (019 932370). Many hotels have their own bikes for rent. It is also possible to cycle and walk along the coast on the seafront to Celle Ligure, 3km west of Varazze. Monte Beigua is a tough terrain but popular with Italian mountain bikers. The roads are relatively quiet, especially during the week, and are fun to cycle. Ask at the tourist office for the useful leaflets *Giovo in MTB* and *Il Giovo in bicicletta*.

TOURIST INFORMATION The **tourist office** (Piazza Beato Jacopo 58; 019 935043; w varazze.com) is in the town hall but like most tourist offices in Liguria its opening hours are limited. There is a useful, if limited, app, SVD Savona e Dintorni, and it is available for both Android and Apple. Be sure to ask about the numerous events held during the summer. Some of them are of the tacky seaside variety but can be fun, while others, especially local church festivals, are steeped in ancient tradition, including a religious procession on 30 April. Particularly charming is that of the *lumini in mare* which takes place at the end of July, when late in the evening, thousands of candles put in wax paper cups are sent out to sea from the beach. Varazze has a top-notch firework display on 15 August when the booms and crackles echo around the mountains in the most theatrical way.

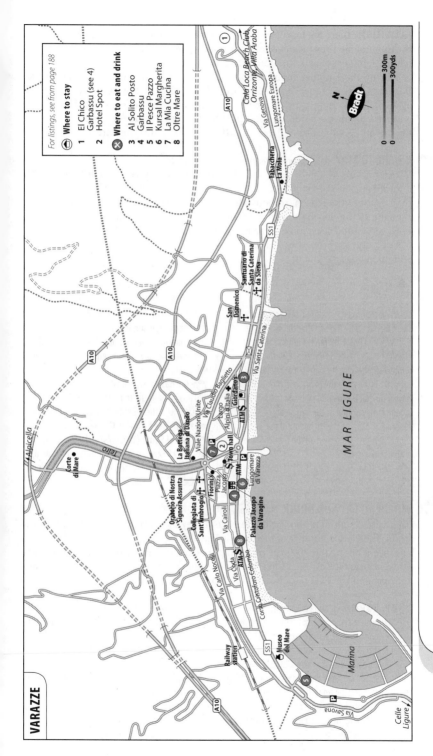

VARAZZE

For listings, see from page 188

Where to stay
1 El Chico
   Garbassu (see 4)
2 Hotel Spot

Where to eat and drink
3 Al Solito Posto
4 Garbassu
5 Il Pesce Pazzo
6 Kursal Margherita
7 La Mia Cucina
8 Oltre Mare

MAR LIGURE

Cala Loca Beach Club
Orizzonte, Villa Araba
Tabaccheria
La Mola
Santuario di
Santa Caterina
da Siena
San
Domenico
Via Santa Caterina
Via Claudio Baglietto
Largo
Alpini d'Italia
Giordanes
Lungomare
di Varazze
Piazza
Jacopo
Fiorinì's
Town Hall
La Bottega
Italiana di Danilo
Viale Nazioni Unite
Oratorio di Nostra
Signora Assunta
Collegiata di
Sant'Ambrogio
Via Cairoli
Palazzo Jacopo
da Varagine
Corte
di Mare
Alpicella
Teiro
Via Carlo Nocelli
Via Oxla
Museo
del Mare
Railway
station
Marina
Via Savona
Celle
Ligure
Via Genova
Lungomare Europa
SS1

0 ——— 300m
0 ——— 300yds

Activities There are lots of sporting activities available along the coast and up in the mountains. They include snorkelling, sailing, fishing, paragliding, climbing and tennis. A full list of activities can be found on w varazzeoutdoor.it.

During the summer months, boat trips run from the port to San Fruttuoso, Portofino, the Cinque Terre and Porto Venere. Pay at the quayside. There are also whale-watching trips (w whalewatchliguria.it), fishing trips (local fishermen advertise on the port-side) and it is possible to enjoy Varazze's impressive firework display on 15 August from the sea (☏ 010 256775; w liguriaviamare.it).

🏠 WHERE TO STAY *Map, page 187, unless otherwise stated*

Varazze is full of hotels, nearly all old-fashioned family-run establishments with a loyal band of guests. Weekends in July and the first three weeks of August are the busiest of the season, so book ahead. Don't expect anything too swanky here, though, as the accommodation on offer is predominantly mid-range. There is, however, a good selection of apartments on w airbnb.com.

Look also for properties in Piani d'Invrea. I have mine on the site, so you might end up in our apartment!

🏠 **El Chico** (38 rooms) Strada Romana 63; ☏ 019 931388; e elchico.sv@bestwestern.it; w www.elchico.eu; ⊕ closed 24 Dec & Jan. Don't be put off by the fact that this is a 4-star Best Western hotel. It's family-run & is the classiest place to stay in Varazze, & with cooling, whitewashed walls, it exudes an atmosphere of calm. It's just east of the town so it's better if you have a car, but it is possible to walk to town. It's a good family option as the large leafy garden is fenced & it has a pool with beautiful sea views. Dinner & b/fast are served on the terrace & there is ample parking. €€€

🏠 **Cas'Alda** [map, page 182] (3 rooms) Via Pini d'Aleppo 22/9b; m 339 112 0759; w bed-and-

breakfast-in-italy.com. Two of the rooms have sea views & the other overlooks the garden. This small B&B is in the smart part of Piani d'Invrea close to the Orizzonte swimming club & the pretty coves along the Lungomare Europa. A lovely peaceful setting, but to stay here, it helps if you have a car. €€

🏠 **Garbassu** (2 rooms) Via Cairoli 3; m 345 770 8653. This is the trendy face of B&B life in Varazze, with the same owners as the eponymous restaurant (see below). €€

🏠 **Hotel Spot** (18 rooms) Viale Nazioni Unite 10; ☏ 019 97270; w hotelspotvarazze.it Modern, trendy & inexpensive, this hotel is a breath of fresh air. €€

✗ WHERE TO EAT AND DRINK *Map, page 187*

There are restaurants all over the town and they have upped their game in recent years. There are a number of nice bars in the old town.

Since it opened in 2007 the modern port-cum-marina, with its waterfront bars and restaurants, is especially lively in the evening. There are cafés on the Lungomare Europa, and the **Cala Loca Beach Club** has a decent restaurant.

✗ **Il Pesce Pazzo** Marina di Varazze; ☏ 019 930032; w ilpescepazzo.com; ⊕ lunch & dinner daily in good weather. A really excellent fish restaurant that serves only local fish. There is a fixed menu, as well as à la carte. Outdoor seating in summer. You can take away a tasty snack of fried fish & a glass of wine from their boat, which is moored in front of the restaurant (summer only) & you can go fishing for your supper as well, as they organise fishing trips. €€€€€

✳✗ **Al Solito Posto** Via Santa Caterina 30; ☏ 019 204 6537. Good menu including meat & fish dishes. They also make the pizza right in front of you, which is fun. It is very popular so be sure to book a table. It has AC, but in very hot weather is a bit stuffy. The good thing about this restaurant is that it is usually open even in bad weather when other places in Varazze are closed. €€

✳✗ **Garbassu** 72 Corso Giacomo Matteotti; m 342 707 6724; ⊕ evenings only. One of

Varazze's top choices. Hip family-run restaurant serving local dishes with a stylish difference. Good for vegetarians. Great shabby-chic atmosphere. Tasty vegetarian options but portions, on the whole, are small. Be sure to book well in advance as it is so popular you have to wait days for a space in high season, but to do so it is best to pop in, as they often do not answer the phone. €€

✳✖ **Kursaal Margherita** Corso Matteotti 15; ☏019 96286; w kursaalmargherita.it. I like this restaurant because it has a lovely terrace overlooking the sea & is usually open out of season. In summer you will need to book. Food is basic but the pizza is good. €€

✖ **La Mia Cucina** Viale Nazioni Unite 15; m 340 820 5169. Mostly fish on the menu at this simple, modern little restaurant in the heart of Varazze. €€

✖ **Oltre Mare** Corso C Colombo 50; ☏019 930235. Specialises in mussels & pizza. Good homemade focaccia & some classy touches to the starters. Trendy décor & nice large outside terrace. Good value for what it is. €€

NIGHTLIFE On Wednesday and Saturday the **Orizzonte** swimming pool (f), in Piani d'Invrea usually hosts a late-night disco by the pool. They run a pick-up service from Varazze. It is a popular spot for weddings with fabulous views across the bay.

SHOPPING Varazze has some excellent food shops. Locals, and my husband, swear by the focaccia from **Giordano's** at Via Goffredo Mameli 10. For fresh pasta go to the **Fiorini's** family shop on Via Lanzerotto Malocello. They make excellent ravioli stuffed with local herbs, called *pansotti*, and use the basil grown in Genova Prà, considered the best in Liguria, to make their pesto.

You can purchase locally produced meat, poultry and a range of pasta, sauces and spreads at **La Bottega Italiana di Danilo** (Via Recagno 2; w www.campagnamica.it).

There is an excellent market on Saturday morning opposite the town hall. It sells all sorts of things from handbags to frying pans. The food market clusters around a small square, the Largo Alpini d'Italia, east of the main car park, some of it in a market hall. Here it is possible to buy eggs and vegetables from old ladies dressed in black headscarves and long black skirts, who come down from the mountains for the morning every week. The best supermarket is the COOP in the Corte di Mare shopping centre on the edge of town. To drive there from the centre, take the road along the river for Alpicella but then turn left at the bridge over the river and loop back towards Varazze along the other side of it.

OTHER PRACTICALITIES There are **ATMs** on Piazza Dante Alighieri, Corso Giacomo Matteotti 8, and in the Corte di Mare shopping centre. The **post office** is at Via Santa Caterina 43, and also has a cash machine. The **pharmacy** is at Via Malocello 47, and the closest hospital is in Savona (page 205).

WHAT TO SEE AND DO Varazze is a typical Ligurian town huddled next to the coast road. From the seafront promenade there are good views of the black-and-white **Palazzo Jacopo da Varagine**. The ochre tower next to it is embellished with the town's crest, below which a small gateway leads into the tiny **Piazza Jacopo**, the heart of the old town.

Testament to Varazze's wealth and Jacopo da Varagine's legacy are a number of historic churches. Just to the left of the square, off Via Sant'Ambrogio is the Romanesque **Collegiata di Sant'Ambrogio**, which was built in the 15th century; the red bell tower with its three arched windows that dwarfs it dates from the 14th century. The ornate neo-Renaissance façade was added in 1916. The courtyard in front is paved with beach pebbles laid out in a geometric style, which is typical of Liguria. Inside is a polyptych by Giovanni Barbagelata and Luca Cambiaso's *Madonna and Saints John the Baptist and Francis*.

The **River Teiro** divides the town neatly in two, although it is channelled under the road, which runs through the centre of the town before it flows out to sea. Just before disappearing the river runs by the front of the **Oratorio di Nostra Signora Assunta**, which is built into what remains of the old 12th-century town walls that protected Varazze from Saracen raids. If visiting in summer, don't be fooled by the tiny trickle of water that runs down the middle of the riverbed making a mockery of the high concrete walls that surround it. In winter it can turn into a raging torrent and sometimes bursts its banks, as it did in 2010, causing widespread damage.

Walk back towards the sea and then plunge into the old town that lies on either side of the **Viale Nazioni Unite**. It is full of old-world charm and narrow pedestrianised alleyways bordered by tall houses painted in red and ochre with pretty trompe l'oeil decorations, a typically Ligurian sight. It is a charming place to stop for a drink and is full of masses of small shops, owned by families for generations, selling everything from dishwashers to buttons. Varazze's new marina is popular in the evening for a stroll and there is the minute **Museo del Mare** on the quayside (⏰ Sep–Jun 10.00–noon & 15.00–18.30 Sat–Sun, Jul & Aug 21.00–23.00 daily; admission free).

It is worth the short walk east on the seafront to see two of Varazze's other churches. On the Via Aurelia is the **Santuario di Santa Caterina da Siena**. The present church dates from the 17th century and is dedicated to the saint who stayed here in 1376 when her prayers seemed to miraculously bring an end to the plague that had ravaged the town. Inside are some giant, highly decorated golden crosses that are paraded around town on her feast day on 30 April. The tiny golden leaves make a shimmering noise and are an impressive sight on a sunny day.

A few minutes' walk to the east along the seafront, take the lower fork of the road after the petrol station. To the left is the red-and-white-striped church of **San Domenico** that dates from 1419, which is home to a silver urn containing the remains of Jacopo da Varagine.

To the right of the church, the road picks up the original path of the railway that once ran along the coast. It was closed in 1970 and has subsequently been turned into the **Lungomare Europa** and runs 5km east to Cogoleto. The promenade goes through the old railway tunnels that are cut into the serpentine rock and is quite atmospheric. A tourist train runs along the path in summer. The maquis landscape is dotted with Aleppo pines and upmarket holiday homes and overlooks a series of small coves with free access to the sea; it is a lovely place to swim. There is a good café just past the local landmark, the white Moorish Villa Araba, which is a private house.

UP IN THE MOUNTAINS BEHIND VARAZZE The mountains above Varazze are stunning and shouldn't be missed. From the centre of Varazze, the SP542 runs along the right bank of the river and up into the mountains. After a 5-minute drive a sign on the right indicates the road to the **Eremo del Deserto**. At the top of the hill the road splits. The right fork takes you to the panoramic tiny white church of the **Madonna della Guardia**, which stands like a beacon above Varazze and which still belongs to the Marquis d'Invrea. It is a 15-minute walk from the road and has great views on a clear day. It is possible to see from La Spezia in the east to the Capo di Noli in the west. I once saw Corsica from here. It is a rare event and was captured so cleverly by Maupassant in his short story *Happiness*.

The right fork in the road continues on to **Eremo del Deserto**, a 17th-century Carmelite friary founded in 1618. It is closed to the public but there are lovely walks in the dense forest and secluded picnic spots by the rocky streams. The road then leads back to Cogoleto and the coast.

Continuing along the SP542, the landscape becomes wild and rugged as the road climbs towards **Monte Beigua** and the olive groves give way to holm oaks and then chestnut trees. Follow the signs for **Alpicella** and a series of hairpin bends to this tiny quaint hamlet, which is tellingly dominated by its war memorial. It always makes me think of D H Lawrence's description in *The Lost Girl* of the day war broke out in a tiny Italian hamlet just like this.

From the church there are lovely views down the wooded valley to the sea. The village dates back to the 4th century and has a small **archaeological museum** (019 97660; by appointment only) in the parish church. In the valley below there are a number of Neolithic standing stones and stone carvings and there's a pleasant walk to a stone bridge built in the year 1000, known as the Bridge of the Saracens.

Where to stay, eat and drink Alpicella has two good restaurants and a traditional bar and is a pleasant place to relax away from the hustle and bustle of the coast. Food up in the mountains here is meaty. The local dish is *zeaia*, a stew of pork, beef and chicken that is cooked so slowly that it produces a thick jelly that envelops the meat, allowing it to be eaten cold.

Agriturismo Castello d'Alpicella (2 apts) Via Ceresa 17; 019 918424; w castelloalpicella. it. Just above the village, it specialises in dishes made from donkeys raised in the nearby fields. It's possible to work in the donkey farm & in the vegetable garden. They also breed boxer dogs. Restaurant set menu, excluding drinks (€€€). Apt for 6. €€

Agriturismo Fonda [map, page 182] Via al Deserto 13; 019 918201; Fri evening; summer & winter lunch & dinner Sat, lunch only Sun. A little restaurant hidden in the woods serving wild boar, lamb, rabbit, homemade pasta & the typical *crostate di marmellata*, jam tart, on the road from Sciarborasca to the Eremo del Deserto. You can also go horseriding. €€€

Trattoria ai Cacciatori Piazza IV Novembre 14; 019 918368; w trattoriaaicacciatori.it. Next to the bar is the place for a meat feast. Set menus €25 & €28, exc drinks. €€€

Baccere Baciccia Via IV Novembre 17; 019 918005; w baccerebaciccia.it; closed Tue. Located on the main square, it serves tasty, large pizza & meat courses. It's popular with locals, so be sure to book in high season. They also rent rooms (€). €€

La Tana degli Orsi [map, page 182] Via Pratorotondo 3, Località Faie; m 349 104 6583. This agriturismo has a seasonal set menu at €30. It has a lovely view across the sea. Classic local dishes like *pansotti* are on the menu. €€

Monte Beigua
From Alpicella take the road on the western side of the main square to the summit of Monte Beigua, which sits at the heart of the **Parco Naturale Regionale del Beigua** (w www.parcobeigua.it), which is the largest protected area in Liguria. Its hairpin bends through the dense forest are some of the best in Liguria before the road opens out into wild moorland. Look out for roe deer and foxes in the thick beech woods and wild boar at night. It's an excellent spot for birdwatching during the spring and autumn migrations. There are lots of outdoor activities to enjoy here, among them climbing and canyoning. For more information take a look at w varazzeoutdoor.it.

On a sultry summer's day, as the road rises above the clouds, the mountain takes on a mystical air as breaks in the fast-moving cloud offer glimpses of the sea and the coastal towns below. It is no surprise that the ancient Ligurians considered Monte Beigua a sacred place and left many carved effigies on the mountain. You can see these in the archaeological museum in Pegli (page 82). Look out for the little herds of goats wandering the mountaintop.

Some of the best walks on the summit start at the mountain refuge, **Rifugio Pratorotondo** (page 194). On the mountaintop you can pick up the **Alta Via dei Monti Liguri**. It is a very easy walk and suitable for all ages. On the last Sunday in July, the local mountaineers, the Alpinisti from Cogoleto, gather at the mountain hut, the Casa della Miniera, to fry savoury doughnuts and sing songs that feature local hero Garibaldi and his exploits in the Risorgimento. From the path on a clear day it is possible to see as far as the Alps as the plain stretches out below the mountain range towards Turin. Wild flowers and butterflies abound and there are plenty of wild raspberries and blackberries in the height of summer growing along the paths. From the *rifugio* the walk to the summit of Monte Argentea takes about 4 hours round trip.

It is well worth taking the bus from Varazze to the *summit of Monte Beigua* and walking back down through the woods. Paths lead from the Albergo Monte Beigua to Sassello and the hamlet of Palo, or you can take a short amble to the Croce del Beigua, the monumental cross. There are often goats here. There is a path that leads down from the hotel to Alpicella as well one that circuits Monte Cavalli. From the top of Monte Cavalli there are often dreamy misty views across the mountains which evoke the druid heritage of the area, as well as stunning views along the coast to Savona, Bergeggi and Capo Noli. A parallel scenic trail begins at the top of Monte Beigua close to the hotel and goes down to Varazze via Faie and through the Passo del Muraglione, which takes about 2 hours to walk. Both walks are easy as they are downhill but parts are steep and you must wear proper walking shoes. Also remember that they will be very slippery if it has rained.

From Varazze you can drive up near to the Santuario della Guardia on the summit of Monte Grosso di Varazze. It is a really beautiful spot with lovely views across the coast and towards Monte Beigua. Take the fork signposted Faie on the road to Alpicella. The SP57 leads up through Casanova after the village the church is signposted to the left. Park the car at the second signpost which is brown and has the symbol of a church.

Local bookshops sell *Vette e Sentieri del Beigua Geopark* by Andrea Parodi. It is in Italian but the maps are clear, as are the length of the walks and their difficulty. The book also details more serious climbing routes.

The summit of Monte Beigua is strategically important, both militarily and commercially, and is as a result sadly covered in a cluster of telecommunication towers. From the small picnic ground at 1,287m above sea level, just before the summit, the views are truly spectacular and you can see almost from one end of Liguria to the other. Here the air is always degrees cooler than on the coast and when it swelters in expectation of a thunderstorm, a trip up to Monte Beigua can be like spending an afternoon in Scotland. This is the heart of the province of Savona, which is the most forested part of Liguria, with 60% of the land covered in trees.

After the **Rifugio Pratorotondo**, the SP31 will take you either to Sassello or Urbe. Both routes are popular with mountain bikers

The road to **Urbe** is beautiful and remote. Here you are right off the tourist track and deep in Liguria's hinterland. Stop to buy jam at **Dalpian Il Sottobosco** (Località Acquabuona; ℄ 010 929298; **w** dalpian.it). Some 15 minutes to the north of the abbey, **Lavagè** (Via Valle Gargassa 100; ℄ 010 925880; **m** 347 307 0662; **w** lavage.it) sell milk, cheese and meat in their farm shop. They also organise tasting sessions of local products, but you must book in advance.

There's a lovely outing to the beautifully preserved 12th-century abbey, **Abbazia di Santa Maria alla Croce** (\ 010 929419; ⊕ 09.30–noon & 15.00–18.00 daily; admission €8). Take the SP41 from Rossiglione to Badia near Tiglieto. The abbey is signposted as the Abbazia di Badia and is close to the car park just after the road forks. The car park is not signposted, so if you hit a dirt track, turn around otherwise you will end up lost in the wilds of Piedmont. The abbey sits in the pretty Val d'Orba surrounded by green fields and was one of the first Cistercian abbeys founded outside of France. It was also once the home of St Bernard of Clairvaux, an extremely important figure in 12th-century Catholicism who also inspired men to fight in the Crusades. The monks abandoned the abbey in the 18th century, after which it became a private property. They returned in 2000 after the monastery was refurbished, only to leave again in 2011. There is a pleasant walk in the woods along the footpath from the car park which, if you do the full circuit, takes 2 hours.

The Valle Stura
The road leads down from the mountains just before Rossiglione in the Valle Stura, which sadly has the A10 motorway running along it, but away from the road there are some interesting sights to stop and see.

Campo Ligure
Campo Ligure is a pretty medieval town with a miniature castle, built in the 12th century by the Spinola family, which offers a lovely view across the town. Campo Ligure was an important staging post on the trade route with Piedmont to the north. The name Campo indicates the town was a military camp in the Roman era. Campo Ligure is off the tourist trail, but is undergoing something of a renaissance since it was added to the prestigious *borghi piu belli d'Italia*, the list of Italy's most beautiful villages.

The **Oratorio di Santi Sebastiano e Rocco** (c1647) has some fine paintings, including one by famous painter Domenico Piola, and at Christmas there is a beautiful mechanical crib.

On the slopes of the hill below the castle is the **Giardino di Tugnin**, an extraordinary collection of sculptures by 79-year-old Gianfranco Timossi, known as Tugnin. There are a number of vast pieces carved out of single olive trees, depicting scenes from Dante's *Inferno* and local mythology. Read more about Tugnin and his creations at w bradtguides.com/campo_ligure.

Most of Campo Ligure burned down in the 17th century and was rebuilt around a charming central square. Don't miss what the locals claim is Italy's narrowest street. It is a tiny alleyway next to Via Saracco 19. The town is also famous for its filigree, the art of twisting threads of gold and silver, and is the only remaining important centre in Italy for this ancient art, which has died out even in Sardinia, once famous for the craft. It is protected by the Made in Liguria label and to make sure you buy a genuine article and not something made in China, look out for this. The town has a small but excellent museum, the **Museo della Filigrana** (Via della Giustina 5; \ 010 920099; w museofiligrana.org ⊕ 15.30–18.00 Tue, Thu, Fri, 10.30–noon & 15.30–18.00 Sat & Sun; admission €4) has a collection that spans five continents. It was originally a private collection put together after World War II by Pietro Carlo Bosio. There is an interesting collection of Jewish artefacts, which, perhaps not surprisingly considering the date the collection was put together, are sadly wrongly labelled. Much of the collection is stunning and includes a huge silver birdcage that was made in Genoa in the 18th century and is believed to be the largest filigree object in the world. On the top floor you can find out

Walnuts are not just whizzed up into tasty pasta sauce, but turned into *nocino* which is a walnut liqueur. Traditionally walnuts were gathered on the eve of the festival of San Giovanni, which falls on 23–24 June, on or just after the summer solstice, a time of year that is shrouded in superstition. Women traditionally gathered the nuts in the evening and left them in the dew overnight. The next day they got brewing and the tipple was ready to drink at Halloween. You can buy it at **Azienda Agricola Le Vallegge di Sivori Anna Maria** (Località Vallegge 1, Rovegno; 010 302 4141; m 339 633 5123), but be sure to make an appointment.

about how filigree is made. The metal is worked much in the same way that pasta is made and it is forced through smaller and smaller holes just like spaghetti.

You can buy filigree from Franquita, a third-generation filigree maker at **Filigrana Bongera** (Via Saracco 1) and handmade jewellery from Hungarian Janos Gabor Varga at Blind Spot Jewellery (w blindspotjewellery.com), who settled in Campo Ligure to live among other artisans. To read more about his jewellery and Franquita's filigree business, and other artisans working in Campo Ligure, see w bradtguides.com/campo_ligure.

Where to stay, eat and drink They make a special focaccia called *revzora* in Campo Ligure which is made with cornflour, which gives it a lovely golden colour. Buy it at **Panificio al Castello** (Via Convento 3) or **Panificio Dal Pio** (Via Trieste 23) in Campo Ligure. Also look out for *crumiri di Masone*, crescent-shaped biscuits that were invented by a carpenter in 1910. Buy them in **Masone at Pasticceria Mosto** (Via Marconi 3) or **Pasticceria Vigo** (Via Roma 19). **Bar Moderno** in the main square has excellent ice cream made from local fruits and is a good place to stop for a drink. The local jewellers are likely to be found at lunchtime in the **Bar Sportive Tonino** on Via Saracco 52.

Affitacamere Barucco (3 rooms) Vico Baruco 1–3, Campo Ligure; m 335 624 6813; w dabarucco.it. Simple rooms that belong to the brother of one of the town's filigree artisans, Franquita. Good place to stay if you want to get plugged into the local craft scene. €€

La Case Inglese (3 rooms) Via Ravugna 36, Urbe; 019 722265; w lacasainglesebb.it; ⊕ Jul–Sep only. B&B with a wonderful view over the forests to the mountains, right off the tourist track. Lovely garden & vegetable plot. Wi-Fi & kitchenette. You will be a welcome addition, as many guests come here for English lessons with the English owners, hence its name. €

Nonno Toni B&B (3 rooms & 2 apts) Via della Giustizia 10, Campo Ligure; m 334 782 0086; w nonnotoni.it. This new B&B is named after the family's grandfather 'Toni', who ran his cobbler's business here in the heart of Campo Ligure. Two

spacious rooms with a shared bathroom & a 1-bedroom flat with kitchen. Common area with a PC & printer & pretty roof terrace with sunbeds & umbrellas. Free Wi-Fi. The owner is an electrical engineer & his pride & joy is the piped-music system. Bikes. €

Rifugio Pratorotondo [map, page 182] (5 dbl rooms, 2 rooms with 6 bunks) Via Pratorotondo 2, Località Pratorotondo; 010 913 3578; e info@rifugiopratorotondo.it; w rifugiopratorotondo.it; ⊕ closed Tue in Sep unless they have reservations. Savour local cheese with honey & other traditional dishes in the restaurant (€€), but beware the portions are as large as ever in Liguria. On Sun in season they make a very good *farinata*. The rooms are basic but the setting is lovely. €

Da Pippi Via Roma 94, Masone; 010 926 9126; ⊕ closed Mon evening & Tue. Traditional mountain food. Don't forget this is mushroom country so choose a dish with *funghi*. €€€

✗ Osteria Vallebona [map, page 182] Via Valle Ponzema 183, Campo Ligure; ✆ 010 920230; ☉ closed Mon. Excellent local cooking. Dishes are seasonal & include their farm's own home-grown vegetables. A meal here is a real Ligurian experience. €€

✗ Taverna del Falco Via Bosco Ing. Luigi 23, Masone; ✆ 010 920264; **f**; ☉ lunch weekdays, dinner Tue–Sun. Pizzeria & wine bar popular with locals. A traditional feel. Also serves local dishes. €€

FURTHER AFIELD The SP165 leads up into the mountains to Capane di Marcarolo, which is actually in Piedmont. It's worth driving across the mountains down into the **Passo di Giovi** to see the Sacrario dei Martiri della Benedicta where Nazi troops massacred two brigades of partisans in April 1944. Also along the road is the memorial to another bloody event that took place a month later when the Nazis shot 59 political prisoners in the Passo Turchino and buried them in a mass grave in reprisal for a bomb attack on the Genoa Odeon that killed five German soldiers. The road back to the coast passes through Masone. This is the blacksmith centre of Liguria, where they used to make the anchors for the Genoese fleet. It is also famous for the *masonine* knife, which is still made here. If you want to buy one, they are made by Ottonello (w ottonello-knives.com). The **Museo Civico di Masone** (Piazza Castello 2; ✆ 010 926003; ☉ 15.00–18.00 Sat & Sun; free) has a collection of objects from the valley and the blacksmith industry.

Sassello The road from the *rifugio* on the top of Monte Beigua goes deep into the chestnut forests on its northern slopes where, close to the border with Piedmont, you'll find **Sassello**, a foodie tourist's dream destination. It's a sleepy place with an interesting old town and virtually no non-Italian tourists (and there aren't many of those either). Locals from the coast come up here on the weekends for a stroll and an ice cream.

🍴 SAVOUR SASSELLO

The Sassello experience is all about food and begins the moment you get to the main square, **Piazza Rolla**, although the food experience here is more one of shopping than eating out. Many of the products keep and make great gifts and souvenirs.

The butchers, **Macelleria Salumeria Giacobbe**, is an old-fashioned shop that sells top-quality local fresh meat; they make their own hams and a lard pate, *pâté di lardo*.

In this part of the hinterland they make little meat patties of pigs' liver and juniper berries, *frizze*, and a bread made with potatoes and flour, *tirotto*. You can buy *tirotti* at **Panificio Tre Torre** (Via Roma 8) or **Pasticceria Rose** (Via Roma 36) who also sell amaretti. **L'artigana del Fungo** (Località Aicardi 9; ✆ 019 720245; w lartigianadelfungo.it) pickle mushrooms and sell jams and dried mushrooms at their small factory near Sassello.

Sassello is the amaretto capital of Liguria; its *amaretti di Sassello* are soft little round biscuits made from almond paste, which have been made here since the 17th century. Buy them in the shops in the old town and not at Bar Jole where they are twice the price. There's an **amaretti festival** in September. Wash them down with a glass of local Amaretto liqueur.

Honey is also a local speciality and you can buy it at **La Bottinatrice di Elisa Merialdo** (Località Bonuzzo 3; ✆ 019 724548). It is a family home, so be sure to check they are there before you go.

Don't be put off when you arrive in the main square, which is simply a car park. The streets behind hide a beautiful tiny old medieval town that hasn't been spruced up and has lots of character. Sassello was the first town in Italy to receive the orange flag, which is awarded by the Italian Touring Club to quality small resorts of the hinterland.

There is a small exhibition about the Beigua Park in the **tourist office** at Via Marconi 165. The **Museo Perrando** (Via dei Perrando 33; ℡019 724100; ⊕ Thu, Fri & Sun 16.00–18.00 Apr–Oct & Sat 10.00–noon; free) is the local history museum and here you can find out about the seven-day Battle of Sassello in the Napoleonic Wars.

If you stay a night here, be sure to take time to visit **Acqui Terme** in Piedmont just over the border. Its hot spring in the centre of town is worth the drive. There is a nice hike along the **Sentierio Natura della Deiva**, which is signposted in Sassello. It is a good walk for birdwatchers and when it snows you can do it with snow shoes. The circuit takes 4 hours and goes past the old 19th-century barracks, the **Forte Lodrino Inferiore**.

🏠 **Where to stay, eat and drink** There are a couple of nice but basic bars by the car park. We nearly always go to **Bar Jole** (avoid the granitas) but I have a soft spot for **Bar Levey** since I once left my handbag there and they kept it safe until I dispatched my husband to collect it.

🏠 **Le Radici B&B** [map, page 182] (3 rooms) Località Albergare; **m** 328 693 3398; **e** eradicisassello@gmail.com. This peaceful B&B is the place to escape from it all. It has a large garden, Wi-Fi & kitchenette. **€€**

🏠 **Cascina Granbego** [map, page 182] (3 rooms) Località Colla Maddalena; ℡ 019 724237; **m** 347 781 0778; **w** granbego.com. For a completely rural experience, stay at this pleasant B&B, which has a rustic atmosphere & its own cottage garden & chickens. **€**

🏠 **La Sorba** [map, page 182] (2 rooms) Località Assorba 1; **m** 333 325 9397; **e** info@lasorba.com; **w** lasorba.com. This agriturismo is in a 17th-century farmhouse surrounded by fields & woods on an organic fruit & vegetable farm. The restaurant serves typical dishes made with the farm's own produce. Wi-Fi. **€**

🏠 **Pian del Sole** (32 rooms) Locandà Pianferisco, Via Pianferioso 23; ℡019 724255; **e** info@hotel-piandelsole.com; **w** hotel-piandelsole.com. Owned by passionate chef Ivano

---

🍴 TRUFFLE TIME

Alba across the border in Piedmont may be famous for its truffles, but Millesimo [map, page 182] is just an hour's drive away. Truffles grow wild in the woods under the roots of oaks, poplars, lime trees and willows. There are both black and the rarer white truffles. The white truffle is usually eaten with rice or eggs. The more common black truffle is less fragrant but stays fresh for longer and should be cooked in butter before being sliced and placed on eggs, or mixed in a pasta dish.

Truffles were once believed to be an aphrodisiac and grow all across Liguria. The prized *scorzone* variety grows abundantly around Finale Ligure and black truffles are also found in the Imperia, Nervi and Prino valleys.

A two-day truffle festival is held in Millesimo in the last week of September and you can buy truffles at **La Bottega dei Sapori** (Piazza Italia 58, Millesimo). All truffles sold in Millesimo carry a certified label that shows the date of collection, the species and its area of origin. If you want to go truffle hunting, contact **Associazione Tartufai e Tartuficoltori Liguria** (Piazza IV Novembre, Millesimo; ℡ 019 57409; **m** 333 103 5799; **e** ass.tartufai.liguria@quipo.it) as hunting for truffles requires a licence.

Ravera, the restaurant (set menu €€€) in autumn serves local, wild mushrooms & chestnuts are used to make the desserts. Large garden that's good for children. The hotel has a swimming pool. Wi-Fi. €

✗ Palazzo Salsole Piazza Concezione 1; ✆019 724359; w palazzosalsole.it; ⊘ closed Mon. In the heart of Sassello is an excellent café, restaurant & wine shop. They serve all the local specialities & it is the best spot in the town to eat. They organise events & themed evenings. €€€

✗ Ca dei Brusco Località Piano 1; ✆ 019 724311; m 349 096 4104. This restaurant in an agriturismo serves all the local specialities including *lardo*, salami & mushrooms. There are set menus at about €30. Rustic atmosphere, classic of the area. Dinner Fri–Sun only. €€

✗ Trattoria Vittoria Via G Badano 8; ✆019 724138. Opened in the 1930s, this is a Sassello institution on the main road near the flour mill. Simple hearty food. The place to try the local mushrooms. €€

Sassello to Millesimo The road back to Varazze from Sassello passes through Stella. Just south of Sassello at Pontinvrea are the ruins of five forts built by the House of Savoy in the 19th century to fend off a French attack on Piedmont.

If you head west, beware the tourist board write a lot of hype about the hills behind Savona and have done their best to dress it up into a Napoleonic trail. Napoleon led the French army to an important victory close to **Cairo Montenotte** in 1796 and it is a nice little place, but if you are only here for a short while, give this one a miss. Old towns abound in this part of the world and this one is surrounded by industry. If you do go, be sure to stop and look at the sports' field. It was once a concentration camp used in the first part of World War II for prisoners of war, but after the German invasion in 1943, it was used for holding Slovene and Croat political prisoners, of whom 1,000 were transported to Mauthausen.

There are some interesting rock formations; one like a giant mushroom, near **Piana Crixia**, which is a national park north of Dego, known for its wild orchids. This is a particularly nice walk in spring, as it has a view across to the Ligurian Alps, which are snow-capped until May, but only go out of your way to do this once you have walked on Monte Beigua. Hazelnut trees grow here and a typical dessert is a tasty hazelnut cake. You can buy sausages and cheese from **Azienda Mario Ferrari** (Località Scorticate 1; ✆019 578088; m 340 231 6732).

Just down the road, the SP42 takes you to **Millesimo**. It has a little fortified bridge with a tower in the middle but how it made it on to the Touring Club Italia's list of the top hundred villages in Italy is a mystery. I fell for the propaganda and took the kids here a few years ago but the outing was a flop. It is industrial and the view from the bridge, which is cute enough, is of the elevated motorway. There's a small Napoleonic museum in the castle but it is usually closed. Its redeeming feature is the tasty little local sweets, *millesimini*, made with chocolate and rum. Just north of Millesimo, Rochetta di Cengio is known not only for its mushrooms but its pumpkins, *zucce* in Italian. It does, however, have a very good, rather chic restaurant.

Cyclists will enjoy a diversion to Cosseria to see the **Museo della Bicicletta** (Località Bosi, Cosseria ✆ 019 519785; w veloretro.it; ⊘ 16.00–19.00 Wed, 09.30–12.30 & 15.00–18.00 Sat–Sun; admission €2), home to over 200 bicycles, the oldest of which was made in 1791.

Altare, 15km northwest of Savona, is a scruffy little town where they used to blow glass. It has a small glass museum but there is absolutely nothing to draw you either here or to the surrounding countryside.

Where to stay, eat and drink

▲ Relais del Monastero (3 rooms) Località Monastero 3, Millesimo; ✆019 560050; e info@relaisdelmonastero.eu; w relaisdelmonastero.

it. Beautifully atmospheric B&B in a former 13th-century monastery with elegant bedrooms. Garden & a traditional restaurant (€€€). €€

🏠 **Villa Eugenia** (5 rooms) Strada Santa Maria 21, Cairo Montenotte; m 340 081 5987; w eugeniabedandbreakfast.com. B&B in an atmospheric 19th-century villa with swimming pool. €

✘ **Pantarei** Piazza Italia 52, Millesimo; ✆ 019 565968. Nice friendly restaurant in the main square serving basic Ligurian & Piedmontese cuisine. €€

ALONG THE COAST TO SAVONA: CELLE LIGURE AND ALBISOLA

CELLE LIGURE Just 2km along a lovely stretch of the Via Aurelia, with great sea views, is the tiny, charming and ever so chic **Celle Ligure,** which is again almost exclusively an Italian resort. It is really two towns. Piani di Celle is a small and pleasant resort with a good, sandyish beach, a minigolf course, and a pretty seafront promenade that leads to the old town. Old Celle is a small, medieval, fortified fishing village that sits right on the beach and will give you a feel of what towns and villages along this coast looked like before the Aurelia was built 200 years ago. The sandy beach is one of the best in the area and has a decent free public area.

Celle is the home of Olmo, which was founded in 1939 by Giuseppe Olmo, the champion cyclist who went by the name of Gepin. The company still makes designer bikes and can create the perfect custom-built bike (Via Poggi 22; ✆ 019 990157; w olmo.it).

🏠 **Where to stay, eat and drink** Shopping in Celle is excellent. Try the fishmonger **Pescheria Nello** (Via Ghiglino 9) and for meat and cold cuts **Celle Carni** (Via Aicardi 19). By the train station, which is behind the old town, there is a good modern delicatessen, **Pappa e Ciccia** (Largo Giolitti 10), and an excellent greengrocer next door if you want to quickly pick up a picnic. **Pescheria Friggitoria Stelin** (Via Ciambrini 28) does excellent takeaway fried fish.

In Carpineto, in the Valle Ellera above Albisola, you can buy honey at **Apicoltura Gaino** (✆ 019 488141; m 347 734 5386; call before going to check they are home). The bees live in multi-coloured hives. Gaino senior started keeping bees as a hobby 30 years ago but his son, daughter and son-in-law have turned the idea into a business. They produce a range of honey and other delicacies, as well as soap.

🏠 **B&B Il Castellaro** (3 rooms) Via SS Giacomo e Fillippo 57; ✆ 019 992995. Three basic rooms in a house with garden. Friendly owners. Bikes, table tennis & table football. €€€

🏠 **La Natta di Monte Tabor** (3 rooms) Via Posetta 37; ✆ 019 991580; w nattadimontetabor. it. This B&B has a beautiful pool, fabulous view & is above Celle. Some of the rooms have kitchenettes. Hosts will organise grocery deliveries. €€€

✘ **Ristorante Torre** (13 rooms) Via Aurelia Ponente 20, Garbasso; ✆ 019 993465; w ristorantetorrecelle.it. This is the place to try many of the local specialities, especially if you opt for the €40 tasting menu. It is not good for vegetarians as the menu is mostly meat & fish. The restaurant

uses produce from Slow Food producers. You can also stay here – rooms are in a cheaper price band (€€€) than the restaurant & are basic. €€€€

✘ **Mose** Via Federico Colla 30; ✆ 019 991 1560; w ristorantemose.it; ◷ lunch & dinner Fri–Tue. A mother & son team run this excellent restaurant that serves veal & fish but sadly little for vegetarians. The tasting menu is €60. €€€

✘ **Ligustico** Località Vetriera 2, Gameragna; ✆ 019 706384. This small restaurant in the centre of the village, a short drive into the hills behind Celle, serves local Stella cheese & some excellent plates of sliced steak mixed with mushrooms, tomatoes & other vegetables. For vegetarians there is tasty pasta with nut sauce. €€

ALBISOLA The road carries on to **Albisola,** a rather soulless place, but famous for its ceramics. They've been making them since the 15th century from local clay and

It is the end of a blistering hot afternoon that we drive up to the Azienda Calcagno Paolo behind Celle Ligure. The greenhouses rise up in steps above the motorway. Paolo Calcagno converted his father's strawberry farm into a small basil empire in 1984 and built his first greenhouse.

He now has 11 greenhouses and 5,000m² of his land are under glass. Today, Paolo supplies some of the best restaurants in and around Portofino and the top tables in Milan and London's most sophisticated eateries, including The River Café.

This is a state-of-the-art farm. Under the steep road that rises alongside the terraces of greenhouses is a large engine room similar to the steam engine on a small ship. From the end of September until mid-May the greenhouses need to be kept at a constant temperature of 22°C.

'We keep the tradition but embrace the new technologies,' he beams as he shows off the orange generator that runs by burning wood chips. It cost Paolo €286,000 to install but has cut the cost of heating the greenhouses by 55%. 'You have to have courage in this business,' he says.

It is not just Paolo's energy that has kept his business sheltered from the economic crisis of recent years. 'Quality functions well,' he says. 'It's like Ferrari or a handmade shirt. Businesses like these do not have a crisis.'

The weather sometimes makes life difficult. 'Last year was a disaster with the rain,' he explains, 'and now it is too hot, but the heat I can deal with. See how the leaves of the basil plants contract with stress in the heat and become dark green. In the cool of the night they will relax.' He lets out a deep breath. As we speak, the mist is creeping in across the mountains behind Celle.

Early morning or late afternoon is the best time to harvest basil. It's 6.30pm and inside the greenhouses are a couple of Senegalese, an Albanian, a Tunisian and a Ukrainian picking the tiny shoots of basil by hand. In his cold storage room Paolo shows us a large orange plastic bag containing the latest harvest of this crop. 'It's the best,' he says tossing the dark green leaves with his hand as the air fills with a strong also peppery aroma. In the warehouse, his sisters are busy packing up the fresh basil. Each box carries the date and the special DOP label showing it's the real thing.

Paolo is keen to welcome visitors to his farm and is one of the few producers who sell directly to the public. 'You must leave your door open to everyone who wants to visit. This is the future of tourism in Liguria.'

Azienda Calcagno Paolo Via Postetta 45a; ℡ 019 993961; m 335 688 3003. The basil is distributed in the UK by w natoora.co.uk. Pesto-making sessions can be arranged in advance. Azienda Calcagno also sell seasonal fruit & vegetables.

traditionally they painted everything in blue and white. The style is known as Antica Savona. There is a small ceramics museum, **Museo della Ceramica Manlio Trucco** (Piazza della Libertà 19, Albisola Superiore; ℡ 019 484615; ⊕ 08.30–12.30 Tue, Thu & Sat, 14.00–18.30 Wed & Fri; summer 09.00–12.30 Tue–Sat; admission charge).

Ignore signs on the Aurelia before the town if you are coming from Celle that point to the birthplace of Pope Sixtus IV. I've hunted for it but never found the house and you are in danger of getting stuck down an impassable Ligurian dirt track if you try.

Ceramiche Mazzotti (Viale Matteotti 29; ☎ 019 489872; w gmazzotti1903.it; ⏱ 09.00–noon & 15.00–19.00 Mon–Sat, sometimes Sun (call to check)) has one thing over the other ceramic workshops in town. Founded in 1903, it played a key part in the second phase of the Italian Futurist movement.

Tullio Mazzotti (1899–1971), known as Tullio d'Albisola, trained as a ceramicist under his father but by the age of 25 he was already exhibiting his work at the *Exposition des Arts Décoratifs et Industriels Modernes* in Paris and was the leading ceramic artist in the Futurist movement, alongside Filippo Tommaso Marinetti, Umberto Boccioni and Giacomo Balla. In 1929 Tullio had an entire room dedicated to his work in the exhibition 'Trentatré Futuristi' held at the Galleria Pesaro in Milan.

Albisola became a hub of Futurism and Tullio boasted that Albisola had surpassed the ceramics of Copenhagen, Meissen, Wedgwood and Sèvres. Tullio was also the creator of books made out of metal, which, in the words of Marinetti, were 'the Futurist expression of our Futurist thought', and his 1933 edition of his poem, *L'anguria lirica*, is fine example of this.

In the 1930s, he commissioned his friend, Futurist architect Nicolaj Diulgheroff to design a house and workshop. Completed in 1934, it became a hotbed of radical artistic ideas through to the 1960s.

Casa Mazzotti is the only example of residential Futurist architecture in its original form and still houses the family business. The shop sells reproductions of the original Futurist ceramics but be warned they are expensive and a coffee set will set you back €700. It is well worth going in to take a look, however. They also sell some fun, modern homeware in bright colours, which is much more affordable.

After a visit have a drink at the **Caffè Bar Testa**, in Albisola's main square, where the artists used to meet to exchange ideas.

Don't miss the magnificent, beautifully preserved 18th-century **Villa Faraggiana** (Località Villa Faraggiana 1; ☎ 019 480622; w villafaraggiana.it; ⏱ 15.00–18.15 daily, but check the website as there are frequent closures; you need to ring the bell on the gate marked 'Ufficio' (office), & they will let you in; admission €8). There's a guided tour that starts in the chapel. The villa was built in the 18th century for the Durazzo family, who originally came from Durres in Albania, which is called Durazzo in Italian. It was then won over a game of cards by the Faraggiana family from Novara in Piedmont. In 1940, in a story reminiscent of the famous Sicilian novel *The Leopard*, Alessandro Faraggiana, a well-known explorer moved into the villa where he lived alone until his death in 1961. He dedicated the later part of his life to restoring the house and, on his death, left it to the city of Novara, which continues to own it, and keeps it up by renting it out for weddings.

The valleys behind Albisola are leafy but workaday. From the little village of Ellera you can walk up to the Alta Via Monti Liguri. The socialist politician Sandro Pertini (1896–1990) was born in Stella. He was imprisoned by the fascists and went on to be President of Italy (1978–85). Stella is, however, more famous for its goat's cheese. It is best eaten with olive oil and salt and pepper. You can buy cheese straight from the farm at **Azienda Agricola Usai Pasquale** (Località Corona; ☎ 019 703137; m 347 544 6819) but be sure to make an appointment. Look out for it in local supermarkets.

Where to stay, eat and drink

🏠 **B&B Lina** (1 room) Corso Vittorio Poggi 50; m 349 497 3020. Just above the beach with a sea view this tiny B&B is a romantic hideaway. Friendly hosts. Kitchenette & private bathroom. €

✖ **La Rosa dei Venti** Via Cristoforo Colombo 80; 📞 338 893 8965. Rose conjures up some magical dishes in an intimate & friendly atmosphere. There is no menu, you just get what Rose feels like cooking & all the ingredients are fresh. If you have a dietary requirement, say so when you reserve a table. The set menu is around €30 & cheaper for children. Booking essential. €€€

✖ **Da Marietta** Via E Schiappapietra 17, Ellera; 📞 019 49059; w trattoriadamarietta.beepworld. it; ⊕ closed Mon & Wed evenings. This restaurant in the quaint village of Ellera serves a number of classic local dishes including *cima*, *gnocchi al pesto*, *ravioli di zucca* & local mushrooms, snails & wild boar in season. €€

SAVONA

Savona, Liguria's third-largest town, with a population of over 61,000, is a lively port city. Once rough and ready, Savona has been undergoing something of a renaissance as the recently massively renovated port in front of the old town is now the starting point for the vast Costa cruise ships. Its centre has been transformed over the last few years from a grimy, rather run-down place into a stylish old town with some excellent gourmet food and elegant little shops. Although it is not somewhere that you would spend your holidays (the beach isn't particularly nice), there's plenty to see here, the food is good, the city has lots of character and is steeped in history. It is worth a day trip or a stopover if you are off on a cruise.

Don't be put off by the suburbs as this used to be one of the chief seats of the Italian iron industry and today the former Roman port is dominated by the two red towers of the electricity station. Coal was brought to the dockyard in buckets on an elevated system, which my kids have dubbed 'flying coal', and which have always been the source of much hilarity in the back seat.

HISTORY Savona has been an important port for over 2,000 years. The city sided with Hannibal in the Punic Wars and was taken by Rome in 180BC. Like practically everywhere else along the coast after the fall of the Roman Empire, it was sacked by the Lombards in AD641, then it changed hands numerous times as first the Ostrogoths, then the Byzantines and then Carolingians, arrived.

Savona was Genoa's arch-enemy and there was a running battle between the two cities for hundreds of years. Savona was attacked by Genoa ten times between 1153 and 1440, and in 1528 Genoa's Admiral Doria, in a final brutal assault, filled in the port with stones, dismantled the castle and sacked the city. Savona became part of the Genoese empire and the city never recovered. They've never forgotten either. There's still anti-Genoese graffiti on the odd wall. The town took another pounding from Allied bombs in World War II, despite the fact that it was a resistance stronghold. As a socialist partisan base in the immediate post-war years, Savona played an important role in the flight of Holocaust survivors from Europe know as Aliyah Bet. The *Josiah Wedgwood* was kitted out in the harbour and sailed secretly from nearby Vado in June 1946 with 1,300 Jewish refugees on board.

One thing that really riles a Savonese is Genoa's claim that the explorer Christopher Columbus was born there. Once when we visited the cathedral, we were taken to one side by the guide. He spoke in a hushed voice because there was a couple he thought were from Genoa also in the church andwas handing out discreet photocopies of academic articles 'proving' that Columbus was in fact from Savona.

On a gentler note, Savona gave its name to soap; the French word for soap is *savon*. The legend goes that a fisherman's wife accidentally boiled olive oil with soda and made the first soap. Thank goodness; she deserves a sainthood.

Savona gave the world two popes: Pope Sixtus IV (1414–84) and Pope Julius II (1443–1513); the latter made it into the British history books for having issued the dispensation allowing Henry VIII to marry Catherine of Aragon, who had previously been briefly married to Henry's brother, who had himself died some years before. There was a lot more to him than that, however, and he was singled out by Machiavelli as a crafty, ecclesiastical prince.

The city was also the home of Leon Pancaldo (1482–1538), who circumnavigated the globe with Magellan, and poet Gabriello Chiabrera (1552–1638), after whom the local theatre is named. Paolo Boselli (1838–1932), Italy's prime minister from 1916 to 1917, hailed from here, as have some of Italy's top footballers: Enrico Cucchi (1965–96), Christian Panucci, Michele Marcolini, Luis Fernando Centi, Renato Dossena and Stephan El Shaarawy.

GETTING THERE AND AROUND

By boat Costa cruise ships leave from the harbour by the old town [203 D2] and ferries for Corsica leave from the suburb of Vado Ligure. The marina [203 C2] has 530 berths (✆ 019 855541; w porto.sv.it).

By bus Buses run along the coast road and leave from Piazza del Popolo [203 B1] for the hinterland.

By car Savona is 40km west of Genoa on the A10 coastal motorway and the A6 leads north to Turin (1½hrs). Park by the harbour next to the citadel [203 C3] or in the port by the NH hotel [203 D2].

By taxi Taxis are available on ✆ 019 827951.

By train Trains to Ventimiglia, Genoa and Turin pass through here. Trains stop at all the resorts along the coast. The train station [203 A1] is an architectural classic and was designed by Pier Luigi Nervi in 1960. There is a bus service to the town centre and a shuttle bus to the cruise terminal.

On foot Savona isn't a large city and the whole historic centre can be accessed on foot.

TOURIST INFORMATION The **tourist office** is in the **Fortezza del Priamàr** [203 C2] (✆ 019 831 05005; w comune.savona.it). There is a limited but useful app, SVD Savona e Dintorni, available for both Android and Apple devices. The tourist office on the port side is open when cruise ships are docked.

Note that businesses and residences have different numbers. Business addresses have an 'r' after the number and that number does not necessarily correlate with private addresses.

Savona is known for its religious procession on Good Friday.

Activities In summer, there are whale-watching trips (w whalewatchliguria.it), and ferry boats (w liguriaviamare.it) leave from the harbour in the old town for Laigueglia, Portofino, San Fruttuoso, the Cinque Terre and Porto Venere. There are also trips to see the firework displays along the coast.

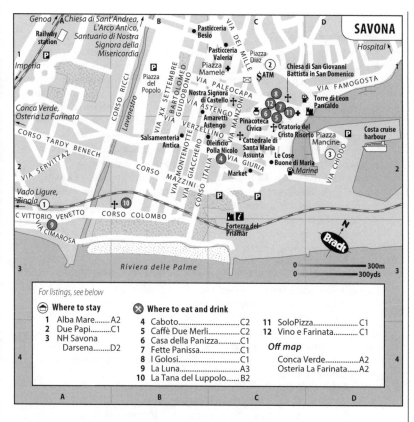

SAVONA

For listings, see below

🛏 **Where to stay**
1 Alba Mare.........A2
2 Due Papi...........C1
3 NH Savona
   Darsena.........D2

✖ **Where to eat and drink**
4 Caboto...........................C2
5 Caffè Due Merli.............C2
6 Casa della Panizza.........C1
7 Fette Panissa.................C1
8 I Golosi..........................C1
9 La Luna...........................A3
10 La Tana del Luppolo.......B2
11 SoloPizza.......................C1
12 Vino e Farinata.............C1

Off map
   Conca Verde...................A2
   Osteria La Farinata.......A2

You can go fishing with a local fisherman, **Savonainpesca** (m 338 962 0713; e info@savonainpesca.it; w savonainpesca.it).

WHERE TO STAY

🏠 **NH Savona Darsena** [203 D2] (92 rooms) Via A Chiodo; ☎019 803211; e nhsavonadarsena@ nh-hotels.com; w nh-hotels.com. Modern hotel in the old port on the quayside from which the Costa cruise liners leave. All rooms have balconies. Functional & quiet. Frankly, if you want a hotel, this is the only decent one in the city at the moment. €€

🏠 **Alba Mare** [203 A2] (3 rooms) Corso Vittorio Veneto 9/4; m 349 479 2511; e albamaresavona@ gmail.com; w bed-and-breakfast-in-italy.com. A nice B&B not far from the citadel, with a sea view. €

🏠 **Due Papi** [203 C1] (3 rooms) Piazza Armando Diaz 7; m 335 668 9372. This self-catering accommodation features free Wi-Fi throughout. Classic-style apartment with B&B accommodation & kitchen. In the old town, within walking distance of the main sights. Free bike rental. €

✖ WHERE TO EAT AND DRINK

Casa della Panizza [203 C1] (Vico dei Crema) sells freshly fried chickpea *panissa*, from a hole in the wall. Stop for a drink and *farinata* at **Vino e Farinata** [203 C1] (Via Pia 15). Locals go to **Fette Panissa** [203 C1] (Vico dei Crema) to eat the chickpea *panissa* and *fugasette*, which are like salty doughnuts. It is traditional street food. **Caffè Due Merli** [203 C2] (Piazza Maddalena 1) is a nice, tiny café with outside tables in a little square in the old town on a pedestrianised street. The café **I Golosi** [203 C1] (Via Paleocapa 64)

A dish that pops up on the menu here is *barbagiuai*, a fried pumpkin ravioli. Pumpkins were brought to Italy after Columbus discovered the New World. Snails are also popular and often cooked with mushrooms in the autumn. Whitebait soup is a tasty starter, *minestra di bianchetti*. The local vegetable tart is made with rice and leeks, *torta di riso e porri*. In the hinterland, *polenta bianca*, made with flour and potatoes, is a popular meal. The local *farinata* is also made with wheat rather than chickpea flour.

Sugo di carciofi, artichoke sauce, is especially popular in Savona with pasta or as a condiment. You will see it stored in jars or make your own:

Slice 12 small artichoke hearts and douse with lemon juice. Meanwhile, fry one garlic clove and two onions in three tablespoons of olive oil until transparent, then add a dash of white wine. Raise the heat to burn off the alcohol. Season with sea salt and a tablespoon of chopped parsley. Add the artichokes and simmer for 15 minutes. Whizz in a blender. It should be creamy, not runny. Frozen artichokes are sold in supermarkets and are excellent for this recipe.

The local cheese, *robiola*, is made from cows' milk and comes from the Val Bormida. *Formaggette savonese* are small, round, soft cheeses that are often added to focaccia to make *fugassette de Sanna*.

Above all, Savona is famous for its tiny, bitter *chinotto* oranges. As they can't be eaten fresh they are made into a liqueur, a soft drink, candied fruit, jams and mustard. The fruit trees were brought from China by merchants in the 15th century. Also look out for the local apricots, which flood the markets in summer.

Finish your meal with a *torta di nocciole* made with nuts and honey, a speciality of the Val Bormida, or *frittelle di San Giuseppe*, sweet knobbly doughnuts. In November for All Saints' Day, little meringue-style biscuits with dried fruit and hazelnuts, *ossa dei morti* and *pane dei morti*, appear in the bakeries.

sells excellent ice cream and delicious fruit lollies. Beer lovers should head for **La Tana del Luppolo** [203 B2] (Via Buscaglia 5r).

❦ A Spurcacciuna [map, page 182] Via Nizza 41r; ☏019 862263; w aspurcacciun-a.it; ⊕ lunch & dinner Thu–Tue. Fish restaurant in the Mare Hotel. The tasting menu is €85 exc drinks. You can taste a lot of local products here including *amaretti* from Sassello & sorbet made with basil from Prà. Romantic beachside location. €€€€

❦ Caboto [203 C2] Via Caboto 25r; ☏019 770 2077. Inexpensive spot that is good for a lunch stop in winter as the inside of the restaurant is nice & cosy. Typical Ligurian food. €€

❦ Conca Verde [203 A2] Via alla Strà 27, Località Conca Verde; ☏019 879063; w ristoranteconcaverde.com; ⊕ evenings Tue–Sun. Meat, fish & great pizza. It's a local hangout & people tend to order large pizzas to share. Good

wine cellar. The view is lovely too as it is up in the mountains behind Savona. €€

❦ La Luna [203 A3] Via Domenico Cimarosa 11r; ☏019 813381; w lunadinner.com. Traditional dishes with a contemporary touch at this relaxed restaurant in an old carpentry shop in the Fornaci district. €€

❦ Osteria La Farinata [203 A2] Via Bonini 1r; ☏019 862299; w osterialafarinata.it. The name is the giveaway as this is the place to eat an array of *farinata* with different toppings. Not in the city centre. €

❦ SoloPizza [203 C1] Via Quarda Superiore 20; ☏019 770 0757. This is Savona's best pizza restaurant. They even serve a pumpkin pizza. It's in a good location on the old port. €

SHOPPING An outdoor **market** is held every Monday in Piazza del Popolo and the daily covered market is by the towers facing the port. Every first Saturday and Sunday of the month, there's an antique market in the arcaded main street.

Part of the fun of exploring Savona is munching as you go. **Amaretti Astengo** [203 B1], on the corner of Via Montenotte 16r and Via Astengo is a fantastic biscuit and pastry shop founded in 1878. **Pasticceria Besio** [203 B1] (Via Sormano 16r), founded in 1902, makes award-winning amaretti. **Pasticceria Valeria** [203 C1] (Via dei Vegerio 52r) is the place for little biscuits, *baci di Savona* and chocolate layer cake, *torta di chinotto*, made with the local *chinotto* jam. **Salsamenteria Antica** [203 B2] (Via Montenotte 64r) is a gourmet food shop and every imaginable Ligurian delicacy is on sale here.

Le Cose Buone di Maria [203 C2] (Via Dei Vacciuoli 27r) sells pesto, pies, fresh pasta and *cima*. Just outside Savona, above Quiliano, **La Magnolia di Ivana** (Località Roviasca, Via Bossolo 2; m 338 265 1926) sells delicious homemade cheeses and is linked to the Slow Food movement, but be sure to call and make an appointment before you go.

OTHER PRACTICALITIES There is an **ATM** at Piazza Diaz 35 [203 C1]. The **post office** is at Piazza Diaz 9 [203 C1]. There is a **pharmacy** at Via Paolo Boselli 24 [203 C1]. The **hospital** is at Via Genova 30 [203 D1] (019 84041, A&E 019 840 4963). Follow the signs from the Via Aurelia heading east out of town towards Albisola. If you do end up here, it's a great little hospital, especially if you have a hand injury, as this is the hospital's speciality. Many of the rooms have sea views.

A WALK AROUND OLD SAVONA Unmissable on the harbour side and by the car park is the huge, stern **Fortezza del Priamàr** [203 C2]. It was built by the Genoese when they conquered the city in 1528 and still looks just as menacing as they intended. It is a superb example of 16th-century military architecture. Symbolically, it is on the site of the old cathedral that dated from AD825 and the original old town founded by the Romans.

The Priamàr was used as a prison in the 19th century and one of its most famous inmates was the revolutionary hero of the Risorgimento, Giuseppe Mazzini, who was held here between 1830 and 1831. There's no charge for walking along the battlements (019 831 0325; ⊕ 09.00–18.30 daily, closes midnight in summer). There is a small museum, the **Museo Archeologico Priamàr** (019 822708; w museoarcheosavona.it; ⊕ 15.00–18.00 Thu, 10.00–14.00 & 16.00–18.00 Sat & Sun, 10.00–13.00 when Costa ships in harbour; admission €2.50), but it isn't very exciting. The fortress is used for cultural events and in summer there is an open-air theatre that has a wide variety of performances, plays, ballet and opera under the stars.

Opposite the castle are two medieval towers (c1100 and c1200) in Piazza Brandale, which was the busy commercial centre during the Middle Ages. Walk round the newly modernised harbour. Boat trips leave from here in summer. The castellated **Torre di Leon Pancaldo** is named after the sailor who accompanied Magellan on his voyage around the world in 1519–22 and died on the River Plate in 1538. The statue on the tower is the Madonna della Misericordia, the patron saint of the city. Now take the elegant arcaded main street, Via Paleocapa, opposite.

There are two churches on **Via Paleocapa**. The **Chiesa di San Giovanni Battista in San Domenico** [203 C1] was built in the 18th century on the site of a much older medieval church. More interesting is the **Oratorio del Cristo Risorto** [203 C2], once part of an Augustinian convent. The high altar is attributed to Francesco Parodi. There are also a number of impressive paintings and three processional floats, which are paraded on Good Friday.

Take a left at **Via Pia**, the old town's narrow main street, where there are some interesting little shops. The **Pinacoteca Civica** [203 C1] (⟨ 019 831 0256; ⊕10.00–13.30 & 15.30–18.30 Thu–Sat, 10.00–13.30 Sun & Wed; admission €6) in Palazzo Gavotti houses one of Liguria's best art galleries. The palazzo was donated by the Gavotti family in the 18th century to house pilgrims visiting the nearby church at the **Santuario di Nostra Signora della Misericordia**. The collection includes paintings from the Ligurian school and works by Picasso, Mirò and Magritte make this a surprising little museum. There are ceramics from the 14th to the 20th centuries, including the valuable 17th-century Albarello ceramic pharmacy jar that was used in the San Paolo hospital. The collection of Slavic icons dates from the 17th to the 19th centuries and was amassed by the surgeon, Renzo Mantero, who was just one of Liguria's many collectors. Don't forget to look up. There are some beautiful frescoed ceilings.

From Via Pia, Vico del Marmo leads to the **Cattedrale di Santa Maria Assunta** [203 C2], which was built by the Genoese in 1589, although the façade dates from 1886. It is well worth visiting as it has a beautiful carved choir stall made between 1500 and 1521, one of the finest in Italy. The Byzantine baptismal font was taken from the old cathedral. The frescoes inside date from the 19th century but those in the chapel off the left-hand aisle are 15th century. Don't miss the masterpiece by Albertino Piazza, *Enthroned Madonna with Child and Saints Peter and Paul.* In the small **Museo del Tesoro** (⟨ 019 813003; ⊕ 10.00–noon & 16.00–17.30 Sat, 16.00–17.00 Sun, 10.00–noon when Costa ships in dock; admission €2) are works by Liguria's star painters, Ludovico Brea and Luca Cambiaso. The cathedral is also home to the relics of St Valentine and, by the door, there is an unusual marble crucifix with the image of the Virgin Mary carved on the back. The shell on the top is the symbol of St James. You can visit the apartment of Pope Pio VII (⊕ 16.00–16.30 Sat, closed Jul & Aug)

The Della Rovere family were the big boys in town and two family members became the popes, Sixtus IV and Julius II. Sixtus ordered the construction of another Sistine Chapel in the cathedral cloister in 1481 to house his parents' tombs, which are on the left-hand side. The Rococo-style ceiling was added in the 18th century. The cloister is much older than the present cathedral and was part of the church of San Francesco that originally stood here. At the start of the 19th century, Pope Pius VII was held here while he was imprisoned by Napoleon. Opposite the cathedral is the Palazzo Della Rovere, commissioned by Julius II in 1495, but never completed.

Nostra Signora di Castello [203 C1] on Corso Italia, the third big shopping street, has the city's main art treasure, a 15th-century polyptych *Madonna and Saints* begun by Lombard artist Vincenzo Foppa but completed by Ludovico Brea. There is also a vast processional float that lives in the oratory.

FURTHER AFIELD In Vado Ligure in **Zinola** is a British military cemetery that contains the bodies of 83 sailors from the wreck of the SS *Transylvania* that was torpedoed off Savona in 1917. The ship was heading for Egypt and was packed with over 3,000 soldiers and 60 Red Cross nurses. Amazingly only 402 people drowned and the majority of the survivors were rescued by the Japanese ships that were escorting the boat and by local fishermen. The survivors were cared for in Finale Marina and Noli, many of them in private homes. Sadly, many of those who survived subsequently perished on the battlefield in Palestine. The wreck was found in 2011 at a depth of 600m.

A 15-minute ride north of Savona at the aptly named village of Santuario is the **Santuario di Nostra Signora della Misericordia** [203 B2] (⟨ 019 879025;

w santuariosavona.eu; ⊕ 09.00–noon & 15.00–18.00 daily). The sanctuary was founded after the Virgin Mary appeared before a local peasant Antonio Botta on the morning of 18 March 1536. The frescoes that adorn the ceiling in the church date from the 17th century and are the work of painter Bernardo Castello. In the votive chapel dedicated to the Madonna there is a precious 13th-century crucifix. Even if you aren't religious, it's worth coming here as it is very atmospheric and, on a Sunday, is bustling with pilgrims.

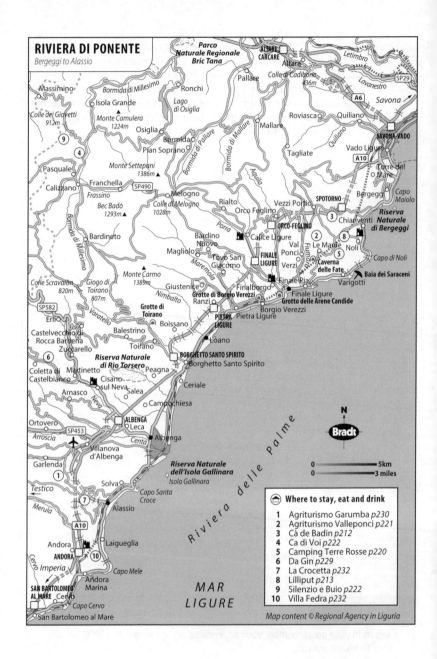

Where to stay, eat and drink

1 Agriturismo Garumba *p230*
2 Agriturismo Valleponci *p221*
3 Cà de Badin *p212*
4 Ca di Voi *p222*
5 Camping Terre Rosse *p220*
6 Da Gin *p229*
7 La Crocetta *p232*
8 Lilliput *p213*
9 Silenzio e Buio *p222*
10 Villa Fedra *p232*

Map content © Regional Agency in Liguria

8

Bergeggi to Alassio

Telephone code 019 (+39019 if calling from abroad); Albenga and Alassio 0182 (+390182 from abroad)

The coast from Bergeggi, about 10km from Savona's old town, to Finale Ligure is some of the best on the Riviera di Ponente. The big draws are the jagged cliffs of the Capo di Noli and its beautiful turquoise bay, chic Varigotti, whose brightly painted houses sit right on the beach, and the walled towns of Noli and Finalborgo. Inland is less to write home about but there is lovely walking at Le Manie above Noli and fantastic rock climbing all year round in Finale. Despite its beauty, it is no longer on the British tourist agenda, although Alassio once had a British population that far outstripped the local one, so you are in for a very Italian experience.

BERGEGGI AND SPOTORNO

Sadly, there's not much to see of old Bergeggi on the slopes of Monte Sant'Elena above the sea. The big attraction is its little uninhabited island, the Isola di Bergeggi off the rocky headland of Capo Maiolo, with its ruined monastery and fortifications. It is a nature reserve (w www.parks.it/riserva.bergeggi), and there are a number of interesting flowers that grow here. Among them are a variety of campanula, *Campanula sabatia*, which although it traditionally grows across northwestern Italy is now endangered. The rare jupiter's beard, *Anthyllis barba-jovis*; and the endemic *Thymelaea hirsuta*, more commonly known by the Arabic name, *mitnan*, a yellow-flowered desert shrub, which is used to make rope in the eastern Mediterranean, also thrive here. This is one of the few nesting sites for the Caspian gull.

The island has some huge caves, one of which, the Grotta Marina, is 37m long and 17m wide, and was inhabited in prehistoric times when the sea level was far lower than it is today. Indeed, many caves along the coast were inhabited in ancient times, but are today well below the water level.

There are snorkelling and canoe tours of the island. If you want to do this, you need to book by calling or stopping at the tourist office on the Via Aurelia (Via Aurelia 2; ✆ 019 859777; ☉ Apr–Jun 09.30–12.30 & 15.00–17.30 daily; Jul–Sep 10.00–12.30 & 15.00–17.30 daily, Sun morning only; budget €16 a head for a canoe tour and €25 for snorkelling). The tourist office rents out snorkelling gear for €5. It takes about 2½ hours to canoe around the island and there are double canoes. Booking is essential. Bergeggi is also a good place to moor your boat and take a dip.

Bergeggi village is home to a Michelin-starred restaurant, Claudio, which has rooms and apartments with fantastic views but is not as good as it should be for the prices it charges, so save your euros. You can also visit the old train tunnels, La Grotta del Treno, which were abandoned in 1970 (✆ 019 257901; temporarily closed at time of writing).

Often what you cannot see teaches you as much about a place as what is on show. As you drive along the coast road just past the fork that leads up to Bergeggi, and enter the bay that is home to Spotorno and Noli, on the other side of the road from the Villaggio del Sole restaurant, there is a nondescript block of modern flats with three pointed red roofs. It was the site of a concentration camp where, after the Nazi invasion of Italy in September 1943, political prisoners and Jews from Savona were held before being deported to the death camps. It is a forgotten footnote in the Holocaust.

Bergeggi has virtually merged with Spotorno, a busy little resort that suffered from overdevelopment in the 1960s and 70s. It is packed to the brim in the summer thanks to its good, sandyish beach and fine palm-lined promenade. It has its tacky side, with a rather crumbling little Lunapark but, like all towns along the Ligurian coast, it has an ancient heart and an interesting history.

Its mass of mediocre hotels makes it an easy place to find a room but service is an issue here, although if you make an effort to speak Italian, it will make a difference. Avoid staying on the eastern side of town, which is the modern part. Italian film buffs may well recognise the older resort, as the Italian film classic *La Spiaggia* was filmed here in 1953. It is based on a real story about a prostitute who takes a holiday in Alassio, further down the coast.

In the past Spotorno was known for its *lembi*, boats that took textiles, wine and lemons to Sardinia and France. The town's history goes back further than it looks. Spotorno once belonged to the bishops of Savona and was sacked by its neighbour Noli in 1227.

Spotorno also has a rich literary legacy. Poet Camillo Sbarbaro spent his childhood summers here with his grandmother and took up residence from

🍴 APRICOTS WITH DOTS

If you are in this part of Liguria at the end of June and during the first weeks of July, look out for a unique type of apricot known as the Valleggia apricot, the *albicocca di Valleggia*. It is a smaller fruit than normal, with a thin skin, that is a delicate orange colour and is speckled with brick-red coloured dots. It has an intense flavour that makes it stand out. It has been grown in Liguria for well over a thousand years and once grew all along the coast from Loano to Varazze. In the 1950s, when the orchards stretched for hundreds of acres, the apricots were exported to Germany and Switzerland on special trains.

The trees are taller than normal apricot trees, which makes pruning and fruit picking more difficult and local farmers found it hard to see off the competition from more profitable orchards in the south of Italy in the 1970s, so many turned to growing flowers in greenhouses or simply sold their orchards for building land.

Some orchards survived in Quiliano, Finale Ligure and Spotorno and they have been at the heart of the revival of this crop that has been backed by the Slow Food Movement.

Look out for signs advertising the Festa di Albicocca, the apricot festival, which takes place in early July. Gourmet jams made with the fruit make a great souvenir.

You can buy the apricots in season at **Ortofrutticola** (Via Fratelli Cervi 2, Valleggia; 🖈 0198 80368; ⊕ 07.30–18.30 Mon–Sat) and **Cooperativa Ortofruticolo** (Località Pilalunga, Via Torcello, Quillano; 🖈 019 886326; ⊕ 08.30–10.00 Fri–Wed).

1951 to 1967. Sbarbaro was also a botanist and up by the ruined 14th-century castle, the multi-coloured lichens he used to collect still grow in abundance. He described Spotorno in the summer heat, 'On the bare bone of the street, on the bald mountains dressed with lime, July is ruthless. With flesh stripped from the bone, the village opens its dry jaws to the sea, who quenches its thirst sprinkling it with bitter foam.'

The old town, which runs parallel to the beach, is split in two by the *caruggiu lungu* on which stands the delicately coloured 17th-century church of the Santissima Annunziata, which has some pretty frescoes by Andrea and Gregorio de Ferrari, Domenico Piola and Giovanni Agostino Ratti. The Oratorio della Santissima Annunziata has lots of maritime *ex-votos*, left by sailors and fisherman to give thanks to the saints for a wish come true – more often than not this meant escaping the wrath of the sea. There are also some interesting 17th-century paintings and a wooden sculpture by 18th-century artist and master carver, Maragliano.

WHERE TO STAY, EAT AND DRINK Buy biscuits and cakes at **Gramegna** (Via Venezia 5, Spotorno) or **Panificio Moderno di Saba Sisto** (Via Garibaldi 61), which is a great little bakery full of tempting cakes, focaccia and sweets packed up in the most tantalising way if you want a quick picnic.

Le Terre del Drago (2 rooms) Via del Carifoglio 13, Località Torre del Mare; m 346 499 3449. B&B on the promontory of Torre del Mare with a nice garden with hammocks. Wi-Fi, pet friendly & parking. Rooms have independent access. €€€

Casa Coreallo (3 rooms) Via Coreallo 26; m 348 135 7979; w bed-and-breakfast.it. A B&B set back from the town on the hills between Spotorno & Noli in a lovely garden where b/fast is served in summer & in the evening is dotted with candles. Really friendly owner who has gone out of her way to create the perfect place to stay. Swimming pool. €€

A Sigogna Via Garibaldi 13; 019 745016; w asigogna.com; Oct–Nov evenings only, closed Tue. Ligurian fish dishes predominate in this simple restaurant in the old town. €€€

Krapfen di Desare Via Garibaldi 50. Top of the cheap eats & sells sugary donuts for €2. €

NOLI

Huddled under craggy Monte Ursino, Noli is a picturesque, miniature, walled town, which is one of the best-preserved medieval cities on this stretch of the coast. Just 4m above sea level, Noli sits quite literally on the beach. There is a small palm-fringed promenade and a good little public beach with rough sand. Pulled up on the beach are rows of little boats belonging to the local fishermen, who set out every night to gather their catch. For more information about the fishing industry at Noli, see w bradtguides.com/noli. Noli has lots of charm, makes a great day trip and is a good place to base yourself for a holiday.

HISTORY Independent minded Noli sided with the Romans against the Carthaginians when most of the local tribes backed Hannibal. It takes its name from the Byzantine Neapolis, or 'new town', and was known as Naboli in the Middle Ages. From 1192 to 1797, as Italy's fifth maritime republic and wielding considerable power, it took its seat next to the big guys of Amalfi, Genoa, Pisa and Venice, but today few people remember its illustrious past.

Noli came to prominence when it took part in the First Crusade in 1096, from which the city grew rich. Its burgeoning economic power enabled the citizens of Noli to buy their independence from the Marquis of Carretto, who had been granted control of the city by Savona and who once had his stronghold in the castle that sits in a commanding position above the town.

Noli was quick to see the advantages of siding with the Genoese against their Ligurian rivals Savona, as well as in their battles with Pisa and Venice. It was a clever move, which ensured that the city remained independent as Genoa's influence spread along the coast. A sign of Noli's growing wealth and prestige was the Pope's appointment of a bishop of Noli in 1239.

Noli's harbour, however, was too small for it to compete with Genoa and Savona as ships grew in size. Feuding with its neighbours, Finalborgo and Savona, and the constant invasions of Liguria by Spain, Milan and Piedmont, undermined the city's economy and contributed to Noli's eventual decline. When novelist Tobias Smollett arrived here in 1764, he dismissed the once mighty harbour as 'of little consequence' and was horrified by the squalor.

GETTING THERE AND AROUND

By bus There is a regular bus service from Spotorno, which has a railway station. Buses link with the towns along the coast, running west to Varigotti and on to Finale Ligure. It takes about half an hour to get to Finale.

By car Noli is on the SS1, the Via Aurelia. Park on the western side of the city walls by the church of San Paragorio, although in summer the car park fills up fast. The nearest exit from the *autostrada* A10 is at Spotorno. The SP8 leads down to the SS1. Noli is 1km west of Spotorno.

By taxi (m 347 793 5942)

TOURIST INFORMATION At Corso Italia 8 (℡ 019 749 9003; w comune.noli.sv.it). Every September the town celebrates its history as the four districts of Noli, the *rioni*, battle it out in the Regata Storica dei Rioni, usually held on the first or second Sunday of the month.

WHERE TO STAY, EAT AND DRINK The tourist trap of restaurants and cafés that lines the city walls on Corso Italia facing the sea are pricey and certainly not the best Noli has to offer. That said, the basic Da Sandro serves good pizza and is inexpensive. On a budget, it is best to buy focaccia and supplies on Via Colombo and have a picnic on the beach. **Pappus** (Via Colombo 12) sells good ice cream. The speciality at **Pasticceria Francesca Scalvini** (Via Colombo 3) is *pane del pescatore*, a sweet cake, and **Pasticceria La Crepe** (Via Colombo 61) sells excellent pastries.

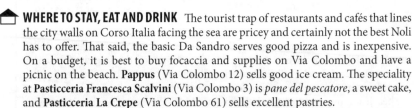

* **Cà de Tobia** (6 rooms) Via Aurelia 35; ℡ 019 748 5845; e info@cadetobia.it; w cadetobia.it. A boutique-style B&B just mins from the sea. There is also a junior suite if you need more space. Decorated almost entirely in white to reflect the sunlight & with specially created works of art. The family also own the Bagni Vittoria beach club (w bagnivittorianoli.it) & can reserve the best sun loungers for guests. Complimentary bikes. Free Wi-Fi. €€€

Il Paradiso di Manu (5 rooms) Regione Chiariventi; ℡ 019 749 0110. This B&B is up in the

hills behind Noli with lovely views across the bay & is attached to an excellent restaurant. Note the restaurant is often closed in low season. Each room has private access. Swimming pool. €€€

Cà de Badin [map, page 208] (2 rooms) Via Canepa 11; m 347 263 8580; e cadebadin.noli@ gmail.com; w cadebadin.altervista.org. Behind Noli near La Manie in Tosse, so it is a peaceful spot set in the olive groves. You need a car here, however. €

Il Vescovado Piazzale Rosselli 13; ℡ 019 749 9059; e info@hotelvescovado.it; w www.

212

Spotorno has its place in literary history and was the home of English writer D H Lawrence and his German-born wife Frieda from 1925 to 1926. Inspired by the scenery, Lawrence wrote, 'The moon shines so brightly, that even the vineyards throw shadows and the Mediterranean Sea gleams so white in the darkness. On the beach the lights of old houses allure softly, above the wall of the promontory the headlights of a locomotive move on …'.

Little remains of the Villa Bernarda where he lived, as it was gutted amid a local scandal to make way for holiday flats in 2002, despite the fact that it was here he found the inspiration for his most famous novel, *Lady Chatterley's Lover*. The elm that Lawrence planted in the garden was also cut down.

While at Villa Bernarda, Lawrence wrote the short story *Sun* and the novella *The Virgin and the Gypsy*. The earthy nature of the Italian way of life and the ferocity of the sun and its power to liberate the sexual inhibitions of the visiting American wife in *Sun* also had an increasingly liberating effect on Frieda. After a visit to Sicily, Lawrence returned to find his wife and the villa's owner, a wartime hero named Angelo Ravagli, were having an affair. Frieda stripped naked and frolicked in the garden with Ravagli and the couple were discovered by Lawrence.

Ravagli was the model for Mellors, the gamekeeper who has an affair with his employer's wife in *Lady Chatterley's Lover*. Lawrence, like Lady Chatterley's crippled husband, was dogged by ill-health and had been recently diagnosed with tuberculosis.

Lawrence and Frieda had a stormy relationship and Frieda had frequent affairs. A visit by Lawrence's sister Ada sparked a serious quarrel and Lawrence left Frieda, having a short affair himself, before a reconciliation after which the couple moved to the Villa Mirenda near Florence.

The year after Lawrence's death in 1930, Ravagli left his wife and children, and joined Frieda in New Mexico. They lived off Lawrence's royalties and married in 1950. When Frieda died, Ravagli inherited her estate, which included all of Lawrence's royalties and returned to Spotorno a millionaire and was welcomed home by his first wife with open arms.

---

hotelvescovado.it; ⏱ restaurant closed Tue. This is one of the best restaurants in Liguria, located in the old bishop's palace above Noli. It has a terrace with a wonderful view across the harbour & is *the* place to eat. Take the lift from the seafront. It specialises in local food. Try the shrimps from Oneglia & artichokes from Albenga. It is also a small hotel (€€€) with rooms furnished in a style that befits the history of the building. €€€€€

✗ **Lilliput** [map, page 208] Regione Zuglieno 49; 📞 019 748009. Family-run place 3km out of Noli, but worth the trip as the seafood in this pleasantly dated restaurant is excellent. A plus for families is the minigolf. Terrace with good view. €€€€

✗ **Controcorrente** Via Colombo 101; m 349 220 8133; w ristorantecontrocorrente.it. Modern restaurant with good seafood. €€€

SHOPPING Noli is famous for both its *trofie*, little worm-sized twists of pasta that are served with pesto, and *cicciarelli*, small anchovy-like fish. Buy them at the fishmonger's **Pescheria Cerisola Clelia** on Via Colombo 106. Market day is Thursday.

OTHER PRACTICALITIES There is an **ATM** at Corso Italia 31. The **pharmacy** is at Corso Italia 10. The nearest **hospital** is in Savona just east of the old harbour (page 205). The **post office** is at Via Monastero 147.

A WALK AROUND NOLI The main attraction is simply Noli itself and the pleasure is to be had wandering through the maze of alleyways that make up the old town. Walk through the frescoed Porta Piazza on the seafront. On the right-hand side is the 15th-century **Palazzo del Comune** with its arched windows and giant sundial. This is where the republic's consuls once met. Towering above it is the 13th-century clock tower, the Torre Comunale. Once the city skyline boasted an incredible 72 towers but today only eight remain. To the right runs the porticoed Loggia del Comune, which was big enough for boats to be hauled into for protection. Just outside the door of the old prison hangs a *strappado*, an iron instrument of torture, whose use Tobias Smollett recounted with gory detail. On the wall of the loggia stone plaques commemorate visits by poet Dante and Christopher Columbus, who called into Noli en route for Portugal, a journey that would eventually take him to the New World. Noli also has its own explorer, Anton da Noli, who discovered some of the Cape Verde Islands.

The old town is a charming rabbit warren of pedestrianised, narrow streets, *caruggi* with suspended arches between the tall houses. The cathedral, the **Cattedrale di San Pietro**, stands on Piazza Manin just beyond the gateway. It is a medieval church wrapped up in a Baroque shell and is the proud owner of a polyptych by the school of Ludovico Brea, whose paintings in bright colours are one of the things to see in Liguria, and paintings by the Spanish artist Vincente Suarez who lived in Noli at the end of the 18th century.

Via Colombo is the town's main thoroughfare and is lined with beautiful 13th- and 14th-century houses. It leads to Piazzetta Morando and the towering **Torre dei Quattro Canti**, the tower of the four singers, which is 38m tall.

Via Colombo opens out into a large square, which is a good spot to stop for a drink and is where the locals hang out. From here there are good views up **Monte Ursino** towards the 12th-century ruined castle that inspired Dante's image of purgatory and of the defensive walls that run down the hillside to connect with the city walls. If you fancy a hike, a path leads up the castle and offers commanding views of the tiny island of Bergeggi and Capo di Noli.

Via Colombo carries on along the left side of the square to the **Porta San Giovanni**, the 14th-century gateway. At the beginning of this section of Via Colombo is the Baroque **Oratorio di Sant'Anna**, which was built in 1771. Be sure to pop inside, as it is adorned with ornate miniature ships, which is typical of churches along the Ligurian coast. On the southern side of the square an arch leads into Via Anton da Noli, once home to the Jewish ghetto.

Cross the small bridge that runs over the old moat into the car park to discover Noli's main attraction, the 11th-century church of **San Paragorio**, one of the finest Romanesque monuments in Liguria. Decorated with typical Lombard arches and pilasters, it was founded in the 8th century and restored in the 19th century. Inside there is a huge Romanesque wooden cross, the bishop's throne dating from the 13th century and fragments of 14th-century frescoes. Along the wall there are also several Gothic tombs made of Finale stone. The church stands outside the city walls but served as Noli's cathedral until it was decided in 1572 that it was far too vulnerable to sacking by Barbary pirates to house the city's treasures, whereupon San Pietro became the new cathedral. Don't miss the altar, which is a Roman sarcophagus that once contained the relics of St Eugene, which were moved to San Pietro in 1602.

CAPO DI NOLI AND VARIGOTTI

The Via Aurelia leads west out of town around the **Capo di Noli**. This is one of the loveliest stretches of the coast road and shouldn't be missed. There's a regular bus service from Noli. The cliff face is covered in rare plants and is home to a flock of peregrine falcons. Capo di Noli was notoriously dangerous as Smollett wrote in 1764, in his book *Travels through France and Italy*:

> It is a very high perpendicular rock or mountain, washed by the sea, which has eaten into it in divers places, so as to form a great number of caverns … When the wind is high, no felucca will attempt to pass it; even in a moderate breeze, the waves dashing against the rocks and caverns, which echo with the sound, make such an awful noise, and, at the same time, occasion such a rough sea, as one cannot hear, and see, and feel, without a secret horror.

Today the Via Aurelia runs past the very same caverns along the old railway path and the sea, which is rich in marine wildlife and is a popular spot for diving.

The road leads to the small crescent-shaped **Baia dei Saraceni**. The railway line originally ran right by the sea here and it was thanks to continual landfalls that it was deemed necessary to build a tunnel deeper inland in 1977. The shallow waters are perfect for small children and unlike most beaches along the coast, it has no bathing concessions and is thus, uniquely, completely free. Despite being only a thin strip of shingle, it is one of the prettiest beaches in Liguria. The bay is dominated by a medieval watchtower that once guarded the seaside village of Varigotti, in the next bay. If you're feeling energetic, it is fun to swim around the headland. If you come by car, beware that the car park is pricey and charges by the day or afternoon. It is more economical to park in the car park on the other side of the tunnel in Varigotti.

The village of **Varigotti** is an upmarket resort and one of the loveliest spots on the Riviera di Ponente. The Via Aurelia runs behind the tiny old town and its colourful pink and yellow houses, all different shapes and sizes, sit right on the beach, just as they did all along the coast before the Aurelia was built at the beginning of the 19th century. It is an unusual village for Liguria with squat square houses that are almost Moorish in appearance. The large shingle beach stretches for almost 2km as it skirts the wide, turquoise bay. The views across to Alassio are quintessentially Ligurian as the mountains tumble down into the sea creating a series of little coves. If you like antiques, visit on the first weekend of the month when there's an antiques market.

The tiny town, with its quaint alleyways, inspired the stories of Hemingway and Cesare Pavese. Founded by the Byzantines, it was originally named Varicottis but the city was sacked and wiped off the map by the Lombards in AD643, only to be rebuilt in the 14th century by the Del Carretto family when the threat from Saracen raiders had subsided. Most of the old houses along the beach date from this period. The castle that stands above the village is the remains of the Del Carretto stronghold. It was destroyed by the Genoese in 1341 when they also filled in the harbour, which stood below in the Baia dei Saraceni. Today, it's a stylish little place but, when travel writer Frederic Lees arrived here in 1912, he found Varigotti desolate and deserted:

> Half-a-dozen inhabitants, at the most, make up its population, and nearly all of these are old people. One of them, a woman with short-cropped hair, sat motionless on the doorstep of a ruined house, and made no reply, nor gave any sign of possessing human intelligence … She might have been a figure in stone, so fixed was her attitude, and the expression in her eyes a statue symbolical of this *città morta*. Only one human being could we find with whom to talk: an ancient man with bowed back and long, gray beard, who mumbled a tale of how all his sons had left him for America, and how all 'the old familiar faces' had departed.

From the old town you can walk up to the castle. From here a path runs along to the Church of San Lorenzo above the Baia dei Saraceni. This path joins the **Sentiero del Pellegrino,** the pilgrims' path, which leads along the clifftop to Noli. There are beautiful views. There is windsurfing at Bagni Mariella (m 347 451 0414; w bagnimariella.it).

🏠 WHERE TO STAY, EAT AND DRINK

🏠 **Albatros** (18 rooms) Via Aurelia 58, Varigotti; ☎019 698039; e info@ hotelalbatrosvarigotti.it. Smart modern hotel with b/fast, Wi-Fi & family rooms. Parking. €€€

🏠 **Miramare** (18 rooms) 019 698018; e info@hotelmiramarevarigotti.com; w hotelmiramarevarigotti.it. Simple beachfront hotel. Wi-Fi & parking extra. €€€

🏠 **Il Gabbiano** (4 apts) Via Al Capo 2, Varigotti; ☎019 698 8187; w bagnialsaracenoresidence. com. Stylish spot in the heart of Varigotti. Be sure to book a room with a terrace overlooking the sea to get the best from your stay. Belongs to the beach club Al Saraceno, which has a nice restaurant & rents canoes. €€

✖ **La Muraglia Conchiglia d'Oro** Via Aurelia 133, Varigotti; ☎019 698015; e r.conchigliadoro@ libero.it; ⏰ closed 15 Dec–15 Jan. This is the place to treat yourself. It's one of the area's best restaurants & serves mostly fish dishes. €€€€€

✖ **Aqua** Via Aurelia 46, Varigotti; ☎019 748754; lunch & dinner Wed–Mon. Mediterranean dishes on the menu at this restaurant, which is right on the beach on the road to Finale. Service can be a bit hit & miss but the location is a winner. Be sure to book a table. €€€

✖ **Bagni Gallo** Via Aurelia 1, Varigotti; m 347 596 4173; w bagnigallovarigotti.com. A beach club on the sand in front of the old town with an excellent restaurant serving simple food. €€

FINALE LIGURE

Finale is the place to come if you enjoy sports. The mild climate makes it a climbing destination all year round and it is noted for the wide variety of climbs on the limestone rocks. There is a wide selection in the valleys behind Finale as well, and combined with the stunning sea-cliff climbs, notably at Capo di Noli, the area has a unique mixture of challenges for climbers. This is also a popular place for mountain biking and diving.

Finale is actually made up of three different tiny towns all with the name Finale that were joined together in 1927. It is a wealthy little place and home to part of the aircraft division of Piaggio, the company better known for its iconic Vespa motorbikes.

HISTORY People have been living in and around Finale for thousands of years. Just outside the city, in the cave of Arene Candide archaeologists in the 1940s found eight hearths, and an important burial site of a teenage boy, whom they named Il Principe, the Prince, as his skull was covered in a cap of hundreds of shells. You can't visit the site but you can see Il Principe in the archaeological museum in Pegli (page 82), which is well worth a visit.

Finale was given its name by the Romans as it marked the end of the stretch of territory that was under the control of the tribe of Vado Sabatia; they called it Ad Fines, or 'On the Border'. In ancient times the settlement marked the boundary between the lands controlled by two of the main Ligurian tribes: the Sabatii in the east, and the Intemelii in the west. It was the stronghold of the Ghibilline Del Carretto family, who were bitter enemies of Genoa. After a fierce battle in 1385 the Del Carrettos were forced to hand over much of their fiefdom to the Genoese, but they didn't give up without a fight. A full-blown war erupted in 1447 and finally the town was taken by Genoa in 1713.

GETTING THERE AND AROUND

By bike Riviera Outdoor (Via Nicotera 3; 📞019 689824) and **No Break** (m 347 627500) offer bike rental and tours.

By boat The marina has 590 berths (📞019 603290; w marinafinaleligure.it).

By bus There are regular bus services from Savona and Albenga. Allow a journey time of 45 minutes each way.

By car The coastal *autostrada*, the A10, passes behind Finale Ligure, which is also on the SS1, the Via Aurelia. It's 60km from Genoa.

By train The town is on the main Ventimiglia–Genoa and Ventimiglia–Turin lines. The station is at the western end of Finale Marina.

TOURIST INFORMATION The **tourist information office** [218 D4] can be found at Via S Pietro 14, in Finale Marina (📞 019 681019; w comunefinaleligure.it). In March there is a regional farmers' market. The Palio delle Compagne Finalesi, an archery contest steeped in tradition, takes place during the second weekend in July; there's a medieval festival in the third week in August in Finalborgo.

Activities For hang-gliding contact **AS Finale Volo Libero** [218 C4] (m 349 423 1930; w finalevolo.freeservers.com); for diving **Peluffo Sport** [219 F7] (Via Molinetti 6; 📞019 207 7248) and **Cycnus Diving Centre** [219 G3] (📞019 601620; w cycnus.net); and climbing, biking and trekking **Rockstore** [218 B7] (Piazza Garibaldi 14, Finalborgo; 📞019 690208; w rockstore.it). Climbing lessons are organised by **Blumountain Guide Alpine** (Contrada Valle 13; 📞019 681 6276; w blumountain.it).

▟ WHERE TO STAY

🏠 **Punta Est** [219 F4] (38 rooms) Via Aurelia 1; 📞019 600611; e info@puntaest.com; w puntaest. com; ☺ closed Oct–Mar. Located high up on the cliff just past Finale Pia & built around an 18th-century villa with spectacular views & a lovely garden. Restaurant, swimming pool & a private beach but there is an additional cost for the beach club. Free Wi-Fi. **€€€€**

🏠 **Albergo Rosita** [219 G3] (11 rooms & 2 apts) Via Manie 67; 📞019 602437; e info@ hotelrosita.it; w hotelrosita.it. A family-run 2-star hotel but a great atmosphere, fabulous restaurant & lovely views. **€€**

🏠 **Ca' Datu** [219 G1] (1 room & 2 cottages) Località La Manie 10, 📞019 698 8010; e cadatu.a@alice.it; w cadatu.com. Up in the hills, this B&B has a children's playground, barbecue & large garden. The farm produces olive oil & olives, which can be brought direct from the farm even if you are not staying here. **€€**

🏠 **Vecchie Mura** [218 B7] Via delle Mura 1; 📞019 691 1268; w allevecchiemura.it. Quaint little hotel with garden in Finalborgo. The only downside is no AC, but great location. **€€**

🏠 **Castello Vuillermin** [219 E7] (69 beds) Via Caviglia 46, Finale; 📞019 690515; e hostelfinaleligure@libero.it. One of Italy's best hostels with a great view back down the valley to the sea. It was used for a long time as a prison & as hostels go, the rules are still strict. Inexpensive restaurant. **€**

🏠 **Erasmo** [218 D7] (3 rooms) Via Colombo 22/4; m 347 840 1707; e info@daerasmo.com; w daerasmo.com. Elegant B&B just 20m from the seafront in Finale Ligure. **€**

🏠 **I Lamoi** [218 C3] (5 rooms) Località Chiappe 2, Monticello; 📞019 204 1386; w ilamoi. it. Farm-stay B&B. They grow organic fruit & veg and sell their products at the farm. **€**

🏠 **L'Allegra Brigata** [218 B2] (3 rooms) Località Aquila 2; m 333 907 7436;

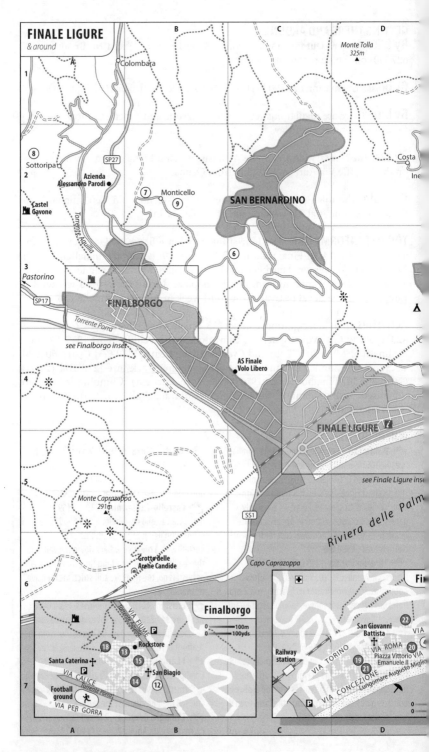

FINALE LIGURE
& around

Colombara

Monte Tolla
325m ▲

(8) Sottoripa

SP27

(7) Monticello

(9)

SAN BERNARDINO

Azienda
Alessandro Parodi ●

Costa
Ine

Castel
Gavone

(6)

Pastorino

SP17

FINALBORGO

Torrente Porra

see Finalborgo inset

AS Finale
Volo Libero

FINALE LIGURE

see Finale Ligure inse

Monte Caprazoppa
291m ▲

SS1

Riviera delle Palm

Grotte delle
Arene Candide

Capo Caprazoppa

Finalborgo

Rockstore

VIA FIUME

P

0 —————— 100m
0 —————— 100yds

(18) (13)

Santa Caterina †

P

VIA CALICE

(15)

(14) † San Biagio

(12)

Torrente Porra

Football
ground

VIA PER GORRA

San Giovanni
Battista †

(22) VIA

VIA ROMA

(20)

Piazza Vittorio VIA
Emanuele II

Railway
station

VIA TORINO

(19)

(21)

VIA CONCEZIONE

Lungomare Augusto Miglio

P

Fi

0
0

A   B   C   D

218

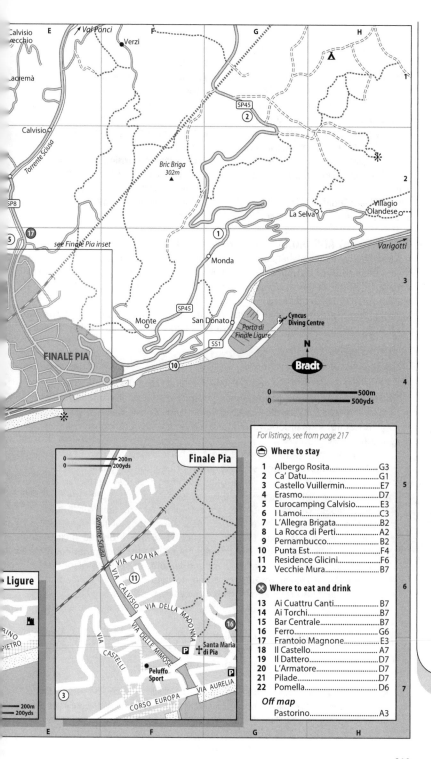

w bballegrabrigata.it. B&B in the pretty valley below the ruined castle, which is a peaceful oasis. Lovely B&B with very good hosts. €

🏠 **La Rocca di Perti** [218 A2] (3 rooms) Località Hiazzari; ☎019 695513; m 389 816 6170; w laroccadiperti.it. Nice rustic setting. This agriturismo produces wine, olive oil & fruit & veg. €

🏠 **Pernambucco** [218 B2] (3 rooms) Via Aquila II 5; m 328 942 3822; w pernambucco. com. In the same lovely valley below the ruined castle. This is one of the nicest spots to get away from it all. €

🏠 **Residence Glicini** [219 F6] (21 apts) Via Bolognani 5; ☎019 600671; e info@glicini.it;

w glicini.it. Modern apts 10mins from the sea in a quiet part of Finale Pia. Good for families. Free Wi-Fi. €

🏕 **Camping Terre Rosse** [map, page 208] Località Manie 40, Finale; ☎019 698473; e info@ terrerossecamping.it; w terrerossecamping. it. Has a restaurant & is located in the beautiful area above Finale famous for mountain biking & hiking. €

🏕 **Eurocamping Calvisio** [219 E3] Via Calvisio 37, north of Finale Pia, Finale; ☎019 601240; e eurocampingcalvisio@libero.it. Has a swimming pool, bar, restaurant, pizzeria & minimarket. Also apts for rent. €

✖ **WHERE TO EAT AND DRINK** Il Dattero [218 D4] (Via Pertica 10) has a Sicilian-trained chef and the sorbets and *granite* are excellent. In Finalborgo, ice-cream lovers flock to **Bar Centrale** [218 B7] (Piazza Garibaldi), with tables in the main square. They use the local *chinotti* to make ice cream. It is a local institution and was founded in 1872. **Pilade** [218 B7] (Via Garibaldi 67) is a great little bar that also serves pizza. Just north, Calice Ligure has an excellent ice-cream shop **Pastorino** [218 A3] (Via Vittorio Veneto 31). **Ferro** [219 G6] (Via Garibaldi 10) is the place

---

🍴 CHIN CHIN

In the lush green valley of Aquila below the ruined castle in Finale Ligure the Parodi family farm has been booming despite the years of economic crisis in Italy. Sixty-nine-year-old Giacomo Parodi and his wife Maria-Stella have been leading a small food revolution reviving the *chinotti* industry, which had almost died out.

These tiny bitter oranges were brought back to Savona from China in the 16th century by a local sailor. In Italian, *cinese* means Chinese. About the size of a golf ball, they once grew all along the coast from Varazze to Pietra Ligure, where there were thousands of trees. Sailors used the fruit to guard against scurvy and the farmers sold them to the French and American navies but a sharp frost in 1956 killed many of the trees just at the moment that mass tourism was about to arrive on the Riviera. Rather than planting new trees farmers either turned to crops that could be safely grown under glass, like basil and lemons, or sold their land for development. However, in 2004 Giacomo decided to take a chance and started to plant new trees and in the last ten years, the Parodis and the Slow Food Movement have brought together 15 local producers who now have 1,300 trees in total.

The Parodis mostly produce *chinotti* for drinks company Lurisia, which makes a clear fizzy drink that tastes rather like tonic and a stronger brown one, which is used in cocktails, which you can taste in the local bars.

Azienda Alessandro Parodi Frazione Finalborgo, Località Aquila; ☎019 690187; m 339 133 7181; w parodichinotto.it. Call and make an appointment before you go. To read more about the Parodi family farm, see w bradtguides.com/chin_chin.

to buy cakes and biscuits. You can buy olives and olive oil from local producer **Frantoio Magnone** [219 E3] (Via Calviso 156; w frantoiomagnone.com).

✗ **Ai Torchi** [218 B7] Via dell'Annunziata 12; 019 690531; w ristoranteaitorchi.com. In Finalborgo, this elegant restaurant serves mainly fish dishes & has a local following. You can eat desserts made with *chinotti* here. €€€

✗ **L'Armatore** [218 D7] Via Barrili 22; 019 692561; w ristorantelarmatore.it; ⊕ closed Tue & Wed. Smart restaurant with stylish presentation. Vegetarian, as well as seafood dishes. Tasting menu €38. €€€

✗ **Agriturismo Valleponci** [map, page 208] Località Verzi, Val Ponci 22; 019 9246619; e info@valleponci.it; w valleponci.it. The food at this rustic agriturismo couldn't be fresher. A simple Mediterranean & Ligurian menu offers plenty of home-grown vegetables. The outdoor dining terrace looks out over surrounding fields & the

indoor dining room is cosy & welcoming during the winter months. There are lots of wild boar up here & if you stay in one of the rooms for the night (€), you might spot one if you go for a late-night walk. You need a car to stay here. €€

✗ **Ai Cuattru Canti** [218 B7] Via Torcelli 22; 019 680540; ⊕ lunch & dinner, closed Mon. Tiny casual restaurant serving traditional homemade Ligurian dishes in the atmospheric streets in Finalborgo. Food is simple & well presented. Be sure to book. €€

✗ **Pomella** [218 D6] Via Ulivi 3; 019 689 8549. Serves excellent traditional dishes & focaccia. €€

✗ **Il Castello** [218 A7] Piazza del Tribunale 8; 019 692474. The best place in town for pizza. €

WHAT TO SEE AND DO Coming from Varigotti you arrive first at **Finale Pia,** which grew up in medieval times around the monastery. It has a lovely church, **Santa Maria di Pia** [219 F7] (c1725–28), which has a Rococo façade and Romanesque-Gothic bell tower. The monks brought their own artists with them from Tuscany and the works that adorn the church are influenced by the della Robbia school. It is a fun place to visit as the adjoining 16th-century Benedictine monastery has a shop where the monks sell their honey and homemade sweets.

Finale Marina is a seaside resort with an old town, a nice seafront and sandyish beach. In Piazza Vittorio Emanuele II, an imposing-looking triumphal arch commemorates the visit here in 1666 by the Spanish Habsburg heiress Margherita. The church of **San Giovanni Battista** [218 D7] is also worth visiting as it has a wooden *Crucifixion* by the master sculptor, Maragliano, dating from the 18th century.

Two kilometres inland, **Finalborgo** is a perfectly preserved walled medieval town that's bursting with character. The 17th-century **San Biagio** [218 B7] is a good example of classic Genoese Baroque. Stick your head inside the doorway and the size of the church will impress you. It is a history lesson in and of itself, as it shows you how important this tiny place once was. It also has an impressive octagonal bell tower dating from the 15th century, which is built into the city walls. The convent of **Santa Caterina** [218 A7], to your left if you enter the city from the western gate, was founded in 1359 but rebuilt during the Renaissance. It was used for a hundred years as a prison until 1965 when restoration work revealed some impressive frescoes in the Tuscan style. It is now home to the **Museo Archeologico del Finale** (019 690020; w museoarcheofinale.it; ⊕ 09.00–noon & 14.30–17.00 Tue–Sun; Jul–Aug 10.00–noon & 16.00–19.00; admission €6), where you can see some of the finds from the cave of Arene Candide.

Above Finalborgo there are two castles. One is the youth hostel and the other is the ruined 15th-century **Castel Gavone** [218 A2]. It was once the fortress of the Del Carretto family and was twice destroyed by the Genoese in the 1180s and in 1713. There's not just climbing, but nice walks at the **Rocca di Perti** [218 A2] north of Finalborgo.

One of the nicest things to do in Finale is to pack a picnic and set off for a walk along the old Roman road, the Via Julia Augusta. In the **Val Ponci** [map, page 208] there are five Roman bridges dating from the 2nd century. Three are in remarkably good condition, especially the Ponte delle Fate, the Fairy Bridge. Follow the signs for Voze from Noli and from Finale take the road to Verzi to pick up the trail. The **Parco delle Manie** is covered in reddish-brown limestone cliffs up to 20 million years old and riddled with caves in which many important prehistoric finds have been made. The park is criss-crossed with paths that run across the meadows and pine forests on the plateau of Le Manie. Primitive drawings on the rockface showing figures, crosses and abstract human forms, have been found here. In **Vezzi Portico** [map, page 208], the **Azienda Agricola Ca da Cruxe** (Via Casa Sparsa Moisio 1; ☎019 742264; m 333 815651) produces goat's cheese, *formaggio di capra*.

Another good spot for a picnic and a walk is the **Colle del Melogno** (1,028m), where there are fortifications built at the end of the 18th century by the Piedmontese and the Austrians. One for the history buffs as there was a major battle here during the Napoleonic Wars. The forts are in somewhat of a state of disrepair and can't be visited but they are quite fun to see all the same; the road runs through the middle of them, so you can get a close-up look. This is also a good place to buy cheese from a roadside stall on weekends in high season.

From here the SP490 runs through thick forests to Calizzano.

CALIZZANO Not an especially interesting village architecturally, Calizzano is notable as one of Liguria's main mushroom centres. A mushroom fair is held on the second Sunday in October, and a chestnut fair the following Sunday. Buy mushrooms at **La Bottega dei Funghi** (Via Pera 40; ☎019 79642; w barberisfunghi.com) and **Santamaria** (Via Sforza Gallo 12; m 335 770 8025; w federicosantamaria.it), who produce mushrooms, jams and preserved vegetables. In Liguria chestnuts were traditionally dried in *tecci*, small single-storey stone buildings. You can see abandoned *tecci* in the hinterland, but in the Val Bormida around Calizzano, the Slow Food Movement is supporting a revival of the old drying method, which can take up to two months. The chestnut harvest is between mid-September and mid-November. They are ground and often used as a substitute for flour. They are also used to make ice cream. You can buy biscuits and cakes made with chestnut flour at **Pasticceria Da Motta** (Via Garibaldi) and **Dolci Valeria Nari** (Via Frassino 31). **Gelateria Pinotto** (Piazza Rocco) sells chestnut ice cream. There are gentle walks from the villages of Massimino and Murialdo.

Take the road back to the coast via Bardineto or the Colle di Melongo. Across the pass is the pretty Lago di Osiglia, an artificial reservoir. You can canoe on the lake.

🏠 **Where to stay, eat and drink** *Map, page 208*

🏠 **Silenzio e Buio** (4 rooms) Regione Barbassiria, Calizzano; ☎019 79202; w silenzioebuio.com. A romantic peaceful B&B in a rustic setting with garden. Rooms have balconies with mountain views. No pets. They are on w booking.com. **€€**

✗ **Ca di Voi** (4 rooms) Frazione Caragna 15, Calizzano; m 333 356 8200; e info@ agriturismocadivoi.com; w www. agriturismocadivoi.com; ⊕ closed Jan–Feb. Produces chestnut flour, biscuits & ice cream. Rooms to rent (**€€**) if you fancy a total chestnut experience. Tasting menu €30. **€**

ALONG THE COAST FROM BORGIO VEREZZI TO ALBENGA

Sadly, this part of the coast to Albenga has been overdeveloped and is not especially attractive. In the historic centres, however, there are some sights worth stopping to see.

WHERE TO STAY, EAT AND DRINK

🏠 **San Martino** (4 rooms) Via Alla Chiesa 18, Borgio Verezzi; **m** 346 807 3438; **w** sanmartinorooms.it. Wonderful views from the terrace. Parking & great b/fast. Wi-Fi. **€€**

🏠 **B&B Il Rudere** (1 room & 1 apt) Via Dari 12, Toirano; **m** 347 052 8606; **e** ilrudere.toirano@gmail.com; **w** ilrudere.tk. B&B close to the caves at Toirano. The owners produce organic honey & also offer sailing trips on their boat. **€**

🏠 **Cà de Berna** (10 rooms) Lucifredi, Balestrino; 📞 0182 988166; **e** info@cadeberna.it; **w** cadeberna.it. The owners have a very good restaurant, Pastorino (**€€€**), in the village. Swimming pool & free Wi-Fi. Some rooms sleep 4 & there are lovely views. **€**

🏠 **Hotel Cà Ligure** (16 rooms) Località Ranzi, Via Concezione 10; 📞 019 625181; **e** info@hotelcaligure.it; **w** caligure.it. Up on the hills 3km from the coast with panoramic views, in a peaceful spot. There's a nice garden & all rooms have balconies with views. There's also a good restaurant (**€€€**). **€**

🍴 **Il Muma** Via Cava Vecchia 2, Borgio Verezzi; 📞 019 610788; **w** ilmuma.com; ⊕ dinner Tue–Sun, lunch Sun only. Serves up traditional Ligurian cuisine on a terrace with a stunning view. **€€€€**

🍴 **Cappero** Via Roma 23, Borgio Verezzi; 📞 019 610958; **w** ilcappero.com; ⊕ closed Mon, lunch Sat & Sun only, otherwise dinner. Vegetarian choices. Lovely atmospheric restaurant with a great terrace. **€€€**

BORGIO VEREZZI **Borgio** sits on the coast and **Verezzi** on the hill above. Borgio has a well-preserved, pretty medieval centre and the cobbled streets run up to the 17th-century church of **San Pietro**. A winding scenic road leads up to Verezzi. The square next to the 17th-century church of **Sant'Agostino** has splendid views over the sea and is used as an open-air theatre in summer. The big draw here are the caves, the **Grotte di Borgio Verezzi** [map, page 208] (📞 019 610150; **w** grottediborgio.it; ⊕ closed Mon; guided tours Oct–May at 09.30, 10.30, 11.30, 15.00, 16.00 & 17.00, Jun–Sep at 09.30, 10.30, 11.30, 15.20, 16.20 & 17.20; the visit lasts about an hour & the temperature is a steady 16°C; admission €9). Set deep in the limestone hills, they were discovered in 1933 by three young boys, but it wasn't until 1950 that the full 5km of caves were properly explored and revealed a hidden underworld of little lakes and multi-coloured stalactites, some so slim that they vibrate when you speak. The remains of sabre-toothed tigers, cave bears and elephants have all been found here.

PIETRA LIGURE In Pietra Ligure [map, page 208], there is a lovely ruined castle, and in the 18th-century church of San Nicolò are frescoes by Antonio Novaro. It was built in honour of San Nicolò di Bari who freed the city from plague in 1525. Inside are two noteworthy paintings: *St Nicholas Enthroned* by Giovanni Barbagelata (1498); and *St Anthony and Paul the Hermit* by Domenico Piola (1671). The 10th-century **Oratorio dei Bianchi** on Piazza Vecchia, also called Piazza del Mercato, is where the bell was rung by St Nicolò to announce the end of the plague.

LOANO Loano has a long sandy beach if you fancy a swim, and a smart seafront promenade, which has definitely come up in the world since the new marina opened in 2011. Enter the town by the clock tower gate, built in honour of King Vittorio Amedeo III who claimed Loano for Piedmont in 1774. The 16th-century **Palazzo Comunale** was built for the Doria family. Across the square, the church of San Giovanni has a copper cupola added after the earthquake of 1887. If you have a car, drive up to the 16th-century **Convento di Monte Carmelo** on the hills above, from which there are lovely views. If you have a sweet tooth, stop at **Pasticceria Renzo e Luca** (Via Stella 16). Olive oil is available from **Polla Nicolà** in Loano (Via Ghilini 46; 📞 019 668027; **w** oliopolla.it; ⊕ closed Sun afternoon).

Loano was the site of Napoleon's historic first victory in Italy. The battle took place on a snowy November day in 1795. Not only was Napoleon seriously outnumbered by the Austrians but his forces weren't really in a fit state to fight a battle and were desperately short of provisions and ammunition. Many of the soldiers had no boots and had to wrap their feet in linen bandages; certainly not ideal for fighting in the snow or marching across rocky crags and stony roads. Luckily, just before the battle, a brig got past the British warships blockading the coast and unloaded 100,000 rations of biscuits and 24,000 pairs of boots, raising morale throughout the camp. These were distributed to the weak and suffering first, then to those who had distinguished themselves in action, but many in the army still remained barefoot. One old grenadier quipped that, from tomorrow, the enemy would be responsible for supplying them with boots. Despite the odds Napoleon managed to win a great victory here, which gave the French a crucial foothold in the Ligurian Alps, which he exploited to the full the following spring in the Montenotte Campaign.

GROTTE DI TOIRANO [map, page 208] The thing to see on this stretch of coast are the caves in the karst rocks of the Val Varatella (✆ 0182 98062; w toiranogrotte. it; ⊕ 09.00–12.30 & 14.00–16.30 daily, museum closes 18.00; by guided tour only; admission €12), which were discovered in 1950. They are among the most beautiful in Italy, full of rare crystals, stalactites and stalagmites, some of which are enormous. One has been dubbed the Torre di Pisa, the Tower of Pisa, and in the Sala del Pantheon, one stalagmite is 8m tall.

Deep in the caves there is an atmospheric pool that looks like something from a fairy tale, but the real importance of the caves comes from the prehistoric remains that have been found here.

All in all, it is quite a mysterious place. In the **Grotta della Bàsura**, the Witch's Cave in dialect, there are the remains of extinct cave bears and traces of Palaeolithic man dating from 80000BC, and a mixture of both paw and footprints can be seen. It is not known if the bears lived here before the prehistoric men moved in or if they came into the cave to hunt them. What is really very strange is the evidence, in one of the caverns, that prehistoric man hurled balls of clay at the cave walls.

In the 1st century BC, Diodorus Siculus described Ligurians still living in caves like this: 'At night they sleep in the country,' he writes, 'and rarely in their wretched hovels or small huts, but generally in those caverns, formed by nature, which offer a convenient shelter.'

Just to add to the mystique, Europe's largest ocellated lizard also lives here; some of them can grow up to 2m long. The grotto of Santa Lucia, which is one of the series of caves, became a place of pilgrimage in the Middle Ages as its spring is supposed to heal eye diseases. Santa Lucia is the patron saint of sight.

You can buy local olive oil from **Frantoio Rosciano** (Via Provinciale 1, Toirano; ✆ 0182 98204; w www.frantoiorosciano.it; ⊕ 08.30–12.30 & 15.00–19.30 daily).

WALKING Ask at the tourist office in Finalborgo about walks on **Monte Carmo**, which at 1,389m is a popular spot for hiking. The Via Ferrata trail from Ca dell'Erscia to Bric dell'Agnellino takes you across a rope bridge over a canyon. There is also a good walk called the Terre Alte trail that starts from Toirano (see above) and intersects with the Alta Via dei Monti Liguri.

At first sight Albenga looks like a not very interesting modern sprawl of a town that floods out over a small, flat plain. Don't be fooled. It is really two towns in one. One part is a rather downmarket seaside resort with no particular draws. The other, however, is one of the best-preserved medieval towns in Liguria, laid out on the original Roman grid system and famous for its medieval towers, of which there were once a staggering 50, which must have made Albenga one of the wonders of Liguria.

As a result, local tourist leaflets have dubbed Albenga the San Gimignano of Liguria. That's a slight exaggeration but Tuscany's San Gimignano is itself not as original as it looks, having been heavily restored in the fascist era and today is so overrun with tourists that it has lost much of its charm. What plays on Albenga's side is that the place is authentic and not very touristy and is well worth stopping to see, although it too was 'restored' in the 1930s. That said, if you look at the old pictures of Albenga and most of Liguria for that matter, if some restoration hadn't been done, there might not be much standing by now.

HISTORY Albenga was originally the stronghold of the Ligurian tribe the Ingauni, who ruled the area that ran from Finale Ligure to Sanremo. Its first recorded mention comes in the 4th century BC. The Romans, quick to see its potential, conquered it in 181BC, rebuilt it, and renamed it Albium Ingaunum. It was an important stopping point on the Via Julia Augusta that ran along the coast to Spain and was a town of fine buildings, villas and triumphal arches.

After the fall of the empire, Albenga was sacked by the Visigoths but was rebuilt in the 5th century AD and went on to become Byzantine Marca Arduinica. The city became an independent commune in 1098 and played an important role in the First Crusade, thus securing trading privileges in the Near East in towns that flew the city's coat of arms.

Albenga fell under the Ligurian curse of factional infighting as powerful families like the Clavesanas and Del Carrettos fought for control and in the 15th century it was seized by Genoa. Nature was also cruel to poor Albenga. The River Centa changed its course, silting up the town's famous harbour and leaving the port prey to a malarial marsh. Today, the town stands 1km from the sea.

GETTING THERE AND AROUND
By car and bus Albenga is just off the Via Aurelia and the A10 *autostrada*, 46km west of Savona. Everything in the city centre is within walking distance. Buses run up into the hills from the train station and along the coast but, to explore the hinterland properly, you need a car.

By taxi For local taxis, call ✆ 0182 0303.

By train Albenga is on the Genoa–Ventimiglia line. Journey time to Savona is 35 minutes, and Imperia 45 minutes. The train station is east of the old town, a 10-minute walk down the tree-lined Viale Martiri della Libertà.

TOURIST INFORMATION The office is at Viale Martiri della Liberta 1 (✆ 0182 568 5216; w albenga.net). The **Palio dei Rioni Ingauni** on the fourth weekend of July is a medieval contest between the town's four districts. On 2 July, on the feast of the **Madonna di Pontelungo**, there is a religious procession and a market with stalls followed by a firework display. An antiques market is held mid-July–mid-August. There is a Jazz Festival in August.

🏠 WHERE TO STAY

☀ 🏠 La Meridiana Resort (25 rooms) Via ai Castelli 11, Garlenda; 📞 0182 580271; **w** lameridianaresort.com. Romantic spot with a great restaurant. Large garden with swimming pool; surrounded by olive groves & vineyards. Next to Garlenda golf course not far from the tiny Riviera Airport. €€€€

🏠 Artemisia (5 rooms) Via Ricci 12; **m** 389 991 4076; **e** info@artemisiaalbenga.com; **w** artemisiaalbenga.com. A very homely B&B in the heart of old Albenga & a very atmospheric place to stay. Use of kitchen included. €€

🏠 B&B Sulle Ali del Tempo Via Erico d'Aste 18; **m** 335 372545; **w** sullealideltempo.it. Lovely palazzo in the heart of the old town. Romantic spot, good for couples. Wi-Fi. €€

🏠 Torre Cepollini (3 rooms) Via Medaglie d'Oro 25; **m** 338 700 3455; **e** info@torrecepollini. it. B&B in the old town run by an Englishman, Michael, & Italian–Croatian Mario, who welcome you as if you were friends. Beautifully decorated, in an old palazzo with a tower. €

🍴 WHERE TO EAT AND DRINK

The plain that surrounds Albenga has been cultivated for over 2,000 years and produces some extremely tasty and unusual vegetables like the trumpet-shaped courgette, *cuore di bue*, beef tomatoes, spiky artichokes and purple asparagus.

In winter, artichokes are cut into wedges and cooked with dried mushrooms, garlic, rosemary and onions. They are sprinkled with flour before a dash of white wine is added and topped off with a rich tomato sauce. Artichokes are abundant in the spring and are a classic Easter dish, but are also sold frozen in the supermarket.

Market day is Wednesday and an organic food market is held in Piazza San Michele every second Saturday of the month.

🍴 Babette Via Michelangelo 17; 📞 0182 544556; **w** ristorantebabette.net. Sophisticated restaurant with views across the sea to the Isola Gallinara. It is popular with locals for special occasions. Excellent spot for lovers of fish. Tasting menu €43. €€€€

🍴 Antica Osteria dei Leoni Via Mariettina Lengueglia 49; 📞 0182 51937; **e** robertodepalo2006@libero.it; ⊕ closed Jan & Tue. A safe bet in the old town with good seafood dishes. €€€

🍴 Pernambucco Viale Italia 35; 📞 0182 53458; **w** ilpernambucco.it. A long-popular restaurant in what was once a minigolf course but is now a pretty garden. This elegant eatery has excellent local fish dishes & a good wine cellar. €€€

🍴 Da Puppo Via Torlaro 20; 📞 0182 51853; **e** puppo.albenga@alice.it; **w** dapuppo.it. In a narrow alley in the northern part of town, this restaurant serves excellent pizza, *farinata*, savoury tarts & stuffed vegetables. It's the place for a quick meal, but expect to queue. €€

SHOPPING The old town has some good local shops, many of which have been in the same family for generations. **Da Claudio e Adele** (Via Palestro 6) is a simple ham and cheese shop in the heart of the old town that sells locally produced sheep and goat's cheese among other delicacies. **Pastificio Fontana** (Via Palestro 24) sells good fresh pasta and sauces including the local *ragù del contadino*, made with artichokes, capers, black olives and sundried tomatoes. **Pescheria Pinto Porta Molino** (Via Medaglie d'Oro 2) is Albenga's best fish shop and sells its own bottled anchovies. **Antico Frantoio Sommariva** (Via Mameli 7) is a gourmet food store built into the walls of the old town and was once an olive mill. It also has a small museum. **Noberasco 1908** (Viale dei Mille 32; **w** www.noberasco.it) sells herbs and dried fruit. You can buy goat's cheese at **Il Boschetto** (Fraz Bastia; 📞 0182 20687).

The asparagus that grows on the lush plain around Albenga is a deep purple colour. It is known as the Violet d'Albenga and is unique to the province of Savona. The alluvial soil has a deep layer of sand and silt, which when combined with the Ligurian microclimate, makes this the only place that the variety has ever been able to grow. It is sweet, soft and buttery to taste and perfect boiled and served with a little extra-virgin Taggiasca olive oil.

The crop began to die out at the end of the 20th century as it is delicate to harvest and the work is tedious and backbreaking. Sadly, but not surprisingly, many farmers replaced the asparagus with less demanding, more lucrative vegetables and herbs, notably basil for the pesto industry.

Preserving the crop has been one of the challenges that the Slow Food Movement in Liguria has taken on. In 1970, the Violet d'Albenga was grown on 61ha, 30 years later this had reduced to just 4ha. Support the local farmers and buy their asparagus and other fabulous vegetables at the shop on Piazza XX Settembre 7 in Albenga. The asparagus harvest is in March through to June and you can buy it from **Azienda Agricola Montano** (Via Prae 1, Ceriale; e aziendamontano@libero.it) and eat it in Albenga at **Pernambucco** (see opposite).

The surrounding hills produce some excellent wines. Try the white Pigato. Outside of Albenga it's possible to buy wine directly from the vineyard at **Le Rocche del Gatto** (Regione Ruato 2, Salea d'Albenga; m 348 2627094; w lerocchedelgatto.it; ⊕ daily, Sun by appointment only).

Don't leave Albenga without going to **Baxin** ✳ (Piazza IV Novembre 1; w baxin. it). It was founded in 1826. Their flagship biscuit, the *baxin*, is made with fennel seeds and lemon and can be eaten without a pang of guilt as it contains no fat.

Pasticceria Pastorino (Via Genova 30, Albenga) opened in 1899 and won prizes for their biscuits in Paris and Rome in the 1920s. They make *amaretti di albenga*, with ground hazelnuts and not almonds and *inguani al rhum*.

OTHER PRACTICALITIES There is an **ATM** at Viale Martiri della Libertà 72. The **post office** is at Via dei Mille 25. There's a **pharmacy** at Via Medaglie d'Oro 42, and the **hospital**, Santa Maria di Misericordia, is at Viale Martiri della Foce 40 (✆ 0182 5461).

WHAT TO SEE AND DO The road directly in front of the railway station leads up to the old town's southern gate on **Piazza del Popolo**. From here, **Via D'Aste** takes you straight to the **Cattedrale di San Michele**, which has been remodelled numerous times over the centuries and is a real mixture of architectural styles. Built as a basilica by order of General Costanzo between the 4th and 5th centuries, restoration work in the 1960s gave the cathedral back its medieval appearance. There's a fine fresco, the *Crucifixon with Saints* (c1500), and a 19th-century organ. The bare-brick tower was attached to the church in 1391.

Alongside the cathedral, the real draw is the octagonal **Baptistry** (⊕ 10.00–noon & 15.00–18.00 Tue–Sun; admission €6). The entrance is in the loggia of the Palazzo Comunale, down a flight of stairs some 2m beneath street level as numerous floods have raised the ground level over the centuries. This is one of the most important early Christian monuments in Liguria and dates from the 5th century. It is believed to have been built on the site of a pagan temple. Unfortunately, it was heavily restored in the 19th century when the original vaulted Byzantine roof was destroyed. An unfinished font stands at the centre of the chapel; 12 doves encircle the monogram of Christ in an important Byzantine mosaic dating from around AD500. Floral work on the tomb by the entrance dates from the Lombard period in the 8th century. The mosaic decorations in the vault are from the 5th and 6th centuries.

The **Palazzo Comunale**, with its towering **Torre Comunale**, was once the town hall. Inside is a small archaeological museum, the **Museo Civico Ingauno** (admission with baptistry ticket & keeps the same hours). The first floor is used for exhibitions and is adorned with frescoes, and has a beautiful carved 16th-century ceiling. Behind the cathedral is **Piazza dei Leoni**, named after three stone lions brought here from Rome in 1608. It is surrounded by medieval houses and one side is formed by the apse of the cathedral.

On the other side of the square from the cathedral, the **Museo Navale Romano** (☎ 0182 51215; ⊕ winter 10.00–12.30 & 14.30–18.30 Tue–Sun; summer 09.30–12.30 & 15.30–19.30 Tue–Sun; admission €3.50) is an excellent little museum, which is housed in the Palazzo Peloso Cepolla, with its Romanesque tower. The star exhibit is the collection of 1,000 amphorae and other objects that went down with a Roman ship that sank off Albenga in the 1st century BC. There is also a collection of pharmacy jars dating from the 16th and 17th centuries that were used in the local hospital. It is well worth visiting not only to see the amphorae but because its 18th-century frescoed interior gives a feeling of how rich the city once was and going inside one of these palaces gives you quite a different perspective on the city.

West of Albenga, near the airport is **Villanova d'Albenga**, a fortified village with a number of interesting little churches dotted around it.

If you are with kids, at Ceriale there is the giant water park, **Le Caravelle** (Via S Eugenio; ☎ 0182 931755; w lecaravelle.com; ⊕ Jun–Sep 10.00–18.30 daily; admission €21.50).

Close to Ceriale is the **Riserva Naturale di Rio Torsero**, which is a palaeontologist's delight as it's full of interesting fossils dating back to the Pliocene period. The reserve has a small museum, **Museo Silvio Lai** (Via Nuova di Peagna, Ceriale; ☎ 0182 990208; ⊕ winter 15.00–18.00 Sat, 10.00–noon Sun, summer 16.00–19.00 Tue–Wed, 21.00–23.00 Fri–Sat, 10.00–noon Sun; admission €2), which has a garden full of plants dating back to the time of the dinosaurs.

The beach in Albenga is not much to write home about, but there is a decent stretch of free beach at the western end of the seafront with a view across to the **Isola Gallinara**. The island, 1km off Capo Santa Croce, is an important nature reserve and home to a large breeding colony of herring gulls and cormorants. Its name translates

FANCY A WALK?

Cross over the bridge by the old town and turn right at the roundabout on to Via San Calogero. Just up the slip road on the left are the remains of the Roman road, the **Via Julia Augusta**, the ruins of the only theatre known to have been built on the western Riviera, and a number of funerary monuments. The largest of these is called **Il Pilone** and was heavily restored at the end of the 19th century.

Watch out! The road was once home to a man-eating serpent that was killed by a thunderbolt sent by the Archangel Michael. If you fancy more Roman remains, the old Roman bridge is east of the old town on the Via Aurelia.

as Chicken Island because in Roman times it was inhabited by wild chickens, *galline*. Once a holy place, it was chosen as a refuge by St Martin of Tours in the 4th century and then settled by Benedictine monks. The ruins of their abbey, destroyed in the 15th century, are still visible. The watchtower was built by Genoa in the 16th century. Boats leave for tours around the island from Andora, Alassio, Diano Marina and Laigueglia in summer. Budget €15 per person (m 333 796 2375).

ZUCCARELLO AND CASTELVECCHIO DI ROCCA BARBENA

The hinterland here is narrow as Piedmont is just 24km from the coast. From Albenga the SP582 winds 12km up into the mountains along the banks of the river Neva to the beautiful medieval village of **Zuccarello** with its perfect, porticoed main street. It passes its days in a sleepy time warp and has hardly changed since the Middle Ages. It was founded in 1248 and originally belonged to the Clavesana family who lost it to the more powerful Del Carrettos. They then gave half of the town to Genoa and half to Piedmont. One is tempted to say it was a poisoned chalice, and it was a move that resulted in the War of Zuccarello, which ended in 1625. In the end the entire village was bought by the Genoese, who used their money and arms to build their empire. The castle has been restored, is used for cultural events and has a pretty medieval gate.

Follow the road from here north to **Castelvecchio di Rocca Barbena**, 18km from Albenga. This is olive oil country and the grey-green leaves of the trees are the backdrop to the village's impressive ruined castle. There are beautiful views, as ever in Liguria, across the valley. A lot of the houses here were abandoned and it looked as if the village was dying, but a number have been done up. If you make an appointment, you can buy the Slow Food jams, oils, pesto and olives produced by **La Baita** in Gazzo (☏ 0183 31083; w labaitagazzo.it).

Alternatively at **Martinetto** just before Zuccarello, you can take the SP14 to the pretty village of Coletta di Castelbianco, known for its cherries and truffles. The mountains here are popular with climbers.

From here the road leads up to the **Colle San Bernardo** (943m) and on to Bardineto and Calizzano, the chestnut and mushroom capital of the Val Bormida. The best time to visit is in the autumn, which is not only chestnut time but also mushroom and truffle season (see box, page 196). If you take this route, cross over the **Colle di Melogno** and drive back to the coast via **Bardino Nuovo**. Around Bormida there are lovely wooded hillsides and mountain streams. The local speciality is *fazeni*, potato flatbreads.

⌐ WHERE TO STAY, EAT AND DRINK

🏠 **Casa Cambi** (4 rooms) Via Roma 42, Castelvecchio di Rocca Barbena; ☏ 0182 78009; e casacambi@casacambi.it; ⏲ Apr–Nov. More a B&B than a hotel, in an old house. The owner, Anna, is a fantastic cook but she is sometimes away so check she is there before you book as this is a remote place in the mountains. Bring everything you need. They also rent apts. €€€

✖ **Da Gin** [map, page 208] (8 rooms) Via Pennavaire 99, Castelbianco; ☏ 0182 77001; w dagin.it; ⏲ closed mid-Jan–mid-Feb. Many of the local fruit & vegetables supported by the Slow Food Movement are on the menu in this family-run restaurant & hotel. Set menus are extensive; €25–35. Nice garden. €€€

ALASSIO

Alassio has a long sandy beach and is one of the nicest holiday resorts along this stretch of coast. Discovered and colonised by the English in the late 19th century, it is still an upmarket place. Its narrow old town runs close to the beach and tiny alleyways link its main thoroughfare to the delightful seafront. It is one of only a handful of towns and villages in Liguria that has no road running alongside the sea. Today, the majority of the visitors who come to Alassio are from Milan and Turin. As a consequence it tends to be busy at weekends and in August, but it also means that the local restaurants serve some excellent food, as these are fussy customers.

HISTORY Alassio takes its name from Aldelasia, the daughter of the 10th-century Holy Roman Emperor, Otto the Great, who eloped to Alassio with her lover Arelamo when it was still a sleepy fishing village. Alassio was taken by Genoa in 1541 but it wasn't until in the late 19th century, when it was discovered by the English Hanbury family who lived up the coast at Villa Hanbury near Ventimiglia, that Alassio hit the big time. Lured by the mild climate, the British flocked here building splendid villas and gardens, their own church of St John and a tennis club. There's even an English lending library on Viale Hanbury 17, which is one of the biggest in Italy, with 30,000 books in its collection.

It was while on holiday here that Elgar composed his overture *In the South*. Carlo Levi, the author of *Christ Stopped at Eboli* spent his summers here and, in the 1930s, it was a celebrity holiday hot spot.

GETTING THERE AND AROUND
By boat The marina has 400 berths (0182 645012; e info@marinadialassio.net; w marinadialassio.net/en).

By car and bus Take the exit for Albenga from the A10 *autostrada* and then the SS1. It is 50km from Savona. Buses run along the coast to Albenga and Andora.

By taxi Taxis are available (0182 640040).

By train Alassio is on the main Genoa–Ventimiglia line.

TOURIST INFORMATION At Via Mazzini 68 (0182 647027; w comune.alassio. sv.it). Alassio's big days are the saint's day of Sant'Anna, 26 July, the fireworks on 15 August and the Miss Muretto beauty contest at the end of August.

WHERE TO STAY
Villa della Pergola (12 rooms & suites) Via Privata Montagù 9; 0182 646130; e info@ villadellapergola.com; w villadellapergola.com. The villa was built by the Scot, General William Montagu Scott McMurdo, who fought in Crimea & in Afghanistan in the late 19th century. It is up above the town surrounded by a lovely exotic garden. It's a fascinating place with lots of memorabilia from Alassio's 19th-century heyday. There's a small swimming pool with a sea view. It's a real experience to stay & worth the price. It also has a top-class restaurant. Wi-Fi. €€€€

Splendid Mare (45 rooms) Piazza Badaro 3, Laigueglia; 0182 690325; e info@splendidmare. it; w splendidmare.it. Simple rooms in an old

monastery on the beach in Laigueglia. Swimming pool & restaurant serving traditional dishes. Free Wi-Fi. €€€

Agriturismo Garumba [map, page 208] (3 rooms) Crocetta-Caso 75, Località Garumba; m 348 449 0262; e avota@email.it; w garumba. eu. If you have a car, you can't beat a meal & a night at Garumba. The restaurant (€€€) is in a peaceful setting in the hills above Alassio & is decorated in soothing beige & white in a rustic style. Dishes are classic local specialities. The rooms are simple & elegant. €€

Beau Rivage (20 rooms) Via Roma 82; 011 19621035; w www.hotelbeaurivage.it. Small family-run hotel on the seafront in a 19th-century villa where the painter Richard West once lived. A few mins' walk to the sea. Parking €20 extra. Restaurant with vegetarian options. €€ 🏠 **B&B Alassio** (2 rooms) Via XX Settembre 23; m 393 963 9876; w bedandbreakfastalassio.

it. Great little B&B with a sitting room & well-appointed kitchen, in the heart of Alassio with the added bonus of a car park. Free Wi-Fi. €

WHERE TO EAT AND DRINK Antico **Caffè Balzola** (Piazza Matteotti 26), in a tiny square near Via XX Settembre, is an Alassio institution with a wonderful turn-of-the-century interior famous for its *baci di Alassio*, small round biscuits made with hazelnuts, egg whites, honey and sugar; the two semicircles are held together with chocolate cream. Beware, they don't display any prices and the biscuits here are twice the price of any other good pastry shop along the coast. The café's big rival is the **Caffè Pasticceria Sanlorenzo** (Via Vittorio Veneto 69), which wraps itself around the pastry shop and on to the lovely seaside promenade.

Don't miss **Caffè Roma**, on the corner of Via Dante and Via Cavour, which has been a popular spot since the 1930s when the owner started making ceramic tiles out of celebrities' signatures to hang on the wall of the garden opposite. Legend has it that this was the American writer Ernest Hemingway's idea. **A Cuvea Gelataria** (Piazza Matteotti 3) has the best ice cream.

Market day is Saturday and if you fancy a picnic, there are lots of good food shops along Via XX Settembre. Some of the best food locally is to be had at the **Agriturismo Garumba** (see opposite).

NIGHTLIFE There's plenty of nightlife in Alassio with bars and discos along the seafront.

OTHER PRACTICALITIES There is an **ATM** at Via Mazzini 95. The **post office** is at Piazza Merlini 2. There is a **pharmacy** at Corso Dante Alighieri. The nearest **hospital** is in Albenga.

WHAT TO SEE AND DO The old town is centred on one long, narrow street that runs parallel to the seafront, known locally as Il Budello, 'the intestine'. The pleasure to be had in Alassio is to stroll along it with an ice cream in hand. There are no must-see sights but to miss the **Muretto**, the wall of celebrity signatures, would be a pity. It is opposite the Caffè Roma (see above).

If you fancy some culture, English painter Richard West lived in Alassio for 20 years and his daughter donated 60 of his paintings to the town. They are in the **Pinacoteca Richard West** (Viale Hanbury 17; ✆ 0182 648076; ☉ winter 15.00–18.00 Wed & Fri–Sun; summer 16.00–19.00 Wed & Fri–Sun; free admission), which is just behind the English library.

Above all, what you do in Alassio is enjoy its fantastic sandy beach. If you want to stretch your legs, walk up to the 13th-century church of **Santa Croce** and follow the old Roman road to Albenga (page 222). On Monte Tirasso the sanctuary of Nostra Signora della Guardia was founded in the 13th century on the site of a Roman fortification and from here the views along the coast are stunning. There are boat trips around the Isola Gallinara and whale-watching excursions from the pier in summer.

BEYOND ALASSIO

South of Alassio is the little resort of **Laigueglia,** which was founded by the Romans. It is a pretty old town that sits right on the beach. It has lots of charm and a series of small piazzas that open out on to the sea, which are the perfect place for a drink. Parking can be an issue in summer so take the train if you are staying along the coast. The town is overlooked by the enormous church of San Matteo. It's a classic example of Ligurian 18th-century Baroque with two bell towers covered in majolica tiles. It was built when Laigueglia was a prosperous coral-fishing town and restored after an earthquake in 1887. Inside is a depiction of the *Assumption* by Bernardo Strozzi, one of Liguria's most famous painters.

On the ridge between Laigueglia and Andora is the tiny hamlet of **Colla Micheri**, once home to Norwegian explorer Thor Heyerdahl, who died here in 2002. His remains were interred in the garden of his home.

Andora is the last coastal town on the Riviera delle Palme. It is a nice place to stroll about or take a dip in the sea. There is a pleasant sandy beach here. For history lovers there's also the Roman Bridge, which actually dates from the Middle Ages. Andora has been a fishing port since ancient times and the port, Andora Marina, has an old Genoese watchtower. Above it are the ruins of the Castello di Andora, which was built by the Clavesana clan around the year 1000.

The sea here is part of the International Cetacean Sanctuary and whale-watching boat trips leave from both Laigueglia and Andora with **Whale Watch Imperia** (m 392 1376120; w whalewatchimperia.it; tickets €32).

For a taste of Liguria's hinterland take the road to **Testico**. It is a good route for mountain-bike enthusiasts as it is quiet; drivers need to beware of speeding bikes on sharp corners. The road follows a wide, fertile valley where you can stop to buy olive oil direct from the producers in **Stellano**. The road rises up the hill to the village of Testico, where there is not only a fabulous view but also a number of cafés.

WHERE TO STAY, EAT AND DRINK

Villa Fedra [map, page 208] (3 rooms) Via Delle Catene 121, Andora; m 348 220 7238; e info@villafedra.com; w villafedra.com. This traditional B&B offers rooms in the owners' house so you are in for a real Italian experience. Wonderful views. €€

✕ **Casa del Priore** Località Castello 34, Andora; ☎ 0182 87330; w casadelpriore.com; ⊕ dinner only. Romantic old stone house in the hills. Simple menu of traditional dishes & pizza made from locally sourced ingredients of the highest quality.

Good list of Italian wines. Nice outdoor terrace with a view down to the sea. €€

✕ **U Baccan** Piazza IV Novembre, Testico; ☎ 0182 668166. This restaurant is the place to try wild boar & rabbit. €€

✕ **La Crocetta** [map, page 208] Via Ottone I 115, near Moglio; ☎ 0182 469220. Cheap & cheerful pizzeria with a wonderful view across Alassio. All day bar serving food at lunch & dinner only. €

Cervo to Taggia and the Valle Argentina

Telephone code 0183 (+390183 if calling from abroad); Taggia and Arma di Taggia 0184 (+390184 from abroad)

There's a lot to see along this stretch of coast and the hinterland is among the best in Liguria. There are great sandy beaches at Arma di Taggia, historic towns like Imperia's Porto Maurizio and Taggia, and an abundance of good food to tempt you. There are olive trees everywhere and you can buy olive oil and wine directly from producers.

You can visit all year round and, when it snows, you can ski in Monesi, even if the facilities are a bit basic. Walking is the big draw in the hinterland. Some of Liguria's highest mountains offer strenuous hiking and wonderful views abound. Late spring and early summer are the best time for walking when the mountains are covered in flowers.

CERVO

Cervo kicks off Imperia Province in style. Once a coral-fishing village, this is a romantic picture-book Ligurian small town perched up above the sea surrounded by ruined walls. What sets it apart from other Ligurian villages is that it is dominated by its enormous church and capped off with a crumbling castle.

Stylish Cervo has lots of charm. Painted yellow and cream houses huddle round the church above the pretty, free, shingle-cum-pebble beach that curls around the bay. It is famous for its international Festival of Chamber Music that takes place in front of the church every July and August. There are also many other musical events throughout the year. Visitors to the region often base themselves here rather than along the coast, which is rather built up.

The hills around Cervo are covered in pinewoods and olive trees where the ancient Ligurians once worshipped woodland gods, until the Romans arrived in 181bc and put an end to that. The wreck of a Roman cargo boat that sunk in the 1st century ad lies 2km off the coast. Although it is a little touristy here, it is a far cry from anything you might have seen in the south of France and there are still little old men and ladies pottering the streets.

GETTING THERE AND AROUND

By boat The closest marina is at San Bartolomeo, with 170 berths (✆ 0183 408089; e info@sanbart.it; w sanbart.it), but it is shallow at between 1.2m and 2.6m.

By car Take the San Bartolomeo exit from the A10 *autostrada* and then the SS1, 1km east.

By train, bus or taxi Few trains stop at Cervo-San Bartolomeo station, so get off at Diano Marina and take either a bus, or taxi (✆ 0183 495210; m 333 385 4141).

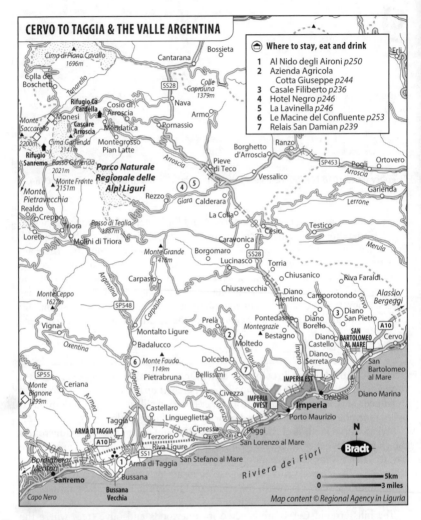

CERVO TO TAGGIA & THE VALLE ARGENTINA

Where to stay, eat and drink
1 Al Nido degli Aironi *p250*
2 Azienda Agricola
  Cotta Giuseppe *p244*
3 Casale Filiberto *p236*
4 Hotel Negro *p246*
5 La Lavinella *p246*
6 Le Macine del Confluente *p253*
7 Relais San Damian *p239*

Map content © Regional Agency in Liguria

WHERE TO STAY, EAT AND DRINK

🏠 **B&B Corallini** (3 rooms) Via Alessandro Volta 6; **m** 331 833 8731; **e** piero@corallini.it; **w** corallini-cervo.it. Beautiful B&B in the heart of Cervo. Be sure to book the room with the terrace. €€

🏠 **Camera con Vista** (3 rooms) Via Silvio Pellico 11; **m** 339 547 9455; **e** info@cameraconvista-cervo.com; **w** cameraconvista-cervo.com. This establishment has a terrace with a beautiful sea view & swimming pool. A bargain at the price. €€

🏠 **Locanda Bellevista** (6 rooms) Piazza Castello 2; **** 0183 408094; **e** bellavistacervo@

infinito.it; **w** bellavistacervo.com; ⏲ closed Nov. Right in front of the old town of Cervo, so a great location, if a bit basic. The hotel also has a restaurant (€€€) serving traditional local dishes & is linked to the Slow Food Movement. €€

✗ **Il San Giorgio** Via Volta 19; **** 0183 400175; **e** info@ristorantesangiorgio.net; **w** ristorantesangiorgio.net. Classy restaurant with a Michelin star, although quality can be a little erratic. Six-course tasting menu, excluding drinks. They also have 2 beautiful suites for rent (€€€). €€€€€

WHAT TO SEE AND DO Cervo is a tiny place and the pleasure is all to be had wandering around the old streets and relaxing in a café. The 12th-century castle was once a key point along the Via Aurelia and is now home to the **Museo Etnografico del Ponente Ligure** (✆ 0183 408187; ⏰ 10.00–13.00 & 15.00–18.00 Tue–Fri, until 23.00 in summer; admission €3), which is quite an interesting little museum laid out in rooms that were once a hospital for the poor and pilgrims, founded by the Knights of Malta, who also founded the Oratorio of Santa Caterina.

Despite its size, Cervo was once a rather rich place and there are several interesting palazzos, among them the 18th-century town hall with its arcaded loggia, **Palazzo Viale**, on Via Nicola. It was the home of Tommaso Morchio, who was the Genoese admiral who captured Malta in 1371.

Narrow alleyways run down from the castle to the huge church, **San Giovanni Battista**, which sits gazing out to sea in front of a pretty little square with a nice café. It is a fine example of the Baroque style; construction began in 1686. It is decorated with 18th-century frescoes featuring a deer, *cervo* in Italian. It is a reference back to the days when the Romans worshipped Diana, the goddess of hunting. Inside, its sheer size is stunning, considering how small Cervo is, and is testament to how wealthy the village once was. There are some impressive paintings by a few well-known Ligurian artists, among them the multi-coloured 17th-century carving by Poggio, *St John the Baptist*, and the 18th-century *Crucifixion*, attributed to Maragliano. The church is known as the *Chiesa dei Corallini*, the church of the coral fishermen, who raised the money to build it and dedicated one of the chapels to their patron saint, Erasmus. Coral fishing came to an end after the terrible storm of 1720.

TOWARDS DIANO MARINA The coast between Cervo and Diano Marina is modern and not very interesting. There are, however, some nice sandy beaches. **San Bartolomeo al Mare**, 2km along the coast from Cervo, has another draw: the excellent pastry shop **Pasticceria Racca** (Via Aurelia 88).

The area behind San Bartolomeo al Mare is good biking country as the roads behind it are quiet. You can ride up to **Riva Faraldi** and if you are used to mountain terrain, on to La Colla and back to the coast via Diano San Pietro to Diano Marina. Don't be put off by the start of this ride, which goes through a scrubby area under the motorway. It is a 21km round trip. Alternatively, you can go from Diano Marina to La Colla then take the road up to Camporotondo. The road winds over the mountains offering fabulous views as you cycle through Diano Arentino and Diano Gorlei on your way back to Diano Marina. It is a circuit of 30km and is one for bikers who like to stretch themselves to the extreme. **Diano Arentino** has a lovely live nativity scene if you are here on Christmas Eve.

If you fancy a walk, take the first downhill path on the right just past the parking lot above Cervo old town. It leads to Il Ciapa, a communal park. There are picnic tables and a children's playground. The walk takes you through some classic maquis shrubland back to the coast at Cassette. It is an easy walk of under an hour. Alternatively, you can walk on up to Castellareto where there are some prehistoric ruins and lovely views. This part of the path is known for its orchids. If you want to take a longer hike from here, the path goes up to the Colle di Cervo, 324m above sea level, and winds back to the coast to San Nicola, a walk of about 3 hours.

From San Bartolomeo al Mare, you can also take a boat trip and go diving with **Krill Diving Club** (📱 335 682 5556; 🌐 krilldiving.org).

DIANO MARINA

Three kilometres from Cervo or a short trip on the bus, the coastal strip widens. Diano Marina spreads along it. The town has a long, sandy, palm-lined beach and is busy both during the day and at night. This is a good place to come if you like watersports. Ask in the tourist office for which beach clubs offer them as it tends to change by the season.

🏠 WHERE TO STAY, EAT AND DRINK
Hotels here are modern, large and geared for beach holidays.

🏠 **Hotel Diana Majestic** (86 rooms) Via degli Oleandri 15; ✆ 0183 402727; e info@ dianamajestic.com; w dianamajestic.com. Large, modern hotel on the seafront with a large swimming pool. The olive groves around the hotel supply the oil for the restaurant. Free Wi-Fi. €€

🏠 **Le Raganelle** (2 rooms & 6 apts) Via Case Sparse, Reg San Siro, Diano Castello; ✆ 0183 401041; e leraganelle@libero; w leraganelle.it. In the hills behind Diano Marina this family-run organic vegetable & olive oil farm has a swimming pool, barbecue & a children's playground. The restaurant serves local dishes & homegrown produce. Cash only. €€

🏠 **Casale Filiberto** [map, page 234] (2 apts) Via ai Prati, Diano San Pietro; m 339 597 5568; e info@casalefilliberto.com; w casalefiliberto. com. This agriturismo is in a lovely restored stone farmhouse with a large terrace overlooking the farm's olive groves up in the hills behind Cervo. €

🏠 **Hotel Gabriella** (50 rooms) Via dei Gerani 9; ✆ 0183 403131; w hotelgabriella.com; ⊕ closed Oct– Feb. Bikes, paddle boats & canoes at no extra charge, children's games area, & a small kitchen for parents

who wish to prepare meals for small children. You can even rent a smart car. The hotel is modern, sits right on the beach & has a swimming pool. Free Wi-Fi. €

🏠 **Liliana** (35 rooms & apts) Località Diano Serreta; ✆ 0183 494743; w hotel-liliana.com. A mini complex high up above Diano Marina, it's a romantic spot & the older rooms are right by the pool. It's also good for families with cars. There are ping-pong tables & games for children. A lovely terrace looks down the valley to the sea & swimming pool. There's a restaurant serving good, home-style cooking. €

✗ **Agriturismo Veggia Dian** Via Gombi San Siro 1; ✆ 0183 400594; e info@veggiadian.it; w veggiadian.it. They produce their own olive oil & serve traditional dishes based on what is in season. Set menu only with wine €30. There is a terrace in summer. They also have 4 rooms for rent (€€) & a swimming pool for guests. They have a shop at Via Milano 40 in Diano Marina. €€€

✗ **Pizza Fra Diavolo** Corso Garibaldi 2; ✆ 0183 494655. This is a good spot for a quick lunch or light supper. They have won awards in pizza-making championships, & have a gluten-free menu. €€

WHAT TO SEE AND DO The town was destroyed in the terrible earthquake of 1887 so it is a mixture of late 19th- and early 20th-century buildings. Only a few things remain from the old town, among them some paintings, including one by the master painter, Luca Cambiaso, the *Death of St Joseph*, and the 17th-century marble altar from the old town that can be seen in **Sant'Antonio Abate**.

There is a Roman wreck just off the coast from Cervo, for diving enthusiasts; the finds from it are in the **Museo Civico Archeologico** (Corso Garibaldi 60; ✆ 0183 497621; w palazzodelparco.it; ⊕ 09.30–13.30 & 21.00–23.00 Tue, Thu & Fri, 09.30–13.30 & 15.00–17.00 Wed & Sat; admission €3), in the late 19th-century Palazzo del Parco. Diano was given its name by the Romans. The ancient Ligurians worshipped woodland gods in the oak forest that once covered the hinterland and, appropriating the local religious site just as they expropriated the port, the Romans dedicated shrines to Diana, the goddess of hunting.

The hinterland is now covered in the olive groves that give this stretch of coast its name, the Riviera degli Olivi, and it's possible to visit some of the local olive oil farms. **Il Colle degli Ulivi** (Località Sant'Angelo 40; ✆ 0183 405583; w colledegliulivi. com; ⊕ daily) is situated on the hillside overlooking Diano Marina. It also rents apartments. Many of the trees here are over a hundred years old and it's worth the drive up to the farm, if only to get a feel for rural Liguria. If you don't have a car, visit the family-run shop in Diano Marina on Via San Francesco d'Assisi 7. They don't just sell olive oil but a vast array of local products, like artichoke spread.

Above Diano Marina is Diano Castello, where the locals used to take refuge from pirates and where the Roman fort was located. The 17th-century fresco on the town hall commemorates the great Genoese victory at Meloria in 1284 when they finally smashed their great rivals Pisa.

At Diano Borello, 2km away, the pretty 14th-century church of San Michele has a polyptych by the famous artist, Antonio Brea. This is where one of Liguria's best wines, Vermentino, is made, so ask for a glass if you stop for a drink.

IMPERIA

Imperia sits at the centre of the Riviera dei Fiori and is the capital of the province. It is not much more than a large town surrounded by green hills and is a surprisingly nice place to stay. It has a historic old town, good restaurants and a sandy beach.

Imperia is actually made up of two cities: the modern workaday **Oneglia**, home of the pasta company Agnesi; and the medieval **Porto Maurizio**. It takes its name from the river Impero, which flows between the two. Oneglia is the more modern, commercial half while Porto Maurizio is the historic centre.

The marriage has been achieved only on paper and the two cities have very different personalities; even two railway stations and two harbours. The area below Porto Maurizio, along the seafront, is known as Borgo Marina and is already home to snazzy yachts and, in the no man's land between the two towns, there were, until recently, plans to build a new marina.

HISTORY In 1923 Mussolini united Porto Maurizo and Oneglia into the fascist-sounding Imperia. The unlikely bedfellows had been rivals for centuries. Porto Maurizio is named after the Byzantine emperor Maurice. It belonged to Genoa while Oneglia belonged to Albenga which sold it to the powerful Doria family. Their most famous son, Admiral Andrea Doria, was born here in 1466. In 1576, the Doria sold it to the house of Savoy and it became their foothold on the sea. It was also left in the front line in the battles between Savoy and Genoa, passing finally to Genoa in 1746. In 1815, when Savoy was firmly back in charge thanks to the Congress of Vienna, it became the provincial capital and a bridge linking the two towns was built in 1848. Porto Maurizio grew in importance after Savoy ceded Nice to France in 1860.

Nationalist writer Edmondo De Amicis spent his early childhood years here and he retained 'a sweet and deep affection' for his hometown, where he played with his brother on the beach. 'My earliest recollection', he wrote, 'is that of a day on which I played on a heap of sand with my little brother, who was my senior by two years, and who died when I was four, leaving me but a vague reminiscence of his face.'

GETTING THERE AND AROUND
By boat Plans to build a new marina between Porto Maurizio and Oneglia have been shelved. The marina in Porto Maurizio has 1,300 berths (`0183 62679; e info@portoimperia.it; w portoimperia.it).

By bus Bus 16 runs up into the mountains to Pieve di Teco, about 40 minutes away.

By car The A10 *autostrada* runs behind the town, which is 117km from Savona.

By lift There is a series of lifts that take you from Borgo Marina to the heart of Porto Maurizio, Parasio.

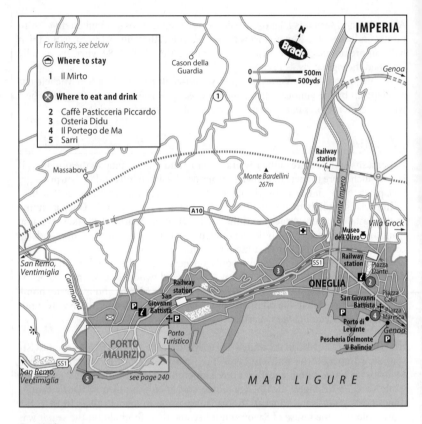

For listings, see below

🛏 **Where to stay**

1 Il Mirto

✖ **Where to eat and drink**

2 Caffè Pasticceria Piccardo
3 Osteria Didu
4 Il Portego de Ma
5 Sarri

By taxi
Oneglia ☎0183 292990   **Porto Maurizio** ☎0183 63311

By train There are train stations at both Porto Maurizio and Oneglia. The tourist train from Borgo Marina runs along the seafront in summer past the marina and the old factories to Oneglia, and functions rather like a local bus service

TOURIST INFORMATION The office is at Piazza Dante 4, Oneglia (☎0183 274982; w rivieradeifiori.com). A wide variety of diving courses are offered by **Borgo Marina Diving Centre** (Via Croce di Malta 59; m 329 221 5647; w borgomarinadiving.com). There is a yachting festival in September every other year, and an olive oil festival in November.

Activities From June to September boats leave the port of Oneglia on half-/full-day whale-watching expeditions arranged by Blu West Imperia (☎0183 769364). These are exceptionally good fun and well worth the expense

 WHERE TO STAY *Map, page 240, unless otherwise stated*

✳🏠 **Il Mirto** [map, above] (2 rooms) Via Cason della Guardia 29; m 347 443 4988; w ilmirto.com. Lovely B&B in the countryside near Imperia with a swimming pool & sauna. Very friendly owners. **€€€**

🏠 **Cà del Vescovo** (3 rooms) Via Carducci 7; m 338 597 7113; e info@cadelvescovo.it; w cadelvescovo.it. B&B on the 2nd floor of an old palace in Porto Maurizio with atmospheric frescoed ceilings & marble floors. Huge romantic rooms make this the place to stay in Imperia. Use of kitchen included. €€€

🏠 **Corallo** (44 rooms) Corso Garibaldi 29; 📞 0183 666264; e info@coralloimperia.it; w coralloimperia.it. Basic rooms with a great view of the sea. Good b/fast & restaurant. €€€

🏠 **Relais San Damian** [map, page 234] (10 rooms) Strada Vasia 47; 📞 0183 280309; w san-damian.com. Close to Dolcedo, a 10min drive up into the hills. This is a great agriturismo B&B with a swimming pool & delicious b/fast. The rooms are

large & elegantly appointed with antique furniture. €€€

🏠 **Hotel Croce di Malta** (39 rooms) Via Scarincio 148; 📞 0183 667020; e info@hotelcrocedimalta.com; w hotelcrocedimalta.com. A little 1970s in style but it has good-sized rooms at a reasonable price. Book one with a sea view. Try to avoid b/fast, which is not good. The hotel has an excellent location in Borgo Marina close to restaurants & shops, & is across the road from a good, free, sandy beach. There is parking but book a space in advance as it is limited. Wi-Fi in the lobby. €€

✘ WHERE TO EAT AND DRINK *Map, opposite, unless otherwise stated*

The speciality of Oneglia is *condiglione*, a sort of salad niçoise made with tomatoes, pepper, olives and anchovies. Pizza dell'Andrea, or *piscialandrea*, is claimed by the Niçoise to be a rip-off of their *pissaladière*. The locals here say that they invented the dish in honour of the great Genoese admiral, Andrea Doria. In fact, it is a good example of the fusion of cuisine across the border with France. After all, Nice was part of Savoy until 1860 and shares a large part of its cultural heritage with Liguria's eastern provinces. Stop for coffee at the **Pasticceria del Teatro** [map, page 240] (Via Cascione 70).

✘ **Osteria Didu** Viale Matteotti 76, 📞 0183 273636; ⏲ lunch Sat–Sun, dinner Wed–Sun. Don't be put off by the location, which is by a busy road, as this place is popular with locals & has excellent seasonal dishes. There is no menu, just a list of about 10 dishes. Style is elegant & simple. If you book in advance & tell them you are vegetarian, they will cook you something tasty. €€€€€

✘ **Osteria dell'Olio Grosso** [map, page 240] Via Parasio 36; 📞 0183 60815. A simple cosy restaurant popular with locals in Parasio. Predominantly fish dishes & an excellent tasting menu at €35. €€€

✘ **Sarri** Via Lungomare Cristoforo Colombo 108, Borgo Pino; 📞 0183 754056 w ristorantesarri.it; ⏲ closed Wed & Thu lunch. Vegetables & olive oil come from the family farm, but that said there is little for vegetarians. Menu is made up of the local catch. Set menu €38. €€€

✘ **Dai Pippi** [map, page 240] Via dei Pellegrini 9; 📞 0183 652122. Small restaurant serving a seasonal menu that consists of only a small number of courses, but all are excellent. €€

✘ **Caffè Pasticceria Piccardo** Piazza Dante 1–2; 📞 0183 293696. An old-fashioned landmark café, pastry shop & *gelateria*. The speciality is *stroscia*, a shortbread flavoured with white vermouth, lemon zest & olive oil, & lollies, *pinguini*, made of ice cream dipped in melted chocolate in moulds that are 100 years old. €

✘ **Il Portego de Ma** Via Calata Cuneo 29; 📞 0183 764147. Pizzeria in Oneglia with a good selection of toppings & tasty homemade desserts. €

✱ ✘ **Oasi La Pizza** [map, page 240] Sant'Antonio 15, Borgo Marina; 📞 0183 666892. This cult pizza restaurant is unmissable. It has no menu: pizza & pasta dishes are simply sent out of the kitchen. They cook up what they fancy & you have to shout out if you want it. It is a really fun experience & not expensive to boot. All dishes are the same price. They keep a tally of how many you have. It's great in a group as you get to try a bit of everything. The top tip is to sit back & relax. Enjoy a drink & watch what's coming out before you decide to pounce. There are also fabulous desserts. €

SHOPPING Pescheria Delmonte 'U Balincio' (Calata G B Cuneo 77) at the eastern end of the arcaded port in Oneglia, was opened in 1960 and sells fresh fish and anchovies salted in the old-fashioned way with only the head and guts removed.

Market day is Saturday and the market held in Piazza Maresca is one of the biggest and most authentic on the Riviera.

OTHER PRACTICALITIES Base yourself in Borgo Marina where there is a **post office**, **bank** and **shops** just behind the seafront. The **pharmacy** [map, below] is on Piazza Marconi. The **hospital** [map, page 238] is at Via Sant'Agata 57 (\0183 5361).

WHAT TO SEE AND DO

Porto Maurizio Porto Maurizio is made of up of three distinct areas. **Borgo Foce** is the seaside area. **Parasio** is the historic centre with its medieval buildings, Baroque churches, romantic arcades overlooking the beach and steep concentric alleys running round the hill. **Borgo Marina** is a lively little resort area with a good, sandy, shallow beach. There's a free section that's perfectly nice for a dip by the Hotel Croce di Malta. Borgo Marina was once a Byzantine port and was used by the Knights of Saint John during the Crusades, who built the church **San Giovanni Battista** [map, page 238].

Borgo Marina is home to the new **Museo Navale Internazionale del Ponente Ligure** (Via Scarincio 2; \0183 651541; ⊕ 09.00–11.00 Tue, 15.30–19.30 Wed & Sat; €7). They have a fascinating collection of seafaring paraphernalia – ships in bottles, maps, uniforms and model boats.

Towering over Borgo Marina is the massive cream-and-white Neoclassical **Duomo di San Maurizio**, the biggest church in Liguria and built between 1781 and 1838 by Gaetano Cantoni. It's decorated with white, ornate carvings and vast marble columns. It tells a lot about just how important this town once was. Construction was delayed by the tumultuous years of the Napoleonic Wars and things had to be modified a bit: the size of the cupola for example being reduced after it collapsed in on itself. The statues of the four apostles from the original church that was

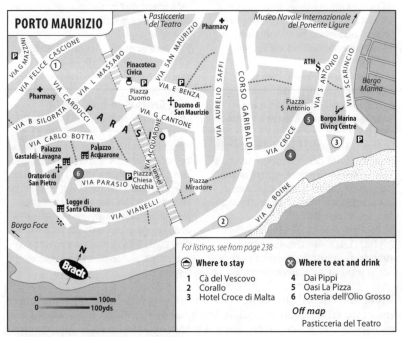

PORTO MAURIZIO

Pasticceria del Teatro
Pharmacy
Museo Navale Internazionale del Ponente Ligure

VIA G MAZZINI
VIA FELICE CASCIONE
P ①
Pharmacy
VIA CARDUCCI
VIA B SILORATA
VIA L MASSABO
Pinacoteca Civica
Piazza Duomo
VIA E BENZA
VIA SAN MAURIZIO
P A R A S I O
VIA CARLO BOTTA
Palazzo Gastaldi-Lavagna
Palazzo Acquarone
Oratorio di San Pietro
⑥
VIA PARASIO
Piazza Chiesa Vecchia
Logge di Santa Chiara
VIA VIANELLI
Borgo Foce
N
Duomo di San Maurizio
VIA G CANTONE
VIA G ACQUARONE
Tunnel
Piazza Miradore
CORSO GARIBALDI
VIA AURELIO SAFFI
ATM
Piazza S Antonio
VIA S ANTONIO
VIA SCARINCIO
Borgo Marina
⑤ Borgo Marina Diving Centre
③ P
VIA CROCE
④
VIA G BOINE
②
Piazza S Antonio

Bradt

0 ___ 100m
0 ___ 100yds

For listings, see from page 238

🛏 **Where to stay**
1 Cà del Vescovo
2 Corallo
3 Hotel Croce di Malta

✖ **Where to eat and drink**
4 Dai Pippi
5 Oasi La Pizza
6 Osteria dell'Olio Grosso

Off map
Pasticceria del Teatro

demolished to make way for the new one are beneath the portico. The paintings inside are by some of Piedmont and Liguria's best artists including Gregorio de Ferrari and Domenico Piola.

On the other side of Piazza Duomo, the **Pinacoteca Civica** (\0183 61136; ⊕ winter 16.00–19.00 Wed & Sat–Sun; admission €5) has a rather uninteresting collection of paintings but a lovely display of nativity figures. Cribs or *presepi* (singular *presepe*) are as popular in Liguria as they are in the south of France.

From the Piazza Duomo **Via Acquarone** leads up to **Parasio** and its steep lanes and steps. It's well worth the climb and the area has been recently restored. Its name derives from the Latin *palatium*, an ancient keep and fortress, hence the Palatine Hill in Rome. The Genoese governor once had his palace in **Piazza Chiesa Vecchia**. There are lots of old palazzos with imposing carved slate doorways.

The **Oratorio di San Pietro**, on Salita Santa Chiara on the southern side of the Parasio, is the town's oldest religious building and dates from the 12th century, although most of the present structure is actually 17th century. Via San Caterina was the wealthiest street in town. Next to it is the **Palazzo Acquarone** decorated with frescoes by de Ferrari. The **Palazzo Gastaldi-Lavagna** was where Napoleon stayed in 1794. Mazzini and Ruffini hid, after the failed 1833 rebellion, in the nearby Palazzo Bensa.

The loveliest place in Parasio is the **Logge di Santa Chiara**, a serene arcaded walkway overlooking the sea. You reach it from the square in front of the convent, through the 13th-century Della Foce Gate. There's rarely anyone here and it is a beautifully restful spot. The convent is working, full of nuns and you can visit the church.

Oneglia **Via Bonfante**, which runs along the western side of Piazza Calvi, has some

wonderfully atmospheric 19th-century arcades. It ends at **Piazza Dante**, known locally as Piazza della Fontana, which is the heart of the city. It is surrounded by neo-medieval 19th-century palazzos.

Down by the sea is the **Porto di Levante**, which dates from the Savoy period and is largely given over to the olive trade. In the afternoon local fishermen land their catch here and in the evening it's a good place to have a drink and soak up the atmosphere. A coastal path, the Via Angelo Silvio Novara, runs east to Diana and the beaches along Galeazza Bay but the beach experience is taken slightly downmarket by the railway line that runs along the seashore here.

In the heart of Oneglia's shopping district, the 18th-century **San Giovanni Battista** [map, page 238], in Piazza San Giovanni, has a 15th-century tabernacle attributed to the Garni school, some beautiful wooden choir stalls and *St Clare drives out the Saracens* by well-known artist Gregorio de Ferrari who was born in Porto Maurizio. San Giovanni, St John, is the town's patron saint and his feast day is still celebrated in style in July. It's worth popping into the town's other 18th-century church on Piazza Ulisse Calvi, to see the *Gloria di San Biagio* by Bocciardo and the wooden *Crucifixion* by the school of Maragliano, one of Liguria's best sculptors.

This is olive oil country and there is a stylish museum, the **Museo dell'Olivo** [map, page 238] (Via Garesso 11; \0183 295762; w www.museodellolivo.com; ⊕ 09.00–12.30 & 15.00–18.30 Mon–Sat; admission €5) by the station. It is part of the family-run Fratelli Carli oil company and both very modern and surprisingly interesting. The museum charts the development of the olive oil industry from ancient times to the present day. Ask for an English guidebook. There's a beautiful collection of oil lamps and cruets. There is also an excellent shop attached where it is possible to watch employees being trained up in the art of olive tasting. The olive and artichoke paste they sell is excellent.

The **Museo del Clown** in the **Villa Grock** [map, page 238] (Via Fanny Roncati Carli 38; ☎0183 704211; ⊕ Mon 14.30–17.30; €5.50) has a magnificent garden and has been recently renovated. It was the home of one of the most famous clowns of the 20th century, the Swiss Adrien Grock, who died here in 1959.

THE MOUNTAINS BEHIND IMPERIA

Olive trees suffuse the hills with a grey-green colour. Just 7km from Imperia, on top of **Montegrazie** is the beautifully frescoed 15th-century **Santuario di Nostra Signora delle Grazie**. Inside is the *Last Judgement* and *Punishment of the Damned* by Tommaso and Matteo Biazaci. The church is built on the spot where a dumb shepherdess suddenly began to speak after a vision of the Virgin and it's worth the journey for the views alone.

If you have a car, it is fun to drive from hilltop village to village. It was in **Moltedo**, once famed for growing myrtle, that Van Dyck took refuge from Genoa with his lover Paolina Adorno. In its Baroque church there are two good paintings: *St Isodore* by Gregorio de Ferrari, and the *Holy Family* by Jan Roos.

Buses run along the SS28 north into the mountains. It is a scenic route and quite a fast one thanks to the new road. **Pontedassio** is where the Agnesi pasta dynasty started life in 1824 and grew rapidly under the directorship of Vincenzo Agnesi (1893–1977), who also wrote a famous history of pasta. Take a 2km diversion eastwards to **Bestagno** to see its ruined medieval castle. Returning to the SS28 continue up the **Val Imperia** following the River Impero to the rather uninteresting village of **Chiusavecchia**. Nearby **Borgomaro**, however, is a good base for exploring the valleys around. It's a pretty, sleepy village on the banks of the Impero and has an excellent hotel, the **Relais del Maro** (page 244). Just above the village **Costantino Tallone** (w oleificiotallone.com) has been making oil since 1924.

From Chiusavecchia, you can drive up through the olive terraces to **Lucinasco**, which hangs on the slopes of a hill above a forest of silvery green leaves. Buy local olive products at **Azienda Agricola Armato Cristina** (Via Roma 17; m 338 147 5966). Just past the village is one of the most important shrines in Liguria: the 15th-century **Santuario di Santa Maria Maddalena**. Surrounded by oak and chestnut trees in front of a small lake, it's an atmospheric place to stop for a picnic, especially in autumn.

FANCY A WALK?

There are a number of easy trails in the area, some along old mule tracks. From the northwest of Dolcedo in Ripalta a path leads up to the hamlet of Orenghi. The path splits just before you get there. Take the path in the direction of Bellissimi. The trail leads back to Dolcedo via Trinchari. The 7km walk takes about 2½ hours. Alternatively, you can walk 1.6km directly back to Dolcedo from Bellissimi in about 20 minutes.

If you drive up to Lucinasco through the olive groves from Chiusanico, just as you arrive in the village there is an old mule path that leads down to San Lazzaro Reale through the olive groves. It is 2.7km and takes about 40 minutes. From San Lazzaro Reale you can also walk 8km along the old cart track to San Bartolomeo through the vineyards and the woods. It takes about 3 hours.

There is an easy and panoramic walk from the Passo del Ginesto to the hamlet of Torria which takes about 1 hour and 20 minutes and is 5km.

Many of the villages in the hinterland, not just in Liguria, but in many parts of Italy, have been in serious decline some for decades as the large towns and coastal resorts tempted young people away.

So what do you do if your family owns an old shop or two and a couple of apartments in a dilapidated village with few full-time residents? One answer to that conundrum, which has brought life back to forgotten villages, is to take a risk and open an *albergo diffuso*.

Albergo diffuso translates literally as 'scattered hotel' or another way of looking at it is to call it a B&B village, with traditional-style accommodation dotted about but managed centrally in a hub where breakfast is served. It offers the perks of staying in an independent room immersed in village life with the facilities of a hotel. And it allows owners of property that is often just one room to renovate it and rent it out.

Elena and her mother run the Relais del Maro in Borgomaro, 20 minutes' drive inland from Imperia (page 237). Elena grew up on the coast but spent her childhood summers in the village with her grandparents and regards it as home.

Her grandparents ran a successful butchers' business and lived above the shop. When her grandmother died in 2005, they were faced with a problem. What would they do with a large building in the heart of the village that was dying? 'It was my love of the place and the houses that made me start the business,' says Elena. 'We got a grant and decided that the place could not be allowed to fall into ruins and that we could do something to help the village.' In addition to the main house they also had the houses where her great grandparents and her great aunt had lived, as well as a barn where her grandfather kept his rabbits.

Today the buildings are all modernised and elegantly decorated and they run a chic boutique hotel where you can relax by the pool and admire the pastel-coloured houses across the tiny river in front of the garden. Kids kick footballs about in the main square. *Alberghi diffusi* often bring a renaissance to village life as they encourage local producers to sell their products through the hotel, bring customers to restaurants and tempt other property owners who live elsewhere to convert their crumbling houses into holiday homes. That's exactly what has happened in Borgomaro. Find out more: w alberghidiffusi.it.

The church dates from 1480 but it has been a place of worship since pagan times. Inside are frescoes of the 16th-century school of Cambiaso, and the seven statues of Christ dating from the 15th century that originally belonged in the church are now housed in the village oratory.

After this the road to Dolcedo is a real Ligurian experience: a classic twisty turning road that's a bumpy and rough drive until the newly paved road takes over past another medieval church; then it's on over Monte Acquarone and down into the Val Prino. All in all it's a classic Ligurian experience.

The highlight here is **Dolcedo**, a pretty town with stone-paved mule tracks and watermills on the banks of the river that date back to the 1100s and were used to make olive oil. The village has five bridges, one of which, the Ponte Grande, is the oldest in Liguria. It was built by the Knights of Saint John in 1292 and still bears their cross.

Cervo to Taggia and the Valle Argentina   THE MOUNTAINS BEHIND IMPERIA

9

Pietrabruna in the San Lorenzo Valley is a picturesque village that used to make a living from lavender but now grows anemones in greenhouses. A walk around Monte Faudo starts from the car park below the town through the remains of the old lavender fields.

🏠 WHERE TO STAY, EAT AND DRINK

🏠 **Azienda Agricola Cotta Giuseppe** [map, page 234] (3 cottages) Via Ameglio 5 Pantasina, Vasia; m 333 798 1164; w agricotta.com. A lavender & olive oil farm on the top of a hill. The family have run the property for generations & a stay here will give you a flavour of life in Liguria. Excellent for families. €€

🏠 **Relais del Maro** (14 rooms) Via A Guglieri, Borgomaro; ☎ 0183 54350; e relais@relaisdelmaro. it; w relaisdelmaro.it. This hotel is excellent. It is an *albergo diffuso*, meaning that some rooms are in the owner's former family home, the Casa Madre, & 8 others are in different parts of Borgomaro. It's a lovely place to relax, with a swimming pool in the garden, which looks out over the village from the terrace. There's even a small library & sitting room. They sell a number of local jams & wine, & even welcome dogs with their own bed & food. Free Wi-Fi. The perfect spot for a wedding party. €€

✗ **Censin da Bea** Via A Gellieri 14, Borgomaro; m 335 821 2982; e info@ristorantecensindabea. com; w ristorantecensindabea.com; ⏲ summer lunch Sat–Sun, closed Mon; winter dinner Thu–Sun. This trattoria in an old mill by the river is definitely an experience & perhaps the maddest place I have ever eaten. There is a set 'tasting' menu. It consists of 12 complete courses & dinner for 2 could feed a family for a week, so although I've put it in the 'Mid-range' price list for the amount of food, it could easily be in 'Rock bottom'. Given the quantity, it's a bit up & down as far as quality goes. It's impossible to see how it makes ends meet & its jolly owner admits times are hard, but despite that, knocked €10 off the bill because I was a vegetarian & had missed out on a couple of things. I was unable to move & couldn't eat the next day! Set menu €35. €€€

✗ **Trattoria dalla Etta** Via Roma 33, Lucinasco; m 339 548679; w dallaetta.com; ⏲ summer for lunch & dinner daily exc Mon, otherwise lunch Tue–Sun, dinner Fri & Sat. This family-run restaurant serves classic Ligurian food. €€€

✗ **Pizzeria Le Logge** Piazza San Giovanni 2 Borgomaro; ☎ 0183 54002; ⏲ summer evenings except Mon; winter Fri–Sun. Has tables outside on the terrace in summer overlooking the village. The pizzas are large, so make sure you are hungry. €

THE VALLE ARROSCIA The villages and mountain passes above Imperia are completely off the beaten track and *the* place to get a feel of the real Liguria. Before you arrive in **Pieve di Teco**, the SP453, the old Via del Sale (salt road) runs west along the Valle Arroscia following the river Arroscia to the plain of **Ortovero** and the rose-growing centre of **Pogli**. Lavender is also grown in the valley and used to make soap.

The road passes through the tumbledown village of **Vessalico**, the garlic capital of Liguria. It looks like it's about to collapse which is a real pity. Modern houses dot the hills and it appears as if everyone has moved out and given up on it. Buy some fresh strings of pink-skinned bulbs to take home in the shop on the edge of town. It's a very exclusive crop, as it is only grown on terraces around the town. It's a common misconception that Italians use more garlic the further you travel south: Ligurians in fact consume more garlic than they do in Puglia down in the heel of Italy. There's a garlic festival in the first week in July, Fiera dell'Aglio Vessalico. They make a very tasty mayonnaise sauce with it, *agliata*.

A little further along the road is the old olive mill town of **Borghetto d'Arroscia** with its arched medieval bridge. Again, it's rather run down, but just south of the village by the side of the road is a beautiful church dating from 1493, **San Pantaleo**. Its porch is covered with 15th-century frescoes of biblical scenes, and worth stopping off to admire, although it is likely to be locked.

Vessalico is a tiny, rather unremarkable, village in the Valle Arroscia but it does have a claim to fame. It is the home to a very rare garlic bulb, which is only grown on the hills around the village. Vessalico's special garlic has a delicate aroma and an intense flavour, which is slightly spicy. Try the local garlic mayonnaise on toasted bread or boiled potatoes.

The garlic is harvested after 20 June and the bulbs are braided into a long lattice. It is something that can only be done in the morning or the evening when the garlic bulbs are damp and the leaves are malleable. It is a method that keeps the garlic fresh until the following spring. Vessalico has been hosting a garlic festival since 1790 and it is held on 2 July unless the date falls on a Sunday, when it is held on the Saturday before.

You can buy strings of garlic in the **Mercato delle Terre** in Cairo Montenotte (page 197) on the second Saturday of the month or directly from the farmers' co-operative: **A Resta** (Frazione Lenzari 15, Vessalico; \ 335 607 9126; w vessaglio.it).

Many of the olive mills here are open to the public; for a full list of oil producers see w consorziodoprivieraligure.it. The popular travel book *Extra Virgin* by Annie Hawes (page 284) is set here, so if you are fan, you will be in your element. At **La Baita** in Gazzo near Borghetto d'Arroscia you can buy farm produce including olive oil (\ 0183 31083; w labaitagazzo.com).

Double back and take the SS28 to the market town of Pieve di Teco. If you are interested in old churches, drive up to **Rezzo** to the sanctuary of Nostra Signora del Santo Sepolcro e di Maria Bambina, which has some more interesting 15th-century frescoes. The valley is lovely and verdant, and makes for another good detour off the beaten track. Stop to buy goat's cheese from the **Azienda Agricola Barbara Saltarini** (Via Al Santuario 3; m 338 424 6595), which also has an excellent restaurant.

Pieve di Teco About half an hour's drive from Imperia, Pieve di Teco was once an important trading town on the salt road that led to Piedmont. It was founded in 1293 by the Clavesana family but its Byzantine origin is given away by its name, which derives from the Greek word for fort, *teichos*. This was once an important border town and was hotly contested by both the Genoese and the House of Savoy, the rulers of Piedmont. It came under Genoese control in the late 14th century. Many bloody battles were fought over Pieve and Napoleon's army laid waste to the town in 1794 as they marched north into Piedmont.

Salt, olive oil and salted anchovies were traded with Piedmont for meat and grain, a business that made Pieve di Teco extremely rich. While some of the villages in this part of Liguria are rather run down, Pieve has recently had a face-lift and is on the up. It was once known for its mountain shoes and tanneries that must have left a certain smell in the air.

A grand high street, the **Corso Mario Ponzoni** runs through the centre of town with colonnaded walkways on either side. Pieve's churches, however, are the main thing to see. The enormous 18th-century parish church of **San Giovanni** was designed by Lombard architect Gaetone Cantoni, who also built the cathedral in Porto Maurizio. The church, like that in Porto Maurizio, is on a vast scale and has a massive Neoclassical dome. Again, it's another tiny place with a massive church that indicates more than anything that Pieve di Teco was not always off the beaten track.

Nearby, on Via Borelli in the **Spazio Aggregativo d'Arte Cultura e Storia**, there's a permanent exhibition of the 'Masks of Ubaga' (⊕ 10.00–noon daily – don't trust these times: I visited late on a Sun afternoon & the artists were swigging wine & eating salami in the courtyard; admission €2), which is a mix of contemporary art and the local eerie tradition of mask making. To the south of the building are the open tubs where the people of Pieve di Teco used to wash their clothes.

On the other side of Corso Mario Ponzoni on Via San Giovanni Battista, the **Oratorio di San Giovanni Battista** was finished in 1234 and is home to a collection of beautiful frescoes including the *Last Supper* (1736) by Pieve artist Giovanni Francesco Sasso. On Sundays (times vary) it's possible to see the impressive religious artwork in the 15th-century church of **Santa Maria della Ripa** further down the same street. Pieve also has a miniature theatre, the **Teatro Salvini** (✆0183 704423). It opened in 1920 and has recently been restored, and puts on a number of performances.

This is wine-growing country and you can visit a number of producers in the area. You can taste wine at **Tenuta Maffone Bruno** in Frazione Acquetico near Pieve di Teco (m 347 124 5271; w tenutamaffone.it) and at **Casina Nirasca** (Via Alle Alpi 4, Pieve di Teco; ✆0183 368067; w cascinanirasca.com).

🏠 **Where to stay, eat and drink** You can find a good selection of rooms and apartments on **w** airbnb.com.

For a quick picnic head for **Panificio Pasticceria Pignone** (Corso Mario Ponzoni 50) and buy the pine nut-studded cake *pinolata* and the local speciality *biscotto fagoccio*, made with ground hazelnuts. The **Panetteria Fratelli Ferrari** (Via Eula 34) makes focaccia with walnuts and the local loaf *pagnotta pievese*.

🏠 **Hotel Negro** [map, page 234] (13 rooms) Via Canada 10, Cenova; ✆0183 34089; e hotelnegro@libero.it; w hotelnegro.com. Although it's in a bit of a time warp, it's the only proper hotel in the area & is quite an eccentric place. It's in the hilltop village of Cenova, which dates from the 11th century & is full of interesting carvings. It's a short drive from Pieve di Teco & you need a car to get here. There's a good restaurant (€€€) & a swimming pool. It's has been run by the same family for over 40 years. €€

✗ **La Lavinella** [map, page 234] Via Scuola 2, Rezzo; ✆0183 34154; w ristorantelalavinella.com. Top-quality homemade Ligurian dishes. €€
✗ **Pizzeria dal Maniscalco** Via O Manfredi 8; ✆0183 366505. This place may not look much outside but is usually buzzing in the evening. It serves good pizza & *fonduta*, the local fondue. It has a real mountain feel & is good value for money. €

Mendatica and Monesi The scenic SS28 leads on to **Pornassio** with fine views across to the Little Dolomites of Liguria and Garessio, known as the pearl of the Maritime Alps. Pornassio is actually famous for its wine but markets it as wine from nearby Ormea in Piedmont, as the name Pornassio has the same connotations in Italian as it does in English.

The SS28 goes up to the **Colle di Nava** which, although it is just 30km from the coast, is covered in beautiful alpine meadows and famous for its honey. The pass is dotted with a number of interesting 18th-century forts built to protect Piedmont's border from the French. There was never actually any fighting here so they are well preserved and the **Forte Centrale** is open to the public on Sundays, in theory at least – it was closed the Sunday I passed by. It is run by the local commune so don't take the opening times, which aren't given, just the day, as written in stone. The road leads on to the **Valle Tanaro** in Piedmont and more stunning mountain scenery but sadly many of the hotels and restaurants stand closed. The road to Piedmont is quite speedy these days and runs past their front doors, which means there's no need to stop off and it isn't an ideal location for a weekend getaway either. The **Alta Via dei Monti Liguri** runs across the crest and is a lovely walk. At the end of July the Festa Croce Bianca, the festival of the white cross, is held on the pass.

A short drive west is **Mendatica**, a medieval mountain town with a number of carved fountains. If you like paragliding, this is the place for you. It's a nice place to visit and is on the up, like Pieve di Teco. Perched above Mendatica is **Monesi**, Liguria's ski resort. If you are looking for a walk locally, you can climb Liguria's highest mountain, Monte Saccarello (2,200m), which typically takes 3 hours. The northern slopes are covered with wild alpine roses in summer.

Another recommended route is the path that leads from Colla dei Boschetti up to Cima di Piano Cavallo, 1,896m above sea level, and then back down to San

(¶) LOST SHEEP

High up in the Ligurian mountains are the old mule tracks along which were once traded oil, salt and anchovies. Until the 1960s the shepherds would guide their sheep up into the mountains in spring and down to warmer pastures by the coast in winter. There the sheep would tidy the olive groves and the vineyards by eating the grass and weeds. The farmers paid the shepherds in oil and wine for the service. They still hold a fair to celebrate *la transumanza,* in September.

The Brigasca sheep, which are hardy with tough legs and sturdy hooves, not only set the rhythm of the seasons but their milk, wool and meat kept the people who lived in the mountains alive. A century ago there were 60,000 of the breed, named after La Brigue, over the border in France. However, the post war world wasn't suited to the Brigasca. When the Val di Roya was taken by France in 1947, it made transhumance more complicated, as it now involved crossing an international border. Unsurprisingly, during the years after World War II young people left for the coast and now there are only 1,800 Brigasca sheep in Liguria and about 800 across the border in Provence.

The Slow Food Movement is working to ensure their survival and has protected the local cheese, *toma di pecora brigasca*. It is pale yellow with hints of walnut and chestnut. The ewe's milk is also used to make *sora*, which is a mixture of sheep's and goat's milk.

Protecting the sheep is not just a gastronomic event. They are crucial to maintaining the natural environment. In springtime they munch the tall, dry grass most likely to catch fire in the summer heat, and wild flower seeds get entangled in their fleece so as they walk they propagate the flowers as the seeds fall. Shepherd Aldo Lo Manto has started making carpets out of the wool his sheep produce (Il Boschetto di Aldo Lo Manto, Regione Boschetto, Bastia; ↖ 182 20687; m 339 416 7938). Look out for his stand at markets and food events along the coast.

Taste the *toma* and more at:

🏠 **Agriturismo Il Castagno** Via Provinciale in San Bernardo 39, Mendatica; ↖0183 328718; m 349 29632; e il.castagno@libero.it. The family still breed Brigasca sheep as they have done for generations & make their own *toma* cheese, which they serve in their farmhouse restaurant (€€€). They rent rooms as well. €€

9

The area around Mendatica is famous for its *cucina bianca*, white cuisine, which is closely linked to its mountain traditions and the ritual of transhumance, the moving of the herds to the high mountain pastures for summer.

It's called white because it is based on pale-coloured cheeses, white beans, leeks, potatoes, cabbage, eggs and milk. There are a number of good local cheeses to look out for. They sell them in the small shop beneath the hotel in Monesi. Sola, also called *sora*, is a mature sheep's cheese. Pecorino, a key ingredient in pesto, is a hard sheep's cheese made throughout the Val Arroscia, as is *brùsso*, a ricotta-style cheese also made with sheep's milk. *Brùsso* is great eaten fresh with olive oil and in *torta di brùsso*, a cheesecake. Toma di Mendatica is a cheese made from both cow's and sheep's milk and it is used to make the local staple potato pie, *frandurà*.

The pasta dish is *sciancà*, thin pieces of pasta similar to lasagne that's torn into pieces and served with olive oil, garlic and Parmesan.

The local *brigasca* sheep take their name from La Brigue in France and have been raised in the valleys around here since Neolithic times. There are engravings of them on Mont Bego in the Valle delle Meraviglie over in France. Their milk is used to produce cheese and the lamb is usually cooked up with artichokes, *agnello con carciofi*.

The root vegetable salsify, *scorzonera*, which tastes a bit like artichoke and has largely disappeared from the Anglo-Saxon table, is popular here. It is boiled and served like asparagus in a white sauce or tossed in olive oil and parsley.

For dessert, try *sciumette*, spoonfuls of whipped egg whites and sugar, cooked in boiling milk or *amaretto di Gavenola*, little round almond biscuits made with honey. The plain biscotti di *semola di Gavenola* are eaten for breakfast. They are sold in long blocks like a loaf.

Bernardo di Mendatica. There is also a path that leaves from the Rifugio Ca Cardella up to the Cascare Arroscia waterfall. This part of the walk is easy and suitable for families but for a real hike take the path that leads up to the top of Monte Fronte, 2,151m above sea level, which takes 5 hours there and back.

The area around Mendatica is famous for its *cucina bianca*, white cuisine (see box, above).

Monesi, however, has seen better days. Hardly anyone comes here anymore and a number of the hotels and restaurants are abandoned, their shutters banging in the wind. There is talk of knocking them down but if there's money to do even that, I would be surprised. The snow, which has been erratic for some decades, is so unpredictable that no-one comes for a proper skiing holiday nowadays; only for day trips if it has snowed. Its popularity as both a winter and summer resort has waned as new roads have made it easier to reach the Alps from the coast, which are only 2½ hours from Savona. It is a pity as Monesi has some lovely scenery and beautiful walks, but on the upside it can offer somewhere to get away from it all if you want to hide away. It is a beautiful part of Italy and there are no tourists, not even Italian ones.

That said, no-one ever lived up in Monesi. The people of Mendatica would move up here for the summer, bringing the priest with them to run a summer school for the children, while they tilled the terraces that now stand unused. It was on the lower levels that they cultivated wheat and on the higher ones lentils. This kind of farming is no longer economic so the mountainside is no longer farmed. The valleys were once part of the same region as La Brigue in France and the local dialect is a mixture of Genoese and French.

Where to stay, eat and drink

🏠 **Il Castagno** (5 rooms, 4 apts) Via San Bernardo 39; 📞0183 328718; e ilcastagno@libero. it. This is the place to try the famous *cucina bianca*. Local food is grown in the valley & the menu (€€€) is based on what is in season. Set menu only, inc drinks. Booking essential. €€

🏠 **La Vecchia Partenza** (8 rooms) Via Provinciale 25, Monesi; 📞0183 326574. A family-run hotel & restaurant (€€) that's open all year. They sell local cheeses in the shop. Everything is homemade, even the pasta, & it's good value. They serve traditional mountain food, rabbit & snails. Granny sits in the corner of the dining room preparing the vegetables. There is a rather good small shop on the ground floor that sells not only local products but also walking guides. €€

ALONG THE COAST FROM IMPERIA TO BUSSANA VECCHIA

CIVEZZA AND LINGUEGLIETTA From Imperia the coast is not really anything to write home about. The resort of **San Lorenzo al Mare** is, however, a place for bikers, as the biking path, which was formally the railway line, runs along the coast to Sanremo from here offering great views across the sea. Stop for a swim or at one of the bars dotted along the route. You can rent bikes at the old train station in San Lorenzo.

Just inland, however, are two lovely villages, neither of which have any particular sights to see but are simply pretty places to stay or stop for a drink or a meal: **Civezza**, which was founded by exiles from Venice and has a church dedicated to their patron saint, San Marco; and **Linguaglietta**, a pretty medieval village, which is one of the top hundred listed in the trusty guidebook *I Borghi più belli d'Italia*, but has lost much of its authenticity as it is now a village of second homes. The church of San Pietro was built in the 13th century and fortified in the 1550s to protect against Barbary pirates.

Where to stay

🏠 **Agriturismo Uliveto Saglietto** (5 apts) Via Carli 21, Poggi; 📞0183 651308; m 339 613 2532; w saglietto.it; ⏰ closed Feb. This agriturismo has a lovely swimming pool & terrace with a great view. The farm produces olives & wine & the apartments are in the old town or in the olive groves. You can also buy their oil & wine online. €€€

🏠 **Hotel Riviera dei Fiori** (44 rooms) 3 via Aurelia, San Lorenzo al Mare; 📞0183 745100; w hotelrivieradeifiori.it The hotel is right on the seashore with its own private beach, restaurant & spa. Free parking. €€€

TAGGIA Here the valley flattens out and, as a result, it is covered in greenhouses and light industry. The Riviera dei Fiori starts in earnest here but don't imagine fields of flowers: the blooms here are all hidden under cover. One's first reaction is to turn tail and run, but that would be a big mistake.

Arma di Taggia has one of the best sandy beaches on this stretch of coast and is a bustling seaside resort. If you avoid the eastern end with its 1960s blocks of holiday flats and stay at the western end by the old town, it's a pleasant place to while away a couple of days. Its medieval twin, Taggia, sits surrounded by its 16th-century walls 3km inland. This is Taggia's cultural face, but it's off the tourist track and bursting with tumbledown charm.

History Arma is a corruption of *barma*, which means 'cave' in Ligurian, and the place has been inhabited since prehistoric times. The original grotto is now a chapel, which was established after the Saracens, who had a base here in the 9th century, had been driven out. There was a Roman fort here to protect the old Roman road, which ran along the Vico Romano in Arma. In 1260 the area was sold to the Genoese by the counts of Ventimiglia and the Clavesana family who controlled Taggia. This was a rich town, which grew wealthy on the back of the olive oil business. The great Genoese family, the Spinolas, owned one of the largest of the town's palaces and retreated here when the political wheel of fortune in Genoa had ceased to turn in their favour.

Getting there and around
By boat The Yacht Club has 140 berths (☏0184 41021). It's dangerous to enter the port when the sea is rough and winds are from a west or southwesterly direction.

By bus There is a good local bus service connecting Arma di Taggia with Sanremo and Bussana, and east to Imperia.

By car Taggia is 10km from Sanremo. Park just off the main square in Taggia. Buy parking tickets in the kiosk. There's a car park in the centre of Arma not far from the beach. It's possible to rent bikes here in summer.

By taxi
Arma di Taggia ☏ 0184 43075

By train The station is in Arma di Taggia, on the main Genoa–Ventimiglia line.

Tourist information The tourist information office can be found at Via Paolo Boselli, Arma di Taggia (☏0184 43733; w taggia.it). The third Sunday in July sees the Festa della Maddalena, when the eerie medieval Dance of Death is performed. On the last Sunday in July, in Arma, during the feast of Sant'Erasmo, an effigy of the saint is put on a traditional boat, a '*gussu*', and pushed out into the sea to bless it. The strange lightning-like phenomenon of St Elmo's fire, which some sailors regard as bad luck, is associated with St Erasmus, another name for Elmo. Diving is offered by **Polo Sub Dive Centre** (Via Lungomare 1; m 333 188 0884; f).

🏠 **Where to stay, eat and drink** There are no good hotels in Arma; the majority are a bit dated. The best bet in the area is to stay in a B&B. There are, however, some excellent upmarket restaurants. In Taggia, buy *canestrelli* biscuits at **Sandro Canestrelli** (Via Mazzini 54; w sandrocanestrelli.com), focaccia at **Panetteria Valeria** (Vico Brea 12), and don't miss the cakes at **Pasticceria Setti** (Via Lungo Argentina 67).

✳🏠 **Al Nido degli Aironi** [map, page 232] (4 rooms) Strada Collette Beulle 12, Bussana; ☏0184 10772; e alnidodegliaironi@tiscali.it. A B&B in the hills just above the greenhouses below Bussana Vecchia, run by the ultra-friendly Anna Maria di Giannascoli. It's a peaceful base from which to visit Sanremo & Taggia. A good option for families with a little play area, cots & high chairs. Some rooms can sleep up to 5 people.

There's a large open dining area with a view of the mountains where, if there are enough guests, they sometimes serve dinner; otherwise you can eat your own picnic if the restaurant is closed. The atmosphere here is great & we even got a kiss when we left. Free Wi-Fi & parking. Advance bookings only. €

🏠 **Giuan** (6 rooms) Via Colombo 290, Arma di Taggia; ☏0184 43059; e info@giuan.it; w giuan.it.

Little family-run hotel that opened in 1863. Simple, modern rooms. Hotel also has a great seafood restaurant (€€€€). Try the ravioli made with stockfish & other stockfish specialities. €

🏠 **Miro** (2 rooms) Via Castelletti 64, Arma di Taggia; m 347 088 1352; e info@bbmiro.com; w bbmiro.com. A B&B on the hill behind the town, a 10min walk to the beach. There's a fully equipped kitchen in a small apt with 1 dbl & 1 sgl room. B/fast served in the garden in summer. €

✗ **La Conchiglia** Via Lungomare 33, Arma di Taggia; ☎0184 43169; e rist.laconchiglia@virgilio.it; w la-conchiglia.it. Restaurant with a terrace in an old fisherman's house by the sea. Great fish dishes such as risotto with Sanremo prawns. Book. €€€€€

✗ **Playa Manola** Lungomare di Ponente 90, Arma di Taggia; ☎0184 460245. Chic beachside restaurant serving predominantly fish dishes. Set menu €35. €€€

Shopping
Along the western coast of Liguria they make a pasta called *corzetti avvantaggiati*: it earns its name 'advantageous' because precious white flour is mixed with the cheaper wholemeal variety.

Also look out for *biscotti di Taggia*, sweet biscuits flavoured with fennel seeds. The local *canestrelli* biscuits are little round twists of dough made with olive oil. The long, flat savoury *ciappe* biscuits found all along the coast from Genoa to Sanremo originate from Taggia.

There is an **antiques market** on the last Sunday of every month in Taggia on Via Soleri. **Market day** is Monday.

Other practicalities
There are ATMs at Via San Francesco 10, Arma di Taggia, and Via Roma 7, Taggia. There are **post offices** at Via Blengino 43, Arma di Taggia, and Piazza Spinola 4, Taggia. There are **pharmacies** at Via San Francesco 10, Arma di Taggia, and Piazza degli Eroi Taggesi, Taggia. The nearest **hospital** is in Sanremo (Via G Borea 56; ☎0184 536301).

What to see and do
There are two faces to Taggia. In Arma, it is all about beach life and this is a particularly good place if you like windsurfing. The beach is sandy and very shallow, making it excellent for young children and the elderly.

The sightseeing is concentrated in the old town of Taggia that sits up on the hill, a few kilometres inland. It's full of all the elements that you would expect in an old Ligurian hill town: narrow, winding streets with old stone houses supported by arches that help to keep them standing in earthquakes. It's far from tarted up: full of cats and old ladies carrying bags of vegetables while old men sit around chatting; how they get away with it I do not know. There's a walking route marked out, often simply with a red arrow painted on the walls. There are surprisingly few tourists up here, a point that hits home when a delivery man asks you for directions!

From the main square **Via Roma** leads into the old town. Walk down **Via Soleri** then take **Salita Sforza** up to the heart of the centre. Look out for the doorway with the crest of the Ligurian Republic of 1797 at Via San Dalmazzo 42. It leads to the 12th-century gateway, the oldest remaining. The **Salita alla Torre** takes you to the ruins of the castle, which was completed in 1564 and used as a place of refuge when Taggia was attacked by Barbary pirates. Down the hill is the church of **Santa Lucia**, which dates from the 1500s. The fountain next to it dates from the 13th century and was once the main water supply. Walk down to the Porta Pretoria and follow Via Bastioni past two watchtowers to Taggia's main sight, the **Convento di San Domenico** (Piazza San Cristoforo; ☎0184 477278; w conventosandomenicotaggia.org; ⊕ 09.00–11.30 & 15.00–17.30 Tue–Sun; admission free). If it's not open, you can peep through the door and still

Badalucco is famous for its unique beans, the *Fagiolo bianco di Badalucco*, which are now protected by the Slow Food Movement. They are like little white pearls and are also known as *rundin*. They are a local variety of the species *Phaseolus vulgaris*, which arrived in Liguria in the 17th century from Spain. They are larger and rounder than cannellini beans and are reputed to be the creamiest beans in Italy. The beans are said to have such a special taste because they are watered by the mountain springs that run through the limestone rock and are thus rich in minerals.

They are often found on the menu served with goat or in a meat and vegetable broth called *zemin* and are made into pancakes, *fritelli*. The simplest way to enjoy them at home is to soak them for 12 hours and then boil for 30 minutes in water with two or three bay leaves and a couple of garlic cloves. Be sure that the beans are not overcooked, as the sensation should be uniform to be authentic. Dress them with olive oil, salt and pepper.

The following shops sell the beans, but to be sure you are buying the genuine article look out for the bags that carry the local Slow Food label.

Azienda Agricola La Casciamèia Via Asplanato 8, Frazione Agaggio Superiore, Molini di Triora; m 348 768 6160.

Agritourismo Al Pagan Regione Pagan Strada Provinciale, leading out of Pigna towards Gouta; m 347 322 3375; w alpagan.it. They also rent out rooms (€). A good spot for families.

---

glimpse the pictures. Founded in 1459, the Convento di San Domenico houses an exceptional series of late medieval polyptychs, many of which are the work of the master Ludovico Brea. Even if religious art isn't your favourite thing, do stop to take a look as Brea's paintings are bursting with colour and light and quite remarkable.

Take the Salita San Domenico back through the **Porta dell'Orso** that once held off an attack by the Barbary pirates. To the north of town is the **Villa Ruffini**. It belonged to Eleonora Curlo, the mother of the Ruffini brothers: Jacopo, a martyr of the unification movement, who killed himself in prison in Genoa, and Giovanni, the writer who transformed this stretch of coast when he wrote the novel, *Doctor Antonio* in the middle of the 19th century. The book was a runaway success and brought a swathe of Victorian visitors to Bordighera (page 264). Below it is a medieval bridge with 15 arches spanning the river Argentina, which runs down the Valle Argentina to the sea.

BUSSANA VECCHIA The coast between Taggia and Sanremo is of not much interest and is rather built up. It does, however, contain an unusual little place, the ruined town of Bussana Vecchia. It sits high up on a craggy hill 2km behind Sanremo, a ghostly reminder of the terrible earthquake that struck on 23 February 1887. The church was packed for a service as it was Ash Wednesday when the roof caved in, killing much of the congregation. Many died in other villages in the area, too. The earthquake led to a mini tidal wave up to 2m high.

For 60 years Bussana was a ghost town and even today it technically no longer exists. In the 1960s, however, a number of artists moved in and now sell their wares to passing tourists. In the last decade the kitsch has started to get a bit out of control in Bussana and it's not as ruined as it was even fifteen years ago. That's a pity but it is still an atmospheric place, especially out of season. There are other ruined churches in the area, however, that capture the moment without making money out of it. Restaurants change hands here every few years and are nothing to go out of your way for either.

UP IN THE MOUNTAINS TO TRIORA From nearby Arma di Taggia, the SP548 leads through the olive groves up the Valle Argentina along the old salt trading road to Triora, a pretty medieval town with a spooky past. The steep and verdant valley starts immediately after Taggia.

Badalucco Just after the Ghimbegna Pass 10km from Taggia, Badalucco is a good place to stop and stretch your legs. There is a pretty bridge with two asymmetrical arches. It's a sleepy little place with old people sitting about on stone benches in the sunshine. It's a striking contrast to the bustle of Arma di Taggia.

It's got an interesting history too. Nearby Montalto Ligure was founded by newlyweds fleeing the Count of Badalucco who insisted on claiming his right to sleep with every new bride on her wedding night. So many villagers fled that he was left penniless and only had dried chestnuts to feed them when they were invited to a reconciliation banquet. Generously, the people of Montalto went home to collect enough food for a feast but never returned to Badalucco and the count learnt his lesson the hard way.

Where to stay, eat and drink Il **Forno** (Via Colombo 6) is a traditional bakery where you can buy typical biscuits and cakes.

🏠 **Agriturismo L'Adagio** (9 rooms) Via Ortai 3-5, Badalucco ⊕ closed mid-Jan–mid-Feb. New B&B, which opened in 2017. Mountain views & use of barbecue. Spa. **€€**

🏠 **Il Poggio di Maro'** (3 rooms) Regione Poggio 10, Badalucco; **m** 347 233 3933; **w** ilpoggiodimaro.it. Stylish, modern bedroom with showers. The farm grows its own fruit & vegetables, which are used in the restaurant (**€€€**). Their tasting menu is €35 & there are vegetarian menus. **€€**

🏠 **Le Macine del Confluente** [map, page 234] (6 rooms) Località Oxentina; **◊** 0184 407018; **w** lemacinedelconfluente.com. Large excellent-value rooms in an old mill in a really romantic spot. There's a swimming pool, big garden & good

restaurant (**€€€**) serving regional dishes. It's a tasting menu based on what is in season so don't plan to stay & eat here for more than a couple of nights as it can get repetitive. **€€**

🏠 **La Finestrella di Montalto** (3 rooms) Via Roma 1, Montalto Ligure; **◊** 0184 407041; **e** info@ lafinestrelladimontalto.it; **w** lafinestrelladimontalto. it; ⊕ restaurant Thu–Tue, closed Nov. A B&B in the pretty village of Montalto, in a converted monastery with an excellent restaurant (**€€€**). In the evening they offer a tasting menu of local specialities at €25–35. **€**

🍴 **Cian de Bià** Via Silvio Pellico 14, Badalucco; **m** 320 662 2079; **w** ciandebia.it; ⊕ lunch & dinner Fri–Sun. Restaurant on a farm. Seasonal dishes include *vitello tonnato*, rabbit & *stoccafisso*. **€€€**

TRIORA

This tiny, teetering stone village is the witch-kitsch capital of Liguria and the locals are keen to cash in on the witch trials that took place here in the 16th century. That aside it is worth a visit for its setting alone in the highest valley in Liguria surrounded by mountains covered in what looks like a thick cloth of green trees. It is also a member of the Touring Club Italiano's 'Orange Flag' club, which means they assess it as one of the best places in the country for tourists to visit. It sits high up over the valley like an eagle's nest. The mountains that surround the village include Monte Saccarello, Liguria's highest peak, and are snow-capped until April. This is a great base from which to explore this beautiful part of the hinterland and visit some of its lovely neighbouring villages. Nearby are some of the most stunning stretches of the footpath, the Alta Via dei Monti Liguri.

HISTORY People have lived here since Neolithic times and this was one of the last valleys to be conquered by the Roman legions. It takes its name from the three sources of water that originate here – 'tria ora' means three mouths in dialect. There is a mosaic of Cerberus, the three-headed dog, in Piazza Regio, as these three sources were once believed to be the gateway to the underworld.

Triora may be remote but it has been fought over for centuries. It was sacked by the Saracens in AD730. It came under the control of Genoa in the Middle Ages when 200 crossbowmen from Triora fought at the Battle of Meloria in 1284. Fortified in 1216, it was ravaged by the Black Death in 1348 and partly burnt by the French in 1498, before it was besieged by the Piedmontese in 1625 and 1671, then occupied by Spanish troops in 1745. Napoleon's troops were welcomed by the villagers and General Massena made the town his HQ in his battles with Piedmont. During the Nazi occupation, there was intense partisan activity in the area.

GETTING THERE AND AROUND
By car and bus Triora sits at the top of the relatively fast SP548 that runs up the valley 25km from Taggia. Four buses run daily from Sanremo and Taggia stations. Don't be put off by the prospect of a long bus journey; it's a beautiful drive. Once there you need a car to explore properly or use the traditional mode of transport: your two feet.

TOURIST INFORMATION Find the office at Corso Italia 7 (\0184 94477; w comune. triora.im.it). There is a witchcraft festival in August and ghost tours; a mushroom festival in September; and inevitably they celebrate Halloween at the end of October. The village of Carpasio, southeast of Triora, celebrates transhumance, when the animals are brought down from the high mountain pastures, every September. In Molini di Triora there's a snail festival every September.

A LOCAL HERO

Francesco Moraldo, who lived in nearby Creppo, hid two Jewish orphans aged nine and 11 during the Holocaust. Moraldo had worked in Nice as the butler to Jewish banker Angelo Donati. He had taken the children in after their parents had been deported to Auschwitz.

In the late summer of 1943, Donati was in the process of organising for all the Jews who had hidden in Nice after the fall of France, as Nice was under Italian control, to be taken to Palestine by boat from Italy. The plan failed as Italy's capitulation was accidentally made public just before the escape plan could be implemented.

Donati, who lived in Nice, took refuge in Switzerland and Moraldo took the boys back home to Creppo. The villagers all helped to protect the children and kept them safe despite the fact that the Germans took vicious reprisals for partisan activity in the area. After the war the boys were adopted by Donati and Francesco Moraldo was awarded the title of Righteous Among Nations by the Yad Vashem Institute in Jerusalem in 1999.

Triora has a rather dark past and is known as the Paese delle Streghe, the village of the witches, after the witchcraft trials held here from 1587 to 1589. In the 16th century Genoa came under the control of Spain, at that time in the throes of the Inquisition. It was believed that witches gathered at a ruined house, *la cabotina* that lay just outside the village. When famine struck in 1587, it was blamed on the witches: 13 women, four girls and a boy. They were hauled before the local magistrates, who began a series of trials and torture sessions. One of them committed suicide by jumping out of a window in the main square and four others were executed. Surprisingly, eight had their sentences revoked. Documents from the trial are preserved in the Museo Etnografico e Della Stregoneria (see below).

WHERE TO STAY, EAT AND DRINK

B&B Triora Medievale (3 rooms) Via Cria 5; m 335 601 1921; w trioramedievale.webs.com. Beautiful views from this atmospheric & romantic B&B in the heart of Triora. The friendly owner offers guided tours of the village. €€

Hotel Ristorante Santo Spirito (10 rooms) Piazza Roma 23, Molini di Triora; \0184 94019; w ristorantesantospirito.com. This family-run hotel has been going for over 100 years & is proof that practice makes perfect. It's a friendly place with an excellent but inexpensive restaurant (€€€) serving local dishes. If you fancy cooking up something yourself, their recipes are on their website (in Italian). They have a farm & sell their produce in the Bottega di Angelmaria. It's below Triora in Molini. €€

La Stregatta (1 room) Via Camurata 24; m 340 559 2494; e lastregatta@tiscali.it; w lastregatta.weebly.com. This B&B in Triora is a cosy place. The room can sleep up to 4 people & has a kitchenette. €

La Tana delle Volpi (3 rooms) Largo Tamagni 5; \0184 94686; m 339 776 4198; e info@latanadellevolpi.it; w latanadellevolpi. it. In an old house built into a watchtower that dates from the 1400s, in the heart of Triora. You are greeted by the smell of cakes baking for b/fast the next day. A very romantic spot, especially in the evening. Daniela's family come from Triora & she has furnished the B&B with her great-grandparents' furniture. There is a terrace with a fantastic view. She also runs the Ricici café in the main square. €

✕ L'Erba Gatta Via Roma 6; \0184 94392; w erbagatta.it A friendly restaurant serving local dishes including rabbit & excellent pizza. Try the famous Badalucco beans (see box, page 252) & the local bread. €€

WHAT TO SEE AND DO Triora is a network of little alleys and once had seven gates, of which only the Porta Soprana survives today. Nearby is the town's oldest fountain, the Fontana Soprana. Just by the entrance to the town is the **Museo Etnografico e Della Stregoneria** (Corso Italia 1; \0184 94477; w museotriora.it; ☉ Apr–Jun 15.00–18.30 Mon–Fri, 10.30–noon & 15.00–18.30 Sat–Sun; Jul–Sep 10.30–noon & 15.00–18.30 Mon–Fri; Oct–Mar 10.30–noon & 14.30–18.00 Sat; 14.30–18.00 Sun; admission €2). There are one or two interesting pieces in the museum, including the display case of Christmas crib figures, but it's rather tacky with a reconstruction of a torture scene. I am inclined to agree with my 13-year-old daughter who found the place was cashing in on what was a really nasty story and thus debasing it. However, the money that the villagers make is paying for much-needed restoration work.

If you carry on straight ahead, the witch's cavern is just outside the town. You need to rise above the kitsch here, which is actually quite minimal but still very unusual for this part of Italy. Turn a blind eye to it as the old town is

This area is especially rich in alpine flowers and butterflies and lovely for walking in the late spring and summer. Some flowers, like the Ligurian gentian only grow here. If you like botany, look out for the detailed guides to the valleys, like *Fiori delle Alpi Liguri* by Gabriele Casazza and Luigi Minuto, sold in tourist shops so you can spot the different varieties. It's in Italian but is illustrated and simple to follow, as it uses Latin names for the plants.

There is a lovely walk from just below the former Colomba d'Oro hotel to Loreto, signposted 'Cetta'. It passes by the pretty church of San Bernardino, which has frescoes from the 15th century.

Another path leads from Loreto along the banks of the Argentina to Molini di Triora. There's a good picnic spot by Lago Degno, a deep pool fed by waterfalls. On a clear day walk the path from Creppo up to **Monte Gerbonte** for spectacular views through a forest of monumental larches and birch trees.

For a real hike, take the path from Realdo that skirts the border with France to the top of **Monte Saccarello**. The imposing statue of **Il Redentore**, the Redeemer, stands on the summit. If the weather is good, you can see all the way to the sea. The round circuit that also crosses Monte Pelegrino takes about 8 hours.

Triora was an important border town in World War II. The Sentiero degli Alpini was hewn out of the limestone rock in the 1930s as a supply route in case war broke out with France.

Keep an eye out for adders when walking.

---

well worth walking around and the views across the countryside and the lush mountains are fabulous.

In the main square, **Palazzo Borelli** was Napoleon's Field Marshal, Massena's, headquarters. The **Palazzo Capponi** is a rather empty cultural centre. With just 400 inhabitants, it is easy to forget that this was once a strategic town on the trading routes north. Yet its highly decorated doorways bearing noble coats of arms, and the artistic treasures in the church, the 16th-century **Collegiata dell'Assunta**, are all testament to Triora's past wealth. Inside the church is a notable work of art, the *Baptism of Christ* (1397) by the Sienese artist Taddeo di Bartolo. In the 17th-century **Oratorio di San Giovanni Battista**, there are paintings by the prolific and talented Luca Cambiaso. A steep path leads from here up to the castle.

Essentially, Triora is all about enjoying the outdoors. There are lots of sporting activities available, among them kayaking along the local rivers. There is plenty of climbing in nearby **Loreto** and **Realdo**. There are also dozens of caves in and around **Monte Pietravecchia** (2,038m) for pot-holing enthusiasts. The breathtaking **Loreto Bridge** spans 120m over the river Argentina and is a popular spot for bungee jumping. In winter there is cross-country skiing. The hotels or the tourist office can advise you on who is currently organising these activities as it is a bit haphazard up here.

Above Triora, but not as picturesque, is what used to be Liguria's highest mountain, **Verdeggia**. Unfortunately, it was destroyed in an avalanche in 1805. Slate is big business here and most of the local houses are built out of it.

Warning: Don't be fooled by the road sign that indicates that you can drive to Monesi from Triora. The road is a very rough dirt track and is virtually impassable, even in a 4x4.

10

Sanremo,
Bordighera and the Val Nervia

Telephone code 0184 (+390184 if calling from abroad)

SANREMO

Set in a wide sheltered bay, Sanremo is a seaside resort that has ballooned into a mini city. It has grand 19th-century hotels and beach concessions, and their uniformly striped umbrellas, but also the bustle of urban living. It's quite a frenetic place and an odd mixture of both savvy, chic, and gritty poverty. It is touristy and attracts a large number of French and Russians in particular and in many ways, it's like a junior Nice.

This is Liguria's fourth-largest city, with a population of over 50,000. Sanremo is the grand old lady of the Italian Riviera and packed with Art Nouveau palaces, most of which are now museums and hotels. In the late 19th century anyone who was anybody holidayed here, politicians, painters, writers, composers, kings and queens. The city still draws wealthy guests but the population of the old town is more authentic.

Even back in 1763, when writer Tobias Smollett visited, he found Sanremo, 'a pretty considerable town', with 'a harbour capable of receiving small vessels, a good number of which are built upon the beach'. Sanremo made a good impression on him and he praised the 'fine fruit and excellent oil', and found the 'women of St. Remo are much more handsome and better tempered than those of Provence. They have in general good eyes, with open ingenuous countenances.' From him this was praise indeed as most of the time he spent in Liguria he was horrified by his accommodation and revolted by the meals he was served.

Sanremo hosts conferences and events throughout the year and is always buzzing. If you're not going to one of its big festivals, it's best to avoid Sanremo when there is one going on, as hotel prices skyrocket. There is plenty to see here and it is worth a stop off if you are travelling by. It's a good base out of season if you want to be somewhere with some nightlife. There are also good facilities for golf, horseriding and watersports. Besides the casino, Sanremo is famous for its flowers, which are shipped all over the world.

HISTORY The city was founded by the Romans, who called it Matuta. It was destroyed first by the Lombards in the 7th century and later by the Saracens. By the time the city got itself back on its feet, it was known as San Romolo. Over the centuries the name became corrupted into Sanremo, which can also be spelt San Remo, which was its official name under fascism.

The Genoese resented the trading competition that they faced from Sanremo and brutally suppressed the city, imposing stringent restrictions on civic rights, and

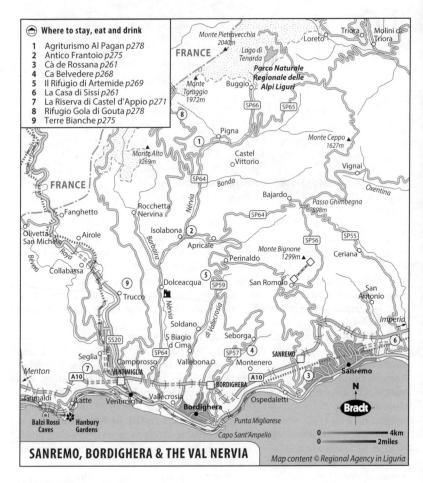

FRANCE

Monte Pietravecchia
2040m

Triora
Molini di
Triora

Loreto

Lago di
Tenarda

**Parco Naturale
Regionale delle
Alpi Liguri**

Monte
Toraggio
1972m

Buggio

SP66   SP65

Pigna

Monte Ceppo ▲
1627m

Monte Alto
1269m

Castel
Vittorio

Vignai

FRANCE

Fanghetto

Rocchetta
Nervina

Bonda

Bajardo

Oxentina

Passo Ghimbegna
898m

SP64

Olivetta
San Michele

Airole

Isolabona

SP64

Apricale

Monte Bignone
1299m ▲

Ceriana

SP56

SP55

Collabassa

Dolceacqua

SP59

Perinaldo

San Romolo

San
Antonio

Trucco

Soldano

di Vallecrosia

Imperia

S Biagio
d Cima

Seborga

SS20

SANREMO

Seglia

Camporosso

SP64

Vallebona

SP57

Montenero

Sanremo

Menton

A10

VENTIMIGLIA

Vallecrosia

A10

BORDIGHERA

N

Grimaldi
Latte

Ventimiglia

Bordighera

Ospedaletti

Bradt

Balzi Rossi
Caves

Hanbury
Gardens

Punta Migliarese

Capo Sant'Ampelio

0 ———— 4km
0 ———— 2miles

SANREMO, BORDIGHERA & THE VAL NERVIA

Map content © Regional Agency in Liguria

even confiscating the bell of San Siro Cathedral, so by the end of the 18th century Sanremo was pretty much a backwater. Its harbour was also too shallow for large ships and the increased trade they brought.

In 1857, things improved dramatically for the Sanremesi when a local medic, Dr Panizzi, embarked on a campaign to make the British aware of the medical benefits that could be derived from spending time in Sanremo's mild climate. He had an article published in *The Times* and wrote a pamphlet extolling Sanremo's virtues. He subsequently went to London to promote his hometown as the perfect place to convalesce and by 1874 Sanremo had become a popular winter resort. The heat of the summer, by contrast, was considered a danger to health.

The first guests who came to the Riviera were housed in a private villa belonging to Countess Adele Roverizio di Roccasterone. The Hotel Londra was built in 1860 and was soon followed by the Royal. The building of the railway in the 1870s opened up this part of the coast and made it easy for people from northern Europe to reach. Just how entrenched the British community was to become here and how much time they spent enjoying the winter sun is evident from one of the first guidebooks written about Sanremo. Among the practical listings section, along with pharmacies and banks are entries on how to deal with births and deaths. One of the first guides to Sanremo in

English, published in 1869, was *San Remo as a Winter Residence by An Invalid*, and indeed many of those who first came to the Riviera were sick or convalescing.

The list of celebrities who stayed here is too long to give every name individually and in the age of limited communication across borders, a holiday on the Riviera gave politicians a chance to have crucial private conversations. The Russian empress Maria Alexandrovna and her son Nicholas II both stayed in Sanremo. Artists and scientists also flocked to the city. Edward Lear spent the last years of his life here but sadly left little work related to the place. Swedish business family the Nobels lived at Villa Nobel, now a museum, and Tchaikovsky was inspired during a holiday in 1878 to compose *Eugene Onegin* and the *Fourth Symphony*.

In 1920, at the Sanremo Conference, the city made its contribution to world history when the allocation of League of Nations mandates was agreed; most notable of these was the British Mandate in Palestine.

ORIENTATION Sanremo is made up of three distinct areas: the shopping district that centres on Corso Matteotti; La Pigna, the old town; and the west end where the hotels cluster next to the casino.

GETTING THERE AND AROUND
By bike Bike hire is available from **NoloBici**, who are located in the main car park near the casino [260 A4] (m 349 491 6209; w nolobici.it). There's a 25km cycling and walking path that runs along the coast to Taggia offering fantastic views.

By boat There are two marinas; the Porto Vecchio to the west, with 450 berths (☏ 0184 505531; e sanremo@guardiacostiera.it); and Porto Sole in the east (☏ 0184 5371; e info@portosolesanremo.it; w portosolesanremo.it). There are whale-watching tours from the harbour in summer (w whalewatchsanremo.com); tours of the bay last 45 minutes and among the species you may see are bottlenose dolphins, striped dolphins, fin whales, sperm whales, Risso's dolphins, pilot whales and common dolphins. There are also excursions to watch the firework displays from the sea: 14 August in Sanremo, 15 August in Alassio, and 29 August in Ventimiglia.

By bus Buses leave from Piazza Colombo for Taggia, taking 15 minutes, and Ventimiglia, taking about 35 minutes. At time of writing a new route, the Costa Azzura, was due to open, linking Sanremo with Monte Carlo.

By car Sanremo is 5km off the main Genoa–Ventimiglia A10 *autostrada*, 34km from Ventimiglia and the French border. The closest airport is Nice, 65km away. Park by the casino; parking tickets are sold in the train station.

By taxi For taxis, call ☏ 0184 541454.

By train The train station [260 E1] is on the eastern side of town and is on the main Ventimiglia–Genoa and Ventimiglia–Turin lines.

TOURIST INFORMATION The office is at Corso Cavallotti 59 [260 E1] (☏ 0184 580353). Sanremo celebrates its flower industry in a parade held at the end of January. The biggest festival is the Sanremo Song Festival, which inspired the Eurovision Song Contest, and is held in late February. There are music festivals in June, July, August and October. In March, the city is the finishing line for the Milan–Sanremo cycle race. There are major firework displays on 14 August and on New Year's Eve.

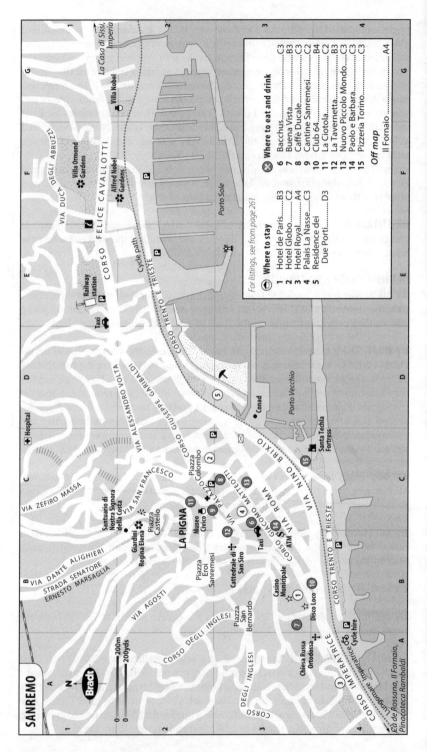

SANREMO

For listings, see from page 261

Where to stay
1 Hotel de Paris......B3
2 Hotel Globo.........C2
3 Hotel Royal.........A4
4 Palais La Nasse....C3
5 Residence dei
   Due Porti............D3

Where to eat and drink
6   Bacchus................C3
7   Buena Vista...........B3
8   Caffè Ducale..........C3
9   Cantine Sanremesi..C2
10 Club 64................B4
11 La Ciotola............C2
12 La Tavernetta........B3
13 Nuovo Piccolo Mondo...C3
14 Paolo e Barbara.....C3
15 Pizzeria Torino......C3

Off map
Il Fornaio...............A4

WHERE TO STAY

Hotel Royal [260 A4] (126 rooms) Corso Imperatrice 80; ☎ 0184 5391; e reservations@ royalhotelsanremo.com; w royalhotelsanremo. com. In a vast tropical garden 5mins from the casino, this hotel is the ultimate Riviera experience with spa & outdoor pool. Once one of the grandest hotels on this coastline where royalty & celebrities holidayed, there is a beach club, sauna, gym & tennis court. Gourmet restaurant. €€€€

Hotel de Paris [260 B3] (28 rooms) Corso Imperatrice 66; ☎ 0184 192 5250; e reservation@ hoteldeparissanremo.it; w hoteldeparissanremo. it. Smart old hotel that has been refurbished to a high standard, situated moments from the casino. There are good-sized rooms, a sauna, spa & gym. Parking, beach facilities & free Wi-Fi. The hotel has a panoramic lift with a lovely view of the Russian Orthodox church. €€€

La Casa di Sissi [map, page 258] (3 rooms) Strada Banchette Napoleoniche 68, Poggio; ☎ 0184 160 0056; m 335 659 5605; e Carmen@ lacasadisissi.com; w lacasadisissi.com. In Poggio above Sanremo, this B&B has a fabulous view & a large garden. €€€

Cà de Rossana [map, page 258] (5 rooms) Via Padre Semeria 490; m 328 400 6839; e rossaprimula7@yahoo.it; w caderossana.com. B&B in a large garden with lovely views. Every room has private access. A 5min bus or car ride to the beach. The friendly owners are full of tips on what to see & do. €€

Palais La Nasse [260 C3] (6 rooms) Corso Matteotti 144; ☎ 0184 543300; m 335 626 0360; e info@palaislanasse.com; w palaislanasse.com. Designer-style B&B in the heart of Sanremo's shopping district. €€

Residence dei Due Porti [260 D3] (33 rooms) Corso Trento e Trieste 21; ☎ 0184 506506; e info@dueporti.it; w dueporti.it. This has 1-, 2- or 3-bed apts overlooking the seafront, 5mins from the town centre & conveniently close to the supermarket. Free bike rental & daily cleaning. Sun terrace. Wi-Fi. Perhaps the best-value accommodation in Sanremo. €€

Hotel Globo [260 C2] (43 rooms) Via Asquasciati 2; ☎ 0184 509485; e info@ hotelglobosanremo.it; w hotelglobosanremo.it. Basic, modern hotel in the centre of Sanremo. An excellent location within easy walking distance of all the sights. Recently refurbished & exceptionally clean. Parking & free Wi-Fi. There are also suites for families. €

WHERE TO EAT AND DRINK

For food 'to go' or in a hurry, buy pizza and flans from **La Tavernetta** [260 B3] (Via Palazzo 129). There are lots of good food shops on Via Palazzo and Via Corradi, and for basic picnic supplies the best supermarket is Conad [260 D3] by the harbour. The **market** is in Piazza Eroi Sanremesi behind the cathedral on Tuesday and Saturday. **Caffè Ducale** [260 C3] (Corso Matteotti 145) is a lovely old-fashioned café and the place for a coffee or a drink. **Il Fornaio** [260 A4] (Corso Matuzia 209) sells excellent fresh pasta. If you like fish, try the Sanremo red prawn.

Buena Vista [260 B3] Corso degli Inglesi 15; ☎ 0184 509060; w ristorantebuenavista.it. A small, unpretentious, Argentine-themed restaurant with simple décor & wooden floor. Specialises in steak & fish dishes. Kids' menu. €€€€€

Paolo e Barbara [260 C3] Via Roma 47; ☎ 0184 531653; e paolobarbara@libero.it; w paolobarbara.it. A small & intimate restaurant with beautifully prepared local dishes that make this the foodie experience of Sanremo. The restaurant is run by a couple who are passionate about food & are more hosts than restaurateurs. €€€€€

La Ciotola [260 C2] Via Santo Stefano 4; ☎ 0184 507609. No-frills family restaurant serving classic local dishes. Good-value set menu. €€€

Nuovo Piccolo Mondo [260 C3] Via Piave 7; ☎ 0184 509 9012; ⊕ closed Sun. Handsome vaulted family-run restaurant specialising in traditional Ligurian dishes. €€€

Bacchus [260 C3] Via Roma 65; ☎ 0184 530990. Great stop either for a drink or a light meal. €€

Cantine Sanremesi [260 C2] Via Palazzo 7; ☎ 0184 572063. The local speciality is *sardenaira*, a pizza without cheese, with olives, garlic & anchovies & probably originally sardines, as the name implies. This is the place to try it. €€

Club 64 [260 B4] Via Verdi 2; ☎ 0184 578192; ⊕ closed Tue. Near the casino, this is another good pizzeria. €€

✗ Pizzeria Torino [260 C3] Giardini Vittorio
Veneto 20; ✎ 0184 990194. Another good pizzeria
that also serves pasta & meat dishes. €€

ENTERTAINMENT AND NIGHTLIFE The **casino** [260 B3] (Corso Inglesi 18; ✎ 0184
5951; **w** casinosanremo.it; over 18s only; admission free) is at the centre of Sanremo's
nightlife. Entrance is only permitted with ID. Dress code is jacket and tie for the
American and French gaming rooms. The cabaret revue **Disco Loco** [260 B3] (Corso
Imperatrice 18) is a popular place. Both the old port and La Pigna are busy after dark.
In summer there are jazz, folk and blues concerts in the parks and the harbour.

OTHER PRACTICALITIES There is an **ATM** at Via Roma 61 [260 C3]. The **post office**
[260 C3] is at Via Roma 158. The **pharmacy** [260 C2] is at Via Palazzo 58, and the
hospital is at Via G Borea 56 [260 C1] (✎ 0184 5361).

A WALK AROUND SANREMO The seafront at the western end of town is named the
Lungomare Imperatrice [260 A4] in honour of Tsarina Maria Alexandrovna, the
wife of Tsar Alexander II, who donated the first palms that lined it. It is here that
you will find the city's most prestigious hotels and it is the place to rub shoulders
with the ghosts of Sanremo's past. It's also the most convenient starting point from
which to discover the city as there is a sizeable car park.

Not far from the tourist information office is the pretty onion-domed **Chiesa
Russa Ortodossa** [260 A4], which dates back to 1920. Proof of just how international
the city was is to be found in the crypt. King Nikola and Queen Milena of
Montenegro (who died in exile in 1921 and 1923 respectively) were buried here
until 1989, when their remains were returned to Cetinje, the old royal capital of
Montenegro. Although their remains are no longer here, the original tombs are.
Their daughter, Elena, was queen of Italy, after she married Victor Emmanuel III
in 1896. It is a very simple little church; be sure to look up once inside. The tiny
window at the top of the ceiling looks beautiful on a bright, sunny day.

Next to the church is the **casino** [260 B3] (see above), built in 1904 and designed
by Eugenio Ferret. It's still the heart of Sanremo's social life and one of the largest
casinos in Europe.

Walk or cycle along the seafront past the harbour and the huge fortress that was
built by the Genoese to keep the Sanremesi in line. Until 2002 it was used as a prison.

At the end of **Corso Trento e Trieste** are the pretty gardens of the **Villa Ormond**
[260 F1], and the Moorish **Villa Nobel** [260 G2] (Corso Cavallotti 116; ✎ 0184
507380; **w** provincia.imperia.it/villanobel; ⊕ 10.00–13.00 Wed–Sun, 15.00–18.00
Fri–Sun; admission €5.50). The house was built in 1874 and is where the famous
Swedish scientist Alfred Nobel lived and died in 1896. It is well worth a visit to
get a glimpse of the way the foreign community lived in Sanremo in the late 19th
century. What is striking is how homely the place is. No surprise, then, that Nobel
returned like a homing pigeon to relax and unwind. In the basement, there is a
small exhibition about Nobel's invention, dynamite. It was absolutely crucial in
making it easier to move around Italy by both train and road. Liguria is full of
tunnels that have been blasted out of the rock and it's thanks to Nobel that they are
there. You can also see his laboratory, where he experimented with nitroglycerine.
Flowers from Sanremo always decorate the Nobel Prize ceremonies in Oslo.

Walk back along Corso Felice Cavallotti and Corso Giuseppe Garibaldi to Via
Palazzo. From here head up into **La Pigna** [260 B2], the old town. It is a maze of
steep lanes, stairways, narrow tunnels and arches that run in concentric circles

from the top of the hill. It's surprisingly ungentrified and, if you only have a short time in Liguria, it will give you a real feel for the place.

John Addington Symonds, an English poet and literary critic who visited Sanremo in 1879, described it as 'a huge glacier of houses poured over a wedge of rock, running down the sides and along the ridge, and spreading itself into a fan between two torrents on the shore below.' The old town is tightly interlaced with a network of arches that are almost tunnels, which are designed to protect against earthquakes.

It is refreshing to walk out of the old town at the top of the hill into the **Giardini Regina Elena** [260 B2] which have views back over the town and the harbour. On the hilltop is the symbol of Sanremo and a landmark for sailors, the **Santuario di Nostra Signora della Costa** [260 C2], founded in the 15th century. The present building dates from 1630. The pebble mosaic outside is the largest in Liguria, and the first gold coin donated to the fund to build the church came from a local sailor who had been saved from drowning.

Walk back down the hill to **Piazza San Siro**, the location of the **Cattedrale di San Siro** [260 B3] which was founded in the 12th century; it has an unusual 15th-century black crucifix inside. This is where the Sanremesi were frequently roused to take up arms against the Genoese.

The **Museo Civico** [260 C3] (Piazza Nota 6; m 328 530 4665; ⏰ 09.00–19.00 Tue–Sat; admission €5). The ticket also covers the entrance to the **Pinacoteca Rambaldi** [260 A4] in Coldirodi (\ 0184 670398; ⏰09.00–13.00 & 14.30–17.30 Thu, 09.00–13.00 Fri–Sat, 14.30–17.30 Sun). This gallery, established in 1865, has a collection of paintings from the 15th to the 19th centuries and 5,000 books, including a number of rare manuscripts. Look out for *The Madonna and Child* by Lorenzo di Credi. Coldirodi is also a nice little village and a good place to stop for a drink. On a hill above the sea, it has great views along the coast.

The funicular up Monte Bignone (1,299m) no longer works, but again, if you have your own wheels, there are some lovely views from the summit.

The cycle path, Pista Ciclabile del parco costiero della Riviera dei Fiori (w pistaciclabile.com) runs 24km along the coast and is a major new attraction. There are nice bars and cafés dotted along the route, which goes as far as San Lorenzo al Mare.

FURTHER AFIELD

Ospedaletti The next town to the west takes its name from the Roman Catholic military order, Knights Hospitallers, some of whom were shipwrecked here at the beginning of the 14th century, and where they built a pilgrims' hospice of which no traces now remain. It is not much to write home about today, but the Villa Sultana was one of the first big casinos on the Riviera and is on Corso Regina Margherita. It is now an apartment block. Katherine Mansfield stayed in Ospedaletti in the early 1900s and the new marina may well bring some glitz back to the town in the same way that other such developments have been doing along the coast. Every other September, in even-numbered years, Ospedaletti hosts a vintage motorcycle race.

🏠 *Where to stay, eat and drink*

🏠 **La Mimosa del Golfo** (2 rooms) Strada Costa dei Pini 23; m 329 978 0747; w lamimosadelgolfo.it B&B 10mins' walk from the beach. Rooms have a terrace & private bathroom. Sea views. **€**

✕ **Acquerello** Corso Regina Margerita 25; \ 0184 682048; w ristoranteacquerello.it. Menus at €45 & €55. **€€€€**

✕ **Byblos Lungomare** C Colombo 6; \ 0184 689002; w ristorantebyblos.com; ⏰ closed Mon. Elegant restaurant famous for its fish but also serves some meat dishes. Lovely sea views. **€€€€**

✕ **Acquolina** Piazza San Giovanni 7; \ 0184 683687. A fusion of Ligurian & Sicilian tastes. **€€€**

Up in the mountains A short drive up in the mountains through the forest, some 23km behind Sanremo, is some beautiful remote mountain country. Take the SP56 that skirts Monte Bignone to the west to Bajardo. The village sits on a hilltop commanding the valley below. It's a beautiful sight and is often above cloud level, which gives it a rather magical appearance.

When we visited, we met an old man who had a little exhibition of photographs he has taken of Bajardo in all weathers. I thought they were so lovely that I asked him if we could have one to use in this guide. 'A guide to Bajardo?' he asked. 'No, Liguria as a whole,' I replied. 'Pah!' he said, shaking his head, 'Why, it's all in Bajardo! No need to write about those places.'

It may be a sleepy little village but the ruined church of **San Nicolò**, where 200 people were killed in the devastating earthquake of 1887, splashed Bajardo across the pages of the world's newspapers. Although it was the middle of the week, the church was full as it was Ash Wednesday. Many of the houses at the top of the village were also destroyed. It is still a rather melancholy and moving place, and fortunately no-one has exploited the tragedy to make money. The church is at the top of the village and there are panoramic views from the terrace across to the Ligurian Alps, which are particularly lovely in winter and spring when they are capped in snow.

Bajardo traditionally made its living felling trees for shipbuilding. There's a local legend that a tree-cutter felling trees for Ventimiglia, which was an ally of Pisa, fell in love with the local count's daughter, who was an ally of Genoa. The father had no mercy and cut her head off, an event that's commemorated in a festival every June. There is also a Druids Festival in July. For a real off-the-beaten-track outing, take the road back to Taggia via Vignai. Alternatively, the SP55 from Bajardo passes the mountaintop village of Ceriana, 12km north of Sanremo. It was built in the Middle Ages on the site of a Roman villa and is a classic example of a Ligurian hill town built in concentric circles.

 Where to stay, eat and drink

🏠 **Le Camelie del Bosco** (3 rooms) Regione Gian Lui 2/a, Bajardo; m 328 765 5982; w cameliedelbosco.it. Top-class romantic B&B with beautiful views of Bajardo. **€**

✗ **Osteria Ra Culeta di Littardi Jose** Piazza Sonnaz, Bajardo; m 389 312 4271. In the main square, this excellent little restaurant serves some great ravioli & simple dishes. They make prize-winning biscuits called *bajoccolio* which are little shortbreads. They also rent an apt if you want to stay longer. **€€**

BORDIGHERA

Bordighera is a sunny, lively resort full of grand 19th-century buildings and Art Nouveau villas. Before World War I, wealthy tourists from northern Europe flocked here to spend the winter, among them Monet who passed three months busily painting away in and around Bordighera. The light entranced him but the way it constantly changed locked him in a personal battle to capture the true essence of Bordighera on canvas.

The miniature old town, Bordighera Alta sits high on the Capo Sant'Ampelio. The elegant 19th-century resort spreads out below, along the sea. This end of town is the best place to base yourself as the urban sprawl of western Bordighera has little charm. This is still an all-year-round resort, with lots of opportunities for watersports, golf and tennis.

HISTORY Bordighera has been inhabited since the 4th century and was for most of its existence a little fishing village of no consequence. Its name is a dialect word meaning a shelter for fishing rods. It was once part of an independent community of eight towns that broke away from Ventimiglia in the 17th century, but, besides this, it was always a bit of a backwater and not much happened here.

It was the publication of the novel *Doctor Antonio,* by Giovanni Ruffini in 1855, which was set in Bordighera, that was to fire the Victorian imagination and rocket Bordighera into the limelight. Ruffini was a supporter of Mazzini, the father of the Risorgimento, and ended up in exile in London where he wrote his novel, not in Italian but in English. It was really intended to whip up popular support for the unification of Italy but also painted such a beautiful picture of Liguria that it was a best-selling advert for the Riviera. As a consequence, by the late 19th century there were far more British citizens in Bordighera than locals. There were plenty of Russians holidaying here too, who came on the 'grand express' from St Petersburg.

The English colony was centred on Via Vittorio Veneto. There's a Via Shakespeare, where the Tennis and Bridge Club was once sited, the first of its kind in Italy, founded in 1872. The Brits even had their own Anglican church on Via Regina Vittoria, which is now a cultural centre.

GETTING THERE AND AROUND

By bike Bikes can be rented at Barale Giorgio Via Emanuele II 479.

By boat The Marina di Sant'Ampelio was at time of writing being expanded (↖ 0184 265656; e ufficioporto@commune.bordighera.it). Beware: the entrance to the harbour can be dangerous in rough weather.

By bus Buses go up into the mountains to the main towns and villages behind Bordighera and along the coast.

By car Bordighera is 7km from Ventimiglia and the French border on the A10 *autostrada*. When you drive down from the *autostrada*, go slowly as there are a couple of dangerous hairpin bends. There's plenty of parking by the seafront.

On foot There are a number of panoramic footpaths that lead up into the mountains to Vallebona, Seborga and Montenero, roughly a 5-hour round trip, but you can catch a bus to or from Seborga.

By taxi Taxis are available by calling ↖ 0184 261574.

By train Bordighera is on the main Ventimiglia–Genoa and Ventimiglia–Turin lines.

TOURIST INFORMATION Find the office at Via Vittorio Emanuele II 172–174 (↖ 0184 262322). They have a useful leaflet that shows you how to trace Monet's footsteps. There are signs with copies of the ten pictures he painted in 1884 dotted around the town. Bordighera celebrates its patron saint, Sant'Ampelio, on 14 May with a religious procession, a party in Piazza Edmondo de Amicis and fireworks. There is a good English information website covering the whole area: w cinquevalli.it.

Activities There are whale-watching trips in summer (m 392 137 6120; w whalewatchimperia.it).

🏠 WHERE TO STAY

🏠 **Grand Hotel del Mare** (66 rooms) Via Portico della Punta 34; 📞 0184 262201; **e** info@grandhoteldelmare.it; **w** grandhoteldelmare.it; ⏰ closed Sep–Feb. Modern hotel on the cliff side that looks right out over the sea. It's on the eastern side of town, 15mins on foot from Bordighera. Parking & spa. It's a complex surrounded by large gardens. All rooms have a sea view. There are 2 restaurants & seawater swimming pool. Minigolf. €€€€

🏠 **Aqua di Mare B&B** (3 rooms) Via dei Pescatori 6; **m** 339 810 8227; **e** info@acquadimare.com; **w** acquadimare.com; ⏰ closed 1st 2 weeks of Feb & Oct–mid-Nov. Just 30m from the sea & close to the old town. Terrace & free parking. €€

🏠 **Hotel della Punta** (18 rooms) Via Portico della Punta, Via S Ampelio 27; 📞 0184 262555; **e** info@hoteldellapunta.it; **w** hoteldellapunta.it. If there isn't room in the Piccolo Lido (see right), this is just across the road. Some rooms have sea views & they are open in the autumn, which is unusual for Bordighera. €€

🏠 **Hotel Parigi** (55 rooms) Lungomare Argentina 16–18; 📞 0184 261405; **e** info@hotelparigi.com; **w** hotelparigi.com; ⏰ closed mid-Oct–23 Dec. The hotel is at the eastern end of Bordighera, which is the nicest place to stay & is on the seafront. Recently renovated, it opened in the early 1900s. It has a rooftop seawater swimming pool & fitness centre. €€

🏠 **Hotel Piccolo Lido** (33 rooms) Lungomare Argentina 2; 📞 0184 261297; **e** info@hotelpiccololido.it; **w** hotelpiccololido.it; ⏰ closed Oct–22 Dec. A very friendly little hotel at the far eastern end of the seafront, which is the nicest place to stay in Bordighera & is close to the Sant'Ampelio church. Some rooms have balconies & a sea view. Sun terrace. Children's playroom. €€

🏠 **Hotel Villa Elisa** (32 rooms) Via Romana 70; 📞 0184 261313; **e** villaelisa@masterweb.it; **w** villaelisa.com. A Victorian villa surrounded by a garden full of lemon & orange trees. Transfers to & from Nice airport available. Restaurant, outdoor swimming pool, playground, playroom & a mini club for kids in high season. €€

🏠 **Villa Maddalena** (2 rooms) Via dei Colli 21; **m** 329 957 9977; **e** contact@villamaddalenabordighera.com; **w** villamaddalenabordighera.com. Elegant renovated villa close to the old town. Private access. Free parking. €€

🏠 **La Terrazza** (3 rooms) Via Pompeo Mariani 4; **m** 388 690 9633; **e** info@laterrazzabordighera.com; **w** laterrazzabordighera.com. B&B in a 17th-century tower in the old town. On 3rd & 4th floor with a terrace with a great view. Excellent b/fast buffet. No credit cards. €

✖ WHERE TO EAT AND DRINK

✳ ✖ **La Reserve** Via Arziglia 20; 📞 0184 261322; **e** lareservebordighera@gmail.com; **w** ristorantelareserve.com. This is really 2 restaurants in 1, & a café. You can stop here for a drink or a light lunch but there is also a top-notch restaurant. Both the bar, the café & the restaurant have a terrace with what is perhaps the best view in Bordighera, as La Reserve is on the seafront next to the pretty Sant'Ampelio church. It is also a beach club & you can swim off the rocks. If you have a boat, you can moor just off the coast & swim in. Bar & café €€; restaurant €€€€

✖ **La Cicala** Via Lunga 16; 📞 0184 261815; **w** lacicalabordighera.it. Traditional restaurant in the old town. €€€

✖ **Osteria Magiargé** Piazza Giacomo Viale 1; 📞 0184 262946; **w** magiarge.it; ⏰ closed lunch Thu, Jul & Aug. In the old town this restaurant is a romantic spot & serves imaginative Ligurian food. Here you can try the famous Perinaldo artichoke & garlic from Vessalico. Good value set menus. €€€

✖ **Coco's** Via Vittorio Emanuele 203. A groovy little ice-cream parlour with zebra-striped seats, which specialises in some unusual flavours alongside the traditional. Fancy a balsamic vinegar ice cream? They also serve a huge variety of different teas. €

OTHER PRACTICALITIES There is an **ATM** at Via Vittorio Emanuele II 157. The **post office** is at Via Goffredo Mameli 89, and there is a **pharmacy** at Via Vittorio Emanuele II 165. The **hospital** is at Via Aurelia Ponente 97 (📞 0184 5361).

WHAT TO SEE AND DO The seafront, the **Lungomare Argentina** runs along the wide bay east to the Capo Sant'Ampelio, on which sits the pretty 11th-century church of **Sant'Ampelio**. According to legend, he arrived here in the 5th century and lived as a hermit in a cave. That cave is now said to be the crypt of the church and in it is a large stone that was supposedly his bed, in which he died in AD428. Sant'Ampelio left his mark on the city as he came from Egypt and brought with him some palm tree seeds. Bordighera has for hundreds of years been famous for its palm trees and has the most northerly palm grove in Europe. Every Palm Sunday, it supplies the Vatican with the palm fronds that adorn St Peter's in Rome.

The church is on a rocky promontory, which is a great place to swim and sunbathe. Across the road rise the gardens that lead up to the old town. Considering that it's been exposed to tourists for over 150 years, it is surprisingly authentic and still full of old ladies and cats. Below the old town to the east is the villa where Charles Garnier, who was the architect of the Paris opera house, lived.

Sadly the **Villa Regina Margherita** that once belonged to Queen Margherita of Savoy, who adored this villa is now no longer open to the public, but the town's other museum, the **Museo Biblioteca Clarence Bicknell** (Via Romana 39; ✆ 0184 263694; ☉ 08.30–13.00 & 13.30–17.00 Mon, 09.00–13.00 Tue & Thu; admission free), is conveniently just across the road. Note: This museum is one of many in Liguria that don't hold to the hours listed. I was told by a lady in the Liguria Institute next door that 'They aren't doing mornings this week but they will be there on Thursday afternoon.' They were not. She then said, 'Ah! Something came up. Try next week.' I did, but something else had obviously come up. I tried a number of times to visit and failed, so good luck and keep us posted if you get in. The museum holds a vast array of books, botanical specimens and some prehistoric carvings from Mont Bego just over the border in France. They were collected by local English vicar and Esperanto speaker, Clarence Bicknell, who was an expert on the botany of the Riviera.

If you fancy a walk or need a playground, head for the **Giardini Monet,** just up the street towards the old town.

UP IN THE MOUNTAINS The SP58 climbs first to **Vallebona**. This is wine and olive oil country. It is a sleepy village and nice to wander around and stop for a drink. The dialect is a mixture of Genoese and French so be sure to listen in to the old men chatting away to get a sense of it.

In 1963, the 14km^2 Principality of **Seborga**, 12km from Bordighera, elected Prince Giorgio I as its ruler. There are only around 350 people who live here, but they briefly instituted their own currency, the *luigino*, print their own stamps and have special Seborga number plates. There is even a little sentry box just outside town.

Seborga was given to the Benedictine monks in AD954 by the Count of Ventimiglia and the Knights Templar ordained their first grand master here on returning from the Crusades in 1118. After their demise, it became the property of the Cistercians in 1309, and it was the monks who struck the first coins here in 1686. In 1729, Seborga was sold to Savoy but the legal document was wrongly drawn up and was thus declared null and void. Tiny Seborga was then overlooked by the 1815 Congress of Vienna, which abolished the state of Genoa and handed the city and her possessions to the King of Piedmont, so the inhabitants claim it still to be an independent country.

In reality, though, Seborga is part of Italy, and its citizens regularly pay taxes, vote in regional and state elections and use the euro. Buses leave six times a day from Piazza Martiri Patrioti, in Bordighera, and there is a pretty footpath that leads back down to Bordighera through Sasso, which takes about 2½ hours to walk. Seborga could have become a tourist trap but the residents were wise enough to know where to draw the line.

⌂ Where to stay, eat and drink

⌂ **Ca Belvedere** (3 rooms) [map, page 258] (rooms) Via Antico Principato 10; m 333 271 9918. In the hills 20mins' walk from Seborga so you need a car to stay at this *agriturismo*. Min 4-night stay. €

✖ **Osteria del Coniglio** Via Verdi 7, Seborga; ☎0184 223820. Serves all the local specialities, among them rabbit & goat. A good little restaurant with fair prices. €€

Perinaldo The tiny town of Perinaldo, at the head of the Val Crosia, is on the hill above Apricale. Take the SS59 from Vallecrosia and as you drive up the valley you can immediately see how imposing this town once was when the coast was empty and wild with only a few fishing hamlets dotted along it. Perinaldo was the birthplace of three celebrated astronomers: Giovanni Domenico Cassini (1625–1712); Giacomo Filippo Maraldi (1665–1729); and Giovanni Domenico Maraldi (1709–88) who were all members of the same family. Giovanni Domenico Cassini discovered the first asteroids, the moons of Saturn, and the speed with which Mars, Venus and Jupiter rotate on their respective axes. He worked for the Sun King, Louis XIV, and his name was given to one of NASA's spacecraft.

A small museum, **Museo Cassini** (☎0184 672001; ⊕ 08.30–14.00 hols, 08.30–noon Sat – guided tours by appointment; free), in the Palazzo del Comune is dedicated to him and has some interesting astronomical documents and personal letters from leading scientists of the day. He is said to have been born in the Castello Maraldi, where Napoleon stayed while fighting in Italy, which is now a private house.

🍽 ORANGE FLOWER POWER

The perfumers of Liguria are an endangered species but, in the quaint village of Vallebona, you can meet one of the Slow Food Movement's warriors. The tradition of distilling bitter orange blossom, which once dominated the local economy, almost died out a decade ago but Pietro Gugliemi is fighting hard to keep local traditions alive. His family's distillery opened in 1856 but closed in the 1960s. The citrus industry was almost wiped out by three terrible frosts in 1969, 1970 and 1985 and by competition from the chemical industry, who began to produce artificial scents at much lower prices.

Pietro like many young Italians is turning back to the old way of life in which he sees a bright future. In 2004 he re-opened the family distillery and began to replant the orchards. He now produces not only bitter orange flower water but a range of flower waters and creams. He uses a modern steam method to extract the oil, know as *neroli*, after Anna Maria Orsini, who was the Princess of Nerola and adored the scent of bitter orange flower water.

A kilo of blossom, which is collected in May, makes about 2 litres of flower water. It is harvested in the early morning and laid out in the sun to dry. It is a delicate procedure and was traditionally a job for girls who had the smallest hands and the lightest touch. The water is also used to flavour cakes and biscuits and was traditionally believed to be a cure for stomach ache. Pop into his distillery and buy some: **Antica Distilleria** (Piazza Liberta 17, Vallebona; m 339 127 7887; e info@levecchiadistilleria.it; w www.lavecchiadistilleria.it; call to make an appointment).

In Perinaldo farmers grow excellent violet artichokes. The *carciofo di perinaldo* arrived here 200 years ago, reputedly introduced by Napoleon Bonaparte during the Italian Campaign of 1796. He stayed with a noble family in the village and was surprised that the purple artichokes native to Provence were not growing in such perfect conditions. After his stay he sent some seedlings to the family. This variety of artichoke only grows here and in Provence between 400 and 600m above sea level. It is thornless, tender and has no choke. Hardy, it often grows at the edges of the stone walls almost like a wild vegetable.

The artichoke harvest is in May and June but it is preserved in oil so they can be eaten throughout the year and you will see them on sale in local shops. It can be eaten raw in salads or cooked as an accompaniment to meat or game or served in crêpes with parmesan cheese and mushrooms, or in simple pancakes with garlic and parsley. The artichoke festival, known as the *sagra di carciofi,* takes place on the second Sunday in May and is one massive outdoor communal kitchen run by volunteers. You can buy in season from two local olive oil producers: **Azienda Agricola Vittorio Cassini** (Strada per Negi 1, Seborga; w vittoriocassini.it).

The modern observatory, the **Osservatorio Cassini** (w osservatoriocassini.it), has regular star-gazing events. Cassini's grandson, who was also an astronomer, designed the sundial near the church. The **Santuario della Consolazione** just outside the village was, on Cassini's initiative, aligned with the Ligurian line of longitude and thus throws no shadow on 21 June.

Despite its popularity with Dutch and German holidaymakers, Perinaldo is well off the beaten track and, in the middle of the day, when everything is closed, you can explore its ancient medieval alleys all alone. There are also beautiful views down the valley to the sea.

Perinaldo is surrounded by olive groves and you can buy 17 different local oils at **l'Anfora** on Via Maraldi 17.

🏠 *Where to stay, eat and drink*

🏠 **Casa Castello** (4 apts) Piazza Castello 9–13, Perinaldo; m 328 913 1146; e info@castellodiperinaldo.com; w castellodiperinaldo.com. Wonderful location in the old fortress with a terrace with panoramic views. Barbecue. The owners produce wine & you can visit the vineyards. €€€

🏠 **Il Rifugio di Artemide** [map, page 258] (4 rooms & 2 apts) Regione Massabò 17, Località Curli, Perinaldo; m 335 695 1203; w ilrifugiodiartemide.it. Stay on a farm that produces vegetables, oil & wine. A really restful spot & an excellent host. If you don't stay here, be sure to eat at the *rifugio* as Cinzia the owner is a fantastic cook. €

VENTIMIGLIA

Whenever we cross the border from France, there's always a loud whoop from the kids at the sight of Ventimiglia. If you are crossing the border and reading this you might well conclude that my family are a rather poor judge of things. Ventimiglia looks like a huge mess and an urban planning disaster. The hills that surround it are covered in greenhouses and the valley is a sweep of roads. In summer there is a huge, dry riverbed running down the middle.

Ventimiglia is one of the places in Italy that has been affected by the vast number of illegal immigrants who have arrived in the country in recent years. You will see young men from Africa all over town. They are migrants and refugees who have crossed the Sahara and paid smugglers to take them on the dangerous crossing from Libya. They have no intention of staying in Italy and want to cross the border into France.

Police watch the cars coming over the border from Italy, and pull some over for questioning. Some of the migrants try to walk along the seafront and to swim along the coast, but the majority tend to gather on the beach in the afternoon before trying to get across the border by train. If you arrive half an hour or so before the train leaves, you will see them on the platform, but just before it leaves they all disappear and are to be found hiding under seats, in cupboards and toilets. Once the train arrives in France the police get on and start searching. It is a game of cat and mouse. No sooner do the French police send the migrants back than they try to cross the border again. The more determined or richer migrants and refugees pay smugglers from the Roya Valley, a mountainous area of the border, to help them trek to France. Many of them have frozen to death as they have tried to do so.

What the kids love is that it looks like the Italians are cocking a snoop at the French, who take such pride and joy in their coast from Nice to Menton with its spick-and-span villages and towns that ooze the stuffy bourgeois side of France. It is like the Italians are saying, 'Why should we make a fuss over that sort of coast? We have mile upon mile of it!' And they do; much of it is just as stunning.

Despite its chaotic first impression, Ventimiglia is well worth a stopover. It is home to one of the world's most famous botanical gardens, the Villa Hanbury, and a pre-eminent prehistoric site, the Balzi Rossi Caves, where some of the first Ligurians lived. The mountains behind Ventimiglia are some of the most beautiful in Liguria and shouldn't be missed. The villages are full of charm and off the tourist track.

That said, don't expect anything chic here. If I was a teacher and Ventimiglia was my pupil, I would give it, 'C+. Could try harder. Presentation sloppy.' This might be set to change with the building of the new marina, which has taken years, as similar developments have spruced up a lot of towns on the Italian Riviera.

HISTORY Ventimiglia was founded by the Romans and was called Albium Intemelium. After the fall of Rome it was sacked by the Byzantines, the Goths, the Lombards, the Saracens and finally the Genoese, who absorbed it into their growing empire in 1139. The town was briefly controlled by the House of Savoy in the 14th and 18th century. Its name means 'twenty miles', and it is approximately 20 miles (32km) from Nice.

GETTING THERE AND AROUND

By boat At time of writing the new marina was still under construction.

By bus Bus 1 runs up to Balzi Rossi and the border with France. Bus 2 runs along the coast to Sanremo, 15 minutes away. Bus 7 goes up the Val Nervia to Dolceacqua, Isolabona and Pigna.

By car Ventimiglia is on the A10 *autostrada*, 41km from Nice and 130km from Genoa.

By taxi Taxis are available via ☎0184 351125.

By train There are hourly trains to Turin (3½ hrs). It is a fun ride through 81 tunnels and over 400 bridges. Journey time to Genoa is 3 hours, and Nice 45 minutes.

TOURIST INFORMATION The tourist office can be found at Lungo Roja Rossi (☎ 0184 351183). Music and flowers fill the streets during the Flower Festival in June, there is a medieval festival in August and a firework display on 29 August. The modern town has a hugely popular Friday **market**.

⬆ WHERE TO STAY, EAT AND DRINK

🏠 **Casa Fenoglio** (3 rooms) Via Garibaldi 20; ☎349 385 4242; w casafenoglio.com. Rooms in a 16th-century palazzo with AC. **€€**

🏠 **La Riserva di Castel d'Appio** [map, page 258] (16 rooms) Località Peidaigo 71; m 329 714 1350; w lariserva.it. This little hotel is in a fantastic location 300m above Ventimiglia under the ruins of a 13th-century castle that was built on the site of a Roman fortress. It's a family-run hotel that opened in 1967 & the service is very friendly. The views are stunning & there is a good restaurant. Fitness centre & swimming pool. Free Wi-Fi. **€€**

✘ **Balzi Rossi** Via Balzi Rossi 2; ☎0184 38132; w ristorantebalzirossi.it; ⊕ closed Mon lunch & Tue. Enrico Marmo is the head chef here & this classy restaurant is the place for a major treat. Menu is predominantly fish-based. **€€€**

✘ **Pasta e Basta** Passeggiata Marconi 12a; ☎0184 230878; ⊕ closed Mon evening. This is a really fun place to eat on the seafront & it's always busy. They show you a plate on which are stuck the different types of pasta that they serve – you choose the one you want & what sauce you fancy to go with it. Great for families with fussy eaters. **€€**

OTHER PRACTICALITIES There is an **ATM** at Via della Stazione 3. The **post office** is at Via della Repubblica 6, and there is a **pharmacy** at Via Cavour 28. The nearest **hospital** is in Sanremo (Via G Borea 56; ☎0184 536301).

WHAT TO SEE AND DO The River Roya divides Ventimiglia in two. The medieval hilltop town lies to the west and the modern town spreads out over the little plain in front of the sea to the east, including a not particularly nice couple of kilometres of 1960s seaside development along the coast to Bordighera. If you want to base yourself here, choose the coast to the west between **Latte** and the French border.

The old town is a bit rough and tumble. The main street, Via Garibaldi, is lined with 15th-century palaces that are a little scruffy, but it hides a few gems. In the old **Teatro Civica**, the **Biblioteca Civico** is one of the oldest public libraries in Italy and was founded in 1648. It has a collection of rare books, and is open in the morning in summer. Via Garibaldi leads to the **Cattedrale dell'Assunta**, a beautiful example of Ligurian Romanesque architecture, which dates from the 11th and 12th centuries. It replaced the original Carolingian 8th-century church, the remains of which are visible in the crypt. Via Garibaldi leads to Piazza Nizza; from here you can climb the fort built by the Genoese in the 11th century on the site of the Roman military camp. There are magnificent views.

The beaches here are pebble and rough sand, and the sea here has the highest concentration of iodine in the whole Mediterranean. The Via Aurelia runs west to Capo Mortola, where there is excellent diving, offered by **Pianeta Blu Diving Centre** (m 347 101 2896; 📘).

10

In true Ventimiglia style, its Roman ruins are in the east of the city squeezed up next to the railway line. Among them are the remains of the 2nd-century **theatre** (Corso Genova 134; ☏0184 252320; f; ⊕ 09.00–14.00 Tue–Sat 1st & 3rd Sun of the month; free), which could seat 5,000 people; it is one of the most significant Roman monuments in Liguria.

The finds from the site are all in the **Museo Archeologico Gerolamo Rossi** in the Forte dell'Annunziata (Via Verdi 41; ☏0184 351181; w marventimiglia.it; ⊕ 09.00–12.30 & 15.00–17.00 Tue–Thu, 10.00–12.30 & 21.00–23.00 (summer only) Fri, 09.00–12.30 Sat, 21.00–23.00 (summer only) Sun; admission €6). The views along the coast here are wonderful.

A little further west is Ventimiglia's chief attraction, the **Hanbury Botanical Gardens** [map, page 258] (Corso Montecarlo 43, La Mortola; ☏ 0184 229507; w giardinihanbury.com; ⊕ Jun–Sep 09.30–18.00 daily; in winter, closes at 17.00; admission €9, animals not permitted). These are the oldest botanical gardens on the Riviera, founded in 1867 by Londoner Sir Thomas Hanbury and his brother Daniel, who was a botanist. Hanbury himself was a wealthy businessman who made a fortune trading silks and spices in the Far East. He came here to recuperate from bronchitis in 1867, and fell in love with the place.

He bought the Villa Hanbury, which was built in the 14th century and extended in the 17th century, and it was his love affair with its huge garden that put him in the botanical history books. During his travels he brought back rare and exotic plants to fill his 30-acre (12ha) garden. Species from South Africa and Mexico in particular flourished. Today, you can see 5,800 different plants. The collection includes 270 different citrus species. Even if you are not especially interested in botany, it is a beautiful place for a shady walk through the gardens, which are dotted with follies and fountains; one, filled with terrapins, slopes down to the sea, where there is a nice little café. In the middle of the garden there is a section of the old Via Julia Augusta. A word of warning though: don't go on a hot day; it is unbearable as it is quite a slog back up the hill and there is no access to the sea at the bottom of the garden. Places like this are best explored in the cooler months of the year.

The Hanbury gardens have had some famous visitors, among them Queen Victoria in 1882. In 1939, Mussolini met Franco here. Unfortunately, during World War II the estate fell into decay. Since 1960 it has belonged to the University of Genoa. Although much restoration work has been done since then, this is no Kew Gardens and it could definitely do with some weeding – things have a tendency to be neglected around here.

Just before the border on the coast road are the **Balzi Rossi Caves** [map, page 258] (Via Verdi 5; ☏ 0184 38113; ⊕ 08.30–19.30 Tue–Sun; admission €4). If you arrived here without any knowledge of the significance of this place, you might either miss it entirely or dismiss it as rather boring. The frontier village of **Grimaldi**, 10km west of Ventimiglia, is in fact one of the oldest settlements in Europe and 200,000 years ago *Homo erectus grimaldi* lived here, as did Cro-Magnon man, 185,000 years ago.

The caves are one of the most important prehistoric sites in the western Mediterranean but that might take some believing. This is another truly Ventimiglian experience, where you have to get into the chaotic style of things and go with the flow to get the best out of it.

There are nine caves but you can only see two and they get their name from the reddish limestone cliffs: *rosso* in Italian means 'red'. Be warned: it is very difficult to find. From the roundabout in front of the old customs post, follow the brown sign indicating an archaeological site. There is a small car park and from here walk past the rather rundown-looking hotel complex.

Buy a ticket in the museum and then you will be sent around the back to walk up a metal staircase that leads over the railway line. It turns out prehistoric man lived on the wrong side of the tracks. It leads to two tiny caves. There is nothing to see here; this isn't Ventimiglia's fault but Sir Thomas Hanbury's, because when he decided to excavate, not enough care was taken. You need to use your imagination. In ancient times the sea level was much lower and these caves would have been perched high above it.

Inside the museum there are a number of historically important exhibits, among them the cave drawing of the small, stocky Przewalski horse, a type that is today found only in Mongolia. On display too is the triple tomb of a boy and a man over 6ft (1.8m), who lie on either side of a 16-year-old girl. The tiny objects found with them are fascinating and include seashells, pendants, deer teeth and necklaces made of fish vertebrae. Also on show are some of the earliest-known works of art: soapstone Venuses.

UP IN THE MOUNTAINS

There are two magnificent valleys behind Ventimiglia, which are the absolute must-see places of this part of Liguria. If you have limited time, the Val Nervia is the one to visit. It is one of the most beautiful spots in Liguria and a great place for walking. To get a real flavour of the atmosphere stay in one of the old towns, which are at their best in the evening and early morning.

THE VAL ROYA The SS20 runs along the Val Roya to **Airole**. It is a journey of less than 10 minutes, depending on traffic from Ventimiglia, on a fast road, but it's another world. It was one of those Ligurian villages that looked as if it was about to fall down until a couple of decades ago and then Germans arrived and bought a number of holiday homes here. Today, it's lacking in the authenticity you find in most Ligurian hill towns but is still very pretty and peaceful. Closer to the French border **Olivetta San Michele** was once a big base for smugglers and **Fanghetto**, the last village in Italy, has a striking stone bridge.

✘ Where to eat and drink
✘ **Ristorante U Carugiu** Via Roma 9, Airole;
☏ 0184 200521. Good, simple restaurant serving local dishes. €€€

THE VAL NERVIA The SP64 runs along the Val Nervia, one of the loveliest parts of Liguria's hinterland. It stretches 20km up from the sea to a range of mountains called the little Dolomites of Liguria. The area has applied to become a UNESCO World Heritage Site. When the Roman Empire collapsed, the population, who lived on the coast, upped sticks and settled in the mountains for safety against invaders and pirates. They built a series of beautiful hilltop villages that were dubbed by the travellers of the Grand Tour 'rock villages', because they had been literally dug out of the mountainside. You can stop and buy oil on the road up the valley from Ventimiglia as there are a number of producers who sell directly to the public.

Dolceacqua A short drive inland, 8.7km from Ventimiglia, is historic Dolceacqua; its name means 'sweet water'. A single-arched 15th-century bridge, the Ponte dei

Romani, similar to the famous Mostar bridge in Bosnia, spans 33m across the river and leads to the old town, known as the Téra, where some of the streets are subterranean passages.

The old town is dominated by the huge ruin of the **Castello dei Doria** (m 337 100 4228; ☉ 10.00–13.00 & 14.30–18.30 daily; admission €6), which towers over the old town on the left bank of the river. It is a steep walk up a dark, atmospheric, narrow little alleyway to the castle. It was damaged by the 1887 earthquake and is said to be haunted; there isn't a great deal to see inside, so if it's closed, you haven't missed much. If you're looking for a fancy place to tie the knot, this is a possible venue as they hold weddings here.

The castle was once the stronghold of the Doria family, who used to enjoy the *jus primae noctis*, the feudal lord's right to sleep with a bride on her wedding night. The resistance of one bride, Lucrezia, is celebrated in the Sagra della Michetta on 15 August, when small lemon biscuits, *michette*, which have been cooked by the villagers, are collected by two women who lead a musical procession through the streets. The biscuits are later handed out to the crowds. You can buy them at Alimentari Francesca on Via San Sebastiano next to the church. The Doria family moved out of the castle in the 18th century and into the Palazzo Doria by the church of **Sant'Antonio Abate,** and had their own private passageway to the church. The church itself dates from 1400 but was altered in the Baroque period. Inside, there is a polyptych by the famous artist Ludovico Brea, which is worth popping in to see.

A visit to Dolceacqua is stress-free tourism at its best. The thing to do here is to sit in a café in the square in the old town on the opposite bank and simply enjoy the view, which Impressionist painter Claude Monet immortalised on canvas. He wrote in his diary, 'The place is superb, there is a bridge that is a jewel of lightness.' The hills around Dolceacqua are covered in vines that produce one of Liguria's best wines, Rossese, a favourite of Napoleon. So order a glass and unwind. The scenery gets better and better as you drive up the valley. Beyond Dolceacqua is **Rocchetta Nervina**. You can stop and buy oil along the road. It is a really pretty little village perched above a babbling little river, with cool breezes even in the height of summer. In the main square is a shop for picnic supplies. Eat by the river and then rent a canoe at weekends in high summer and mess about on the water under the bridge. The more adventurous should go canyoning upstream.

Beyond Rocchetta is down-to-earth **Isolabona**, once a key defensive point on the crucial trading route north, which was protected by the Doria Castle, built in 1277. It is a pretty little spot to stop for a walk around and to have a drink. The real gem of the valley, Apricale, lies above it.

Where to stay, eat and drink There are lots of stylish B&Bs in Dolceacqua and it makes a great base from which to explore the area by car. To try the local wine go to the **Enoteca Regionale della Liguria** (Via Castello 27; 0184 229507). **Pastissi** (Via Patrioti Martiri 16; closed Nov–Feb) sells excellent ice cream.

Antico Frantoio [map, page 258] (7 apts) Via Molini 38, Isolabona; 0184 208485; w frantoioligure.it. Old mill converted into apts, each with its own garden, rented by the week or w/end. Hotel is surrounded by olive groves 13km from the sea from which the owners produce their own olive oil, which can be bought by guests. All-year swimming pool. Cookery courses, tasting sessions, themed events & boat trips. €€€

B&B Agapantus (1 room) Piazza Garibaldi 11; m 333 866 9323; e agapantus@aol.it; w agapantus.it. Owned by the same family who own Le Gemme (see below). €€

Le Gemme (3 rooms) Via Castello 2, Dolceacqua; m 333 866 9323; w le-gemme.it. In a typical Ligurian house in the heart of Dolceacqua with a terrace with a great view of the castle. There are 2 large rooms that sleep 4. €€

Talking Stones (4 rooms) Via San Bernardo 5; 0184 206393; m 333 662 4255; e info@ talkingstones.it. In the heart of the old town with lovely atmospheric rooms. €€

Terre Bianche [map, page 258] (5 rooms) Località Arcagna; 0184 31426; e terrebianche@ terrebianche.com; w terrebianche.com; closed Nov. Produces wine & extra-virgin Taggiasca olive oil. They are part of the Slow Food Movement.

Splendid view of the Val Nervia. The b/fast is made from their farm produce. €€

Dei Doria (3 rooms) Via Barberis Colomba 40; 0184 206343; m 347 260 6689; e info@ deidoria.it; w deidoria.it. B&B accommodation. Some rooms have a view of the castle. Shared kitchen. €

La Villetta (1 cottage) Via San Bernardo 17; m 334 349 9985. Pretty little cottage with its own garden & terrace in the narrow streets of the old town. Belongs to an Italian-British couple. €

A Viassa Via della Liberazione 13; 0184 206665; w ristoranteaviassa.it; Tue–Sun. Fresh & modern menu varies according to the season. €30 for the set menu exc wine. A Slow Food restaurant & they serve the local purple artichokes from Perinaldo. €€€

La Rampa Via Barberis 11; 0184 206198. Traditional trattoria, sometimes a bit hit & miss but getting a table on the terrace that looks across at the castle is a must. Good menu with pizza & local Ligurian dishes. €€

U Fundu Via Doria 12; 0184 206784; closed Jan. This fabulous restaurant is in the *carrugi*, the narrow alleyways, & is affiliated with the Slow Food movement. No credit cards. €€

THE EMPEROR'S FAVOURITE

The wine produced here was Napoleon's favourite tipple according to legend and the area is famous for its Rossese.

You can taste and buy some at:

Roberto Rondelli Località Brunetti 1, Camporosso; m 328 034 8055. They rent rooms & also have a restaurant (€€).

Terre Bianche Località Arcagna, Dolceacqua; 0184 31426; w terrebianche.com. They hold tasting sessions & also rent apts (€€).

Apricale Apricale tumbles down a crag, a short drive above Isolabona in the Val Merdanzo. This is the place to base yourself to explore the area. The village takes its name from the Latin *apricus*, meaning sunny. Many of the buildings date from the 11th century and the town hosts theatrical events, some in medieval and Renaissance costume in summer. The **Castello della Lucertola** (✆ 0184 208126; ⊕ May–Jun 14.00–18.00 Tue–Sun; Jul–Aug 16.00–19.00 & 20.00–22.00 daily, also 10.30–noon Sun; admission €5) has an exhibition about the history of the town and holds a copy of the town's statutes dating from 1267. There are panoramic views from the pretty **Piazza Vittorio Emanuele**, where there are two good restaurants (see below).

What is lovely about Apricale is that it has only just opened up to tourists and has lots of charm. Less and less of the village sits abandoned these days as the town resounds to the sound of restoration as builders hammer away. Living was hard in the hinterland and many people upped and moved to the coast where there were jobs, schools and hospitals. Without tourism it is possible that the village would have been totally abandoned so it is good to see it coming back to life. It is great fun to explore Apricale's dark alleyways, which are more like tunnels. It is full of cats and uneven cobble stones. You'll soon notice that most of the foreigners are Swedish. That's because a Swedish artist came here in the 1960s and painted the town. His work inspired his friends to buy houses here and they now own about 20% of the property in Apricale.

 Where to stay, eat and drink You can buy a selection of local products at **La Bottega delle Meraviglie** (Via Roma 10; f).

Apricus Locanda (5 rooms) Via IV Novembre 5; ✆ 0184 209020; m 339 600 8622; e apricuslocanda@libero.it; w apricuslocanda. com. In Apricale, this B&B has a terrace & swimming pool. They also have 2 houses. The properties were ruins when the owners bought them just over 15 years ago & they have been tastefully restored. €€

☀ **Munta e Cara** (23 rooms) Piazza Vittorio Veneto 2; ✆ 0184 209030; e info@muntaecara.it; w muntaecara.it. This is an *albergo diffuso*, a hotel that is scattered around a village, & something that is getting increasingly popular in Liguria. The hotel has some fabulous designer rooms that are completely private, with their own front door in different places around the village. Some have

---

🍴 APRICALE ON A PLATE

The food is excellent in Apricale and there are three top restaurants, where they serve classic local dishes. Main courses are meaty: boar, *cinghiale*, rabbit, *coniglio*, and goat, *capra*. Beans are an important part of the local diet and are often served boiled and seasoned with extra virgin olive oil, garlic, bay leaves, sage and peppercorns, or used to prepare tasty soups. The white beans that grow in nearby Pigna are now protected by the Slow Food Movement. The local ravioli is *barbagiuai*, filled with rice, pumpkin and yet more beans. Look out for sausages made in nearby Ceriana, *la salsiccia di ceriana*. The classic pasta dish is *sugeli*, which is tiny pieces of pasta made with just water and flour served in a white sauce made from a local ricotta called *brusso*.

For dessert, the things to eat here are the almond brittle, *cubàite*, and *pansarola di Apricale*, little sweet doughnuts. There is even a *pansarola* festival in September. Also try the *barbajai*, little fritters made with ricotta cheese. Eat them at **La Favorita** (Strada San Pietro 1; w lafavoritaapricale.com).

Wash it all down with a glass of Rossese wine from the hills of the Nervia Valley.

kitchenettes & all are beautifully presented with antique furniture & old-fashioned baths. B/fast is served in a small restaurant in the centre of town & reception is near the car park. The owners are very friendly & full of advice. I couldn't recommend this hotel more highly & it has to be in my top 10 places to stay in Liguria. €€

✗ **La Capanna da Bacì** Via Roma 14; 📞0184 208137; e info@baciristorante.it; w baciristorante.it; ⏲ closed Mon–Wed evening. This is the classy option, with traditional dishes, among them rabbit & wild boar. The restaurant has a fantastic view. They also rent rooms (€€€). €€€€

✗ **Da Delio** Piazza Vittorio Veneto 9; 📞0184 208008; w ristoranteapricale.it; ⏲ Wed–Sun lunch & dinner. Lots of local specialities appear on the menu like rabbit ravioli & *stoccafisso*. Good place to try the local Slow Food products. There's a pleasant terrace & good-value set menus. Even if you don't eat here you might want to try the rather good rabbit recipe on the website. €€€

✗ **Trattoria A Ciassa** Piazza Vittorio Emanuele II 2; 📞0184 208588; e simionecassini@gmail.com. A simple, friendly restaurant in the main square. When the weather permits, there are tables outside with amazing views. All dishes are local & seasonal. Be sure to book as it's very popular. €€€

Pigna and Buggio
Take the road to Isolabona and then the SP64 to the spa town of **Pigna**. It is a small, fortified village that for hundreds of years was an outpost of the House of Savoy. There is a small terrace just after the gate, where there is a café if you fancy a break. It looks across to Pigna's traditional rival, the hilltop town of **Castel Vittorio**, which was a Genoese stronghold. The latter is literally teetering on the top of a crag and the views here are classically Ligurian.

There's a faint smell of sulphur in the air here. There are thermal springs that have been used to cure skin ailments since Roman times, but sadly the spa has closed.

There is a remarkable 15th-century porticoed loggia, from which an alley on the left leads you to the main square, which again has fabulous views across the mountains. Take the passage to the right and you come to the church of **San Michele**, which has a notable 16th-century marble rose window and a golden polyptych of San Michele by the Piedmontese artist Giovanni Canavesio that shows the influence of the master painters, the Brea family. There are beautiful frescoes by the same artist that adorn the small church of San Bernardino.

Before you arrive in Pigna, as you drive up the valley there is a left turn to the Rifugio Gola di Gouta. From here there is a fairly easy circular walk across the summit of Monte Simonasso. It takes about 5½ hours. If you fancy a strenuous hike up the mountainside, you can pick up the footpath by the Church of San Bernardo, which leads to the Passo Muratone. It takes 7 hours there and back.

The tiny village of **Buggio** at the head of the valley feels remote enough to be the last little village in Italy, which indeed it is as the mountains that rise above it form the border with France. This is a great spot for mountain biking as there are tarmacked roads up into the mountains and there is very little traffic.

Above Buggio there is also a mountain lake if you fancy a hike. The path starts at the lower square. It finishes at the **Rifugio Allavena** (📞 0184 241155) at Colla Melosa, 1,540m above sea level. It has a good restaurant and you can also stay here. Accommodation is in dormitories. If you are lazy, you can come all the way up by car. To do this you drive back out of Buggio and take the SP65 in the direction of Triora. There are two circuits of steep footpaths. One leads to the Rifugio Grai and takes 3½ hours and the other 7-hour walk actually dips into France as it winds its way to the summit of Monte Toraggio. Full details of the local walks are on the *rifugio* website: w nuovorifugioallavena.it.

Just before Buggio the road forks and leads up the mountain pass to Molini di Triora. This is a lovely drive over the Colle di Langan, with yet more beautiful views across the Ligurian landscape of mountains and deep lush valleys. It's a quiet road if you decide to walk it, but it's closed if it snows. You can then pick up the Alta Via dei Monti Liguri at the **Rifugio Sanremo** (w caisanremo.it), which also has 30 beds.

🏠 *Where to stay, eat and drink*

🏠 **B&B Via Col Tempo** (3 rooms)   Via Colla, Pigna; 📞 0184 241216; e nadia.ughetto@tiscali. it; w viacoltempo.it. B&B furnished with beautiful antiques in the heart of Pigna. Spacious rooms with views across the valley. **€€**

🏠 **Agriturismo Al Pagan**   [map, page 258] (5 apts) Località Pagan; m 347 322 3375; w alpagan.it. The farm grows the local beans & you can buy olive oil here, too. There is a children's playground & they are pet friendly. Great mountain views. **€**

🏠 **Rifugio Gola di Gouta**   [map, page 258] (21 beds) Località Sella di Gouta, Pigna; 📞 0184 241068; m 329 493 9978; e rifugiogoladigouta@virgilio.it.

This *rifugio* has excellent homemade dishes. Try the ravioli. Restaurant **€€**. Dorm rooms **€**

✖ **Agriturismo Ca De Na**   Via IV Novembre 34, Buggio; 📞 0184 241731. Eating in this lovely farmhouse is a treat. Set menu of seasonal dishes, which with a never-ending supply of wine comes in at €35 a head – a bargain for the quality of the food. **€€€**

✳ ✖ **Osteria del Portico**   Corso Umberto I 6, Castel Vittorio; 📞 0184 241352; ⏱ Tue–Sat lunch & dinner, Sun lunch only; w osteriadelportico.it. This is a 5th-generation-run family restaurant & the place to taste some of the local specialities like wild boar. **€€€**

Appendix 1

LANGUAGE

PRONUNCIATION Italian is one of the easiest European languages to pronounce: the key rule is that words are pronounced exactly how they are written. Unlike other languages, every letter (with the exception of the silent 'h') is pronounced. The stress is usually on the penultimate syllable. Accents indicate if the stress is on a different syllable (eg: *città*).

The alphabet Italian is based on the Latin alphabet and has 21 letters. The letters j, k, w, x and y do not feature, although they are used in foreign words that have been absorbed into the language, eg: 'taxi'.

a	as in **ah**
b	as in **b**ag
c	as in **c**at when preceding a, o, u and h
	as in **ch**eer when preceding e or i
d	as in **d**og, but without aspiration
e	two sounds: as the closed 'e' in p**e**t, or as an open sound, as in air
	eg: closed – m**e**la (apple); open – *bello* (beautiful)
f	as in **f**un
g	as in **g**o when preceding a, o, u and h
	as in **g**eneral when preceding e or i
h	always silent
i	as in **i**t
l	as in **l**ie
m	as in **m**an
n	as in **n**o
o	two sounds: as the closed 'o' in r**o**se, or as in the open 'o' in l**o**t
	eg: closed – c**o**n (with); open – *otto* (eight)
p	as in **p**et
q	as in **q**uick
r	the Italian 'r' is rolled or trilled, with the tongue against the forward palate and gums of the upper teeth
s	before vowels and c, f, p, q, s, t as the 's' in **s**on, and then usually as the 's' in clo**s**ed
t	a hard sound, as in **t**ell but with no aspiration
u	as in r**u**le
v	as in **v**an
z	as in the 'ds' in la**ds** or the 'ts' in lo**ts**
gli	as in the 'lli' in mi**lli**on
gn	as in the 'ny' in ca**ny**on
sc	followed by 'e' or 'i' as the 'sh' in **sh**oot

Stress and accents A word's natural stress usually falls on the penultimate syllable:

*Ro**ma***   Rome   *an**dare***   to go

However, stress can also occur on the first syllable of a word:

*pu**bblico***   public   *ma**ndorla***   almond

The presence of an accent at the end of a word means that the stress is placed on the last syllable:

*Pap**à***   dad (whereas *Papa*   *caf**fè***   coffee
                                means pope)

WORDS AND PHRASES
Basic phrases

yes	*sì*
no	*no*
Good morning	*Buongiorno*
Good afternoon/evening	*Buonasera*
Goodnight	*Buonanotte*
Hello/Goodbye (informal)	*Ciao*
Goodbye	*Arrivederci*
Please	*Per favore*
Thank you (very much)	*Grazie (mille)*
Excuse me (to pass someone)	*Permesso*
Excuse me (attract attention/apologise)	*Mi scusi*
I'm sorry	*Mi dispiace*
You're welcome	*Prego*
Help!	*Aiuto!*
I don't know	*Non lo so*
I don't understand (Italian)	*Non capisco l'italiano*
Does somebody here speak English?	*C'è qualcuno qui che parla inglese?*
How are you?	*Come sta/stai?*
I'm fine	*Bene*
I'm tired	*Sono stanco/stanca*
I feel unwell	*Mi sento male*
My name is …	*Mi chiamo …*
What is your name?	*Come ti chiami?*
I am … from England	*Sono … dall'Inghilterra*
What?	*Che?*
Who?	*Chi?*
Where?	*Dove?*
Why?	*Perché?*
How?	*Come?*

Transport

I would like …	*Vorrei …*
a one way ticket	*un biglietto di solo andata*
a return ticket	*di andata e ritorno*
I want to go…	*Voglio andare…*
What time does it leave?	*A che ora parte?*

The train has been delayed/has been cancelled	Il treno è in ritardo/è stato cancellato
How long does it take?	Quanto ci vuole?
Is this the road to … ?	È questa la strada per … ?
Where is the service station?	Dov'è il benzinaio?

platform	binario	I'd like to hire …	Vorrei noleggiare …
ticket office	biglietteria	a car	una macchina
from… to…	da… a…	a bicycle	una bicicletta
railway station	stazione	Please fill it up	Il pieno, per favore
train	treno	diesel	diesel
bus	autobus	unleaded petrol	senza piombo
bus stop	fermata dell'autobus	driving licence	patente di guida
airport	aeroporto	parking	parcheggio
plane	aereo	No parking	Sosta vietata
boat	barca	centre	il centro
ferry	traghetto	main square	la piazza principale
first class	prima classe	Turn left/right	Giri a sinistra/destra
second class	seconda classe	Go straight on	Vada sempre diritto
car	macchina		

Food and restaurant basics

restaurant	ristorante
Do you have a table for … people?	Ha un tavolo per … persone?
Could I see the menu, please?	Posso vedere il menu?
I am a vegetarian	Sono vegetariano/a
Could you bring me a glass of still water/fizzy water?	Mi porta un bicchiere di acqua liscia/acqua gassata?
The bill, please	Il conto, per favore

bread	pane	leeks	porri
butter	burro	mushrooms	funghi
cheese	formaggio	onion	cipolla
egg	uovo	peppers	peperoni
oil	olio	potato/crisps	patata/patatine
pepper	pepe	tomato	pomodoro
rice	riso	fish	pesce
salt	sale	clams	vongole
sugar	zucchero	mussels	cozze/muscoli
ice cream	gelato		(dialect)
fruit	frutta	octopus	polpo
apple	mela	sea bass	branzino
banana	banana	tuna	tonno
grapes	uva	steak	bistecca
orange	arancia	meat	carne
pear	pera	chicken	pollo
vegetables	verdure	pork	carne di maiale
artichokes	carciofi	lamb	agnello
aubergine	melanzana	sausage	salsiccia
beans	fagioli	wild boar	cinghiale
garlic	aglio	drinks	bevande
courgettes	zucchine	water	acqua

beer	*birra*	milk	*latte*
red/white wine	*vino rosso/bianco*	tea	*thè*
fruit juice	*succo di frutta*	coffee	*caffè*

Shopping basics

How much is it?	*Quanto costa?*
I would like…	*Vorrei…*
Cash only	*Solo contanti*
credit card	*carta di credito*

Accommodation

Where is a good hotel?	*Dov'è un buon hotel?*
Do you have any rooms?	*Avete delle camere libere?*
I would like…	*Vorrei…*
a single room	*una camera singola*
a double room	*una matrimoniale*
a room with two beds	*una camera con due letti*
a room with a bathroom	*una camera con bagno privato*
Is breakfast included?	*La colazione è compresa?*

key	*chiave*	campsite	*campeggio*
shower	*doccia*	hostel	*ostello*
first floor	*primo piano*	hotel	*albergo*
ground floor	*piano terra*		

Signs

entrance/exit	*entrata/uscita*	open/closed	*aperto/chiuso*
arrivals/departures	*arrivi/partenze*	pull/push	*tirare/spingere*
free entrance	*ingresso libero*	cash desk	*cassa*
gentlemen/ladies	*signori/signore*	out of order	*guasto*
WC	*gabinetto/bagno*	ring the bell	*suonare il campanello*
vacant/engaged	*libero/occupato*		

Times, days and months

What time is it?	*Che ore sono?*	Wednesday	*Mercoledì*
It's four o'clock	*Sono (le) quattro*	Thursday	*Giovedì*
today	*oggi*	Friday	*Venerdì*
tomorrow	*domani*	Saturday	*Sabato*
day after tomorrow	*dopodomani*	Sunday	*Domenica*
yesterday	*ieri*	January	*Gennaio*
now	*adesso*	February	*Febbraio*
later	*più tardi*	March	*Marzo*
in the morning	*di mattina*	April	*Aprile*
in the afternoon	*nel pomeriggio*	May	*Maggio*
in the evening	*di sera*	June	*Giugno*
spring	*primavera*	July	*Luglio*
summer	*estate*	August	*Agosto*
autumn	*autunno*	September	*Settembre*
winter	*inverno*	October	*Ottobre*
Monday	*Lunedì*	November	*Novembre*
Tuesday	*Martedì*	December	*Dicembre*

Numbers

1	*uno/una*	18	*diciotto*
2	*due*	19	*diciannove*
3	*tre*	20	*venti*
4	*quattro*	21	*ventuno*
5	*cinque*	22	*ventidue*
6	*sei*	30	*trenta*
7	*sette*	40	*quaranta*
8	*otto*	50	*cinquanta*
9	*nove*	60	*sessanta*
10	*dieci*	70	*settanta*
11	*undici*	80	*ottanta*
12	*dodici*	90	*novanta*
13	*tredici*	100	*cento*
14	*quattordici*	101	*centuno*
15	*quindici*	200	*duecento*
16	*sedici*	1,000	*mille*
17	*diciassette*		

Timetables *Feriale* means Monday–Saturday and is represented by two crossed hammers. *Festivo* means Sunday and public holidays and is represented by a Christian cross. *Estivo* means summer, and *invernale* winter.

Appendix 2

FURTHER INFORMATION

BOOKS
Travel books

Countess of Blessington *The Idler in Italy* Henry Colburn, 1839. The Countess of Blessington's account of her travels in Italy. She travelled by mule and spent a lot of time wining and dining with her friend, the poet Byron. Downloadable at w archive.org.

Dickens, Charles *Pictures from Italy* Bradbury & Evans, 1846. Dickens spent nine months living in Genoa, appalled by the squalor but enchanted by the beauty of the place. Downloadable at w gutenberg.org.

Hawes, Annie *Extra Virgin* Penguin, 2001. Hawes and her sister move to the hills behind Imperia and learn how to live like the natives.

Hawes, Annie *Ripe for The Picking* Penguin, 2003. More tales from the hills of Liguria.

James, Henry *Italian Hours* Heinemann, 1909. James spent 40 years exploring Italy and this is a collection of his essays about the country he fell in love with. Downloadable at w gutenberg.org.

Lees, Frederic *Wanderings on the Italian Riviera* Little, Brown & Co, 1913. Lees walks the length and breadth of Liguria. An enchanting book full of historical detail. Downloadable at w archive.org.

Smollett, Tobias *Travels through France and Italy* (1766). The English novelist Smollett, who now is little read, was not only one of the world's first tourists but his work also had considerable influence on Dickens. Downloadable at w gutenberg.org.

Walton, Nicolas *Genoa "La Superba": The Rise and Fall of a Merchant Pirate Superpower* Hurst, 2015. An easy to read history travelogue.

Old travel guides

Fitzroy Hamilton, Frederick *Bordighera and The Western Riviera* Stanford, 1883. Available on iBooks.

Miller, William *Wintering in the Riviera* Longmans, Green & Co, 1879. Available on iBooks.

Other Western Europe guides For a full list of Bradt's Europe guides, see w bradtguides.com/shop.

Bird, Angela and Stewart, Murray *The Vendée and surrounding area* (1st edition) Bradt Travel Guides, 2018

Di Gregorio, Luciano *Italy: Abruzzo* (3rd edition) Bradt Travel Guides, 2017

Facaros, Dana and Pauls, Michael *Northern Italy: Emilia-Romagna including Bologna* (1st edition) Bradt Travel Guides, 2018

Robinson, Alex *Alentejo* (2nd edition) Bradt Travel Guides, 2019

Stewart, Murray *The Basque Country and Navarre* (2nd edition) Bradt Travel Guides, 2019

Literature
Literature set in Liguria
Two short stories by Guy de Maupassant: *Happiness* and *The Idyll*, as well as D H Lawrence's short story, *Sun* are well worth reading while you are in Liguria. There are a number of e-versions of these stories online, notably at **w** gutenberg.org.

Aciman, Andre *Call Me By Your Name* Macmillan, 2017. The hit Hollywood film was made in Lombardy, but in the original novel this story of a coming of age gay romance was set in Bordighera.

Dwyer Hickey, Christine *Last Train from Liguria* Atlantic, 2009. The introspective daughter of a London surgeon finds herself in Mussolini's Italy.

von Arnim, Elizabeth *Enchanted April* Virago Modern Classics, 1991. Four women come to terms with their unhappy lives and find rejuvenation in Castello Brown in Portofino. Originally written in 1922, it inspired the 1996 film of the same name.

Walter, Jess *Beautiful Ruins* Penguin, 2012. A clever, witty story of fame, desire and fate set in Hollywood, Rome and Liguria. The perfect summer read.

Literature by Ligurian writers in English
Calvino, Italo *The Path to the Spiders' Nests* Penguin, 1998; *The Baron in the Trees* Mariner, 1977; *The Cloven Viscount* Random House, 1962; and *Invisible Cities* Vintage Classics, 1997. Calvino, who was born in Sanremo, is one of Italy's most famous 20th-century novelists.

Montale, Eugenio *Collected Poems, 1920-54* Farrar Straus Giroux, 2000. Liguria's Nobel Prize-winning poet.

Ruffini, Giovanni *Doctor Antonio* Gaglignani, 1855. A love story set in Bordighera, which was a smash hit in Victorian Britain and prompted a mass winter English emigration to the Italian Riviera. Available on iBooks.

History and politics
Emmott, Bill *Good Italy, Bad Italy* Yale University Press, 2012. The former editor of *The Economist* takes a close look at how the Italian economy functions and dysfunctions. A highly readable description of modern Italy.

Foot, John *The Archipelago: Italy since 1945* Bloomsbury, 2018. Lively post-war history of Italy.

Gilmour, David *The Pursuit of Italy* Penguin, 2011. A lively and entertaining history of Italy that's full of colourful characters.

Le Mesurier, E A *Genoa: Her History As Written In Her Buildings* Donath, 1889. It's available in printed form from Nabu Public Domain Reprints. Although it's an old book, it is immensely readable and unravelled the confusing threads in Genoese history for me.

Steinacher, Gerald *Nazis on the Run: How Hitler's Henchmen Fled Justice,* OUP 2011. Fascinating account of how top Nazis fled Europe through Genoa.

People and culture
Barzini, Luigi *The Italians* Penguin, 1964. Barzini was a well-known Italian journalist and this in-depth look at Italian culture was a ground-breaking book when it was written. Many of his observations are still valid.

Downie, David and Harris, Alison *Enchanted Liguria* Rizzoli, 1997. An illustrated coffee table-style book that celebrates the culture, lifestyle and food of the Riviera.

Hooper, John *The Italians* Penguin, 2016. *The Economist* correspondent's take on Italian society.

Plotkin, Fred *Recipes from Paradise: Life and Food on the Italian Riviera* Little, Brown and Co, 1997. It is now out of print but is a great recipe book with lots of information about the regional culture. Second-hand copies are available online if you want to recreate some of the delicious food found in Liguria.

FILM

Come September (1961) A classic romantic comedy starring Rock Hudson.

Genoa (2008) Starring Colin Firth as a young widower who comes to Genoa with his two daughters to start a new life, but one of them soon sees the ghost of their mother walking in the streets of the city.

WEBSITES

w culturainliguria.it Events and festivals.

w ilsecoloxix.it, w lastampa.it Local news.

w lamialiguria.it, www.liguriaguide.com Tourist information.

w liguriasport.com, w escursioniliguria.com, w liguriasci.it, w canyoning.it, w federcanoa.it, w federvela.it All are useful sport websites.

w motorbikeinitaly.it A useful site for bikers.

w www.regione.liguria.it The official regional site.

w visitgenova.it Information on Genoa.

FOLLOW US

Tag us in your posts to share your adventures using this guide with us – we'd love to hear from you.

- ⨍ BradtTravelGuides
- ▾ @BradtGuides & @rosiewhitehouse
- ▢ @bradtguides & @rosieawhitehouse
- ℗ bradtguides
- ▶ bradtguides

LIGURIA ONLINE

For additional online content, articles, photos and more on Liguria, why not visit **w** bradtguides.com/liguria?

Index

Page numbers in **bold** indicate main entries; those in *italics* indicate maps.

INDEX OF ADVERTISERS